FIGURING IT OUT

THIS BOOK WAS PUBLISHED IN ASSOCIATION WITH
THE CENTER FOR AMERICAN PLACES, SANTA FE,
NEW MEXICO, AND HARRISONBURG, VIRGINIA (WWW.
AMERICANPLACES.ORG)

INTERFACES: STUDIES IN VISUAL CULTURE
Editors Mark J. Williams and Adrian W. B. Randolph, Dartmouth College

This series, sponsored by Dartmouth College Press, develops and promotes the study of visual culture from a variety of critical and methodological perspectives. Its impetus derives from the increasing importance of visual signs in everyday life, and from the rapid expansion of what are termed "new media." The broad cultural and social dynamics attendant to those developments present new challenges and opportunities across and within the disciplines. These have resulted in a trans-disciplinary fascination with all things visual, from "high" to "low," and from esoteric to popular. This series brings together approaches to visual culture—broadly conceived—that assess these dynamics critically and that break new ground in understanding their effects and implications.

FIGURING IT OUT

Science, Gender, and Visual Culture

Edited by

Ann B. Shteir and Bernard Lightman

DARTMOUTH COLLEGE PRESS

Hanover, New Hampshire

Published by University Press of New England

Hanover and London

DARTMOUTH COLLEGE PRESS
Published by University Press of New England,
One Court Street, Lebanon, NH 03766
www.upne.com
© 2006 by Dartmouth College Press
Printed in the United States of America
5 4 3 2 1

A portion of the chapter by Barbara T. Gates, "Those Who Drew and Those Who Wrote: Women and Victorian Popular Science Illustration," has been reprinted by permission of the Publishers from "Shifting continents, shifting species: Louisa Anne Meredith at 'home' in Tasmania," in *Intrepid Women: Victorian Artists Travel* ed. Jordana Pomeroy (Aldershot: Ashgate Publishing, 2005), 77–87. Copyright © 2005.

An earlier version of the chapter by Lorraine Code, "Images of Expertise: Women, Science, and the Politics of Representation," has been published as chapter 7, "Public Knowledge, Public Trust: Toward Democratic Epistemic Practices," in her book *Ecological Thinking: The Politics of Epistemic Location* (New York: Oxford University Press, 2006), © Oxford University Press. Used with permission.

Library of Congress Cataloging-in-Publication Data
Figuring it out : science, gender, and visual culture / edited by Ann B. Shteir and Bernard Lightman. — 1st ed.
    p.   cm. — (Interfaces : studies in visual culture)
Includes bibliographical references and index.
ISBN-13: 978-1-58465-602-9 (cloth : alk. paper)
ISBN-10: 1-58465-602-6 (cloth : alk. paper)
ISBN-13: 978-1-58465-603-6 (pbk. : alk. paper)
ISBN-10: 1-58465-603-4 (pbk. : alk. paper)
1. Visual communication in science. 2. Gender identity in science.
I. Shteir, Ann B. II. Lightman, Bernard V., 1950–
Q223.F545 2006
500.82—dc22   2006022093

Contents

Part Three: The Twentieth Century and Beyond: Changes or Continuities?

Acknowledgments

Generous funding from the Gerstein Foundation for the 2001–2002 York University Seminar for Advanced Research and from the Social Sciences and Humanities Research Council of Canada for a conference at York University on "Figural Vocabularies of Gender in 19th-Century Science" made it possible for us to organize the formal institutional features of a research seminar and a conference that led to developing this book and supporting its publication. We also acknowledge with gratitude conference funding from the School of Women's Studies and the Division of Humanities at York University. The funds activated networks of scholarly interest and have led to informal and ongoing academic connections that enrich university communities. For stalwart assistance on the seminar series and conference, we thank Judith Anderson Stuart. Jan Golinski, the discussant on the conference papers, pushed us all to think further about our topic, and we are grateful for that. For funds toward publication of this volume we extend many thanks within York University to: Office of the Vice-President (Academic), Office of the Vice-President (Research), Dean of the Faculty of Arts, Dean of the Atkinson Faculty of Liberal and Professional Studies, Centre for Feminist Research, and Division of Humanities Academic Initiatives Fund. Research grants in support of publication came as well from the Faculty of Arts, York University, and the Social Sciences and Humanities Research Council of Canada. For his work on behalf of this project we thank George Thompson of the Center for American Places.

Contributors

NAOMI ADELSON, Associate Professor and Chair, Department of Anthropology, York University, is a medical anthropologist with particular interest in cultural conceptualizations of the body. From a critical interpretive perspective, she examines the ways in which cultural interpretations of the body and, by extension, of health/normalcy reflect larger socio-political realities. *Being Alive Well: Health and the Politics of Cree Well-Being* (2000) is a study of the meanings and practices of health in a First Nations Canadian context.

ALAN BEWELL is Professor of English at the University of Toronto. His primary interest is in employing postcolonial theory and environmental history to study the literature, science, and medicine of the Romantic period. Author of *Wordsworth and the Enlightenment* (1989) and *Romanticism and Colonial Natural History* (1999) and Editor of the collection *Medicine and the West Indian Slave Trade* (1999), he is currently completing a book on colonial natural history during the Romantic period.

ANNETTE BURFOOT is Associate Professor of Sociology at Queen's University, where she teaches feminist science studies and visual culture. She edited *The Encyclopedia of Reproductive Technologies* (1999) and co-edited with Susan Lord *Killing Women: The Visual Culture of Gender and Violence* (2006). She has published numerous articles and chapters on gender and science, reproductive and genetic engineering, science fabulation, and the visual cultural of medical science.

LORRAINE CODE is Distinguished Research Professor of Philosophy at York University and a Fellow of the Royal Society of Canada. Her most recent book is *Ecological Thinking: The Politics of Epistemic Location* (2006). She is General Editor of the *Routledge Encyclopedia of Feminist Theories* (2000) and Editor of *Feminist Interpretations of Hans-Georg Gadamer* (2003), and with Kathryn Hamer has translated Michèle Le Dœuff's *Le Sexe du savoir* (1998) as *The Sex of Knowing* (2003).

BARBARA T. GATES is Alumni Distinguished Professor of English and Women's Studies Emerita at the University of Delaware. She is author of *Victorian Suicide: Mad Crimes and Sad Histories* (1988), *Kindred Nature: Victorian and Edwardian Women Embrace the Living World* (2002), and numerous essays, reviews, and edited books. She is currently at work on an electronic edition of the manuscripts of Emily Shore's journal (Virginia Rotunda Press).

MARGO S. GEWURTZ is Professor of Humanities and Master of Founders College at York University. She has published numerous essays on Canadian missionaries in China and their Chinese partners and is currently researching the history of medical missionaries in China and the search for Kala Azar.

SALLY GREGORY KOHLSTEDT, Professor in the History of Science and Technology Program at the University of Minnesota, teaches courses on science in American culture, on women, gender and science, and on science in colonial settings. She has recently published "Nature not Books: Scientists and the Origins of the Nature Study Movement in the 1890s," and "Thoughts in Things: Modernity, History and North American Museums" in *Isis,* and she is currently pursuing further works on both topics.

BERNARD LIGHTMAN is Professor of Humanities at York University and Editor of the journal *Isis.* His publications include *The Origins of Agnosticism* (1987) and the edited collection *Victorian Science in Context* (1997). He is currently completing a study of scientific authorship in the Victorian period.

JANINE MARCHESSAULT holds a Canada Research Chair in Art, Digital Media and Globalization in the Faculty of Fine Arts at York University. Her most recent publications include *McLuhan: Cosmic Media* (2005), *Wild Science: Reading Feminism, Medicine and the Media* (with Kim Sawchuk, 2000), and *Gendering the Nation: Canadian Women Filmmakers* (with Kay Armatage, Kass Banning, and Brenda Longfellow, 1999), as well as *Fluid Screens, Expanded Cinema* (with Susan Lord, 2006).

JAMES A. SECORD is Professor of History and Philosophy of Science at the University of Cambridge. His most recent book is *Victorian Sensation: The Extraordinary Publication, Reception, and Secret Authorship of Vestiges of the Natural History of Creation* (2000). He is currently researching the relations between science and the nineteenth-century newspaper press in New York, London, and Paris.

SUZANNE LE-MAY SHEFFIELD is the Associate Director (Programs) for the Centre for Learning and Teaching at Dalhousie University. She is the author of *Revealing New Worlds: Three Victorian Women*

Naturalists (2001) and *Women and Science: Social Impact and Interaction* (2004) in the ABC-Clio Science and Society Series.

ANN B. SHTEIR is Professor of Humanities and Women's Studies at York University. She is author of *Cultivating Women, Cultivating Science: Flora's Daughters and Botany in England 1760 to 1860* (1996) and essays on eighteenth and nineteenth-century gender and science and is co-editor, with Barbara T. Gates, of *Natural Eloquence: Woman Reinscribe Science* (1997). Her current research is a historical study of gender, iconography, and botany.

JONATHAN SMITH is Professor of English and Director of the Science and Technology Studies Program at the University of Michigan—Dearborn. His book *Charles Darwin and Victorian Visual Culture* was published by Cambridge University Press in 2006.

JOAN STEIGERWALD is an Associate Professor in the Science and Technology Studies Program in the Division of Humanities at York University. She is the author of articles on Schelling, Goethe, and Kant and the life sciences and is currently editing a special issue on Kantian philosophy and living beings for *Studies in the History and Philosophy of the Biological and Biomedical Sciences*. She is working on a book on the problem of the organism in German idealism, Romanticism, and science.

JENNIFER TUCKER is Associate Professor of History, Women's Studies, and Science Studies at Wesleyan University. She is the author of *Nature Exposed: Photography as an Eyewitness in Victorian Science* (2005).

Introduction

Ann B. Shteir and Bernard Lightman

This book stands at the intersection of research on science, gender, and visual culture. It focuses on visual and figural images as a way to study the workings of gender in science, and on gender as a way to examine how images in science contain and convey meanings. Contributors examine illustrations in books, magazines, art, museums, television, medical advertising, and digital formats, and discuss historically inflected ideas about women and men that long have been part of cultural practices in science and medicine and continue so into our day. They move through a consideration of images that are both pictorial and verbal out into analysis of intersections of science and gender. How, we ask, can a study of visual features help us understand better the subtle and complex ways that the modern Western culture of science developed and how cultural norms of gender were part of this development?

The focus on pictures in this book comes at a time of heightened interest in visuality in its many forms. Issues of representation and power have been central to many recent studies in the humanities and social sciences, and form part of what W. J. T. Mitchell has termed "the pictorial turn," bringing poststructural theory into visual analyses across media and the arts.[1] Mitchell has been particularly influential in bringing to the study of pictures the kinds of sophisticated tools that scholars have developed for the study of language. Visual Culture and Visual Studies now are interdisciplinary fields in themselves, and anthologies introduce readers to themes, key writings, and historical and theoretical approaches in the study of visual subjects.[2] The visual orientation of modern mass culture has led scholars in numerous fields to trace the origins of our fascination with images and to analyze their impact on us. Writing in the early 1990s, Martin Jay shed light on what he labeled an "antiocularcentrism" among notable twentieth-century French intellectuals, who mistrusted sight as a clear path to knowledge.[3] Over the past decade, the impact of computers and other digital technologies on our notions of representations and images, particularly our ability to manipulate images, has led to more critical perspectives on the correspondence between image and reality. We encounter advertising, video games, movies, and photography with some savvy, yet with some misgivings about their power over us. Political dimensions of all this are apparent in the visual spectacles of recent Image Wars, in which visual symbols of religion, science, and nationhood are destroyed as objects and as images. Bruno Latour argues that since 9/11, with its searing image of the destruction of the twin towers of the World Trade Center, there has been a "state of emergency" proclaimed on how we deal with all images, as we in the West frantically "search for the roots of fanaticism" that has led to the violent smashing of Western idols.[4] Television and newspaper images of the destruction of the Bamiyan Buddhas by the Taliban in Afghanistan, of American tanks racing across the desert toward Baghdad, and of the havoc wreaked by the current controversy over the Danish images of the Prophet Muhammad are other potent symbols of these Image Wars.

Over the past two decades, scholars within the history of science and science and technology studies have taken up visual dimensions of science and examined the use of visual materials in relation to science and its various local and disciplinary cultures. There is now a substantial body of work about pictures in the cultures of science as forms of illustration, and also as forms of education, demonstration, and aesthetic delight.[5] Some scholars have studied scientific instruments and other visual objects used to teach and promote science.[6] Others have visited portraits of scientists and doctors as a way to examine changing representations of individuals and institutions.[7] In the new area of book history, researchers have been scrutinizing books as material objects to be touched, looked at, and consumed, and the study of technologies for producing images is yielding new insights about print culture.[8] Interest recently in the history of collecting, including of natural history curiosities and early illustrated science books, has focused attention on pictures and art work as ways to reconstruct the social circumstances of production of images, and many stories still remain to be told from the living history of science and visual culture.[9] Over the ages, images have been central to Western culture. As a result, we have become image-making beings who think laterally and associatively, and our patterns of thought often are implicit and frequently unexamined. Pictures are tools for us to use in discerning social and cultural factors at work in the broad worlds of science and medicine. These factors often impinge on who practices in these areas of knowledge, and how they and their work are positioned as creators and disseminators of knowledge.

The social, cultural, and political circumstances behind the production, dissemination, and reception of images also have been themes in feminist work on visual culture over the past three decades. Feminist critics and art historians have looked, for example, at representations of women in various media, and critically examined theoretical issues of women as objects of the male "gaze" and the colonizing eye. They have studied women as makers of art, and analyzed institutional practices in the high culture of art as well as in the world of crafts, photography, and new media as these shape women's art production and the reception of this work. In due course, a focus on women's experiences as working artists shifted into more theoretical discussions about gender as a productive analytical category in visual culture, and ideas about masculinity and femininity became tools for exploring the formation and practices of social systems such as disciplines and types of work. The intersectionality of gender with analytical categories such as race, sexualities, and ethnicities has further expanded the vocabulary for feminist researchers in visual culture.[10]

Vision, visualities, and metaphors of sight have been a rallying point for critical analyses in the field of gender and science as well since the 1980s, when Evelyn Fox Keller began elucidating psychosocial and epistemological aspects of detachment, objectivity, and "subject-object" relations in science.[11] Stimulated by the work of Fox Keller, Donna Haraway, and others, a generation of feminist writers have inquired into gendered features in the history and philosophy of science, and have made feminist science studies one of the most provocative areas of knowledge production. Recent topics for feminist work in gender and science have included rhetoric within science and technology, issues of access and advancement for women in scientific fields, gendered practices, new pedagogies, bodies and sexualities, critical epistemologies, and colonial and postcolonial facets of science.[12] Turmoil about controversial pronouncements made in 2005 by President Lawrence Summers of Harvard University concerning sex differences between men and women and the aptitude of women for work in science has given fresh urgency to work in gender and science.[13] Much is at stake for the present and for the future in identifying, diagnosing, and addressing attitudes within science culture that relate to both women and men in science. The field of gender and science can offer methodological tools for current challenges, and visual tools are among these.

Our collection brings visuality into the foreground for contemporary studies of gender and science. Building upon work in visual culture and studies of illustration in science as well as on analyses of gender and science, chapters highlight gender dimensions of visual images in the cultures of modern science. By integrating gender issues into the analyses of science and visual culture, our contributors step onto the scholarly terrain that Ludmilla Jordanova and Londa Schiebinger have mapped in their historical work on science and medicine that educates researchers and students alike about visual resources for historical study. Jordanova has explored gendered languages of nature, particularly the multiple ways that visual and figural images of sex differences in the biological and medical sciences have worked over the past several centuries and can be thought about now. Her study of a nineteenth-century statue of *Nature Unveiling Herself Before Science,* for example, both clarifies and complicates links between science and gender, and a rich essay about a 1797 print entitled *Nature Display'd, shewing the Effect of the Change of the Seasons on the Ladies Garden* challenges any easy translation from gendered images to specific historical realities.[14] Schiebinger has used frontispieces, illustrations, and metaphors in early modern books about nature to unpack heavily gendered norms at work in the developing culture of science from the seventeenth century on, and has used gender productively as a tool for analyzing historical styles of science that in turn have shaped women's access to scientific education and activities. Her accounts of eighteenth-century maternal norms in Linnaean botany, and of gendered, sexualized, and racialized ideas about apes across the eighteenth and nineteenth centuries demonstrate how metaphors and visuals in natural history are pathways into cultural histories of wide contemporary pertinence.[15] In Schiebinger's view, decoding language and iconographic representation is one of a number of methodological tools of gender analysis that have great potentiality for producing new knowledge and practices in the sciences.[16]

Like Ludmilla Jordanova and Londa Schiebinger, contributors to our book use gender to study the visual face of the complex histories and cultures that have shaped modern science and medicine. The trajectory of chapters in this volume is through images to meanings and cultural interpretation. Our interest is in the pictorial as depicted through both images and words. All the contributors have their own analytic perspective on the period, the person, and the venues for science that they have studied. But, equally, all are cognizant of how complex it is to read an image that creates pictures for our mind's eye.

Issues of tools and methods for studying gender in images were on the table during a year-long faculty research seminar on the theme "Figural Vocabularies of Gender in Science and Medicine" held at York University during the academic year 2001–2002. With funding from the Gerstein Foundation, fifteen colleagues gathered for biweekly sessions under the directorship of Ann Shteir and Bernard Lightman to explore the theme from the vantage points of their interdisciplinary interests. Since the inquiry into visual dimensions of gender and science took all the contributors to this book into relatively unexplored scholarly territory, we identified several basic questions about methods as guides for research. These questions included the following:

- Do we read visual images in/about science and medicine in the same way that we read verbal images, or images conveyed through language?
- Do visual images perform the same functions in science and medicine as verbal images?
- How do issues of gender shape the production of visual images in science and medicine?
- How do issues of gender shape how scholars read and write about those visual images?
- What other factors overlap with gender in shaping the production and reception of those images in science and medicine?
- How have visual images about gender in science and medicine changed over time or varied from culture to culture?

These questions shaped our discussions as well as the nine chapters in this volume that developed from papers prepared for the York Advanced Research Seminar. Following on from the research seminar, a small working conference in May 2003 brought to York a number of scholars whose work focuses on nineteenth-century aspects of our topic. Presenters in turn heard commentaries prepared by participants in the York Advanced Research Seminar. Six papers in this volume developed from conference presentations at "Figural Vocabularies of Gender in Nineteenth-Century Science."

Chapters in this collection arose, therefore, out of interdisciplinary inquiry by scholars steeped in a variety of disciplines who welcomed the opportunity to discuss visual methodologies for approaching their topics. The result is an exploratory volume rather than a comprehensive study or a pedagogical overview of tools for analysis of visual images.[17] We are not charting a well-explored field. Instead, the chapters suggest topics and methods. Geographically, this collection clusters mainly in England, with forays to Italy, Germany, China, New York, and Toronto, and into global domains of the internet. While many contributors are in historically oriented areas of research and teaching, others work on contemporary topics in women's studies, anthropology, philosophy, and film studies. Some contributors anchor themselves in analyses of language and concepts, others in historical recovery work on individuals. Some work with digital images, and still others are at home in the print culture of popular science. Common to all the chapters, however, is an emphasis on representation, and how we can use images and verbal figures to understand more about intersections of science and cultural values, particularly how ideas about gender can enhance analyses.

The research that is showcased here displays the persistence of gender norms in the sciences, including in medicine. Ideas about men and women in the sciences, and ideas about values ascribed to and associated with men and women, enter into science culture in deep and often unarticulated ways. It is not just that ideas about sexual difference show themselves in figurative ways. Hierarchies of value enter into thinking about these matters, and have much to do with the inclusion or exclusion of women in the sciences, including the medical sciences. One can see, for example, how clusters of associations to what was tagged "feminine" or "masculine" became cultural cards to be played by a range of stakeholders in the professionalizing decades of nineteenth-century science.

Of course, using images to make explicit the often hidden cultural connotations in a work of science is inevitably problematic, and not just because we lack a substantial body of scholarship exploring the relations binding together science, gender, and visual culture. Figuration of any kind, and in any medium, is a complex form of cultural storytelling. The interpretation of visual images is fraught with difficulties by its very nature, due to the kind of objects that are the subject of our analysis. Portraying an aspect of Darwinian evolution in a work of persuasion for the Victorian scientific elite, for example, may call for using images differently from those in a popular magazine for general readers, or in a television series from the 1990s. That is, various literary, artistic, and technological vocabularies inevitably mediate how authors or artists present their material. Images dealt with in this volume include hieroglyphs, frontispieces, caricatures, anatomical models, museum displays, geographical charts, literary metaphors, photographs, and pictures in magazines. Is it necessary to create different interpretive techniques for each type of image? Are certain types of images easier to interpret than others? Are iconographic images from the late eighteenth and early nineteenth centuries, such as those discussed by Joan Steigerwald, more transparent in their meanings than scientific photographs and similar images from the later nineteenth century, which often hide their artefactual character in the process of presenting themselves as duplications of nature?

Similarly problematic are the various formats for works on science in which images can be found. Some images appear as freestanding pictorial illustration in a book or magazine. Others are textual descriptions of an image, designed to create a picture in the reader's mind. More often, we find a format where the two are combined—verbal images can stand side by side with a visual image. In this format, there is potential for gaps between the meaning of the verbal and the visual image. Which image more transparently conveys an author's intentions? Does the visual image hold the key to interpret the verbal image? Is it the other way around? Or can the meaning of both only be determined by using each image as a guide to interpreting the other?

Other sets of interpretive problems revolve around related issues of agency and identity, and fluidity and destabilization. The case of agency in relation to the production of visual images in science poses a number of difficult questions. Who was responsible for the creation of a particular image? If a group of people was involved, how much of a role did each of them play? How much was this connected to their attempt to establish an identity for themselves within a world of science in which gender norms were often implicit features of activities and practices? Determining the answer to these questions often can be tricky and can depend on whether or not the creators wished their roles to be recognized. On the one hand, visual images have allowed marginalized groups to participate in scientific activities and to establish a scientific identity for themselves. As Jennifer Tucker, Barbara Gates, Bernard Lightman, and Suzanne Le-May Sheffield discuss, women were able to continue to participate in scientific activities through their involvement in scientific photography and illustration, even though the latter half of the nineteenth century was a period when male professionals were trying to push them out of science. For these women, images provided a sense of agency and a scientific identity as popularizer, scientific illustrator, or photographer. In a similar vein, Sally Gregory Kohlstedt deals with the attempt of zoological field naturalists and taxidermists to transform nineteenth-century museum exhibits into displays of masculine power. In this context, the creators of an image could desire to assert their agency and obtain credit for their contributions. On the other hand, some creators could choose to conceal their own roles in the production of a scientific image and mask the gender norms that may have been at work in the product of their labor. The creators of the Visible Human Project, as Naomi Adelson explains, wanted most of all to present their dissections of the human body as objective and natural, despite their tendency to treat the male anatomy as the standard.

In the case of photographs, as both Lorraine Code and Margo Gewurtz show, it is not certain if the photographer or the photographer's subject is responsible for creating the potential meaning of the image. Does Dr. Nancy Olivieri, and not the photographer, control the presentation of her identity as a woman in medicine? Is Dr. Jean Dow stage-managing the photographs taken of her and her assistants so that they reflect her own agenda and not that of the photographer or the missionary society that uses the pictures in their publications? How are we to know when either the subject or the photographer is trying to subvert traditional notions of gender in producing the image? Answering these questions requires sophisticated and indirect analysis that is sensitive to the ways that gender may operate in different cultural settings.

If the issues of agency and identity raise a host of difficulties, so too does the attempt to understand to what extent the meaning of an image evolves in different contexts. The fluidity of meanings of images heightens their tendency to act as destabilizing influences. Images introduce the potential for radical destablization because they often incorporate older images that contain within them previous cultural connotations. As James Secord vividly reveals in his chapter on composite caricatures, the consumer of visual images is free to take images out of their original context and place them together, creating new meanings with consequences for the participation of women in science and for the conception of women by scientists. Keeping track of volatile images from earlier centuries, such as Ann Shteir's Flora or Alan Bewell's natural history collector, as they endlessly transmute into new visual objects while circulating in new social and cultural contexts, seems like an almost impossible task. When Annette Burfoot traces scientific images of reproduction from the early modern period to the present, and when Janine Marchessault discusses the evolution of the medical drama as a genre on recent American television, each scholar is uncovering how the transmutation of an image can lead to the disappearance of women from the picture.

While the interpretation of images presents a challenge for scholars working at the intersection of science, gender, and visual culture, so too does the thematic richness of the topic. Arranging the chapters in a collection is always a case of sorting through a number of possible structural configurations—like viewing the many interesting patterns produced by a kaleidoscope. In the case of this collection, the task was difficult because the scarcity of scholarship in the area left us with relatively few established patterns to pick from, and also because the diversity of the individual chapters ruled out the possibility of quickly identifying a set of neat groupings. As we refined the focus and looked for pleasing and intriguing patterns, we considered first a thematic organization of materials, and later a chronological and historical one. A thematic structure offers many insights by bringing into view four key ways that science, gender, and visual culture overlap with one another.

audience, analysts of images pay attention to audiences for visual images in science, try to identify the effects intended for specific audiences, and gauge how these images may be experienced. But, to what degree can one read from an image to a historical actuality or reality? How broadly can one generalize about the significance of an image for a time and place? As much as our contributors might want to map large patterns about "patriarchy" or "Victorian culture" in relation to gender and science, particularities and multiple voices emerged in their analyses again and again. Universalizing patterns are alluring, but greater insights come from reading in local and historically specific ways, against the backdrop of broad cultural iconographies.

Since sensitivity to historical contexts is a key to interpreting visual images, we chose, therefore, to group the chapters chronologically and historically rather than thematically. An historical structure allows us to see patterns across time, both in the development of visual culture and in notions of gender. Viewing scientific images across the centuries raises some interesting questions about how they have been transformed and how they may reflect changes, continuities, and tensions in notions of gender. Do newer visual technologies intersect with gender in different ways than earlier visual forms, or do older issues and relations carry on in newer vocabularies? To stimulate consideration of this question, and to affirm our historical grounding, three chapters about texts and images from the late eighteenth century form Part One of the volume. Part Two brings together seven chapters about the nineteenth century, and Part Three contains five chapters about twentieth-century and contemporary materials.

The first section, titled "Frontispieces," focuses on the importance of actual frontispieces in scientific texts. By ranging from antiquity into the early nineteenth century, it establishes a framework for inquiry about science, gender, and visual images. All three chapters highlight the importance of classical themes in science and in conceptions of gender. Frontispieces are a rich resource for understanding how the changing depiction of Flora as botanical icon paralleled the evolution of gendered ideas about women and nature; how predominantly male natural history collectors found a figural language for expressing the nature of scientific desire in Ovid's *Metamorphoses;* and how Alexander von Humboldt and his contemporaries drew on classical myths surrounding Diana and Apollo to articulate their views on the scientific disclosure of female and male nature and of nature more generally. The "frontispiece" chapters for this volume set the scene for the historically inflected analyses that follow. They show representations of sexed and gendered identities in tension with social practices. They study practices that take place both inside and outside historically specific cultures of science, and that are displayed across nationality and modes of visualization. Their interdisciplinary scholarship calls upon literary history, philosophy, and social theory as ways to read visual and figural images.

Titled "The Nineteenth Century: Technologies and Gender Politics," the second part explores the move away from ornate images and metaphors based on classical themes, to those that were designed to represent the natural world realistically. The complex frontispieces of the previous period began to disappear in the early nineteenth century at the same time that visual images were circulating more widely, in part because of technological developments. This was also a period when science began to be dominated by male professionals, who claimed that their expertise gave them privileged insight into the interpretation of nature, the representation of nature in images, and the natural basis of gender. Darwin picked his illustrations for his *Descent of Man* carefully, as he wanted to present the process of sexual selection at work in nature, while male natural history museum curators and taxidermists arranged their exhibits to emphasize the way animals conformed to traditional human domestic patterns. Scientific photography, which made its claims to objectivity by denying that human agency was a part of the process, established the public image of Victorian science as a middle-class masculine practice.

Although the professional scientist emerged as a powerful force during the nineteenth century, he did not manage to exclude women completely from the scientific enterprise. Visual images offer eloquent testimony to the struggle of women to preserve a role for themselves in science. Both the flowering of composite caricatures in the 1820s in England and the illustrations in the works of female popularizers of science in the second half of the century point to the continued participation of women in science. For those women who could paint or draw, illustrating the work of scientifically inclined husbands also offered a route into science. Despite the masculinization of scientific photography, some women made, circulated, and consumed photographs.

In Part Three, "The Twentieth Century and Beyond: Changes or Continuities?" chapters explore how the politics of gender in science plays itself out in visual images in such diverse fields as philosophy, film studies, and anthropology. One chapter deals with the hidden narrative within the photographs of women missionaries and doctors in China in the early twentieth century, a narrative that speaks of a collectivity of women working together as scientific professionals. Another chapter explores the use of photographs depicting male and female expertise in a controversy about medical ethics to show how Dr. Nancy Olivieri attempted to defy the medical establishment. Other chapters deal with the powerful impact of new technologies and visual mediums that reinforce the gender status quo. Medical television programs largely have reflected the gendered division of labor that pictures men as doctors and women as patients. Magazine ads in support of reproductive technology depict the process of birth as a matter between skilled doctors and newborn infants; the role of the mother is so secondary that she rarely appears in these ads in human form. New technologies mask the perpetuation of traditional gender norms as their proponents claim to render a hidden reality more visible. Thus, the Visible Human Project, with its creation of the model digital man and woman to further medical research, takes the male as the model of humanity. These powerful new technologies are even more effective than the nineteenth-century ones in presenting themselves as creators of images that are realistic and objective, thereby hiding the cultural and gendered connotations embodied in their representations.

The chapters in this book are themselves figures in the fabric of science culture, with shadings and overwriting, a triptych in which past, present, and future overlap with sometimes surprising results. Intricate references to traditions of knowledge, notably mythology and religion, carry across the centuries and sound unexpected echoes and depths that relate to women and men as well as to complex ideas about masculinity and femininity. Reading chapters in this collection that take us back into early modern Europe and forms of anatomy and print culture, and up into digital technologies of the late twentieth century, one may wonder whether new technologies bring new approaches regarding gender, or continue to replicate older messages. The analyses in the visual culture of science and gender that form this book point to new work to be done. For example, further scrutiny of visual languages of masculinity in scientific work and scientific cultures will reward attention. Contributors to our collection examine female figures as diverse as the iconic goddess of flowers and the woman whose body is one of the digitized Visible Humans. They study the male figure of Apollo as well as the men figured as Macaroni naturalists and as television's Dr. Kildare. Exploring mixed gender messages about knowledge, science, and sexuality found among classical figures and in icons of our day, they bring into visibility some startling continuities in gender ideas and agendas. From classical mythology and Roman popular practices, into cultural struggles about naturalized male and female identity, and on into changing ideas about medical heroism, cultural vocabularies in science call upon gender norms and features in ways that we benefit from recognizing. We will read visual and figural languages of nature more insightfully and energetically if gender is part of our analytic tool chest.

Notes

1. W. J. T. Mitchell, *Picture Theory: Essays on Verbal and Visual Representation* (Chicago: University of Chicago Press, 1994), 13. On the history of the study of visual culture and its frameworks and methodology, See Margaret Dikovitskaya, *The Study of the Visual after the Cultural Turn* (Cambridge, Mass.: MIT Press, 2005).

2. See, e.g., Nicholas Mirzoeff, ed., *The Visual Culture Reader,* 2nd ed. (London and New York: Routledge, 2002); and Vanessa R. Schwartz and Jeannene M. Przyblyski, eds., *The Nineteenth-Century Visual Culture Reader* (New York and London: Routledge, 2004).

3. Martin Jay, *Downcast Eyes: The Denigration of Vision in Twentieth-Century French Thought* (Berkeley: University of California Press, 1993).

4. Bruno Latour and Peter Weibel, eds., *Iconoclash: Beyond the Image Wars in Science, Religion, and Art* (Karlsruhe and Cambridge, Mass.: Center for Art and Media and MIT, 2002), 37.

5. See, e.g., Ludmilla Jordanova, *Nature Displayed: Gender, Science and Medicine 1760–1820* (London: Longman, 1999); Alex Soojung-Kim Pang, "Visual Representation and Post-Constructivist History of Science," *Historical Studies in the Physical and Biological Sciences* 28 (1977): 139–71; Caroline A. Jones and Peter Galison, eds., *Picturing Science, Producing Art* (New York and London: Routledge, 1998); Martin Rudwick, *Scenes from Deep Time: Early Pictorial Representations of the Prehistoric World* (Chicago: University of Chicago Press, 1992); Gill Saunders, *Picturing Plants: An Analytical History of Botanical Illustration* (Berkeley: University of California Press, 1995); Barbara Maria Stafford, including *Artful Science: Enlightenment Entertainment and the Eclipse of Visual Education* (Cambridge, Mass., and London: MIT Press, 1994); Ann Shelby Blum, *Picturing Nature: Nineteenth Century Zoological Illustration* (Princeton: Princeton University Press, 1993); Jonathan Crary, *Techniques of the Observer: On Vision and Modernity in the Nineteenth Century* (Cambridge, Mass., and London: MIT Press, 1990); Michael Lynch and Steve Woolgar, eds., *Representation in Scientific Practice* (Cambridge, Mass.: MIT Press, 1990); Gordon Fyfe and John Law, *Picturing Power: Visual Depiction and Social Relations* (London: Routledge, 1988); and Allan Ellenius, ed., *Natural Sciences and the Arts: Aspects of Interaction from the Renaissance to the 20th Century: An International Symposium* (Uppsala: S. Academiae Upsaliensis, 1985).

6. See Frances Terpak, *Devices of Wonder: From the World in a Box to Images on a Screen* (Los Angeles: Getty Research Institute, 2001). See also Anke Te Heesen, *The World in a Box: The Story of an Eighteenth-Century Picture Encyclopedia,* trans. Ann M. Hentschel (Chicago: University of Chicago Press, 2002); and Thomas L. Hankins and Robert J. Silverman, *Instruments and the Imagination* (Princeton: Princeton University Press, 1995).

7. See, e.g., Ludmilla Jordanova, *Defining Features: Scientific and Medical Portraits 1660–2000* (London: Reaktion Books and National Portrait Gallery, 2000); and Patricia Fara, *Newton: The Making of a Genius* (New York: Columbia University Press, 2002).

8. See, e.g., James Secord, *Victorian Sensation: The Extraordinary Publication, Reception, and Secret Authorship of "Vestiges of the Natural History of Creation"* (Chicago and London: University of Chicago Press, 2000); and Marina Frasca-Spada and Nick Jardine, *Books and the Sciences in History* (Cambridge: Cambridge University Press, 2000); also Lorraine Daston and Katharine Parks, *Wonders and the Order of Nature 1150–1750* (New York: Zone Books, 1998).

9. See, e.g., David Freedberg, *The Eye of the Lynx: Galileo, His Friends, and the Beginnings of Modern Natural History* (Chicago and London: University of Chicago Press, 2002); and Ray Desmond, *Great Natural History Books and Their Creators* (London: British Library, 2003).

10. See, e.g., Amelia Jones, ed., *The Feminism and Visual Culture Reader* (London and New York: Routledge, 2003); Fiona Carson and Claire Pajaczkowska, eds., *Feminist Visual Culture* (Edinburgh: Edinburgh University Press, 2000); and Lisa Bloom, ed., *With Other Eyes: Looking at Race and Gender in Visual Culture* (Minneapolis and London: University of Minneapolis Press, 1999). Two notable earlier works of feminist visual cultural analysis are Griselda Pollock, *Vision and Difference: Femininity, Feminism and the Histories of Art* (London and New York: Routledge, 1988); and Lisa Tickner, *The Spectacle of Women: Imagery of the Suffrage Campaign, 1907–1914* (Chicago: University of Chicago Press, 1988).

11. See Evelyn Fox Keller, *Reflections on Gender and Science* (New Haven: Yale University Press, 1985); Evelyn Fox Keller and Christine Grontkowski, "The Mind's Eye," in *Feminism and Science,* ed. Evelyn Fox Keller and Helen E. Longino (Oxford: Oxford University Press, 1996), 187–202.

12. See Donna Haraway, *The Haraway Reader* (New York and London: Routledge, 2004); also Sandra Harding, *Is Science Multi-Cultural? Postcolonialisms, Feminisms, and Epistemologies* (Bloomington: Indiana University Press, 1998); and Lorraine Code, *What Can She Know? Feminist Theory and the Construction of Knowledge* (Ithaca and London: Cornell University Press, 1991), ch. 4. Anthologies include Muriel Lederman and Ingrid Bartsch, eds., *The Gender and Science Reader* (London and New York: Routledge, 2001); and Maralee Mayberry, Banu Subramaniam, and Lisa H. Weasel, *Feminist Science Studies: A New Generation* (New York and London: Routledge, 2001). See also Paula Treichler, Lisa Cartwright, and Constance Penley, *The Visible Woman: Imaging Technology, Gender, and Science* (New York: NYU Press, 1998).

13. For the text of a debate about "The Science of Gender and Science" that took place at Harvard University on April 22, 2005, see "Edge: The Third Culture," http://www.edge.org/3rd_culture/debate/05/debate05_index.html.

14. Ludmilla Jordanova, *Sexual Visions: Images of Gender in Science and Medicine between the Eighteenth and Twentieth Centuries* (Madison: University of Wisconsin Press, 1989), ch. 5; and *Nature Displayed,* ch.2. See also her *Defining Features,* ch. 3 ("Gender and Scientific Heroism").

15. Londa Schiebinger, *The Mind Has No Sex? Women in the Origins of Modern Science* (Cambridge, Mass.: Harvard University Press, 1989), esp. ch. 5, and *Nature's Body: Gender in the Making of Modern Science* (Cambridge, Mass.: Harvard University Press, 1993).

16. Londa Schiebinger, *Has Feminism Changed Science?* (Cambridge, Mass.: Harvard University Press, 1999), 188–89. Other methodological tools for gender analysis in science discussed in the conclusion to this book include analyzing scientific priorities, institutional arrangements, and the cultures of science, and thinking about definitions of science and theoretical frameworks.

17. A helpful overview of methods for analyzing visual images of many kinds can be found in Gillian Rose, *Visual Methodologies: An Introduction to the Interpretation of Visual Materials* (London: Sage, 2001).

Part One

FRONTISPIECES

Chapter 1

ICONOGRAPHIES OF FLORA

The Goddess of Flowers in the Cultural History of Botany

Ann B. Shteir

Erasmus Darwin loved both botany and mythology, and it is therefore not surprising that his two-part scientific poem *The Botanic Garden* (1791) opens with the image of a goddess gazing into a mirror, surrounded by ethereal beings that adorn her with flowers. The frontispiece, entitled *Flora Attired by the Elements,* depicts the goddess of flowers as preoccupied with her appearance (figure 1). Her body position appears to be modest, yet she is shown as sinuous and sexualized and aware of being on display. This alluring image was designed by the Anglo-Swiss Romantic artist Henry Fuseli as the point of entry into a literary work that itself was meant to entice readers into knowledge of nature, particularly the expansive vitality of the Vegetable Kingdom. Erasmus Darwin was an intensely visual writer who used pictures, metaphors, and analogies of many kinds "to inlist Imagination under the banner of Science" in this work.[1] In the first part of *The Botanic Garden,* "The Economy of Vegetation," nymphs of fire and water, gnomes of the earth, and sylphs of the air guide readers through teeming Nature, in which "LIFE buds and breathes from Indus to the Poles."[2] The second part of the poem is the better known "Loves of the Plants" in which playful verses and anthropomorphic flowers explain the Linnaean system for classifying the plant kingdom, based on the reproductive parts of flowers and on normative ideas about love, marriage, and heterosexuality. The pictorial representation of the goddess of flowers in the frontispiece to Darwin's *Botanic Garden,* blending classical allusion with exuberance and rhetorical ornament, is well suited to a work that combines rhapsodic poetry and scientific information in a curious mix of Enlightenment and Romantic values.

Flora was an appropriate icon for a literary work from a time when the Linnaean sexual system had brought botany to widening

1.1 *Flora Attired by the Elements*, frontispiece to Erasmus Darwin, *The Botanic Garden* (1791), designed by Henry Fuseli and engraved by Anker Smith.
Courtesy Thomas Fisher Rare Book Library, University of Toronto.

audiences in England that were interested in polite and sociable activities relating to the plant kingdom. As the goddess of flowers, Flora links science with mythology, popular culture, literature, and art history. Her presence in the cultural history of botany as a visual and verbal figure has an immediate relevance for analyzing Darwin's poem, for she helps to open up Darwin's work to analyses of women, gender, and nature in relation to the science culture of the late eighteenth century. More than that, Flora gestures broadly to a history of representations of women and nature. From the time of Roman writers, into Renaissance painting, early modern horticultural books, and eighteenth-century poetry, Flora had been a symbol of fecundity and sexuality and was used widely in figural and visual forms. With the development of empirical and experimental sciences, however, when nature increasingly was approached technically rather than poetically, personifications like Flora lost ground within scientific culture. Languages of nature that formerly had resonated with symbolic meanings were challenged by technical scientific vocabularies during the eighteenth and nineteenth centuries, and one result was the erasure of symbols associating women with science. By the nineteenth century, Flora had disappeared from the world of technical botany as a personified and mythic figure. She had an ongoing active afterlife, though, in the gendered culture of polite and sociable botany.

Flora's career as a botanical icon intersects, therefore, with issues of interest to scholars of women's studies, gender and science, cultural history, and visual studies. Pictorial and figurative images of the goddess of flowers are a diagnostic tool that can be used to study practices within disciplines and across cultural forms. Within art history, iconographies of Flora reflect several traditional images of women in the Western imagination and underscore the power of representations in shaping and naturalizing ideas about women. Within the history of science, Flora participates in the history of science writing and is also part of visual traditions within early modern science that routinely incorporated personifications, emblems, and poetic ornaments into book design. Verbal and visual forms of Flora also can stimulate ways of thinking about normative concepts of gender that have been used to position both women and men in relation to knowledge of nature. Although the goddess of flowers is only a representation in the cultural imaginary, Flora does not exist in a completely separate universe from the material realities of women within science culture; rather, she continues to be used by writers, artists, and others, and to do their quite varied gendered cultural work. How historical contingencies might shape such representations, however, is far from simple or easily translatable. Based in her studies of gender in relation to science and visual culture, Ludmilla Jordanova rightly has urged caution when interpreting historical images of women, particularly abstractions and personifications. One should not expect to find clear and direct links between iconic representations of "feminine figures" and the status of women in a time and place, but, she argues, historical images can work well methodologically as motifs and forms of cultural mediation.[3] There is indeed still much to learn about how historical ideas about women, gender, and science overlap so as to shape access by women and men to scientific knowledge. Insofar as a gendered science culture has channelled women's access to knowledge and women's scientific practices, a figured Flora can serve as a guide through some of these historical domains.

This chapter studies two aspects of Flora's story within the historical culture of science: how she serves as a cultural icon in book illustration, and how her story works as a genre within the history of modern science writing. Pictorial forms of Flora as the goddess of flowers were integral to the early history of botanical publications, yet the term "flora" came to refer mainly to a type of technical botany book. I focus here on England during the late eighteenth and early nineteenth centuries, when botany was a prominent area of natural history, part of fashion and part of general knowledge. A popular topic for conversation as well as a form of self-discipline and path to spirituality, the study of botany featured in the culture of self-improvement and national reform at that time. Botanical study was promoted widely for women, who participated in a range of social, intellectual, and artistic activities relating to the Vegetable Kingdom. The goddess of flowers began her metamorphoses in the history of Roman culture, and over the centuries into the time of Erasmus Darwin carried layers of cultural associations that connected closely to gendered ideas about women and nature. Many cultural sources provide resources for studying Flora in the cultural history of science. These include textual references dating back to antiquity as well as associations to the goddess of flowers within popular writing. In addition to textual sources, visual materials abound from iconographic traditions in Western art since the Renaissance.[4] Accordingly, the visualized figure of Flora serves as an excellent leitmotif for complexities of gender and science as these in turn inform institutions and practices in modern science. Flora's metamorphosis from myth into genre, and from pictorial into verbal form, parallels transformations in the masculinizing culture of the sciences by the nineteenth century that favored specialization and professionalization over aesthetics and general knowledge.

Flora's History

Flora steps into twenty-first-century analysis trailing millennia of associations. Her history traces back to nature worship and the Great Goddess and to agriculture-based rituals about the flowering of cereals, vines, and fruit trees.[5] Italic peoples celebrated her as a fertility goddess, and beginning in the third century B.C., Rome held six days of public religious festivals in the springtime, during the last three days of April and first three days of May, that were intended to maintain the good will of Flora. The popular Floralia, or games of Flora, were theatrical performances of "cheerful sexiness" and included "notoriously licentious" activities by prostitutes who danced, mimed, and took off their clothes on audience demand.[6] Satirists and moralists of the Augustan period often censured these ludic celebrations. Seneca, for example, singled out the "naked actresses" at the Floralia in an essay "On the Degeneracy of the Age" (A.D. 63–65), and early Christians condemned the activities and their participants as well.[7]

But the Roman poet Ovid saw the games of Flora in a different light, and his account of the goddess of flowers in the *Fasti* (c. A.D. 8–17) is a key literary source for later stories and for the writers and artists who shaped Flora's legacy. The *Fasti* is a poem about the Roman calendar and the origins of rituals across the Roman religious year that blends mythology, literary reference, anthropological observations, and political commentaries about imperial power in Augustan Rome. Ovid took this work with him into exile from Rome when banished by the Emperor Augustus to a remote site on the Black Sea. From his sad perch on the periphery of Roman culture, he elegiacally celebrated the richness of Roman practices. In *Fasti* book 5, Ovid narrates a history of Flora as goddess and defends and celebrates the popular religious events in her honor. Because Augustan writers before Ovid had ignored Flora in what was, according to Elaine Fantham, perhaps "a pattern of studied neglect," the *Fasti* was particularly influential in shaping myths about the goddess of flowers. [8] Structuring his account as an interview between a poet and the goddess herself, Ovid begins by calling into his presence Flora, "mother of flowers."[9] What is her story? How did she get her name? We learn that Flora was once a beautiful Greek "nymph of the happy fields" whose Greek name was Chloris. The god Zephyr pursued and abducted her, and then married her. He gave her power and jurisdiction over a wide domain; it was she who "scattered new seed across countless nations" and brought color to flowers.[10] Flora's power of fertility also benefited the gods; she provided the flower that enabled Minerva to conceive her son Mars. But like other gods, Flora was insulted easily by a lack of proper attention, and we learn that Rome established an annual festival to secure her good will and protection. The poet in the *Fasti* is enchanted by the lustre and scent of Flora and by all the gifts of the goddess who "warns us to use life's beauty as it blooms."[11]

Flora carried special power for Ovid as a goddess of fertility and celebration, and she in turn was an apt subject for this Augustan poet who celebrated the transformative powers of love and sexuality in his other writings, notably the *Metamorphoses* and *The Art of Love*. But it has been argued that Flora served quite a different purpose outside of literary domains and within Roman religion, gender ideology, and state formation. A classicist who charts a deep-seated misogyny in the foundational myths and rituals of Rome has connected Roman religious practices to the patriarchal subordination of women during the Augustan era. Ariadne Staples argues that cults dedicated to Flora and to Ceres (goddess of the grain and harvests) illustrate the polarization of gender roles within Roman religion. The cults had a complementary relationship to one another, marking the beginning and end of agricultural festivals. But they also expressed a deep division of women into ritually distinct groups of prostitute and wife. Flora was the "meretrix," the prostitute, representing exuberance and a ludic lack of constraint. Ceres was the "matrona," representing sober Roman gender norms of female conduct, including the ideal of the wife as well as the overall regulation of sexuality by marriage.[12] In such a reading of female icons, Roman religious practices worked reciprocally with beliefs about gender and sexuality.

Ovid's glorification of the goddess as enchanting woman, powerful goddess, and mother of flowers is, in part, a deliberate corrective on bifurcated Roman beliefs about women's nature as either licentious "meretrix" or regulated "matrona." But Ovid's affectionate and respectful vision of Flora did not prevail. The association of Flora and the games of Flora with prostitution and lewd self-display became the main legacy of the goddess from Roman culture to Renaissance and early modern literature and art, mediated as well by early Christian beliefs and institutional practices. Giovanni Boccaccio, for example, describes Flora as a prostitute in his *Famous Women* (1362), a collection of biographical pieces about women of earlier times in history and mythology. Boccaccio traces the origin of the Floralia to an actual prostitute, seductive and available, childless and rich, who named the Roman people as her heir and stipulated that public birthday celebrations should be held annually in her name.[13] While this account can be read as celebrating Flora for her strategic self-fashioning, Boccaccio focusses only on woman as body and on woman using her body. His representation of Flora parallels mainstream ideas about woman's nature in canonical Western philosophical, religious, and medical writings over many centuries. Embodying mixed messages as an icon of sexuality, Flora represents reproductive fertility and also practices that have to do with pleasure and profit, not reproduction.

The gendered heritage of the goddess of flowers became part of English and European cultural vocabularies. Art historians interested in meanings ascribed to the figure of Flora have characterized the main iconographic traditions for the Roman goddess of flowers within visual culture as "Flora primavera" and "Flora meretrix." "Flora primavera" is understood to be Flora as springtime, renewal, and fertility; she is a procreative Ovidian "mother of flowers." "Flora meretrix" is Flora as the prostitute and courtesan, who uses her sexuality and manipulates others in ways that are not tied to reproduction. Indeed, in a classic iconographic study published in 1961, the art historian Julius Held, having traced images of Flora across canonical Western paintings, argues that "Flora primavera" is an overlay on a more eroticized tradition, and that the "true nature" of the goddess Flora is to be found in accounts of her as a Roman courtesan.[14] It is problematic to essentialize the figure of Flora in this way. Nevertheless, Held's analysis points to cross-references that would have been familiar to Renaissance and Baroque viewers and that have remarkable iconographic staying power for images of the goddess in various media in more recent times.

Sandro Botticelli's painting *Primavera* (1477–1478) illustrates these traditions of Flora within visual culture as well as the challenges for interpreting imagery of Flora (figure 1.2). Presenting a series of mythological figures as an allegory of spring, Botticelli portrays Venus, the goddess of love, standing in a garden filled with flowers, flanked on one side by three Graces and the god Mercury, and on the other side by Flora and by the nymph Chloris who is seized by Zephyr, god of the wind. Above Venus, Cupid shoots an arrow of love. Moving from right to left, the figures tell a story that generally is understood as a series of actions that involve transformation, development, and fertility. Flowers issue from the mouth of Chloris as she changes into Flora, and Flora's rounded belly in turn displays her fecundity as she strews flowers from her lap. By contrast to the physicality of this group, the three Graces on the other side of Venus are figures of ethereal delicacy. Art historical interpretations of this painting find quite different emphases in Botticelli's work. Some highlight connections to Renaissance Humanist culture and close knowledge of Ovid's *Fasti*, others to Neoplatonism, and still others to social history and vernacular culture. The art historian Charles Dempsey, for example, writes about Botticelli's painting as layered with allusions to secular songs and popular festivals in fifteenth-century Florence.[15] In an analysis that interpolates gender ideology,

(Ed. Alinari) N. 1455. FIRENZE - R. Galleria Uffizi. Allegoria della Primavera. (Botticelli).

1.2 Sandro Botticelli, *Primavera* (1477–1478). *Alinari/Art Resource, NY; Uffizi, Florence, Italy.*

the feminist art historian Lilian Zirpolo has suggested that the painting also illustrates models of behavior for a newlywed noblewoman to follow in her life as a chaste wife and virtuous mother. "Works of art such as the *Primavera*," she writes, "served as visual tools to provide women with models of expected behavior and, at the same time, as reminders of their lesser role in society." [16] The contrast between wild, animal-like Chloris and a domesticated Flora is evidence for her point. Zirpolo's iconographic reading of this painting differs from the account of Flora's "true nature" in writing by an earlier generation of art historians.

Across the early modern period, the genealogy of Flora as fertility goddess, Ovidian "mother of flowers," Roman prostitute, and wealthy progenitor of a popular religious festival, offered artists a diverse cultural palette. A few examples must suffice to indicate uses of the figure of Flora at that time. A court opera entitled *La Flora* from Florence in the 1620s presents Chloris and Venus as powerful and active female symbols of renewal; these have been read allegorically in relation to a Medici marriage and to a transfer in political power in Tuscany at that time.[17] Nicolas Poussin figured

Flora in allegorical paintings that celebrate springtime, notably *Triumph of Flora* (c. 1627) and *Realm of Flora* (1631).[18] Flora is also a central thematic in the visual vocabulary of European paintings of women, with all the layers of meaning and association that one would expect from representations of female figures. Rembrandt, for one, depicted Flora at several stages in his career, sometimes with specific reference to his wife Saskia, but generally as an idealized female figure in pastoral dress. His 1634 painting of *Flora* shows a young woman, flowers in hand, posed as a lovely and sensuous figure of fertility; a tulip in her hair gives a Dutch flavor to the Roman goddess (figure 1.3).[19] Other seventeenth-century portraits of women as Flora highlight the iconographic legacy of the goddess as a "meretrix" figure.[20]

1.3 Rembrandt, *Flora* (1634). *The State Hermitage Museum, St. Petersburg.*

Flora and Botany Books: From Icon to Genre

Examples from the fine arts show the flexibility of the Flora thematic and provide historical contexts for versions of the goddess of flowers in the visual and figural culture of science. During the sixteenth and seventeenth centuries, the goddess of flowers was featured in botanical and horticultural books, characteristically with flowers in her hand and around her head. Recalling Ovid's powerful deity, elaborate pictorial title pages and frontispieces presented Flora as majestic, endowed with considerable authority. On the title page of William Turner's *A New Herball* (1551–1568), for example, Flora stands near the royal arms of King Edward, atop an initialed tablet (figure 1.4).

1.4 Frontispiece to William Turner, *A New Herball* (1551). *Reproduced with the kind permission of the Director and the Board of Trustees of the Royal Botanic Gardens, Kew.*

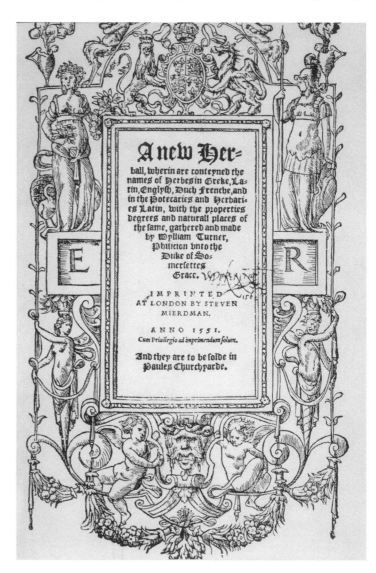

1.5 Frontispiece to Simon Paulli, *Flora Danica* ([1647]–1648).
Courtesy of Hunt Institute for Botanical Documentation, Carnegie Mellon University, Pittsburgh, PA.

She holds flowers, and, like Botticelli's fecund Primavera, wears a garment tied so as to accentuate her belly. William Turner wrote *A New Herball* for physicians and apothecaries in England, many of whom were unable to read Greek or Latin. This influential book by the "Father of English Botany" lists the names of medicinal plants in Greek, Latin, English, Dutch, and French, and describes their properties in English, based on the author's own observations and experience.[21] An equivalent publication in Germany and Scandinavia was *Flora Danica* (1648), an illustrated book of medicinal plants compiled by Simon Paulli, botanical teacher and physician to the King of Denmark. The frontispiece depicts a flower-bedecked Flora who holds a quill-like frond in her hand instead of the conventional floral bouquet (figure 1.5). In no way a "Flora meretrix," Paulli's goddess of flowers is "Flora primavera" with a pen. Indeed, the picture suggests that Flora is writing her own account of the plants of Denmark. Flora also occupied center stage in books about how to cultivate flowers. The title page of John Rea's *Flora: Seu, de Florum Cultura* (1665) features an engraving of Flora as a queen seated on a pediment, with Ceres, the goddess of the grain, and Pomona, the goddess of fruits, standing below her as maids of honor (figure 1.6). Rea was a horticulturalist celebrated for his gardening skills, who wanted to show how to grow fruit trees and flowers such as tulips in the cold climate of England. The regenerative power of his goddess of flowers recalls Ovid's figure of renewal. In a poem accompanying the engraved title page, Rea describes Flora as the "Gracious Queen . . . [who] sweetly smiling casts a ray / From her bright Eyes, which like Sol's cheering Fire, / Dries up cold dewes, and drives away / The Frosts."[22] In all the instances of seventeenth-century books about plants, the goddess of flowers is figured in the tradition of "Flora primavera." She embodies regenerative fertility and is visualized as an icon of power with command over her part of nature.

By the eighteenth century, a visual tradition of Flora as goddess of flowers began to fade in books that construed themselves as scientific. "Flora" metamorphosed from a mythological and allegorical goddess into a literary genre of science writing. As still used now, the term "flora" came to designate a specific type of botany book in an inventory tradition. Neither a compilation of medicinal information about plants nor an assemblage of descriptions of ornamental flowers, a flora lists and describes indigenous plants that can be found in a specific geographical region, and gives botanical characteristics for identifying the plants. As a botanical genre, floras may contain illustrations of defining features of plants, but for the most part they are a resolutely verbal form. William Hudson's *Flora Anglica* (1762) exemplifies this verbal form (figure 1.7). The standard late eighteenth-century book of British botany for many decades, *Flora Anglica* describes plants indigenous to England, groups them into classes and orders according to Linnaeus's sexual system, and adopts Linnaeus's convenient practice of binomial nomenclature. It was written in Latin, and carries neither an engraved title page nor a frontispiece of any kind. Hudson was a well-placed botanical enthusiast in London who is credited widely with being the first to introduce Linnaean principles successfully into British botany.[23] Although 'the term "flora" had appeared a century earlier in publications that incorporated botanical information, it became particularly popular with Linnaean botanists over the course of the later eighteenth century and soon was adopted universally.[24]

1.6 *Flora, Ceres and Pomona*, frontispiece to John Rea, *Flora: seu, de florum cultura. or, a complete florilege* (1665), engraved by David Loggan.
Reproduced with the kind permission of the Director and the Board of Trustees of the Royal Botanic Gardens, Kew.

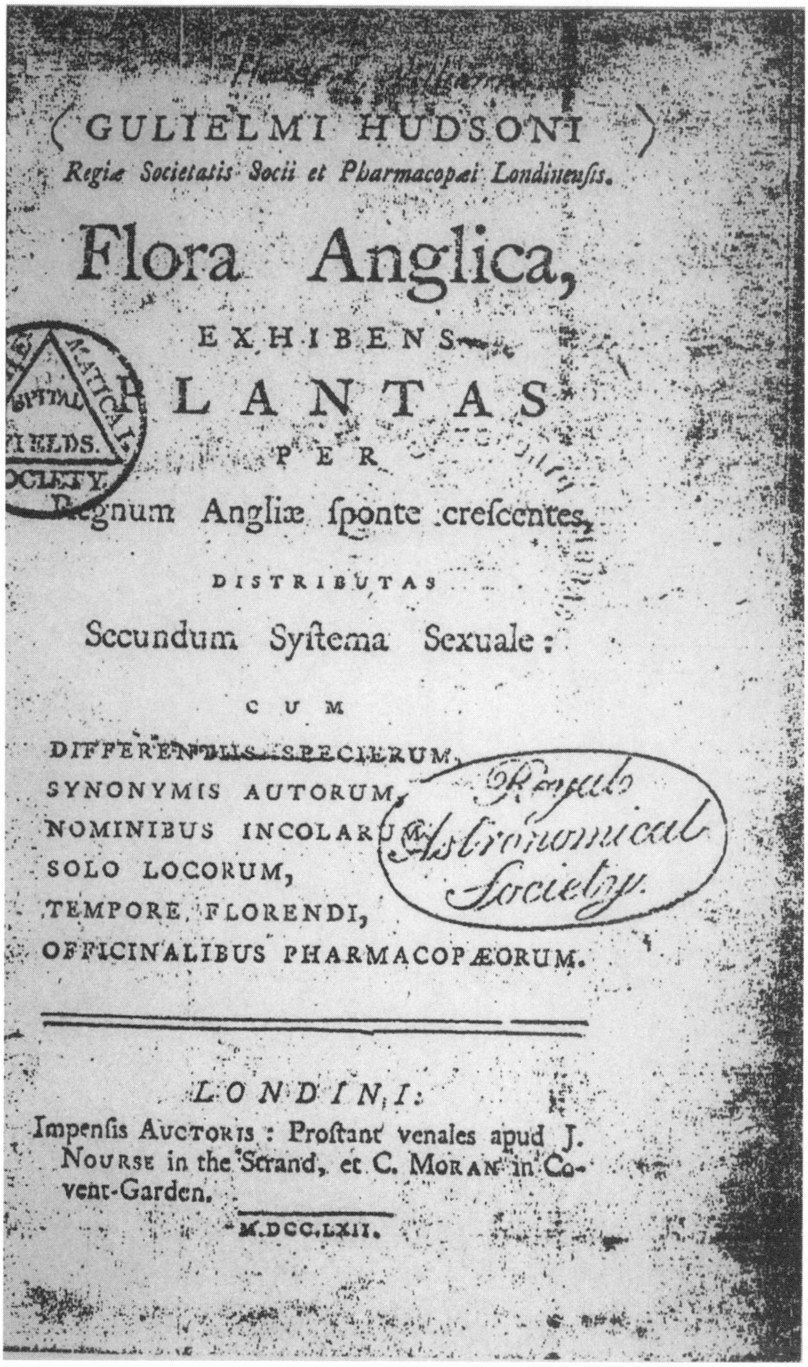

GULIELMI HUDSONI

Regiæ Societatis Socii et Pharmacopæi Londinensis.

Flora Anglica,

EXHIBENS

PLANTAS

PER

Regnum Angliæ sponte crescentes,

DISTRIBUTAS

Secundum Syftema Sexuale:

CUM

DIFFERENTIIS SPECIERUM,
SYNONYMIS AUTORUM,
NOMINIBUS INCOLARUM,
SOLO LOCORUM,
TEMPORE FLORENDI,
OFFICINALIBUS PHARMACOPÆORUM.

LONDINI:

Impenfis AUCTORIS : Proftant venales apud J.
NOURSE in the Strand, et C. MORAN in Co-
vent-Garden.

M.DCC.LXII.

1.7 Title page, William Hudson, *Flora Anglica* (1762).
Reproduced with the kind permission of the Director and the Board of Trustees of the Royal Botanic Gardens, Kew.

The disappearance of the goddess Flora from botany books is part of a larger pattern of disappearance of female icons and also of iconographic material within scientific writings. During the Renaissance and early modern period, as several feminist scholars have shown, female figures were used extensively to embody abstract ideas.[25] Philosophy, Nature, Science, and Peace all were personified in female form in Cesare Ripa's *Iconologia* (1593), an influential collection of emblematic figures that could be used in allegorical representations, and it was commonplace for early modern books on the sciences to carry frontispieces with such allegorical visualizations. But a different scholarly style came to prevail as the culture of modern science moved across the seventeenth century and into eighteenth century, and female icons no longer had a place in scientific publications. This seems to have been particularly the case in England, perhaps because of the ascendancy of an empirical, Baconian, and practical type of science, as embodied in the goal of the Royal Society of London "to raise a Masculine Philosophy," in contrast to the speculative, rhetorical, and "feminine" style of French courtly and intellectual culture. In a richly evocative analysis, Londa Schiebinger connects the disappearance of "feminine icons" to "battles over scholarly styles" that have much to do with struggles over national identity during the seventeenth and eighteenth centuries.[26]

The history of science writing in England from the later seventeenth century is a history of the turn away from ornament, rhetoric, and literary features. An ideal of technical writing came to prevail in which poetic tags and metaphoric language not only were extraneous but also were contradictory to a "modern," "scientific," and "objective" tone and manner. Barbara Maria Stafford has written about the shift from visual traditions within early modern science, and has celebrated the energy and diversity of seventeenth- and eighteenth-century performances of knowledge in spectacles, card games, illustrated books, and automata that brought natural history, mathematics, and natural philosophy to audiences at the French court and in the English middle-class parlor. Images had been the key means for communication, but texts, she explains, came to replace images both quantitatively and qualitatively.[27] However, the relationship between text and image was fraught at that time. Gotthold Lessing argued famously in *Laocoön* (1766) that visual and verbal representations are different and that the spatial and temporal arts should be kept firmly apart. W. J. T. Mitchell identifies here a fear of the image, an iconophobia, as one characteristic in the history of aesthetics, and points to a political aspect of this in the late eighteenth century. To the counterrevolutionary Edmund Burke, images were a sign of "the racial, social, and sexual other, an object of both fear and contempt," and connoted the sphere of things feminine, barbaric, and French.[28] For these ideological reasons, Burke prescribed sharp generic distinctions between domains that he considered proper for the arts and those for other modes such as poetry. Burke's frame of mind can help us understand how naturalists and natural philosophers of that day, giving credence to empirical accounts rather than to rhetorical features, separated out literary dimensions of their work from the technical parts.

With regard to gendered icons, the disappearance of a visualized Flora in technical books about botany was part of a series of cultural changes linked to the development of disciplinary knowledge practices, and these cultural changes had an impact on attitudes toward women and toward women in the sciences. Entries for "botany" and "Flora" in *The New Royal Encyclopedia* (1789) nicely illumine such emerging distinctions between science and the arts at that time. William Henry Hall's multivolume "Repository of Universal Knowledge" contains a long account of "the science of botany" that rehearses arguments for and against the Linnaean system of classification, and includes descriptions and line drawings as well as discussion of methods for drying and preserving plants, all meant "to conduct the young botanist, by easy gradations to a complete theoretic knowledge of the subject." By contrast, the entry for "Flora" consists of one paragraph that recapitulates the saga of "Flora meretrix" as found in Boccaccio—but without so naming it: this "lady of pleasure, who, having gained large sums of money by prostituting herself, made the Roman people her heir, on condition that certain games, called floralia, might be annually celebrated on her birthday." The brief account then updates the story for more Romantic and artistic tastes: "the modern poets and painters have been more lavish in setting off her charms, considering that no parts of nature offered such innocent and exquisite entertainment to the sight and smell, as the beautiful variety which adorns, and the odour which embalms, the floral creation."[29] Hall's representation excludes Flora from any resonance for "the science of botany," and places her in an aesthetic domain where she is a fragrant object of entertainment. The distinction between "botany" and the goddess Flora sharpened as time went on, and mythological figures came to have less of a place in botanical works for scientific readers. Within the print culture of nineteenth-century botany, floras of authoritative standing among botanical experts did not include emblematic frontispieces, and often stepped away from visuals altogether. John Sibthorp's ten-volume *Flora graeca* (1806–1840) is an example of the disappearance of icons and allegorical figures from books of scientific botany. A beautifully illustrated work with many colored plates, the *Flora graeca* features colored vignettes on the title pages, but these portray landscapes rather than Flora and her mythological entourage. Brian Ford points out that some works of high science later in the nineteenth century carried no illustrations at all, one example being J. D. Hooker's seven-volume *Flora of British India* (1875–1897).[30]

Gendering Science Culture: Flora during the Later Eighteenth Century, and Beyond

During the later eighteenth century, however, as the frontispiece to Erasmus Darwin's *Botanic Garden* demonstrates, the goddess Flora continued to be a verbal and visual presence in books in England. Publishers and authors capitalized on enthusiasm for natural history study, particularly for Linnaean botany, by promoting plant study for many levels and types of readers. A small botanical manual to carry on walks into the countryside exemplifies this cultural moment. William Mavor's *The Lady's and Gentleman's Botanical Pocket Book* (1800) lists native plants in groups according to Linnaean categories of class and order and provides blank space on each page for fledgling botanists to enter information about the specimens they find. The title page portrays Flora, accompanied by a winged Cupid, presenting the flowers of her kingdom to a fashionable couple (figure 1.8). Here Flora is a figure of pleasant and decorous invitation to an activity that will be circumscribed by civility and sociability. At a remove from seductive rococo allure, Mavor's goddess is well suited to an eighteenth-century aesthetic that blended amusement with instruction, and many writers adapted her for their own purposes. There are striking instances of Flora as a mother who keeps a wayward family under her firm command. A botanical poem from the 1780s entitled "The Backwardness of the Spring Accounted For" portrays Flora descending to Earth in May to find her kingdom in disarray because her floral subjects have consorted with species different from themselves and abandoned their positions in nature's plan. The poem probably was written on the occasion of a translation of Linnaeus's *System of Vegetables*, for Flora confidently announces a return to social and natural order by declaring that Linnaeus's ideas about system in the plant kingdom soon will guide her "children" back into line.[31] Similar portrayals of a teacherly and maternal Flora who represents entrenched values and traditional family patterns are found in books for women and children that set out models of conduct, one example being J. H. Wynne's poem "Zephyrus and Flora, a Vision" in *Fables of Flowers for the Female Sex* (1773). As cited earlier in this chapter, a classicist has argued that Flora served

1.8 Title page, William Mavor, *The Lady's and Gentleman's Botanical Pocket Book* (1800).

THE
LADY'S AND GENTLEMAN'S
Botanical Pocket Book;
adapted to
Withering's Arrangement of
BRITISH PLANTS.
Intended to facilitate and promote
the Study of
Indigenous Botany.
By William Mavor L.L.D.

Flora dispensing her favours.

London Printed for Vernor & Hood Poultry.

Roman gender ideology by sharply demarcating types of womanhood and placing women within firm constraints of patriarchal marriage and family. It is almost to be expected that a Roman goddess from the age of Augustus would feature in British botanical storytelling during the Augustan Age of British literature. Eighteenth-century British culture worked hard to demarcate sexual difference and, fearful of uncontrolled female sexuality, put art and literature into the service of virtue and morality. Writers across spectrums of religion, class, and sex elevated marriage, motherhood, and family values, stigmatized learned women, and promoted domestic ideologies. In this cultural context, botany books could contribute to programs of social reform, and a representation of Flora not as a boisterous prostitute but as a wise and orderly mother could be positioned so as to work on behalf of regulating women.

I return now to Erasmus Darwin's *Botanic Garden* and the frontispiece *Flora Attired by the Elements*. Darwin's capacious poem ranges fluently over aspects of nature, science, and technology, and sets out a vision of nature as energy and fecund change. The second part of the work is Darwin's exposition of Linnaean theories of plant sexuality. In "The Loves of the Plants" Darwin draws out analogies between erotic, conjugal practices in the plant kingdom and human social relations. Based on belief in fundamental sexual differences between males and females, he tours readers through the sex lives of plants, showcasing "Beaux and Beauties" who "woo and win their vegetable Loves."[32] Within such a reading, the enticing Flora in the frontispiece to *The Botanic Garden* recalls Ovid's figure of fertility and might well be considered a "Flora primavera," a prelude to springtime and to life-enhancing connection in a Romantic holism. Yet, as we have seen, Flora is iconographically also a prostitute whose erotic involvement is not necessarily to be celebrated, and who can be used as a negative exemplar within gender ideology. The Flora figured in the frontispiece to *The Botanic Garden* indeed can be considered paradoxical, and scholars have offered divergent readings.[33] In my view, gaps in the poem between depictions of idealized feminine traits and powerful female sexual appetites and practices support a reading of Darwin's images of women that have more to do with containment, gender norms, and regulation than with exultant fertility figures. Interestingly, though, whether Flora is "primavera" or "meretrix," fertility or sexuality, celebrated or vilified, Darwin's versions of woman focus only on woman as body. At a time of changes in the cultures of both gender and science, Darwin's Flora resembles her iconographic ancestors by embodying a vision of womanhood with no reference to an interest in, or access to, the life of the mind.

Darwin's Flora is "attired by the Elements" at a layered moment in gender history and also at a transition point in the literary culture of science. The representation of the goddess of flowers in a frontispiece dating from 1791 reads differently from William Turner's frontispiece to *A New Herball* in 1531, for contexts to the symbolism have shifted. Whereas Turner's Flora invites readers into a scientific work, Darwin's invites readers into a poem. Darwin's Flora belongs more to a world of literature, and less to a world of science. *The Botanic Garden* is an expository work that combines verse and information and incorporates technical material, and thereby amply illustrates the extent to which botany was part of British popular culture. In the first instance, however, the poem aims to amuse and please its readers. Anne Secord has argued persuasively that pleasure should be integrated into the historiography of popular science because it was on the agenda for early nineteenth-century naturalists and educators who used images as a recruitment strategy and took seriously visual methods for training the eye and the mind.[34] Within such a context, the visual and verbal pictures in Darwin's poem can be read as a way for Darwin to invite "the Generality of Readers," as he put it in the advertisement to *The Botanic Garden,* into "the vestibule" of science—though only into the vestibule.[35]

The "pleasure" of such scientific pursuits as stimulated by Darwin was more appropriate at the threshold of scientific knowledge and practice, and less so at higher levels of technical and utilitarian work distinct from polite botany. By the mid-nineteenth century, figures of the goddess of flowers within botanical publications would have signalled domains of knowledge that were literary rather than scientific. An author or publisher's choice of types of illustration was one way to delineate the level or form of science being presented, as well as the types of audience being addressed. For that reason, women authors of botanical textbooks generally excluded any illustrations that could be construed as decorative rather than pedagogical. Thus, Priscilla Wakefield's widely reprinted *An Introduction to Botany* (1796) includes drawings of the parts of plants and flowers as an aid to identifying and naming plants according to the Linnaean system. But personifications would not have been appropriate for the earnest botanical instruction that she, as a Quaker writer of didactic natural history books, aimed to provide for her intended audience of female and general readers.[36] Mythological figures likewise would have been inappropriate for the teacherly purposes of later female-authored botany books such as Maria Jacson's *Sketches of the Physiology of Vegetable Life* (1811), Sarah Fitton's, *Conversations on Botany* (1817), and Jane Marcet's *Conversations on Vegetable Physiology* (1829).

The decorative and seductive Flora in the frontispiece to Darwin's *Botanic Garden* has little in common with the earnest female agency represented by women writers of botany books from that time. *Flora Attired by the Elements* is a vision of Romantic womanhood, one that genders the female subject and naturalizes her absorption in worlds of desire and personal attention that increasingly were removed from technical practices in the sciences as well as from encouragement to female learning. As we have seen, associations of Flora with sexuality and feminine ornament echo long traditions that were much inflected by mythology, arts, and letters. More importantly for my discussion, the iconographic Flora in Darwin's widely read poem points to associations between women and botany that were soon to become a problem for some parts of the botanical community in England and elsewhere. By the early nineteenth century, mythological figures in rococo poses connoted precisely the type of feminized botany that serious professionalizers such as John Lindley, the first professor of botany at the newly established London University, worked to dislodge. Their aim was to distinguish between "science" and "polite accomplishment," and put disciplinary forms of utilitarian botany firmly in place.[37] When viewed in that light, *Flora Attired by the Elements* serves as a pivotal image in a gendered history of science. It visually represents a moment when ideas about women and the "feminine" figured in the complex process of changes during the nineteenth century that slowly would exclude women from mainstream social and institutional practices in the sciences.

Moving into the Victorian era, figurations of Flora demonstrate a growing gap between literary and technical depictions of nature. Flora continued to bear witness to nature in children's books such as Walter Crane's *Flora's Feast: A Masque of Flowers* (1889) and among painters and designers such as John William Waterhouse and Edward Burne-Jones, who celebrated mythological dimensions of art and life in their work. But Flora had no resonance in the world of scientific botany with its bifurcation between literary and scientific traditions. One likely reason for this was that emblems of nature represented old-fashioned science, part of a language ill-suited to mainstream technological progress narratives. Additionally, many newer scientific professionalizers may not have received a classical education that would prepare them to understand the learned references and humanistic associations expressed in emblems and allegories. The diversifying popular audiences for science during the nineteenth century themselves often lacked a type of education that would have made classical tags familiar and fun, and they likely had a more direct hands-on relationship with nature that had little to do with metaphors and philosophy.

With the disappearance of emblematic frontispieces from many books about botany, natural history, and science, a personified Flora fades into the wings of science culture. Yet, as this chapter has shown, her iconography can re-route the student of gender, science, and visual culture into powerful terrain. Flora, the goddess of flowers, took shape and changed shape from heterogeneous traditions across the history of Western culture. She provides historical perspectives on women and nature, and illustrates gendered tensions about the female figure as both material and symbolic. Flora's metamorphoses are not marginal to the history of women in relation to science, for this iconic goddess embodies connections among representations and realities for women in science that echo historically and into our own day as well. As a way to monitor changing cultural registers across time, place, and media, Flora thus can help us examine relations between aesthetic and technical aspects of sciences, as well as between visual and verbal languages of nature.

Acknowledgements

I am grateful to the Social Sciences and Humanities Research Council of Canada for research funding that made possible trips to libraries to study early illustrated botany books. Special thanks go to the Library of the Royal Botanic Gardens at Kew, and to Marilyn Ward, for opening cupboard doors to their treasure trove of books with frontispieces. Siobhan Neville provided excellent research assistance in support of this project. Thank you to members of the Gerstein Advanced Research Seminar at York University for energetic inquiry on topics of shared interest. Bernard Lightman, my co-editor, asked incisive questions that improved my analysis and gave me much to think about for further development of my cultural history of Flora.

Notes

1. Erasmus Darwin, *The Botanic Garden, A Poem in Two Parts* (1791) (London: Scolar Press, 1973), v.

2. Ibid., "Economy of Vegetation," IV: 407. Darwin used ideas from Rosicrucian philosophy to represent the elements hieroglyphically. He believed that Greek and Roman mythology developed out of earlier Egyptian allegories, and makes frequent reference in *The Botanic Garden* to Jacob Bryant's *A New System; or Analysis of Ancient Mythology* (London, 1774–1776), a widely read source for mythographers at that time.

3. Ludmilla Jordanova, *Nature Displayed: Gender, Science and Medicine 1760–1820* (London: Longman, 1999), 44–47.

4. While cultural studies of flowers in literature and art have much to offer for analyses of gender and visual culture, they are not my topic here. Examples of scholarship in this area are: Beverly Seaton, *The Language of Flowers: A History* (Charlottesville: University Press of Virginia, 1995); and Vibeke Woldbye, ed., *Floral Motifs in European Painting and Decorative Arts* (The Hague: SDU Publishers, 1991). For a discussion of the "describability" and "imaginability" of flowers in literature, see Elaine Scarry, *Dreaming by the Book* (New York: Farrar, Straus and Giroux, 1999).

5. Jack Goody, *The Culture of Flowers* (Cambridge: Cambridge University Press, 1993), 17. See also Georges Dumézil, *Archaic Roman Religion,* trans. Philip Krapp (Chicago: University of Chicago Press, 1970), I: 270–71.

6. T. P. Wiseman, *The Myths of Rome* (Exeter: University of Exeter Press, 2004), 307; and "The Games of Flora," *The Art of Ancient Spectacle,* ed. Bettina Bergmann and Christine Kondoleon (Washington, D.C.: National Gallery of Art, 1999), 197.

7. See Seneca, Epistle XCVII, "On the Degeneracy of the Age," *Epistulae Morales* [A.D. 63–65], trans. Richard M. Gummere (Cambridge, Mass.: Harvard University Press, 1953), III: 108–17.

8. Elaine Fantham, "Ceres, Liber and Flora: Georgic and Anti-Georgic Elements in Ovid's Fasti," *Proceedings of the Cambridge Philological Society* 38 (1992): 50.

9. Ovid, *Fasti,* trans. A. J. Boyle and R. D. Woodard (London: Penguin Books, 2000), 5: 183–84.

10. Ibid., 5: 221–23.

11. Ibid., 5: 351–53.

12. Ariadne Staples, *From Good Goddess to Vestal Virgins* (London: Routledge, 1998), ch. 2.

13. Giovanni Boccaccio, *Famous Women,* trans. Virginia Brown (Cambridge, Mass.: Harvard University Press, 2001), 265–69. Boccaccio's version of Flora's story echoes the origin account found in *The Divine Institutes* of the Christian apologist Lactantius (trans. Sister Mary Francis McDonald, Washington, D.C.: The Catholic University of America Press, 1964, pp. 75–76).

14. Julius Held, "Flora, Goddess and Courtesan," *Essays in Honor of Erwin Panofsky,* ed. Millard Meiss (New York: New York University Press, 1961), I: 201–18, II: 69–74.

15. Charles Dempsey, *The Portrayal of Love: Botticelli's "Primavera" and Humanist Culture at the Time of Lorenzo the Magnificent* (Princeton: Princeton University Press, 1992), esp. ch. 2. For an overview of interpretations, see also Frank Zoellner, *Botticelli: Images of Love and Spring* (Munich: Prestel, 1998).

16. Lilian Zirpolo, "Botticelli's Primavera: A Lesson for the Bride," in *The Expanding Discourse: Feminism and Art History,* ed. Norma Broude and Mary D. Garrard (New York: Icon Editions, 1992), 108.

17. See Kelley Harness, "La Flora and the End of Female Rule in Tuscany," *Journal of the American Musicological Society* 51 (1998): 437–76.

18. See Thomas Worthen, "Poussin's Paintings of Flora," *The Art Bulletin* 61 (1979): 575–88; and Troy Thomas, "'Un fior vano e fragile': The Symbolism of Poussin's *Realm of Flora," Art Bulletin* 68, no. 2 (1986): 225–36.

19. Other paintings by Rembrandt on the theme of Flora are *Flora* (1635), *Saskia as Flora* (1641), and *Hendrickje Stoffels as Flora* (ca. 1654). See Julia Lloyd Williams, *Rembrandt's Women* (Munich: Prestel, 2001), 104, 116, 208.

20. On Flora in seventeenth-century portraits, including court portraiture, see Ursula Weber-Woelk, "'Flora la belle Rommaine': Studien zur Ikonographie der Göttin Flora im 17. Jahrhundert" (Ph.D. dissertation, Cologne, 1995); Susan Shifrin, "'A Copy of My Countenance': Biography, Iconography, and Likeness in the Portraits of the Duchess Mazarin and Her Circle" (Ph.D. diss., Bryn Mawr College, 1998); Held, "Flora, Goddess and Courtesan."

21. William Turner, *A New Herball,* Part I, ed. George T. L. Chapman and Marilyn N. Tweddle (Cambridge: Cambridge University Press, 1989), 8. On Turner, see also Blanche Henrey, *British Botanical and Horticultural Literature before 1800* (London: Oxford University Press, 1975), I: 21–28.

22. John Rea, *Flora: Seu de Florum Cultura. Or, A Complete Florilege* (London, 1665), "The Mind of the Front." On John Rea, see Henrey, *British Botanical and Horticultural Literature before 1800,* I: 193–98.

23. Henrey, *British Botanical and Horticultural Literature before 1800,* II: 109–11. There was no British flora written in English until the publication in 1776 of William Withering's *Botanical Arrangement of All the Vegetables Naturally Growing in Great Britain.*

24. In *Historical and Biographical Sketches of the Progress of Botany,* Richard Pulteney traced the first use of "flora" as a term for a general list or description of plants of a specific area to Simon Paulli's 1648 catalogue of plants of Denmark (London, 1790, I: 169). James Edward Smith linked the popularity of the term "flora" to "the Linnaean school of Botany" in *The New English Flora* (2nd ed., London, 1828, v). Examples of books that "naturalized" this new generic term are John Hill's *Flora Britannica* (1759) and Charles Abbot's *Flora Bedfordiensis* (1798).

25. For analyses of iconic traditions of female figures in the history of science, see Carolyn Merchant, *Death of Nature* (San Francisco: Harper, 1983), ch. 1; Londa Schiebinger, *The Mind Has No Sex? Women in the Origin of Modern Science* (Cambridge, Mass.: Harvard University Press, 1989), ch. 5; and Ludmilla Jordanova, *Sexual Visions: Images of Gender in Science and Medicine between the Eighteenth and Twentieth Centuries* (Madison: University of Wisconsin Press, 1989) and *Nature Displayed: Gender, Science and Medicine 1760–1820,* ch. 2. Marina Warner explores wide cultural uses of female figures in her classic *Monuments and Maidens: The Allegory of the Female Form* (Berkeley: University of California Press, 1985).

26. Londa Schiebinger, *The Mind Has No Sex?* ch. 5.

27. Barbara Maria Stafford, *Artful Science: Enlightenment Entertainment and the Eclipse of Visual Education* (Cambridge, Mass.: MIT University Press, 1994). The early modern period, Stafford suggests, also can be characterized by an "antiocular impulse" that "grew out of a virulent anti-Catholicism" (p. 282).

28. W. J. T. Mitchell, *Iconology: Image, Text, Ideology* (Chicago: University of Chicago Press, 1986), 151. See also W. J. T. Mitchell, *Picture Theory: Essays on Verbal and Visual Representation* (Chicago: University of Chicago Press, 1994), ch. 5.

29. William Henry Hall, *The New Royal Encyclopedia; or Complete Modern Dictionary of Arts and Sciences* (London, 1789), vol. 1.

30. Brian Ford, *Images of Science: A History of Scientific Information* (London: The British Library, 1992), 104.

31. On "The Backwardness of the Spring Accounted For," see Ann B. Shteir, *Cultivating Women, Cultivating Science: Flora's Daughters and Botany in England 1760 to 1860* (Baltimore: Johns Hopkins University Press, 1996), 15–16; also Sam George, "'Not Strictly Proper For A Female Pen': Eighteenth-Century Poetry and the Sexuality of Botany," *Comparative Critical Studies* 2, no. 2 (2005): 201–204.

32. Erasmus Darwin, "The Loves of the Plants," I: 9–10, in *The Botanic Garden.*

33. For a reading of the emancipatory potential of Darwin's delight in female sexuality in "The Loves of the Plants," see Janet Browne, "Botany for Gentlemen: Erasmus Darwin and the Loves of the Plants," *Isis* 80, no. 4 (1989): 593–620. For an account of Darwin's writings about botany for women as "a disciplinary program designed to shore up the gendered hierarchies of the existing social order," see Elizabeth Heckendorn Cook, "'Perfect' Flowers, Monstrous Women: Eighteenth-Century Botany and the Modern Gendered Subject," in *"Defects": Engendering the Modern Body,* ed. Helen Deutsch and Felicity Nussbaum (Ann Arbor: University of Michigan Press, 2000), 253.

34. Anne Secord, "Botany on a Plate: Pleasure and the Power of Pictures in Promoting Early Nineteenth-Century Scientific Knowledge," *Isis* 93 (2002): 28–57.

35. Robert N. Ross, "'To Charm Thy Curious Eye': Erasmus Darwin's Poetry at the Vestibule of Knowledge," *Journal of the History of Ideas* 32 (1971): 386.

36. Shteir, *Cultivating Women, Cultivating Science,* 83–89.

37. See Ann B. Shteir, "Gender and 'Modern' Botany in Victorian England," in *Women, Gender, and Science: New Directions,* ed. Sally Gregory Kohlstedt and Helen E. Longino, *Osiris* 12 (1997): 29–38.

Chapter 2

A PASSION THAT TRANSFORMS

Picturing the Early Natural History Collector

Alan Bewell

Metamorphosis is a dominant theme in eighteenth- and early nineteenth-century natural history. As naturalists argued for the social and intellectual importance of this new scientific field, they employed visual figures in order to represent the change that they envisioned would take place in the world through their activity. Particularly in the field of botany, where the identification and collection of plants suggested both the recovery of the original Edenic garden through science and the possibility of acquiring new natural commodities and luxuries through commerce, frontispiece illustrations seek to figure concretely the new world that would be brought into being by a new science of nature. Eighteenth-century natural history was never just about collecting and displaying natures; its great promise, at the heart of its modernity, was that it would transform the Creation. In often allegorical depictions of a metamorphosed nature, the naturalist frequently occupies an ambiguous position. Since scientific knowledge was bound up intimately with collecting and the globalized exchange of knowledge, the naturalist stood at the center of a rapid expansion of knowledge horizons, particularly those of science and empire.[1] Scientific collections were a key tool in the discovery of the order of nature, as they facilitated the naming and systematizing activities of the naturalist. Knowing and possessing thus were linked intimately. At the same time, beneath the more positive and idealized representations of the naturalist as a figure who was ushering into being a new order of nature—not unlike the original Creator—there was an undercurrent that the collecting job of the naturalist exhibited too close, too detailed, too passionate an absorption in things and the mechanism of life. A seeing made possible through the possession of nature, the methods of early naturalists were often equated with the curiosity of the virtuoso, dilettante, and connoisseur. The attention to detail produced a revolution in science, yet it also could be seen as being too caught up in surfaces or preoccupied with the miniscule, the unique, or the rare. Such knowledge could be seen as a luxury, an affectation, or an eccentricity. Early natural history texts struggled with the nature of the desire that motivated collecting, particularly as the close connection between seeing, possessing, and knowing also could evoke anxieties about deeper and darker modes of knowledge, linked to death, sexuality, luxury, and desire.[2] The pleasures of collecting are a subterraneous aspect of the cultural representation of early modern natural history, yet they are nevertheless an important element in the formation of scientific culture. As Lorraine Daston and Katharine Park have observed, "the passion of wonder itself—visceral, immediate, vertiginous—also had its history."[3]

The elaborate self-reflexive title pages and frontispieces of the late seventeenth century and eighteenth century are a particularly valuable resource for examining early ideas about the relationship between natural history and collecting. Because natural history as a science was in the process of emerging, its value and objectives had to be represented and promoted graphically, particularly in regard to the role that the naturalist might play in the production of "useful knowledge." Since the subject of so many of these engravings is the transformation of knowledge and society brought about by the activity of the naturalist, metamorphosis is not only a thematic concern, but something performed by the illustrations themselves. Although they are pictorial, these frontispieces are intrinsically narratives about change, for they adopt figural language and visual imagery in order to portray the transforming power of science. The explicit focus of these plates is often on science as the public advancement of knowledge, so the Goddess Minerva, as a figure of wisdom, is frequently portrayed alongside various allegorical representations of Europe, its states, or its cities. When these plates speak about science as a transformative activity or passion, they have recourse to Ovid. As the poet of metamorphosis, Ovid provided early naturalists with a figural language for talking about change. Ovid was the self-conscious poet of modern myth-making, but he was also the poet whose main theme was love in all its complexity, and it was in this capacity that Ovid played a central role in providing writers and engravers with a figurative language for talking about the relationship between scientific knowledge and its desires.

Famous was Ovid's account of the how the "laurel" came to be seen as the sign of achievement and honor among poets and scientists alike. Typical of Ovid's technique, he makes a figurative quest into a literal one. He tells how Apollo, the god of medicine and poetry, smitten with love for the maiden Daphne, chased her through the forest. Daphne's beauty, like nature's, has put her at risk, inciting Apollo's desire to possess her. The fleeing girl, "more beautiful than ever in her flight," anxiously prayed to her father to "Change and destroy the body which has given / Too much delight."[4] Hardly are these words spoken than a transformation takes place, and she becomes a laurel:

> Her limbs grew numb and heavy, her soft breasts
> Were closed with delicate bark, her hair was leaves,
> Her arms were branches, and her speedy feet
> Rooted and held, and her head became a tree top,
> Everything gone except her grace, her shining.[5]

Too late, yet still in the throes of desire, Apollo reaches her. He

>   placed his hand
> Where he had hoped and felt the heart still beating
> Under the bark; and he embraced the branches
> As if they still were limbs, and kissed the wood
> And the wood shrank from the kisses. . .[6]

Daphne's metamorphosis into a tree makes little difference to Apollo, for he kisses her bark and embraces her branches, declaring, "Since you can never be my bride, / My tree at least you will be!" The tree thus stands in for the woman, as sexual desire gets metamorphosed into something else. In what will become an enduring myth of the desire that underlies natural history collecting, Apollo announces that if he cannot possess the woman, he can at least wear her as an ornament. He relinquishes his status as lover to become a collector:

>   Let the laurel
> Adorn, henceforth, my hair, my lyre, my quiver:
> Let the Roman victors, in the long procession,
> Wear laurel wreaths for triumph and ovation
>   . . . and as my head
> Is always youthful, let the laurel always
> Be green and shining.[7]

In Ovid's account, a Daphne who could not bear to be possessed by Apollo as a woman seems to consent to this new arrangement, though she hardly has much choice in the matter: "He said no more. The laurel, / Stirring, seemed to consent, to be saying *Yes*."[8] Such is Ovid's account of the emergence of science as a metamorphosis of failed romance. And the quest for love leads to the discovery (in fact, the literal production) of a new plant, the laurel, which, having achieved its own immortality through science, will never age or die, but always will be "green and shining."

Ovid questions a simple separation of science from love, of nature from the desires of Apollo, suggesting that a male naturalist's love for a plant and quest for fame may not be separated so easily from his love of women and beauty. Fame itself—the laurel—is quite literally the embodiment of displaced desire. Characteristically, Ovid narrativizes these relationships by literalizing figures, by taking metaphors literally. To understand the relationship between Apollo, Daphne the maiden, and *daphne* the laurel, one must think within a figure, for Apollo's love for the tree cannot be understood without also seeing it as a figural transformation of his relationship to the maiden. To understand Apollo's love for nature, to understand why a scientist crowns himself with laurels, one needs to read nature with a dioptric form of vision, seeing the laurel as both a plant and a woman at the same time. Also, one must read the narrative in dynamic terms, recognizing that what one eventually sees is itself the outcome of a narrative process, a metamorphosis. Apollo's love of nature cannot be separated from his love of women, nor can that love be seen apart from the history that brought it into being. In this, one of the earliest myths about the collector, Ovid already suggests that the love that motivates the desire to know nature is not separated easily from violence. Ovid's *Metamorphosis* suggests that anxieties about the gendered desire of the collector are not as modern as one might otherwise think. The early literature on natural history collecting reflects on the relationship between knowledge and desire, and when it does so, Ovidean modes of figuration, structured by the gendering of science and its object of inquiry, almost inevitably appear. To introduce Ovidean figurality into the history of science is to begin to recognize the extent to which early science drew upon classical figures in attempting to understand scientific curiosity and its promised transformations. Science, for Ovid, indeed is built on a failed romance and the metaphoric substitutions that transformed a failed possession into fame. A darker reading of the contemporary sciences of nature would seek to recover the ghostly presence of violence that appears to have brought nature into being for the scientist in the first place.

One of the most striking early eighteenth-century frontispieces was the one designed by Jan Wandelar for Linnaeus's 1737 catalogue *Hortus Cliffortianus* (figure 2.1). There, George Clifford's garden is represented in highly allegorical terms that mix myth and realism in surprising ways. In the center, Europa is portrayed seated on a lion, while cupids play with various horticultural items such as a thermometer, a garden plan, a shovel, and a watering can. The patron Clifford does not appear in the frontispiece in bodily form, but instead as a marble

bust, which is being decorated with flowers by a personified Amsterdam. Like Daphne, he has been transformed, apotheosized by the
very flowers that he has collected and by the book *Hortus Cliffortia-*
nus that records that collecting, its title written on the plinth encir-
cled by the symbol of immortality, the snake with its tail in its mouth,
the ouroboros. Behind Europa is Minerva, while beside her the allegorical figures of America, Asia, and Africa are shown willingly

bringing horticultural specimens to Europe, so that they too will be given names and find a place in this garden. These evoke the tradition of "tributes," but this earlier model has been displaced by one that emphasizes a global participation in the production of Clifford's garden: the colonial world is portrayed as freely exchanging its plants for European knowledge, primarily in the fields of agriculture and medicine. The most extraordinary figure in the plate is Linnaeus, who appears as a naked Apollo, with his cloak and his bow and arrows, wearing the laurels of scientific achievement. The violence that makes this triumph possible is registered in the body of the dragon he has vanquished. Set within this botanical context, however, in which plants are not just signs, but also the material reality that is being collected and displayed, one cannot avoid recognizing the deeper relationship that Linnaeus shares with laurels. He wears them because he has named them. The two figures of collector and naturalist, transformed by their activities into classical heroes, promise a European remaking of the Earth as garden.⁹ Gender is important here, for despite the centrality of Europa in the frontispiece, she is essentially a passive power, receiving the gifts of science and nations, notably provided by the power of males.

The frontispiece to Johannes Miller's *Illustratio systematis sexualis Linnaei* (1770) also presents an elaborate allegory on collecting, further illuminating issues of gender (figure 2.2). At the center of the picture, Ceres, the goddess of agriculture, and probably Flora, with a wreath in hand, are shown together. The pedestal on which they stand comes complete with an oak tree and the inscribed words from Genesis 1:12: "And the earth brought forth grass, and herb yielding seed after his kind, and the tree yielding fruit, whose seed was in itself, after his kind: and God saw that it was good." The image suggests that the botanic garden is a recovery of Eden made possible by botany. On the left side stands Britannia, who seems like a spectator looking at a theatrical tableau, while beside her stands Minerva. Allegorical figures from other regions of the world—China, Africa, Southeast Asia, America, the Middle East—are bringing horticultural tributes to her. Knowledge is linked to obeisance, for the Middle Eastern figure has placed his offerings at the foot of the pedestal and is bowing toward her (as did the American native in the Wandelar engraving). Through a framing device, the illustrator draws attention to the role that naturalists have played in making this event possible. In niches in the far wall are the busts of the two men who played the most significant role in botanical classification in the period preceding Linnaeus, Joseph Pitton de Tournefort and John Ray. On the lintel of the archway immediately facing the reader, who looks through it as into a courtyard, are two large medallions of the translator Miller, seated

2.2 Frontispiece from
Johannes Miller, *Illustratio
systematis sexualis Linnaei*
(1770).
*Courtesy of the John W. Graham
Library, Trinity College, University of Toronto.*

beside Health and the cock of Aesculapius, and of Linnaeus, who is
being crowned by Minerva. As in the Wandelar engraving, myth and
realism are fused together in the portrayal of the new world that is
being brought into being by botany, for the realistic portrayal of Linnaeus and Miller, one crowned with laurels, the other with wisdom,
distinguishes them from the classical and mythological allegories that
they have set in motion. Desire is registered in the plate (how could it

be otherwise, given that this is the frontispiece to a translation of Linnaeus's *Systema sexualis*), but rather than portraying *sexual* desire, the plate speaks of the fulfilment of *social* desire, that is, of knowledge and the benefits that flow from it. It portrays the re-creation of the Edenic garden through the creative powers of science. As in the Wandelar engraving, collecting is presented in positive terms, as a global activity, in which the gathering and botanical naming of plants is portrayed as something desired by the rest of the world. Apollo's sexual desire has been displaced into an imperial social desire, and women are portrayed as the ostensible beneficiaries of this activity.

The appearance of non-European people in these frontispieces reflects the increasingly global reach of natural history during this period. In the frontispiece to Pierre Sonnerat's *Voyage à la nouvelle Guinée* (1776), the division of labour shaping colonial natural history is quite clear (figure 2.3). In it, the naturalist is portrayed at the center of the engraving, busy drawing a pet parrot that is being shown to him by a native woman. Behind him, two native males look on intrigued. One clearly occupies a subservient position, holding a banana leaf to shade the working naturalist. Sonnerat's frontispiece, like others, sharply differentiates European scientific culture from native societies, yet it nevertheless presents the two as being engaged in a shared activity, one that ostensibly has resulted in the book whose title page is displayed in the lower right-hand corner of the plate. It is clear that Sonnerat (like the reader) is observing not only the parrot, but also the naked woman who displays it. A domestic setting is implied, with the young child reaching for the parrot, and perhaps the young woman's husband looking on. Nevertheless, the scientific gaze does not entirely exclude the erotic gaze; the naturalist's interest in nature is not separate from his interest in the woman and her culture. Furthermore, the same pen that—in creating the frontispiece—represents the naturalist looking at the parrot also represents the native people looking on. Sonnerat's is, indeed, a narrative of "anti-conquest," for it is critical of an earlier form of colonialism that spoke of a necessary aggression against indigenous peoples.[10] It almost seeks to transform colonial contact, with all its violence, into a domestic tableau. Both the woman and naturalist are on familiar terms (both have removed their hats). Nevertheless, the illustration still speaks of the violence of natural history, now registered in the enormous pile of dead animals that litter the foreground.

In the late seventeenth century and early eighteenth century, the work of Maria Sibylla Merian (1647–1717) stands out in the field of natural history, and offers us the opportunity to consider how a female naturalist understood collecting. Merian was a gifted flower painter, but is best known for her extraordinary insect illustrations,

particularly her concern with representing their complete life cycles.
She raised the insects herself, so that she could illustrate them prop-
erly, usually portraying them on their host plants. Merian's entomological illustrations are superb aesthetically, yet they also convey a
substantial amount of scientific information. Although she began
with illustrations of native lepidoptera, she recognized the commercial opportunities available in the portrayal of the life cycles of non-
European moths and butterflies. Extraordinary for her time, she
travelled to Surinam in 1699, accompanied by a daughter, to paint its
flora and insects. Natalie Zemon Davis describes Merian as one of
her "women on the margins."[11] In the only extant portrait of Merian,
one looks to see some sign of that unusual courage and strength of

character that would lead a woman at the age of fifty-two to sell her art and her entomological collection in order to do natural history research in the tropics (figure 2.4). Instead, there is only a fairly conventional representation of a European naturalist: behind her can be seen a globe, books, a picture of a curlew with a snake in its mouth framed by the ouroboros, and a writing quill and ink; beside her are examples of her artistic work, her flora and seashell illustrations (the latter done for Rumphius). Meanwhile, she points to her most significant achievement, her studies of insect metamorphosis, signified by a butterfly and a potted plant upon which one can see a chrysalis and a caterpillar. Timeworn and sad, Merian seems a far cry from the kind of woman one expected to see, yet perhaps there is a hint of another women registered in the engraving: on the flower vase, sculptured in

2.4 Frontispiece from Maria Sibylla Merian, *Erucarum ortus, alimentum et paradoxa metamorphosis* (1717). *Courtesy of the University of Toronto.*

relief, is a depiction of the naked Daphne being chased by Apollo. It is fitting that the author of the most famous eighteenth-century book on metamorphosis would recognize her debt to Ovid. Occupying a place on the margin, as she did when she was a travelling naturalist, this vase speaks of a desire not elsewhere represented in this portrait of the naturalist in her study.

The frontispiece to the posthumous 1719 edition of her most famous work, the *Metamorphosis Insectorum Surinamensium,* portrays Merian at work in Surinam in quite different ways (figure 2.5). Love and pleasure dominate this illustration, for her work-room is filled with Renaissance *putti.* Instead of bringing the world's natural curiosities to her, as happens so frequently in this kind of illustration, however, these *putti* seem intent upon destroying her work. Gender plays a powerful role in this representation for, although the *Metamorphosis* lies open at her feet and a plant is in a pot behind her, she looks more like a mother of sextuplets, than a natural history illustrator. With downcast eyes to heighten her feminine attractiveness and modesty, she seems more intent upon making a flower nosegay than on preserving the precious insects that her cherubin children are busily demolishing.

One goal of this frontispiece is to reduce the social anxieties raised by the unconventional aspects of Merian's life by suggesting that ultimately her primary commitment as a female naturalist was to domestic family life, not to the study of nature. In this regard, it exemplifies the frequent concern in these engravings with the changes that took place in naturalists not only as a result of the acquisition of knowledge and fame, but also from their contact with strange and exotic cultures and natures. Much of the literature of early natural history derives its power from the complex exchanges—of artifacts, knowledges, cultural attitudes, and specimens—made possible by contact. In pictorial terms, this exchange of cultures and the transformations that it produces often are represented pictorially as cross-dressing. On returning from his botanical expedition to Lapland in 1732, Linnaeus posed for a portrait in the dress of a Laplander, an image that celebrates an exotic identity made possible by travel to foreign countries (figure 2.6).[12] Linnaeus appears dressed in reindeer skin, complete with boots and a girdle from which hang a Laplander's drum, a needle for making nets, and a knife. However, other items, notably a ruler, a magnifying glass, and a botanist's vasculum, indicate that he also stands outside of the culture that he is wearing. As a further assertion that his identity is not equivalent to his dress, Linnaeus holds a plant that he has named (*Linnaea borealis*), complete with identificatory tag, while his elbow rests on a stack of books that he has written. The setting is obviously not a Laplander's yurt, but the naturalist's study.

2.5 Frontispiece from Maria Sibylla Merian, *De Europische Insecten*. Amsterdam, 1730.
Courtesy of Hunt Institute for Botanical Documentation, Carnegie Mellon University, Pittsburgh, PA.

2.6 Linnaeus in Laplander Clothing. From Robert John Thornton, *New Illustration of the Sexual System of Carolus von Linnaeus . . . and the Temple of Flora, or Garden of Nature . . .* London, 1807. *Courtesy of Hunt Institute for Botanical Documentation, Carnegie Mellon University, Pittsburgh, PA.*

The theatricality of this portrait and its overt self-consciousness powerfully demonstrate the culturally disruptive power of eighteenth-century natural history, as the same methods that were applied to the description of plants and peoples also came to be applied to the naturalist himself. Shortly after his return from having served as botanist on Captain Cook's first voyage, Joseph Banks, who was soon to become President of the Royal Society, posed in traditional Tahitian dress in a painting by Benjamin West.[13] In both instances, the adoption of a different culture's dress might be interpreted as simply a form of cultural dress-up. In many ways it is. However, underlying this adoption of dress was an implicit recognition of cultural hybridity, that contact with other cultures and environments can change a naturalist's perspective on his or her own culture. Where Apollo donned a knowledge of nature in explicitly gendered terms, cross-dressing points here to different desires, to the possibility that the naturalist might be transformed culturally, having undergone, at the very least, a change in how he sees the world and his place within it.

Anxieties about the possible dangers that lay in the pleasures of collecting can be seen in another contemporary engraving, the 1773 *Aurelian Macaroni* (figure 2.7).[14] The drawing is part of a larger group of artistic and literary satires that appeared during the 1770s about the members of the "Macaroni Club," a fashionable set of urban dandies, who drew their inspiration from the continent. Elegantly dressed in shoes with buckles, donning elaborate wigs and tricorn hats, sporting walking sticks, spy glasses, and nosegays, the Macaronis embodied a new culture that celebrated luxury. The dangers of the adoption of foreign dress are an ongoing concern of these satires. In Robert Hitchcock's play *The Macaroni*, also first performed in 1773, Lord Promise complains that the young gentleman Epicene has been corrupted by his journey to the continent. "I wanted you to be a man of spirit," he declares. "Your ambition was to appear a first-rate Macaroni; you are returned fully qualified, and determined, I see, to shew the world what a contemptible creature an English-man dwindles into, when he adopts the follies and vices of other nations." The adoption of the dress, taste, elegance, and fashion of a different culture—cultural cross-dressing—here is viewed as a form of gender bending. Meeting Epicene in his dressing room, Lord Promise asserts that "You make such large advances to the feminine gender, that in a little time 'twill be difficult to tell to which sex you belong."[15] The *Oxford Magazine*, in June 1770, agreed, declaring that "there is indeed a kind of animal, neither male nor female, a thing of the neuter gender, lately started up amongst us. It is called a Macaroni. It talks without meaning, it smiles without pleasantry, it eats without appetite, it rides without exercise, it wenches without passion."[16] The *Aurelian Macaroni* expresses similar anxieties about the danger of the naturalist collector, whose relationship to butterflies is linked to exoticism, luxury, and gender-crossing. The illustration points to the cultural association between natural history and consumerist fashion. Like Ovid's Apollo, but without the sense of masculine possession implied by it, the young man wears his avocation on his sleeve: his hat is a butterfly, while his elaborately arranged coiffure is, in fact, composed of caterpillars. He is preoccupied with dress and decoration, notably in the snail motif for his coat buttons. Even the manner in which he displays his insects emphasizes their

2.7 The *Aurelian Macaroni*. Published by M. Darly, July 5, 1773.
© *Copyright The British Museum.*

2.8 *The Fly Catching Maca-*
roni. July 12, 1772.
© *Copyright The British Museum.*

aesthetic arrangement rather than classificatory order.[17] The overt allusion in these caterpillar hairs to the classical Medusa suggests that the illustration touches on deep-seated cultural anxieties about the impact of natural history collecting upon males. The drawing probably satirizes Moses Harris, a member of the first entomological society in Britain, the Society of Aurelians, whose important book on insect collecting, *The Aurelian or Natural History of English Insects* (1766), was published only seven years earlier. The book's frontispiece portrays the butterfly collector as a fashionably dressed young man, reclining beside a woodland path. Like a *putti,* he points toward another collector who is busy employing the bat-fowling net, popular among the English.

The young botanist Joseph Banks did not escape these gendered satires. With the publication of John Hawkesworth's account of his activities in Tahiti (1775), botanical knowledge became powerfully associated in the public mind with a kind of worldly freedom from moral restraint; knowledge of other cultures made the botanist all too aware of the relativity of British customs. The botanist submerged in nature was tempted to return to it. An article in the September 1773 number of the *Town and Country Magazine* portrays Banks as a man who combined in his circumnavigation of the globe the pursuits of both the naturalist and the rake. Exploration and plant collecting were expressions of a particularly dangerous form of curiosity:

> That curiosity which leads a voyager to such remote parts of the globe as Mr B—has visited, will stimulate him when at home to penetrate into the most secret recesses of nature . . . As nature has been his constant study, it cannot be supposed that the most engaging part of it, the fair sex, have escaped his notice; and if we may be suffered to conclude from his amorous descriptions, the females of most countries that he has visited, have undergone every critical inspection by him.[18]

Not surprisingly, both Banks and his assistant, the Swedish botanist Daniel Solander, became the subjects of verbal and graphic satire. On July 12, 1772, there appeared on the Strand an engraving entitled *The Fly Catching Macaroni,* which portrayed Joseph Banks standing astride the two poles, trying with two rackets to catch a butterfly (figure 2.8). Two ass ears project from under his feathered hat, emphasizing his connection to that other famous Shakespearean lover of nature, Bottom, from *Midsummer Night's Dream.* The caption reads: "I rove from Pole to Pole, you ask me why / I tell you Truth, to catch a— Fly." The next day there appeared another, entitled *The Simpling Macaroni,* which presented Solander with a pruning knife in one hand, and a plant pulled from the ground by its roots in another.

The caption compares him to a wandering goose that is fattening itself on Sir Joseph Banks: "Like Soland-Goose from frozen zone I wander / On shallow Banks grows fat Sol*****."[19] As pastiche taxonomic descriptions, the two plates, in effect, turn the tables on the voyager-naturalists, making them into a new variety of human being, worthy of scientific observation.

The satiric portrait of the naturalist as Macaroni was shortlived. Probably its most important legacy for natural history was that it led to the 1777 naming of the Macaroni Penguin (*Eudyptes chrysolophus*) for its bright yellow headfeathers. These issues of cultural and gender cross-dressing, however, were not simply following the conventions of satire, but conveyed popular fears that the naturalist was being changed by what he studied. In the frontispiece to Fusée Aublet's *Histoire des plantes de la Guiane françoise* (1775), a Native American is shown reclining in full headdress, with a blowgun quiver on his lap and a spear, bow, and arrows at his side (figure 2.9). Around him are a selection of plants from French Guiana, each numbered with the corresponding scientific name supplied below the engraving. The native has not been assigned a number, but he is just as much on display. Into this tropical scene, the engraver has introduced a medallion portrait of Aublet, with his head crowned with laurels. Like Sonnerat's inclusion of the title of his book in his frontispiece, the medallion serves a metacritical purpose, for it speaks of the author's role in the creation of the book. Its introduction makes the engraving seem less a scientific print than a natural history tableau, somewhere between a museum and a virtuosi cabinet, with its emphasis upon the collection of curiosities, among them medallions. The collector himself thus becomes part of his collection, his fame as author displayed in the very book that constitutes his achievement.

The medallion raises intriguing interpretive questions about Aublet's relationship to what he observed, for the plate calls into question, in very striking ways, the conventional power relations that shaped colonial natural history. Most clearly, the pen that normally would mark Aublet's difference from native culture, the writing that largely defined the difference between scientific and indigenous knowledge, is in this instance being held by the native. The engraving accords native culture a far greater role in the production of natural history than was commonly the case during the eighteenth century. That the book we are reading is a product of shared labor is emphasized by the fact that the native holds Aublet in his arm (as a medallion). This reference to colonial natural history as a shared activity is in keeping with the importance that Aublet gave to recording native people's knowledge and use of specific plants. As Mark J. Plotkin, Brian M. Boom, and Malorye Allison argue, Aublet "carried out what

2.9 Frontispiece from Fusée Aublet, *Histoire des plantes de la Guiane françoise* (1775). *Courtesy of the Library of Congress.*

are probably the first detailed and extensive ethnobotanical studies of South American rainforest plants," drawing much of his knowledge from information provided to him by African creoles, Caribs, and Galibis.[20] Aublet seems to be doubly crowned, for standing above the laurels on his head is a secondary laurel produced by the combination of the native's feather boa, his hand (whose fingers spread out like the laurel), and the native's bracelet, which repeats the pattern of the laurel. And in relation to Aublet, the palm pen seems less a writing instrument than a headfeather. Where most naturalists maintained the difference and distance between themselves and those they observed, Aublet seems to have been on intimate terms with native culture, so much so that his head ultimately seems to be no less dressed with feathers than that of the native. Even the positioning of the native

American, as it echoes popular classical portraits and sculptures of reclining nudes, seriously raises gender instabilities, further complicated by the emphasis, by both men, on fashionable dress.

During the Romantic period, natural history collecting became a popular leisure activity among the middle classes. Particularly after the publication of Gilbert White's *History of Selborne* (1789) and William Paley's *Natural Theology* (1802), it also was viewed as a suitable recreational activity for clergymen. It was seen as well as an important part of children's education, a field of writing where women were increasingly dominant.[21] Nevertheless, collecting, especially of zoological specimens, retained those darker, more radical associations that I have been tracing, partly as a result of the popularity of Erasmus Darwin's Ovidean *Botanic Garden* (1791), a poem that increasingly was seen as being linked to Jacobin radicalism and to the radical claim that desire was the fundamental force of nature.[22] The consequences of cross-cultural contact continued to be a concern, particularly those relating to freethinking and moral relativism. In Wordsworth's *The Borderers* (1798), a play that deals symbolically with English revolutionary culture, Oswald, the Iago-like villain who ultimately destroys the hero's faith in a transparent truth guiding political action, first appears with "*a bunch of plants in his hand,*" as if his being a botanist was all that an audience would need to know to draw conclusions about his character.[23] We learn that this man is "guilty of some dark deed" and has been "a Voyager . . . in Palestine," where "he despised alike / Mahommedan and Christian." The naturalist, for Wordsworth, is someone who stands apart from culture, looking upon others' moral beliefs with rational disdain. He applies the principles that guide natural history to the study of society and the human mind: "We dissect / The senseless body, and why not the mind?" (1166–67). The naturalist here appears as a social anatomist, a comparison that Wordsworth would return to in the 1805 *Prelude,* describing himself, during his Godwinian phase, as someone who

> took the knife in hand,
> And, stopping not at parts less sensitive,
> Endeavoured with my best of skill to probe
> The living body of society
> Even to the heart. I pushed without remorse
> My speculations forward, yea, set foot
> On Nature's holiest places.[24]

Wordsworth describes this new social anatomizing mentality as a disease. It is criminal, perhaps even perverse, as the language of "A Poet's Epitaph" suggests, where the enlightenment physician is portrayed as being "all eyes, / Philosopher!—a fingering slave, / One that would peep and botanize / Upon his mother's grave" (17–20).

This vision of the naturalist as a threatening figure detached from social values and mores reappears in other Romantic texts. In Mary Shelley's *Frankenstein,* natural philosophy violates nature and produces sterility and death everywhere. In *Cain,* Byron rewrote Genesis, suggesting that Cain's overreaching desire to know what it means to be human has set him against his society. Strikingly, Lucifer uses natural history to undercut Cain's communal and religious faith, introducing him to contemporary geology and to the many worlds that were created and destroyed before the creation of human beings, a knowledge that ultimately leads to the destruction of his brother and the fragmentation of the Adamite family.

Death always has been an important aspect of natural history collecting. During the Romantic period, with the rise of the animal rights movement, the contradictions within this activity increasingly became manifest, even if, in the colonial world, hunting and collecting continued unabated.[25] Where earlier collecting had been seen as performing primarily a social role in expanding human knowledge of the creation, nineteenth-century narratives about the collector often emphasize its importance to the biographical history of the collector.[26] For many, it was a popular source of adventures. As hunter or heroic adventurer, the nineteenth-century collector occupies an ambiguous place in a science that increasingly was distancing itself from field study. Particularly in the colonial arena, collecting provided opportunities for the reassertion of traditional gender and social relations. In *The Naturalist on the River Amazons* (1863), for instance, an encounter with a flock of Curl-crested Toucans allows Henry Walter Bates to act out what seems almost an adolescent misogyny. "I had an amusing adventure one day with these birds," he writes.

> I had shot one from a rather high tree in a dark glen in the forest, and entered the thicket where the bird had fallen, to secure my booty. It was only wounded, and on my attempting to seize it, set up a loud scream. In an instant, as if by magic, the shady nook seemed alive with these birds, although there was certainly none visible when I entered the jungle. They descended towards me, hopping from bough to bough, some of them swinging on the loops and cables of woody lianas, and all croaking and fluttering their wings like so many furies. If I had had a long stick in my hand I could have knocked several of them over. After killing the wounded one I began to prepare for obtaining more specimens and punishing the viragos for their boldness; but the screaming of their companion having ceased, they remounted the trees, and before I could reload, every one of them had disappeared.[27]

How Bates could see this story as "amusing" is difficult to imagine. Adopting the language of "adventure" and referring to the bird as "booty," he enlarges on what seems a mock-heroic battle, pitting himself against the birds. Natural history and colonial contact are inscribed upon each other, as if, indeed, he were a colonial conquistador, yet Bates also clearly sees this battle in terms of gender, describing the birds as "so many furies" and as "viragos," that is, "scolds." Violence here is portrayed as the appropriate masculine response to being "upbraided" or "berated." Yet the threat of female dominance is only temporary. It only appears in the brief period while Bates is "reload[ing]" his gun. In the published engraving that served as the frontispiece to the second volume of his book, the social dimensions of this encounter are quite clear, as Bates appears to be struggling against the superior forces of a parlor-room of female birds. Whereas the frontispiece to Merian's *Metamorphosis Insectorum Surinamensium* seeks to domesticate the female naturalist in a colonial setting, Bates's goes in the opposite direction, using the jungle as an arena for violently reasserting masculinity.

During the latter part of the eighteenth century, the journeys of François Levaillant in South Africa and Humboldt in South America established the paradigm of the heroic Romantic naturalist, an image that would be reinforced by the publication of Darwin's *Voyage of the Beagle* (1839). This association of the collector with colonial adventure, in which travel is used to augment the personality of the naturalist, is strongest in the writings of Charles Waterton, whose *Wanderings in South America* (1825) set a new standard in the transformation of the scientific narrative into an adventure story, and, with it, the metamorphosis of the travelling naturalist into an imperial adventure hero. Waterton was a sophisticated taxidermist, who brought together a collection of about 750 specimens, now housed at the Wakefield Museum in Yorkshire. In his second trip to South America, he returned with "some rare insects (though none new to science), two hundred and thirty birds, two land tortoises, five Armadillos, two large serpents, a sloth, an ant-bear, and a Cayman."[28] The latter, a ten-and-one-half-foot crocodile, was his most talked-about specimen, not for its rarity, but for how it was captured. Waterton claimed that in order to prevent it from being damaged by arrows, he actually had wrestled and rode it onto shore: "I vaulted, so that I gained my seat with my face in a right position. I immediately seized his forelegs, and, by main force, twisted them on his back; thus they served me for a bridle."[29] This was a new, if bizarre, image of the masculinized naturalist-collector, one that has returned recently to television in the figure of the Australian crocodile hunter Steve Irwin. William Swainson spoke for many naturalists in dismissing Waterton as someone who combined "the greatest love of the marvellous, . . . [with] a constant propensity to dress truth in the garb of fiction," and, indeed, it would be mistaken to suggest that Waterton conformed to the dominant cultural image of the scientist during this period.[30] A contemporary review described Waterton as a "gentleman of fortune" who was "merely an adventurous naturalist."[31] Waterton denied that his tale was fiction, yet his claim was undercut by his having already included as the frontispiece to the first edition of *Wanderings* (removed from the second edition), the engraving of a nondescript, half-man, half-animal, which he claimed to have discovered on his fourth voyage. It was, indeed, a hoax, a missing link made from the backside of a howler monkey. It discredited his claims as a scientist, even if it demonstrated his great skill in taxidermy.

Waterton's own portrait is probably the most uncanny image of the collector to appear in the first half of the nineteenth century (figure 2.10). It was painted in 1824 by Charles Willson Peale, the creator of Peale's Museum, the first museum of natural history in America. Peale had a flair for the dramatic, and was quite willing to display himself, as a naturalist in his appropriate habitat, that is, the museum. In his self-portrait *The Artist in his Museum,* Peale portrays himself pulling aside drapery to expose the Long Room Gallery of the museum. Even more extraordinary, he produced a life-size wax figure of himself, which was also on display at the museum. For Christoph Irmscher, it presents an "image of the naturalist who creates a collection and then puts himself into it . . . the collector who is both *apart from* and *a part of* his collection."[32] In the Waterton portrait, Peale did something quite similar. The English naturalist is shown standing in a study with a tropical Red-Crested Finch on his finger, the bird looking up to him as if hoping to be fed. This familiar and apparently harmless relationship between the man and bird is deconstructed, however, by the presence of the stuffed head of a cat, whose somewhat quizzical look draws attention, through its uncanny lifelike qualities, to the taxidermic skill of its owner/creator, Waterton. The control of nature is, indeed, always one aspect of the pleasure of keeping pets, but here, in this cat turned paperweight, it is a pleasure that extends beyond life.[33] The engraving is certainly about death and collecting, but more particularly it is about Waterton's power to mimic life. Manifestly, it is a display of taxidermic magic, of heads that speak to us in the silence of lives transformed into specimens and curios. It was, indeed, in the art of taxidermy that Waterton sought to achieve fame, a goal announced in *Wanderings* through its subtitle: *With original instructions for the preservation of birds, &c. for cabinets of natural history* (1825). Throughout his life, Waterton continually crossed the boundary between pet and specimen, making

2.10 Charles Willson Peale, *Charles Waterton* (1824).
National Portrait Gallery, London.

pets into specimens, and, as the notorious story of his riding a crocodile suggests, specimens into pets, and he played an important role in
the development of wildlife reserves. This engraving, however, is not
about preserving life, but about the transforming passion of the collector, that strange world in which nature must die in order to be preserved. Ovid's Apollo reappears as a modern taxidermist, his Daphne
now a stuffed bird specimen, so life-like you might almost think that
she were about to sing. The engraving speaks of the illusion of total
control, the total transformation of nature into the hyperrealist
products of the taxidermist's study. A masculine passion to possess is
immortalized by a dead nature that lives forever through the illusion-
ary skill of the collector, his ability to make those that have been
transformed seem "to consent, to be saying *Yes.*"

Natural history provided Waterton with the opportunity to engage
in his two favorite preoccupations—those of collecting and of self-
display. Visitors to Walton Hall, in fact, were greeted by two door-
knocker grotesques of Waterton's face, "one laughing, the other [that
received the knocker] in a mock grimace of pain."[34] Peale must have
recognized this aspect of Waterton's character, so close to his own,
for the head of the cat sits on a leather-bound book authored by WA-
TERTON, even though in 1824 Waterton had not yet written a book.
The title of the book, METHOD, is also, one might argue, a clue to the
subject of the painting, for it is actually about the art of taxidermy. A
very stiff Waterton appears in the painting, clothed in full formal
dress, with a perfectly groomed face and head, as if he were as much
on display as his specimens. More than most portraits, this one is
particularly rigid and static, as if Waterton were himself only a man-
nequin, a suitable perch for a living bird. The vague gaze of his eyes
toward the side of the painting, detached from both his viewers and
uninterested in the bird, suggests that the difference between this collector and his collection is not as great as one might think. In this
portrait, Peale employed art to allow Waterton to act out one of the
deepest desires of a collector—that of becoming as immortal as his
collection. Ovid's Apollo responded to the transformation of
Daphne into a laurel by dressing himself in her leaves to signify
achievement. Perhaps following the example of Jeremy Bentham,
who requested that he be stuffed after his death, the two taxidermist/
naturalists—Peale and Waterton—must have realized that the advance of time required a more radical investment on the part of the
collector. Beyond the permanence provided by a book not yet even
written, the naturalist had to be willing to enter the cold silence of his
own collection, joining the others as its most unique specimen.

The naturalist did not stand apart from this myth-making activity,
but also often was portrayed as having undergone an apotheosis, an

access to almost divine power, signified by the laurels of scientific achievement. In an age far more literary than our own, at a time when natural history was as much literary as scientific, naturalists knew the classical meaning of scientific laurels; the original myth of Apollo and Daphne remained as a constant reminder of the achievement, as well as the possible costs, of scientific fame. Ovidean figures provided them with a language for talking about this new field and the desire that motivated their participation in it. As a narrative about gender and scientific desire, and about the mutual transformations that take place both in nature and in the naturalist/collector, this myth provided a model for new visual figurations, some celebratory, some very dark indeed, of changes that this new scientific activity was making in nature and naturalists during this period.

Notes

1. For current work on collecting and material culture, see *The Cultures of Collecting*, ed. John Elsner and Roger Cardinal (Cambridge, Mass.: Harvard University Press, 1994); Paula Findlen, *Possessing Nature: Museums, Collecting, and Scientific Culture in Early Modern Italy* (Berkeley and Los Angeles: University of California Press, 1994); Brenda Danet and Tamar Katriel, "Glorious Obsessions, Passionate Lovers, and Hidden Treasures: Collecting, Metaphor, and the Romantic Ethic," in *The Socialness of Things: Essays on the Socio-Semiotics of Objects*, ed. Stephen Harold Riggins (New York: Nouton de Gruyter, 1994), 23–61; Susan M. Pearce, ed. *Interpreting Objects and Collections* (London: Routledge, 1994); and *Museums, Objects and Collections: A Cultural Study* (Leicester: Leicester University Press, 1992); Anthony Shelton, ed., *Collectors, Individuals and Institutions* (London: Horniman Museum: Museu Antropológico da Universidade de Coimbra, 2001); and Philipp Blom, *To Have and to Hold* (London: Allen Lane, 2002).

2. For a study of collectors' passions, see Susan Stewart, *On Longing: Narratives of the Miniature, the Gigantic, the Souvenir, the Collection* (Baltimore: Johns Hopkins University Press, 1984). For early modern scientific curiosity, see Lorraine Daston and Katharine Park, *Wonders and the Order of Nature, 1150–1750* (New York: Zone, 1998), 303–28. For the late eighteenth and early nineteenth centuries, see Nicholas Thomas, "Licensed Curiosity: Cook's Pacific Voyages," in Elsner and Cardinal, *The Cultures of Collecting*, 116–36; and E. P. Hamm, "Unpacking Goethe's Collections: The Public and the Private in Natural-Historical Collecting," *British Journal for the History of Science* 34 (2001): 275–300. For pleasure and science, see Anne Secord, "Botany on a Plate: Pleasure and the Power of Pictures in Promoting Early Nineteenth-Century Scientific Knowledge," *Isis* 93 (2002): 28–57.

3. Daston and Park, *Wonders and the Order of Nature*, 11.

4. Ovid, *Metamorphoses*, trans. Rolfe Humphries (Bloomington and London: Indiana University Press, 1955), 19.

5. *Ibid.*, 19–20.

6. *Ibid.*, 20.

7. *Ibid.*

8. *Ibid.*

9. See the discussion of this illustration by Victoria Dickenson, *Drawn from Life: Science and Art in the Portrayal of the New World* (Toronto: University of Toronto Press, 1998), 169–71. For gardens and imperialism, see John M. Prest, *The Garden of Eden: The Botanic Garden and the Recreation of Paradise* (New Haven: Yale University Press, 1981).

10. See Mary Louise Pratt, *Imperial Eyes: Travel Writing and Transculturation* (London: Routledge, 1992), esp. 38–68.

11. Natalie Zemon Davis, *Women on the Margins: Three Seventeenth-Century Lives* (Cambridge, Mass.: Harvard University Press, 1995).

12. Originally drawn at Clifford's estate, the portrait is best known through the mezzotint engraving produced by H. Kingsbury for Robert Thornton's *Temple of Flora* (London, 1805). For cultural cross-dressing, see Lisbet Koerner, *Linnaeus: Nature and Nation* (Harvard University Press, 1999); and Beth Fowkes Tobin, *Picturing Imperial Power: Colonial Subjects in Eighteenth Century British Painting* (Duke University Press, 1999).

13. The portrait can be seen in the Usher Gallery, Lincoln, Lincolnshire; it is available in Patricia Fara's informative "Benjamin West's Portrait of Joseph Banks," *Endeavour* 24, no. 1 (2000): 1–3.

14. *The Aurelian Macaroni* was published by the print seller Matthew Darly. His *The Botanic Macaroni* (1772) is reprinted in Fara's "Benjamin West's Portrait of Joseph Banks."

15. Robert Hitchcock, *The Macaroni: A Comedy* (York: A. Ward, 1773), 5, 4.

16. See *Oxford English Dictionary* (2nd ed.) entry for "macaroni."

17. A. S. Byatt draws attention to the gendering of natural history display in "Morpho Eugenia." Harold Alabaster apologizes for the fact that his insects have not been ordered "upon quite scientific principles," his daughter Eugenia preferring instead an "elegant arrangement of the Lepidoptera": "I am particularly taken with the idea of punctuating the rows of butterflies with the little iridescent green scarabs. Eugenia says she got the idea from silk knots in embroidery" (*Angels and Insects: Two Novellas* [New York: Random House, 1992], 17).

18. *Town and Country Magazine; or, Universal Repository of Knowledge, Instruction, and Entertainment,* September 1773, 457–58.

19. For a discussion of James Gillray's satiric portrayal of Joseph Banks as the "The great South Sea Caterpillar," see my "On the Banks of the South Sea," in *Visions of Empire: Voyages, Botany, and Representations of Empire,* ed. David Philip Miller and Peter Hanns Reill (Cambridge: Cambridge University Press, 1996), 189–91.

20. Mark J. Plotkin, Brian M. Boom, and Malorye Allison, *The Ethnobotany of Aublet's "Histoire des Plants de la Guiane Françoise" (1775)* (St. Louis: Missouri Botanical Garden, 1991), 1–2.

21. See Ann B. Shteir, *Cultivating Women, Cultivating Science: Flora's Daughters and Botany in England 1760–1860* (Baltimore: Johns Hopkins University Press, 1996).

22. See my "'Jacobin Flowers': Botany as Social Theory in the 1790s," *The Wordsworth Circle* 20 (1989): 132–39.

23. *The Borderers,* ed. Robert Osborn (1842; reprinted, Ithaca: Cornell University Press, 1982), 43.

24. *William Wordsworth,* ed. Stephen Gill (Oxford: Oxford University Press, 1984), 10.872–77.

25. See esp. Keith Thomas, *Man and the Natural World: A History of the Modern Sensibility* (New York: Pantheon, 1983); Harriet Ritvo, *The Animal Estate: The English and Other Creatures in the Victorian Age* (Cambridge, Mass.: Harvard University Press, 1987); Christine Kenyon Jones, *Kindred Brutes: Animals in Romantic Period Writing* (Aldershot: Ashgate, 2001); and John M. McKenzie, *The Empire of Nature: Hunting, Conservation, and British Imperialism* (Manchester: Manchester University Press, 1988).

26. See in this volume, Sally Gregory Kohlstedt's "Nature by Design: Masculinity and Animal Display in Nineteenth-Century America," 110–39.

27. *The Naturalist on the River Amazons* (Berkeley: University of California Press, 1962), 411–12.

28. Charles Waterton, *Wanderings in South America, the North-West of the United States, and the Antilles, in the Years 1812, 1816, 1820, and 1824* (Oxford: Oxford University Press, 1873), 137.

29. Ibid., 133–34.

30. William Swainson, *The Natural History of Fishes, Amphibians and Reptiles* (London: Longman, Orme, Brown, Green and Longmans, 1838–1839), 2.111.

31. *Monthly Review* 108 (September 1825): 66.

32. Christoph Irmscher, *The Poetics of Natural History: From John Bartram to William James* (New Brunswick, N.J.: Rutgers University Press, 1999), 2; see also 56–100.

33. See Ritvo, *Animal Estate.*

34. Brian W. Edginton, *Charles Waterton: A Biography* (Cambridge: Lutterworth Press, 1996), 118.

Chapter 3

FIGURING NATURE/ FIGURING THE (FE)MALE

The Frontispiece to Humboldt's *Ideas Towards a Geography of Plants*

Joan Steigerwald

The frontispiece to Alexander von Humboldt's 1807 *Ideas Towards a Geography of Plants* (*Ideen zu einer Geographie der Pflanzen*) is a complex image (figure 3.1). It depicts Apollo, god of art and reason, unveiling a statue of Diana, the multi-breasted goddess of nature. Figurative inscriptions in the form of Egyptian hieroglyphs cover the statue's lower body, and a stone tablet inscribed with the title of Johann Wolfgang von Goethe's treatise *Metamorphosis of Plants* rests at the statue's base. Humboldt commissioned the frontispiece as a dedication to Goethe from Bertel Thorwaldsen, who proposed the vignette "alluding to the union of poetry, philosophy and natural knowledge" that Humboldt regarded as the characteristic of Goethe's *Geist*.[1] The frontispiece seems a strangely iconic engraving for a text that offered a detailed account of plant forms in relationship to their characteristic environments, the physical parameters of which were determined through exhaustive scientific measurements. What is the significance of this mythic imagery fronting a work of science, and drawing a study of plant geography out into a context of fascination with antique cosmotheism and the figure of unveiling the goddess of nature? What role is played by this ornamental *parergon,* as a supplement to the work, the *ergon*? This chapter will attend to the frontispiece of Humboldt's *Ideas* and try to understand its meanings in relation to nature, science, and gender.

Immanuel Kant discussed the *parerga* of art in his 1790 *Critique of Judgment.* He took as examples of ornamental *parerga* the frames of paintings, the garments veiling statues—extrinsic additions that do not "belong to the whole [representation] of the object as an intrinsic constituent," yet are able to augment that representation.[2]

3.1 Dedication to Goethe, Frontispiece to Alexander von Humboldt, *Ideas Towards a Geography of Plants* (*Ideen zu einer Geographie der Pflanzen* [1807]), after a drawing by Bertel Thorwaldsen.
Courtesy of Beinecke Rare Book and Manuscript Library, Yale University.

He extended his analysis in a note to his 1794 *Religion within the Limits of Reason Alone*. Here he introduced additions, such as mysteries or miracles, as "*parerga* of religion within the limits of pure reason; they do not belong within it but border upon it. Reason, conscious of [its] inability to satisfy [its] moral need, extends [it]self to [transcendent] ideas capable of supplying this lack."[3] Such additions are risky, in being uncritical. The *parerga* of art threaten to degrade the work and to degenerate into mere adornment and sensory attraction; the *parerga* of religion threaten to degenerate reasonable religion into superstition or fanaticism. Jacques Derrida draws attention to such marginalia, to ornaments or notes, which although supplementary to the proper domain of a work, "intervene in the inside only to the extent that the inside is lacking from itself."[4] *Parerga* draw a work outside of itself, extending its meaning into unintended realms. Neither simply inside nor outside of a work, standing out against both a work, as ground, and the milieu of a work, as background, they raise the problem of drawing a boundary around any work. The issue of what is essential and what accessory to a work warrants continual interrogation, and thus these framing *parerga* have a thickness worth investigating.

At the turn of the nineteenth century, philosophies of nature acquired significance as new modes of religious expression or as alternatives to religion. Humboldt's work is situated in a complex relationship with such philosophies—with deism, pantheism, masonry and atheism, Goethe's studies of nature, Schelling's *Naturphilosophie*, and Romanticism. None of these philosophies of nature can be equated simply with one another, nor can Humboldt's work be understood in terms of any one, if taking inspiration from many. For the modern reader, his work is of interest because it engaged the philosophies of nature surrounding it, while offering a singular vision of the dynamic unity of nature. Humboldt offered a portrait of nature informed by both aesthetic and instrumental readings of nature, a portrait whose expression in his many writings, maps, and diagrams was also a means of self-formation. The frontispiece provides a figurative framing of these characteristics of his vision of nature, its complex iconography at once enhancing the meaning of the text and destabilizing it by drawing it into broader associations.

The first part of this chapter examines the sources and significances of the imagery of the frontispiece. It is consequential that nature is figured and figured as a goddess. For Humboldt and many of his contemporaries, the essence of nature remains indefinite; all knowledge of nature is a figurative representation of its appearances. The contemporary fascination with antique cosmotheism, in which Humboldt's frontispiece participated, was in part due to a recognition among adherents that the goddess of nature is but a figure of the nameless power permeating the cosmos. The veil represents debates regarding whether or not the truth of nature might be revealed, the god Apollo suggests that nature is best comprehended through the cultivation of both reason and aesthetic sensibility, and the hieroglyphic inscriptions draw attention to the figures produced in the reading of nature's script. Each of these elements of Humboldt's frontispiece was a common contemporary motif.

The second and third sections of this chapter examine the role of figurative languages in representing nature and representing male and female nature. Through his maps and diagrams, Humboldt tried to develop a graphic vocabulary that could represent nature's empirical laws—his contribution to contemporary initiatives to develop visual scientific languages. A product of both instrumental reasoning and aesthetic appraisal, it offers a means of visual thinking, of figuring out the form of such laws, without thus claiming to go beyond figures to nature itself, to reveal the naked essence of the goddess. This reading of nature as necessarily figured provides a basis for reconsidering the figures of male and female nature at the turn of the nineteenth century. Aesthetic explorations of self-formation emphasized a development from an unformed or ill-defined to a well-formed character. But contemporary play with gender and sexual ambiguity, whether in artistic appraisal or in new literary forms, suggested a performativity to figuring self. The aesthetic was thus a means for exploring nature, and male and female nature. But as the god of art and science unveils the goddess of nature what can be uncovered is only nature in its figurative form.

Unveiling the Goddess of Nature

It is important to note that Humboldt's frontispiece was part of a genre of frontispieces figuring works of science through mythic imagery. The frontispiece of Carolus Linnaeus's 1746 *Fauna of Scandinavia*, for example, has a statue of the goddess of nature—multibreasted, veiled, and encased by figurative inscriptions—now represented as the Nordic Diana (figure 3.2). Above her shines the light of reason, while in one hand she holds a snake biting its tail as a symbol of the eternal return of life and in the other the moon as a symbol of her original significance as an ancient Italian moon goddess. The motif of the unveiling of the goddess of nature also can be found in seventeenth-century works, such as the frontispiece to Gerhard Blasius's 1681 *Anatomy of Animals* (figure 3.3). Here it is zoology, also personified as female, who unveils nature through the instruments of science, a lamp guiding her head and a scalpel and a magnifying glass her hands. Surrounded by diverse animals, two *putti* at her feet study them through dissection. A statue of the veiled goddess of nature similarly is found in the frontispiece to Georg Forster's 1790 *Views of the Lower Rhine,* his account of his travels with Humboldt (figure 3.4). The image of Apollo also appears in frontispieces of eighteenth-century texts on natural history and

3.2 Frontispiece to Carolus Linnaeus, *Fauna of Scandinavia* (1746).
Courtesy of Georg-August–Universität Göttingen.

natural philosophy. In the frontispiece of Linnaeus's 1747 *Hortus Cliffortianus,* for example, Linnaeus is depicted as Apollo unveiling Minerva, the Roman goddess of wisdom and the arts.[5] One could multiply examples of such frontispieces containing imagery similar to Humboldt's, indicating the thickness of the significances attached to its figures.

The background to the proliferation of such frontispieces was a revival of interest in antique cosmotheism through new historical studies of ancient Egypt and polytheism in the late seventeenth and eighteenth centuries. Such scholarship was a part of debates regarding the relationships between reason and revelation, nature and scripture, stimulated by controversies surrounding Spinozism, deism, atheism, and masonry. These studies of antique cosmotheism

3.3 Frontispiece to Gerhard Blasius, *Anatomy of Animals* (1681).
Courtesy of Georg-August–Universität Göttingen.

3.4 Frontispiece to Georg Forster, *Views of the Lower Rhine* (1790). Copperplate by Paul Malvieux, after a drawing by Jacob Asmus Carstens.
Courtesy of Georg-August–Universität Göttingen.

should be distinguished from the fascination with Egypt during the Renaissance. The Renaissance revival of Egypt through individuals such as Marsilio Ficino and Athanasius Kircher reconstructed Hermetic philosophy as ancient Egyptian theology and celebrated it as an originary wisdom older than Moses and as a counter to Biblical tradition. Jan Assmann emphasizes that once Isaac Casaubon exposed the *Corpus Hermeticum* as a late compilation and possible Christian forgery in 1614, a new phase of interest in Egypt and antique cosmotheism occurred in the late seventeenth and eighteenth centuries. These later scholars worked through the criticism of Casaubon and the hostile reactions of orthodoxy, and built their reconstructions on careful historical criticism. Ralph Cudworth and William Warburton, for example, were interested in Egypt as the historical background of Moses, and in questions of the relationships between monotheism and polytheism, revelation and idolatry. They argued that the hidden truth of antique polytheism was that there is only one God, and also found in the idea of nature the basis of an original, non-revealed monotheism.[6] These scholars drew upon classical authors who presented an engaging picture of intercultural translatability or syncretism and cosmotheism among the diverse religions of antiquity. Although languages, the shapes of gods, and forms of worship varied from one culture to another, the deities of different religions were recognized as having common roles, especially those with cosmic functions.[7] For example, one can find in the *Metamorphosis* of Apuleius the equation of Diana with Isis and other nature goddesses. Similarly, Plutarch, in his treatise *Isis and Osiris,* argued that behind the differing names is always a common cosmic phenomena.[8] Egyptian theology in particular was represented as based on the principle of "One and All." The relativization of different names of deities as surface phenomena to be set off against the background of a common universal religion, as figurative representations of a supreme and hidden cosmic power that remained nameless, was thus understood to be typical of antique cosmotheism.

The idea of nature as the source of an original, non-revealed monotheism and of an ancient cosmotheism with uncovered knowledge of nature appealed tremendously to deists and pantheists and those developing new philosophies of nature in the late eighteenth century. Karl Leonhard Reinhold, for example, used the ideas of Warburton in his 1786 masonic treatise *The Hebrew Mysteries, or the Oldest Religious Freemasonry.* Reinhold wrote this work before converting to Kantianism and taking a position as a professor of philosophy in Jena. In it he offered a positive image of antique religions, arguing that the problems of idolatry, superstition, and animal worship are only surface phenomena, and praised the priests of ancient Egypt for their knowledge of the foundations of physics, mathematics, astronomy, and geography. Friedrich Schiller, a colleague of Reinhold's in Jena, developed an interest in secret societies through close friends who were masons. In his 1790 essay *The Mission of Moses,* he drew upon Reinhold's work, emphasizing his claim that the god of philosophy and Enlightenment rationality was identical to the deity of the Egyptian mysteries.[9] Especially in Germany, the late eighteenth century was a time of distinction between true and false religions, and a time of secrecy for supporters of Spinoza and deism. To those rejecting official religions or even the need for religion, antique cosmotheism or philosophies finding the source of truth within nature and esoteric insights reserved for initiates offered important alternative systems of meaning. New philosophies of nature often invoked the iconography of antique cosmotheisms; hence the appeal to the goddess of nature as a figuration of a nameless cosmic power, to her veil as an image of the hidden essence of nature, to Egyptian hieroglyphs as representing the secret knowledge of ancient cosmotheism and nature's own script, and to the role of both art and science in the unveiling of nature, as in Humboldt's frontispiece.

The Egyptian goddess Isis was identified with the Italian goddess Diana and the Greek goddess Artemis, all being regarded as nature goddesses. Artemis, as the goddess of wild nature and animals, often was depicted with animals. Wild and uncanny herself, she was inviolable and vindictive to those who thwarted her. Associated with transitional marginal places, and with transitions in life and natural death, she presided over the transformation of youths into adulthood. A virginal goddess, with jurisdiction over virgin nature, hunting, and war, she demanded of hunters that they be pure and chaste. She also presided over the transformation of girls from virginity to fully acculturated and tamed womanhood, and over childbirth. The goddess thus became a female face of nature—at once wild, fecund, and virginal. Diana took over these associations from Artemis.[10] In European art, the goddess Diana has been a symbol of nature since the Renaissance. Raphael, for example, depicts the goddess of nature on the steps of the throne of philosophy as a representation of the physical part of philosophy in a 1508 fresco. Thorwaldsen could have taken as his model the statue in the Villa Albani in Rome in the Temple of Ephesian Artemis, or the frontispiece of Giovanni Piranesi's influential 1765 work on the ruins of antiquity.[11]

The image of Apollo stands in sharp contrast to that of Diana in Humboldt's frontispiece. Apollo is figured as a graceful youth of harmonious beauty, Diana as a grotesque form; the god is depicted as a living man in the act of unveiling, the goddess as encased in stone, more a statue than a living being. In classical mythology, the beautiful Apollo has numerous love affairs with nymphs and mortals. Standing on the threshold of manhood, he presides over the initiation of youth into society. He is the god of healing and purification, and of poetry and music—his instrument is the lyre, with its harmonious, well-ordered rhythms. Apollo is Artemis's twin brother, although few mythical stories mix the two. Nevertheless, Apollo is depicted with Diana in several sixteenth- and seventeenth-century Italian paintings, as well as in paintings by Dürer, the elder Cranach, and Poussin.[12] Apollo acquired particular import in the eighteenth century through the writings of the German art historian Johann Joachim Winckelmann, who claimed the Apollo Belvedere as the highest exemplar of antique art. Winckelmann highlighted the aesthetic indeterminacy of the statue, its masterful incorporation of a tension between an ideal marble form and a sensual, graceful, living body, between art and nature. As the face of the aesthetic, Winckelmann contends Apollo is only ambiguously male, representing rather adolescent sexual liminality.[13] Thorwaldsen would have been familiar with both the Apollo Belvedere and Winckelmann's characterization. In Humboldt's frontispiece, Apollo is figured as high culture, a refined rationality and sensibility.

The iconography of the veil was foreign to Artemis and Diana in antiquity, but many antique sources, such as Apuleius's *Metamorphosis*, depict Isis with a veil or robe. Plutarch's treatise *Isis and Osiris* places the goddess before the Temple at Saïs, on which is found the inscription: "I am all that has been, and is, and shall be, and my robe no mortal has yet uncovered."[14] In antiquity, the veil thus was read as a symbol of a distinction between inner truth and outer appearance, between the hidden and the visible. The idea that the nature wisdom of antiquity in general and Egypt in particular was veiled behind figurative modes of expression was taken up by eighteenth-century scholars of antique cosmotheism. In Germany, the veiled figure of nature became a common trope in the literary and critical texts. Schiller, for example, published the poem "The Veiled Image at Saïs" in 1795, which warned against attempting to lift the veil of the goddess before becoming fully spiritually uplifted. In a fragment from 1800, Friedrich Schlegel also represented the difficulty of unveiling the goddess and the shock of the hidden truths unveiled: "It's time to tear away the veil of Isis and reveal the mystery. Whoever can't endure the sight of the goddess, let him flee or perish."[15] By the late eighteenth century, the depiction of the veiled goddess of nature, either Isis or Artemis/Diana, also became common in works of science as an allegory of the secrets of nature, emphasizing either their impenetrability or the possibility of their penetration through new instruments of inquiry.[16]

Humboldt's depiction of the unveiling of Diana is but one example of such representations, with the revelation now mediated by art and science rather than by a priest.

The figurative inscriptions surrounding the base of the statue of Diana in Humboldt's frontispiece reflect the association of Artemis/Diana with animals and wild nature, but they also can be read as Egyptian hieroglyphs, in accordance with the association of the goddess with Egyptian cosmotheism. An interest in hieroglyphs was a part of studies of Egypt in the eighteenth century and they were regarded as a potential source of ancient natural knowledge. The hieroglyphic script was not deciphered until 1822 by Françoise Champollion. Prior to that, most scholars read them as expressing religious concepts and natural knowledge, but put in the form of iconic symbols to conceal these mysteries from the vulgar folk as a means of maintaining social and political stability. In keeping with the motif of veiled truth, the hieroglyphs were a symbol of the distinction of idolatrous surface phenomena from esoteric, intrinsic truth. In other words, they acted like carnal frontispieces, ornamental *parerga* to the meaning in the interior.[17] Warburton, however, argued that the development of symbolic hieroglyphs for the purposes of secrecy was a late development in Egypt, provoked by extraneous factors, a foreign invasion of Egypt and the decision of priests thus to conceal their learning.[18] He fit hieroglyphs into the universal and necessary development of language—moving from pictorial, representational images, through hieroglyphs, to arbitrary marks and eventually alphabets—and thus as a "natural way" for humans to communicate thoughts. To explain their continued use by the Egyptians, Warburton appealed to the notion of the distinct genius of its people, arguing that the Egyptians were extremely imaginative and thus naturally inclined to symbolic figures. He noted that the Egyptian hieroglyphs, which pictured things and used the properties of things to denote undepictable meanings, required a vast knowledge of physics. As opposed to other scripts, Egyptian hieroglyphs remained a "script of nature" and thus a codification of cosmological knowledge; other forms of writing, by turning to conventional codes, lost this connection with the natural world. Warburton took as his example of a symbolic hieroglyph the multi-breasted Diana, interpreting it as a hieroglyph of universal nature. Although he was mistaken—in that this image never appeared as a hieroglyph and was not Egyptian—it was identified with the veiled image of Saïs and the iconography of the goddess of nature.[19]

Building on Warburton's work, as well as on his brother Wilhelm's study of the natural development of language as intertwined with the development of the mind and culture, Humboldt discussed hieroglyphs at length as a part of his research on Mexican artifacts in his 1810 *Views of the Cordilleras and Monuments of the Indigenous Peoples of America*.[20] He compared the graphic scripts of the new world unfavorably with those of the old. He noted in particular that Mexicans were unfamiliar with simple hieroglyphs and hence needed a large number of symbols to convey ideas, that they mixed real hieroglyphs with natural depictions of action, and that they had failed to develop an alphabetic script. More generally, Humboldt was critical of the crude depiction of figures in Mexican paintings, arguing that it was an art still in its infancy, dominated by mechanical representation rather than a cultivated aesthetic sensibility. Thus, although demonstrating an interest in the arts and traditions of non-European cultures unusual for his time, he argued that the primitive state of Mexican art and writing indicated a low state of cultural development.[21] The more cultivated aesthetics of the old world had enabled more refined languages of nature, first in simple and pure hieroglyphic scripts, later in the development of alphabetic languages and languages of science.

It is now possible to begin to see how complex the frontispiece used by Humboldt to frame his text on the study of nature is. It should be read through the context of a fascination with ancient Egypt and cosmotheism, through the understanding of deities such as Diana as specific figurations of an indefinite cosmic divine power, through the image of Apollo as a representation of a refined science and aesthetic, and through notions of veiled truths and symbolic scripts. If Humboldt was not a mason or religious, his interest in nature as a source of meaning suggests that the iconic image is not at odds with his text. In the frontispiece, nature is figured as female and the act of her unveiling as a male activity. The rather grotesque form of the goddess was due partly to the historical accrual of symbolic significances—the many breasts, the figures of wild animals, the feminine as wild and fecund. But in the frontispiece Humboldt also can be seen as presenting the argument that nature should not be left in its crude appearances, nor could it be known in its essence, but is unveiled through the "union of poetry, philosophy and natural knowledge," through the cultivated sensibility of art and reason, largely male domains at the time.[22] Humboldt's geography of plants was to be such a figuring of nature. He introduced diagrams and maps as a means of representing and thinking about nature's empirical laws. As Egyptian hieroglyphs were a part of the natural development of human language and thought, Humboldt's figures were to be a part of the development of scientific language and thought.

In Humboldt's frontispiece, a stone tablet resting at the feet of the statue of the goddess of nature is inscribed with the "Metamorphosis of Plants," in reference to Goethe's study of plant formation. Goethe's work provided directives for the study of plants based on their perceptible forms disciplined through aesthetic appraisal. Humboldt's geography of plants expanded Goethe's project by seeking an aesthetic view of the collective phenomena of vegetation and combining it with their instrumental investigation. Humboldt developed new graphic techniques to harmonize his aesthetic vision with precise measurement and to write nature's laws in a figurative language. He used his diagrams and maps as analytic as well as communicative instruments, as a way of figuring out nature's empirical laws, and as a new graphic form of representation. But Humboldt made no claim to reveal the naked figure of the goddess of nature, nature in its essence; his figurative language of nature aspired to articulate nature solely in its phenomenal appearance.

In *The Metamorphosis of Plants,* Goethe sought to determine the laws of metamorphosis, "the laws of [transformation] by which nature produces one part through another, creating a great variety of forms through the modification of a single organ." Goethe regarded primordial forms [*Urformen*] as the necessary forms of organic bodies in which the specific forms realized by specific organisms are contained as possibilities. Identifying the leaf as such an *Urform,* he described how it can be discerned in the seed, and traced in its successive metamorphoses into the stem, leaves, flower, and organs of fructification: "By the transformation of one form into another, it ascends . . . to the pinnacle of nature: propagation through two [sexes]." Goethe "investigated the outer expression of the forces by which the plant gradually transforms one and the same organ, without any pretence of uncovering the [fundamental or internal forces] behind natural phenomena."[23] He deemed speculation regarding hidden or essential forces as too subjective, emphasizing instead perceptible and hence objective forms of plant formation. Significant to Humboldt's project as represented in his frontispiece, Goethe developed his method for the study of metamorphosis by appeal to notions of aesthetic appraisal. He argued that the ideal forms of nature could be intuited on a similar basis as the ideal forms in art. He first developed these ideas in his study of classical art during his Italian journey (1786–1788) under the guidance of Winckelmann's writings, admiring in particular his emphasis upon combining sensible response with rational study, the sensual and the formal, through a disciplined perception of works of art such as the Belvedere Apollo.

Goethe's study of metamorphosis, developed in the years after his return from Italy, was to provide a similar method of disciplined perception for making evident the primordial forms in nature. Such a rational empiricism would make intuitable how phenomena necessarily appear. The *Urform* that is the basis of all plant forms and formation was a "symbolic plant," a primordial image, *Urbild*, representable in a concrete visual figure. In a symbolic plant, "the particular represents the general" law, so appearance is transformed into an idea, and the idea into an image [*Bild*]. It was a figurative form for both perception and intellect.[24] These precepts guided Humboldt's study of plant form in his *Ideas*.

Humboldt's geography of plants argued that there is a physiognomy peculiar to every region of the earth, based on a few original forms that determine the overall "character of the vegetation and thus the impression that the sight of plants and their groups make on the observer."[25] In this appeal to *Urformen*, the influence of Goethe's *Metamorphosis of Plants* on his geography of plants can be seen. But unlike Goethe, Humboldt proceeded to investigate how the plants of a specific region deviate from the basic plant forms under the influence of the environmental parameters of that region. In emphasizing the collective vegetation of a region, Humboldt drew upon the ideas of his teacher Karl Ludwig Willdenow, Kant's lectures on geography, and Johann Reinhold Forster's observations during his travels with Cook; the term "physiognomy" for the collective impression of phenomena as a measure of its character had been popularized by Johann Caspar Lavater.[26] Humboldt was interested in how vegetation and physical conditions combine to produce the character of a region, and in how the collective phenomena of vegetation varies across time and space with changing environments. His geography of plants was a part of his larger project of a physics of the earth, which tracked the laws of nature in the interactions of forces, to provide a unified portrait of nature.[27]

Like Goethe, Humboldt argued that the impression that the vegetation of a geographical region makes on the mind of an observer is an aesthetic impression. Indeed, the unique character of the plants of a specific environment is to be found in the influence that the plants have on the fantasy and artistic sensibility of the people of that region. In characterizing this visual aesthetic, however, Humboldt appealed to the contemporary developing fashion for landscape painting rather than the individual classical masterpieces that Goethe studied. He claimed that the value of landscape painting lay in its more "earthly tendency" in combining the contemplation of nature with the forces of the imagination, an aesthetic sensibility particularly suited to portraying the collective phenomena of vegetation that interested him in his geography of plants.[28] In his appreciation of landscape painting, Humboldt was influenced by the landscape artist Joseph Anton Koch whom Humboldt met in Rome in 1805; Koch emphasized the interrelationships of the phenomena of nature in his art and the close relationship between the environment of a people and their cultural development.[29] The contrast that Humboldt perceived between the aesthetics of the new world and the old he similarly attributed to their respective environments. Humboldt argued that in the new world the vegetation is so lush that it overwhelms inhabitants and thus they have not been able to develop beyond simple forms of aesthetic sensibility and representation.[30]

Kant linked aesthetic judgments to judgments of the collective phenomena of nature in his 1790 *Critique of Judgment*. In aesthetic judgments, imagination plays a predominant role; lacking a concept for a given intuition, judgment holds the imagination up to the understanding so that a concept can be exhibited and a harmonious relation sensed between the two cognitive powers. In judgments where a concept is available to determine phenomena, the imagination still plays a role, but unconsciously, providing schemata as mediators between intellect and intuition. In judgments of nature in its wholeness, a concept also is lacking and hence judgment provides itself with a principle, the principle that nature is purposive for our intellect, to guide its reflective movement between phenomena and its conceptualization. Although for Kant nature cannot be known in itself, schemata and the principle of purposiveness act as instruments of judgment, enabling the relation of concepts with phenomena corresponding to the limited capacities of human understanding. In a note to his *Critique of Judgment,* Kant refers to the frontispiece of Johann Andreas von Segner's 1770 *Natural Science* that depicts "The Sciences, Measuring the Footprints of Nature" through the iconography of Isis (figure 3.5). The frontispiece emphasizes that although the face of the goddess cannot be regarded directly, or nature known in itself, her footsteps, the manifest phenomena of nature, can be studied through the instruments of science, as depicted by the three *putti* measuring her movements.[31]

Humboldt would seem to agree with Kant and Segner. On his travels, he carried with him an impressive array of the latest scientific instruments, investing considerably in their purchase, in the acquisition of the requisite skills for their use, and in transporting them through the often inhospitable environs of the tropics. With these instruments, Humboldt measured exactly all accessible physical parameters of the different regions he visited, at different altitudes and different times of day.[32] Humboldt used these measurements as instruments of judgment—instruments for reading the

3.5 Frontispiece to Johann Andreas von Segner, *Natural Science* (1770).
Courtesy of Georg-August Universität Göttingen.

QVA LICET.

various physical conditions of the natural world and translating those diverse phenomena into an image of the total impression of a region in which diverse forces interacted.

A tension exists, however, between Humboldt's aesthetic view of the collective phenomena of vegetation and his detailed instrumental measurements. This tension is illustrated by the *tableau physique* that accompanied the *Ideas*, in which the central portrait of the Andes is framed by tables of measurements (figure 3.6). In producing this image, Humboldt struggled with the opposing requirements of scientific precision and painterly effect, of representing the exact environmental parameters of basic plant forms and the impression of the collective phenomena of vegetation. Given Humboldt's shared appreciation with Goethe of aesthetic judgment as a highly cultivated perception, the two facets of Humboldt's tableau cannot be read simply as the view of the layman in contrast to the scientific expert. Indeed, the figure of Apollo in the frontispiece of the work represents the refined sensibility of European culture and the role of both art

3.6 "Tableau physique" accompanying Humboldt, *Ideas Towards a Geography of Plants, with a Natural Painting of the Andes* (1807). Drawing by Lorenz Schönberger and Pierre Turpin, after a sketch by Humboldt. Engraving with watercolor, by Louis Bouguet.
Courtesy of Hamburger Kunsthalle, Hamburg, Germany. Bildarchiv Preussischer Kulturbesitz / Art Resource, NY.

and science in disclosing nature's laws. Humboldt's ambition seems to have been to combine mensurative and aesthetic judgments, and to represent the interconnection of phenomena in an image that encompasses both their precise empirical measurement and artistic appreciation. He was seeking a figurative vocabulary as an instrument to guide judgment and to depict the linkage of phenomena described in his text, a language that was neither solely mathematical nor solely artistic, but a new graphic form of representation.

Humboldt's efforts to develop a "script of nature" were not isolated. At the turn of the nineteenth century, different forms of visual representations—from thematic maps and diagrams to tabular data and graphs—were being explored. These new figurative languages of nature only became articulate during the nineteenth century, and lacked precise conceptual form let alone categorical distinctness at the end of the eighteenth century. Yet the power of these visual scripts to depict natural knowledge and as instruments of thinking was recognized by those advocating their use.[33] Novalis, for example, argued that such figures are not just representations of experiments or illustrations of texts, but an "instrumental language" or nonverbal argument. As experiments are a means of theorizing phenomena and of experiencing a theory, so these symbolic inscriptions stand in for both thoughts and phenomena. They thus help the investigator to visualize ideas and to re-experience and reflect upon experiences.[34] Humboldt similarly did not understand these forms of symbolic writing as nature speaking directly, for they were dependent for their expression on the cultivated sensibility of European art and science. Like Goethe's symbolic images, they combined percept and intellect; like Kant's schemata, they were imaginative instruments of judgment linking phenomena and their conceptualization. Humboldt saw these figures as a means to make visible the laws of nature at once aesthetically and instrumentally.

In later publications, Humboldt developed a figurative depiction of the instrumental readings framing his view of the characteristic vegetation of the geographical regions of the Andes. It had become standard practice during the eighteenth century to organize measurements taken during sea voyages, results from experimental trials, and statistical information on human populations in tabular displays. Humboldt's isothermal map of 1817 demonstrated how such tables of numbers might be transformed into a graphic figure displaying the patterns between phenomena, giving an impression of the laws of heat distribution at a glance (figure 3.7). In developing his map, Humboldt cited the influence of Edmond Halley's maps of magnetic declination from the early eighteenth century, which introduced isolines to represent the spatial variation of magnetic phenomena.[35] As Anne Godlewska has noted, Humboldt's isothermal map, constructed on a plane chart and showing only a few place names, is a systematic rather than geographical space structured to reveal the relationships between phenomena.[36] In fact, it has the appearance of a graph, simply substituting space for time. In developing his "map," Humboldt was influenced by Johann Heinrichs Lambert, who was one of the first to make use of graphical displays of

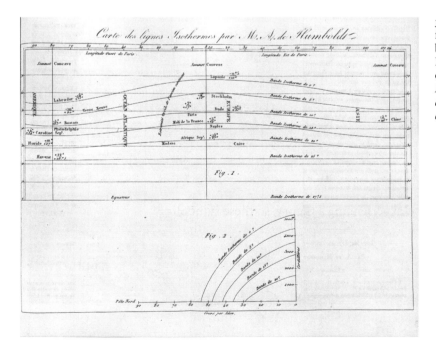

3.7 Map of isothermal lines, from Alexander von Humboldt, "On the Isothermal Lines and the Distribution of Heat on the Globe," *Memoires de physique et de chimie de la Societé d'Arcueil* (1817).

3.8 Graph of solar heat reaching Earth's surface at different latitudes at different times of the year, from Johann Heinrich Lambert, *Pyrometrie*, Figure 35, published posthumously in 1779.
Courtesy of Georg-August–Universität Göttingen.

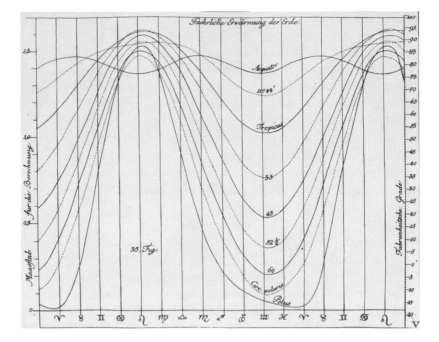

measurements. In *Pyrometrie,* a study of heat published posthumously in 1779 upon which Humboldt drew, Lambert offered his most elaborate graphs (figure 3.8).[37] Lambert argued that his graphs could be used not only to display data figuratively, but also to reveal regularities of nature by tracing smooth curves averaging a mass of measurements.[38] Like Lambert, Humboldt saw his figure as representing physical laws, in this case the differential variation of average annual temperature with latitude. Humboldt also drew upon graphic techniques developed in the late eighteenth century by William Playfair and August Friedrich Wilhelm Crome, who presented graphs of the gradual progress and comparative amounts of the commercial products and populations of nations. Playfair saw in such figures the possibility of a universal language, analogous to figurative languages like Egyptian hieroglyphs, which offered abstract pictographs that could be read in any language.[39] Humboldt's isothermal map also might be read as an attempt at such a universal figurative script, analogous to the hieroglyphs found in his frontispiece. Rather than nature's own script, it was its symbolic inscription, drawing upon both cultivated sensibility and systematic empirical science, combining percept and intellect. Only thus was the impression of the whole, the laws of the phenomena of heat, to be discerned.

In the preface to the German edition of *Ideas,* Humboldt distinguished his investigations of nature from Friedrich Wilhelm Joseph Schelling's *Naturphilosophie,* which promised a portrait of "a higher sort" in seeking to penetrate to the hidden fundamental forces of nature.[40] Kant's note on Segner's frontispiece alluded to the impossibility of attaining such higher knowledge by invoking the "sublime" inscription at the Temple of Saïs associated with the goddess of nature: "I am all that is, that was, and that will be, and no mortal has lifted my veil." For Schiller, the sublimity of the veiled goddess of nature lay in her anonymity; being beyond language "[a]ll names are (in)appropriate."[41] The essence of nature thus remains nameless, without figurative representation. In *The Novices at Saïs*, Novalis also spoke of the ultimate indecipherability of nature, the impossibility of articulating its essence in any other language than nature's own figures:

> Many are the paths that human beings travel. Whoever traces and compares them will see strange figures taking shape; figures that seem to belong to that great cipher script that one sees everywhere on wings and on egg shells, in clouds, snow, crystals and rock formations, . . . on sheets of glass when stroked, in iron filings around a magnet, in oddities of coincidence. One has the presentiment in these figures of the key to this wondrous script, of its very grammar; but the presentiment will not adapt itself to any fixed form, and seems to resist becoming a higher key.[42]

These lines speak to how the language of nature, its figures, defies any simple reading. One is left with *Schein*, appearances in which nature in its essence appears to shine through, but which remain mere appearances rather than nature in its essence. The language of nature resists understanding because that understanding can be expressed only in another language; one cannot get beyond language to the thing itself.[43] One remains caught in the gesture of unveiling.

Humboldt regarded the value of his geography of plants as lying in its combination of instrumental and aesthetic judgments of nature, as figured by Apollo. His maps and graphs were an attempt to develop a figurative language that could assist in both displaying and figuring out nature's laws. But the script of nature thus articulated, if representing nature's empirical laws, did not claim to unveil the naked truth of the goddess of nature. The significance of Humboldt's frontispiece lies in its expression of the figurative form that knowledge of nature apparently necessarily takes.

Figuring the (Fe)male

Humboldt's frontispiece appears to give the male figure, the god Apollo, the active role as unveiler of nature. The goddess of nature appears to be depicted in a familiar form—wild, fecund, mysterious, to be penetrated by the higher light of male reason and art—

her passivity only accentuated by being figured as a statue. Such a reading of the frontispiece conforms to then-dominant conceptions of the roles that males and females should play in society, and necessarily play in biological reproduction. But in light of Humboldt's own ambiguous sexuality—his close friendships with men, his purported homosexuality, always veiled—how did he understand the representation of the god and goddess in his frontispiece? What alternative forms of self-figuring were being explored at the turn of the nineteenth century with regard to gender and sexual identity? As studies of nature questioned whether nature could be unveiled in its innermost essence, so the disclosure of an essential male or female nature was questioned in German aesthetic theory. As Humboldt's geography of plants offered a reading of nature's script based on a wedding of instrumental to aesthetic judgment, and an articulation of that reading in an explicitly figurative form, so representations of males and females in Romantic literature dressed their nature in a performative play with different figurative forms, both veiling and unveiling identity. Aesthetics and literature offered spaces for exploring different gender and sexual roles, and the possibility of confounding the binary opposition of male and female nature.

Historians writing about gender and sexuality at the turn of the nineteenth century predominantly have described a growing entrenchment of differences between males and females. Thomas Laqueur, for example, claims that the shift to a two-sexed model of reproduction established the female reproductive sexuality as different from the male, and gave it a more passive and vegetative role. Londa Schiebinger contends that Linnaeus reified the differences between males and females by reading the laws of nature through the lens of the sexual hierarchies, implicitly by using gender to structure botanical taxonomy and explicitly by using human sexual metaphors to depict plant reproduction.[44] Lisbet Koerner argues that Goethe "postulated as natural fact" the association between women and nature and raised to a founding axiom "the essentialist theory of gender complementarity that gathered force in the Romantic era."[45] Wilhelm von Humboldt also grounded sexual difference in biological necessity—casting the masculine as the active and independent and the female as the receptive and dependent—and made this difference the foundation of natural and social order. Both he and Schiller utilized sexual metaphors for figuring aesthetic theory as the union of form and matter, freedom and necessity, male and female characteristics.[46] New social functions of the marriage vow also reconfigured relationships between males and females; making marriage a choice made in the name of love, it also led to an expectation to realize oneself through one's lover and spouse, and in the process censored alternative sexual or gender relationships.[47]

But new scholarship attending to aesthetic theory and its expressions in literary forms suggests a more complex understanding of male and female at the time. As Catriona MacLeod has argued persuasively, just at the point when sexual difference appeared to be inscribed as a scientific fact and social concern, the androgyne became an important figure in German aesthetic theory. Winckelmann's influential figuring of Apollo articulated an androgynous ideal of beauty. Although lying outside nature as a purely aesthetic construct, Winckelmann argued that the Apollo Belvedere approaches this ideal through the statue's duplicitous character—its rigidity and fluidity, hardness and softness, petrification and animation—and through its representation of adolescent sexual liminality. His descriptions of the statue of Apollo are highly erotic and emotional, reflecting his own well-known proclivity for beautiful boys. In classical myths, Apollo also was known for his boy lovers. Winckelmann's aesthetic androgyny at first suggests all possibilities of development and self-figuration; his beautiful boys, however, are fit into a hierarchy of life stages conceived wholly from a male developmental perspective. Nevertheless, Winckelmann established the mystique of androgyny, with its aesthetic and erotic indeterminacy, as an important figure in German aesthetics and literature.[48]

Goethe's attitudes toward gender and sexuality are also more complex than Koerner claims. Indeed, his literary works offer interesting arrays of female characters, such as those found in *Wilhelm Meister's Apprenticeship,* his seminal *Bildungsroman* published in 1795. The novel is set in the context of a theatrical troupe, a group of actors presenting works of art in human form at the same time as they play with the nature of human identity. Living at the margins of social respectability in the eighteenth century, actors were able to transgress entrenched social boundaries and norms. MacLeod draws attention to the particularly provocative role that Goethe gave to the costumes that the female characters in the troupe adorn as a veil, allowing them to disguise their sex and to adopt different gender roles. Transvestism, as Judith Butler has noted, reveals the performativity of gender and sexuality in the contingent link between the purported original and its imitation. This perpetual displacement allows a fluidity of identities, an openness to resignification and recontextualization, that deprives the dominant culture of its claims to naturalized gender identities. Mignon, the radically androgynous figure in Goethe's text, continually resists dress that would fix her amorphous identity as female and feminine. The fruit of a monstrous, incestuous love, the hideous secret of this unnatural being is veiled throughout the novel.

Wilhelm understandably takes some time to identify her as female and to decide the nature of his relationship to her, and even the narrator of the tale seems perplexed by her disguises, referring to her in both pronominal forms.[49] Like the metamorphosis of plants, Wilhelm develops through a series of transformative relationships to a final sexual pairing with an idealized female, Natalie. This conventional closure seemingly supersedes the play with alternative gender roles that had taken place earlier in the text. Indeed, Mignon dies, suggesting that she, like the garments of her cross-dressing, are false elements in Wilhelm's self-figuring, a process now revealed to be guided by a masonic society to its true fulfillment. Yet Goethe treats the elements of this closure ironically, and Wilhelm and Natalie never consummate their love, leaving the ending ambiguous.[50] In such literary texts, Goethe thus presents a complex figuration of gender and sexuality.

Schlegel's 1799 novel of sexual self-figuring, *Lucinde,* offers the most scandalous contemporary exploration of male and female figures. During the course of the novel, the main character, Julius, engages in highly polymorphous sexual explorations. He develops relationships with all manner of women—from a mother to a pubescent girl, from a prostitute to a reserved woman—like Goethe's Wilhelm Meister, all as an apprenticeship for manhood. But Julius also develops passionate friendships with men that are tainted with homoeroticism. Although his novel unfolds from a male, heterosexual perspective, MacLeod claims that what concerns Schlegel is again the radical aesthetic and sexual possibilities opened up by the figure of the androgyne.[51] *Lucinde* also suggests Butler's performativity of gender and sexuality, but in a far more radical form than Goethe's transvestite females. Perhaps, as Marc Redfield argues, the real scandal of Schlegel's text is its unruliness, its ironic treatment of male and female nature; its obscenity is its absence of form. "The text thematizes a sexual, aesthetic, and hermeneutic 'obscenity' that . . . it also performs."[52] In "A Reflection," near the end of *Lucinde,* Schlegel gave a cosmic dimension to the problem of figuring of the (fe)male:

> The life of cultivated and meditative [human beings] is a continual cultivation and meditation on the lovely riddle of [their] destiny. [They are] continually defining it anew for [themselves], for that is precisely [their] whole destiny, to define and be defined. . . . But what, then, is the definer or the defined itself? For the man it is the [nameless]. And what is the [nameless] for the woman? The indefinite. . . . Who can measure and who can compare two things that are infinitely valuable, when both are joined by the real definition that is destined to fill all lacunae and be the mediator between the individual man and woman and eternal [humankind]? . . . The universe is only a plaything of the definite and the

indefinite; the real definition of the definable is an allegorical miniature of the warp and woof of ever-flowing creation.

The passage parodies the excesses of German idealism and suggests an affirmation of pantheism: "the omnipresence of the [nameless] unknown Godhead."[53] But through the question of gender, Schlegel highlighted the performative character of the transformation of the indefinite into the definite. Man and woman are opposites capable of creating a universe. But as Redfield notes, sex and gender are always figures, manifold and mutable, and since "the inscription of the figure occurs via the uncertainty of the [nameless], [it] names the impossible condition of the production of meaning." Schlegel praised antiquity for finding a good way to name the nameless through the language of myth.[54] He turned to new literary forms and aesthetics for a similar figurative vocabulary.

The nameless in Schlegel's text is sex; same-sex desire in particular remained unnamed at the turn of the nineteenth century. There remains a continued reluctance to name Humboldt's sexual orientation, or to examine its relationship to his work. Eve Sedgwick argues that veiling or unveiling same-sex desire, or inevitably being caught in the gesture of veiling or unveiling with each new encounter, is defining for identity. She also discusses how ignorance, or the posture of ignorance, can be determinative of dynamics of power.[55] For most of the eighteenth century, male sexual relationships had no distinct denomination, but were included with diverse forms of anatomical penetration of women and beasts categorized as sodomy, designating religious blasphemy and a crime punishable by death. At the end of the century, the laws concerning private sexual behavior were liberalized, however, and the category of sodomy began to intersect with concepts of the homoerotic, homosocial, and homoplatonic. Goethe reportedly commented during a discussion on contemporary same-sex relationships that "Greek love" was as old as humanity and thus seems to be at once rooted in nature and against nature.[56] Humboldt kept his sexuality veiled, yet his passionate male friendships were known. His most intense male relationship was with Lieutenant von Haeften, an infantry officer he met in 1794. As Michael Shortland has discussed, the two travelled and lived together, maintaining a close intimacy until Haeften married late in 1795, and even then Humboldt expressed a desire to continue that intimacy in some form.[57] Perhaps it was the nature of those friendships that led Forster to object to the frontispiece for his work on his travels with Humboldt (figure 3.4); produced by his publisher without his consent, it included a vignette of a temple of friendship in the background. Such friendships were an important mode of sexual and self-expression in the eighteenth century, and certainly important in Humboldt's self-figuring.[58] Shortland has suggested that Humboldt also explored his self-figuring through the rigors of travel, which allowed for the expression of both the masculine virtue of heroism and feminine virtues of endurance, perseverance, and resignation, and an aesthetic of negative pleasure.[59] Certainly it was through the aesthetic that different figures of male and female could be expressed as Humboldt undertook a study of nature and his own nature.

What, then, is to be made of Humboldt's vignette for his frontispiece, of Apollo unfrocking Diana? In classical myths, the figure of Apollo is duplicitous—he was Artemis's twin, and he was known for his relationships with young men as well as women and nymphs. Thus Winckelmann's reading of Apollo as a figure for sexual indeterminacy is not simply a product of his own sexual preferences or his response to the Belvedere Apollo. But his emphasis on the androgynous, ambiguous aesthetic of Apollo stimulated various ways of figuring sexuality and gender at the turn of the nineteenth century that challenged dominant normative and naturalized conceptions of the male and female. As attempts were made to define gender and sexual nature, an aesthetic developed that represented their definite forms as but figures of an indefinite essence. Humboldt's own self-figuring could draw upon these alternative articulations.

Humboldt's frontispiece, with the antique image of the god of art and reason unveiling the goddess of nature inscribed with a hieroglyphic script, seems not merely part of a fashion for Egyptian iconography at the turn of the nineteenth century. What lay behind that fashion, and behind Humboldt's frontispiece, was an appreciation of the symbolic significances of that iconography. The fascination with antique cosmotheism was with its figuration of the problem of knowing nature and of finding a language in which that knowledge could be expressed.

Humboldt's figurative languages of nature were both a means of displaying empirical laws formed through mensurative and aesthetic judgments, and a means of figuring out those laws. They were modes of visual thinking that were also modes of instrumental and artistic experimentation in conceptualizing phenomena, and a central part of Humboldt's vision for a unity of "poetry, philosophy and natural knowledge." Aesthetic explorations of different forms of self-figuring offered similar experiments with conceptualization, but in this case of male and female nature. These figures played with the various expressions that gender and sexuality might take, enabling a veiling and unveiling of the self. In both cases, the contrast was drawn between the unknown, unnamed essence of nature and the figurative form of what could be known and named.

1. Letter to Goethe February 6, 1806; reprinted in Ludwig Geiger, ed. *Goethes Briefwechsel mit Wilhelm und Alexander von Humboldt* (Berlin, 1909), 297. The frontispiece is a copperplate engraving by Raphael Urbain Massard after a design by Bertel Thorwaldsen. Humboldt met Thorwaldsen in Rome among the circle of his brother Wilhelm's friends during the summer of 1805. Christa Lichtenstern, *Die Wirkungsgeschichte der Metamorphosenlehre Goethes* (Weinheim: Acta Humaniora, 1990), 28–34.

2. Immanuel Kant, *Critique of Judgment,* trans. Werner S. Pluhar (Indianapolis: Hackett, 1987), 72.

3. Immanuel Kant, *Religion within the Limits of Reason Alone,* trans. Theodore M. Greene and Hoyt H. Hudson (New York: Harper, 1960), 47-48.

4. Jacques Derrida, *Truth in Painting,* trans. Geoff Bennington and Ian McLeod (Chicago: University of Chicago Press, 1987), 56.

5. See Alan Bewell's chapter in this volume, "A Passion that Transforms: Picturing the Early Natural History Collector," 28–53.

6. Jan Assmann, *Moses the Egyptian: The Memory of Egypt in Western Monotheism* (Cambridge, Mass.: Harvard University Press, 1997), 80–90, 96–102; James Steven Curl, *The Egyptian Revival* (London: George Allen & Unwin, 1982), 63–106; Margaret C. Jacobs, *Living the Enlightenment: Freemasonry and Politics in Eighteenth-Century Europe* (Oxford: Oxford University Press, 1991).

7. Assmann, *Moses,* 44–54; R. Gordon, "Syncretism," in *The Oxford Classical Dictionary,* 3rd ed, ed. Simon Hornblower and Anthony Spawforth (Oxford: Oxford University Press, 1996), 122–23.

8. Apuleius, *The Golden Ass,* trans. E. J. Kenney (London: Penguin, 1998); Plutarch, *Isis and Osiris,* in *Moralia V,* trans. Frank Cole Babbitt (Cambridge, Mass.: Harvard University Press, 1984), §§66–67.

9. Karl Leonhard Reinhold, *Die Hebräischen Mysterien oder der älteste religiöse Freymauerey* (Leipzig, 1788); Friedrich Schiller, *Die Sendung Moses,* in *Schillers Werke,* ed. Julius Petersen and Gerehard Fricke (Weimar: Hermann Böhlaus, 1943), 17: 377–97; Frederick C. Beiser, *The Fate of Reason: German Philosophy from Kant to Fichte* (Cambridge, Mass.: Harvard University Press, 1987), 229–32.

10. Walter Burkert, *Greek Religion* (Cambridge, Mass.: Harvard University Press, 1985), 149–52; C. Sourvinou-Inwood, "Artemis"; H. J. Rose and J. Scheid, "Diana"; and R. L. Gordon, "Isis," all in *Classical Dictionary,* 182–84, 463, 768–89; Pierre Grimal, *The Dictionary of Classical Mythology,* trans. A. R. Maxwell-Hyslop (London: Blackwell, 1980), 61–62.

11. Pierre Hadot, *Zur Idee der Naturgeheimnisse. Beim Betrachten des Widmungsblattes in den Humboldtschen "Ideen zu einer Geographie der Pflanzen"* (Wiesbaden: Franz Steiner, 1982), 4–7; Jane Davidson Reid, *The Oxford Guide to Classical Mythology in the Arts, 1300–1990s* (Oxford: Oxford University Press, 1993), 1: 216–34; C. Gasparri, "Die Skulpturen der Sammlung Albani in der Zeit Napoleons und der Restoration," in *Forschungen zur Villa Albani,* ed. H. Beck and P. Bol (Berlin: Gebr. Mann, 1982), 395, fig. 37.

12. Burkhert, *Greek Religion*, 143–49; P. Graf, "Apollo," in *Classical Dictionary*, 122–23; Grimal, *Classical Mythology*, 47–50; Reid, *Oxford Guide to Classical Mythology*, 1:162–69, 216–27.

13. Catriona MacLeod, *Embodying Ambiguity: Androgyny and Aesthetics from Winckelmann to Keller* (Detroit: Wayne State University Press, 1998), 29–37; Alex Potts, *Flesh and the Ideal: Winckelmann and the Origins of Art History* (London: Yale University Press, 1994), 199–231.

14. Plutarch, *Isis and Osiris*, §9; Hadot, *Idee der Naturgeheimnisse*, 7–10.

15. Friedrich Schiller, *Schillers Werke*, 1: 254–56; Friedrich Schlegel, *Philosophical Fragments*, trans. Peter Firchow (Minneapolis: University of Minnesota Press, 1991), 94.

16. Ludmilla Jordanova, *Sexual Visions* (London: Harvester Wheatsheaf, 1989), 87–110.

17. Assmann, *Moses*, 19, 73, 77, 84, 97–99, 114, 117–19, 127–28.

18. William Warburton, *The Divine Legation of Moses Demonstrated* (London: Garland, 1978), 3: 121–69.

19. Warburton, *Divine Legation*, 3: 69–89, 90–93, 142–43; Assmann, *Moses*, 104–108.

20. Wilhelm von Humboldt, "Denken und Sprechen," in *Wilhelm von Humboldts Werke*, ed. Albrecht Leitzmann (Berlin: Behr, 1903); Kurt Müller-Vollmer, "From Sign to Signification: The Herder-Humboldt Controversy," in *Johann Gottfried Herder: Language, History, and the Enlightenment*, ed. Wulf Koepke (Columbia: Camden House, 1990), 9–24.

21. Alexander von Humboldt and Aimé Bonpland, *Researches Concerning the Institutions and Monuments of the Ancient Inhabitants of America*, trans. H. M. Williams (New York: Da Capo Press, 1972), 1: 145–69; Renate Löscher, "Alexander von Humboldts Bedeutung für die Altamerikanistik" and "Alexander von Humboldt und die mexikanischen Bilderschrift," in Wolfgang-Hagen Hein, *Alexander von Humboldt: Leben und Werk* (Frankfurt: Weisbecker), 249–62, 263–72; Mary Louise Pratt, *Imperial Eyes: Travel Writing and Transculturation* (New York: Routledge, 1992), 111–43.

22. Letter from Bertel Thorwaldsen to Goethe, February 6, 1806: Geiger, *Goethes Briefwechsel*, 297.

23. Johann Wolfgang von Goethe, *Scientific Studies*, ed. and trans. Douglas Miller, in *Goethe: The Collected Works* (Princeton: Princeton University Press, 1995), 12: 76, 90.

24. Goethe, *Gedankausgabe der Werke, Briefe und Gespräche*, ed. Ernst Beutler (Zürich: Artemis, 1948–1963), 16: 867; *Goethes Werke* (Hamburg: Christian Wegner, 1948–1960), 12: 470–71, 13: 23–25.

25. Alexander von Humboldt, *Ideen zu einer Geographie der Pflanzen, nebst einem Naturgemälde der Tropenländer*, in *Schriften zur Geographie der Pflanzen*, ed. Hanno Beck (Darmstadt: Wissenschaftliche Buchgesellschaft, 1989), 64.

26. Malcolm Nicolson, "Alexander von Humboldt, Humboldtian Science and the Origins of the Study of Vegetation," *History of Science* 25 (1987): 172–74; Michael Hagner, "Zur Physiognomik bei Alexander von Humboldt," in *Geschichten der Physiognomik*, ed. M. Schneider and R. Campe (Freiburg: Rombach, 1996), 431–52.

27. Michael Dettelbach, "Introduction," in Alexander von Humboldt, *Cosmos: A Sketch of a Physical Description of the Universe* (Baltimore: Johns Hopkins University Press, 1997), 2: xx.

28. Alexander von Humboldt, *Views of Nature, or Contemplation on the Sublime Phenomena of Creation with Scientific Illustrations,* trans. E. C. Otté and H. G. Bohn (London: George Bell, 1902), 346–47, 221, 59–62.

29. Timothy F. Mitchell, *Art and Science in German Landscape Painting, 1770–1840* (Oxford: Clarendon, 1993), 127–43.

30. Humboldt, *Views,* 59–62.

31. Hadot, *Idee,* 9–10.

32. Michael Dettelbach, "The Face of Nature: Precise Measurement, Mapping, and Sensibility in the Work of Alexander von Humboldt," *Studies in History and Philosophy of Biological and Biomedical Sciences* 30, no. 4 (1999): 475–81; "Global Physics and Aesthetic Empire: Humboldt's Physical Portrait of the Tropics," in *Visions of Empire: Voyages, Botany, and Representations of Nature,* ed. David Philip Miller and Peter Hans Reill (Cambridge: Cambridge University Press, 1996), 261–72.

33. Jane Camerini, "The Physical Atlas of Heinrich Berghaus: Distribution Maps as Scientific Knowledge," in *Non-Verbal Communication in Science Prior to 1900,* ed. R. G. Mazzolini (Florence: Olschki, 1993), 479–89.

34. Novalis, *Schriften,* 3: 91, 435.

35. A. H. Robinson and H. Wallis, "Humboldt's Map of Isothermal Lines: A Milestone in Thematic Cartography," *Cartographic Journal* (1967): 119–23; Patricia Fara, *Sympathetic Attractions: Magnetic Practices, Beliefs, and Symbolism in Eighteenth-Century England* (Princeton: Princeton University Press, 1996), 105–17.

36. Anne M. C. Godlewska, *Geography Unbound: French Geographic Science from Cassini to Humboldt* (Chicago: University of Chicago Press, 1999), 254.

37. Alexander von Humboldt, "Von den isothermen Linien und der Verteilung der Wärme auf dem Erdkorper," in *Schriften zur Physikalischen Geographie,* ed. Hanno Beck (Darmstadt: Wissenschaftliche Buchgesellschaft, 1989), 26–30.

38. Thomas L. Hankins and Robert J. Silverman, *Instruments and the Imagination* (Princeton: Princeton University Press, 1995), 118–25; Laura Tilling, "Early Experimental Graphs," *The British Journal for the History of Science* 8, no. 30 (1975): 200–207.

39. Tilling, "Early Experimental Graphs," 155–57; Hankins and Silverman, *Instruments,* 125–27; Sybilla Nikilow, "'Die Versinnlichung von Staatskräften': Statistische Karten um 1800," *Zeitschrift für Geschichte/Revue d'histoire* 3 (1999): 63–82.

40. Humboldt, *Ideen,* 43–45.

41. Kant, *Critique of Judgment,* 185; Assmann, *Moses,* 134–36.

42. Novalis, *Schriften,* 1: 79.

43. William Arctander O'Brien, *Novalis: Signs of Revolution* (Durham: Duke University Press, 1995), 198–213.

44. Thomas Laqueur, *Making Sex: Body and Gender from the Greeks to Freud* (Cambridge, Mass.: Harvard University Press, 1990), ch. 5; Londa

Schiebinger, "Why Mammals Are Called Mammals," in *Feminism and Science,* ed. Evelyn Fox Keller and Helen E. Longino (Oxford: Oxford University Press, 1996), 137–53.

45. Lisbet Koerner, "Goethe's Botany: Lessons of a Feminine Science," *Isis* 84 (1984): 473–74.

46. Wilhelm von Humboldt, "Ueber den Geschlectsunterschied und dessen Einfluss auf die organische Natur" and "Ueber die männliche und wiebliche Form," in *Wilhelm von Humboldts Gesammelte Schriften,* ed. Königlich Preussischen Akademie der Wissenschaften (Berlin: Behr, 1903), 1: 311–34, 335–69; Friedrich Schiller, *On the Aesthetic Education of Man,* trans. Elizabeth M. Wilkinson and L. A. Willoughby (Oxford: Oxford University Press, 1967).

47. Alice A. Kuzniar, "Introduction," in *Outing Goethe and His Age* (Stanford: Stanford University Press, 1996), 17–19; Warren Johansson Jones, "Friendship, Male," in *Encyclopedia of Homosexuality,* ed. Wayne R. Dynes (New York: Garland, 1990), 445–46.

48. MacLeod, *Embodying Ambiguity,* 25–66.

49. Judith Butler, *Gender Trouble: Feminism and the Subversion of Identity* (New York: Routledge, 1990), 137–38; MacLeod, *Embodying Ambiguity,* pp. 97–109.

50. Nicholas Boyle, *Goethe: The Poet and the Age* (Oxford: Clarendon, 2000), 367–425.

51. MacLeod, "The 'Third Sex' in an Age of Difference: Androgyny and Homosexuality in Winckelmann, Friedrich Schlegel, and Kleist," in *Outing Goethe,* 203–206.

52. Marc Redfield, "*Lucinde*'s Obscenity," in *Rereading Romanticism,* ed. Martha B. Helfer (Amsterdam: Rodopi, 2000), 110–16, 121.

53. Friedrich Schlegel, *Lucinde: A Fragment,* trans. Peter Firchow (Minneapolis: University of Minnesota Press, [1799] 1971), 119–20, 118.

54. Redfield, "*Lucinde*'s Obscenity," 129–30; Schlegel, *Lucinde,* 119.

55. Eve K. Sedgwick, *Epistemology of the Closet* (Berkeley: University of California Press, 1990), 1–90.

56. Kuzniar, "Introduction," 4–8; Robert D. Tobin, "In and Against Nature: Goethe on Homosexuality and Heterosexuality," in *Outing Goethe,* 95.

57. Michael Shortland, "'Was He or Wasn't He?' Eros and Kosmos in the World of Alexander von Humboldt," Lecture at York University, October 7, 1997.

58. Wolfgang-Hagen Hein, "Growing to Maturity," in *Humboldt,* 25; Kuzniar, "Introduction," 14–16; Johansson, "Friendship, Male," 45–46.

59. Shortland, "'Was He?'"

Part Two

THE NINETEENTH CENTURY

Technologies and Gender Politics

PICTURING SEXUAL SELECTION

Gender and the Evolution of Ornithological Illustration in Charles Darwin's *Descent of Man*

Jonathan Smith

Charles Darwin's *Descent of Man* (1871) is one of the nineteenth century's most important scientific texts for the representation of gender and sexuality. The bulk of Darwin's book is devoted to his theory of sexual selection, an account of the origin of the differences in secondary sexual characteristics between males and females that are so common throughout the animal kingdom. According to Darwin, the larger pincers of the male lobster, the horns of the stag, the tail of the peacock, and the facial hair of male monkeys are all the products of mate selection. In most cases, the "law of battle" prevails: Males compete violently for the right to mate with the female of their choice, sometimes against the female's will. In other cases, and especially among birds, male competition takes other, non-violent forms—display, "antics," and song—and the female is the selector. So important are birds to Darwin's discussion of sexual selection that he devotes twice as many chapters to them as he does to either mammals or humans, and one-third more pages to them than to mammals and humans combined. Darwin justifies this attention on the grounds that secondary sexual characteristics in birds are more various and conspicuous, but he also notes that birds are ideal for considering the source, development, and character of the human aesthetic sense. "On the whole, birds appear to be the most aesthetic of all animals, excepting of course man," Darwin writes in the opening of the first bird chapter, "and they have nearly the same taste for the beautiful as we have."[1] Not surprisingly, Darwin's exposition of sexual selection was thus insistently visual. While the *Origin* contained just a single illustration, and the section of the *Descent* devoted to human evolution only two, the first edition of the *Descent* was illustrated by

4.1 "Bower-bird, *Chlamydera maculata,* with bower (from Brehm)." Figure 46 in Charles Darwin, *The Descent of Man, and Selection in Relation to Sex,* vol. 2 (London: Murray, 1871), 70. Darwin had this illustration copied from A. E. Brehm's *Illustrirtes Thierleben* (1864–1869), but Brehm had copied it from John Gould's *Birds of Australia* (1840–1848). *Special Collections Library, University of Michigan.*

seventy-four wood engravings. Of these, bird illustrations were by far the most numerous, comprising almost one-third of the total.

Two of these bird illustrations were of the spotted bower bird (figure 4.1) and the Assam peacock pheasant (figure 4.2), the former providing the "best evidence . . . of a taste for the beautiful" in birds and the latter constituting one of the most important examples of male display in courtship.[2] Darwin borrowed both of these illustrations from German naturalist A. E. Brehm's popular *Illustrirtes Thierleben* (1864–1869), although the bower bird had itself been copied from John Gould's *The Birds of Australia* (1840–1848). Gould, commissioned by Darwin a generation earlier to classify and illustrate the bird specimens from the *Beagle* voyage, had been Britain's leading ornithologist-illustrator since the 1830s, and Darwin relied heavily on his publications and his advice for the bird chapters of the *Descent*. Why, then, did Darwin not make direct use of Gould's bird illustrations for the *Descent*? And why did Darwin retain the bower bird illustration in the second edition of the *Descent* in 1874 while replacing that of the peacock pheasant with a completely new rendering (figure 4.3)? To answer these questions is to engage in an analysis simultaneously intervisual and intertextual, one concerned not merely with the rhetorical function of illustrations but with the difficulty of controlling their meanings. The scientist who offers a new theory, as Darwin was, can destabilize existing illustrations by appropriating and reinterpreting them, but if he chooses to illustrate his own theory, as Darwin did, he must either work within prevailing visual traditions or create new ones. In either case, the interplay between text and image is crucial, but the words that are needed to shape the response of the reader/viewer to an illustrated text are themselves subject to challenge, destabilization, and counter-appropriation. When a new theory is scientifically controversial and culturally unsettling, as sexual selection was, that instability is especially evident.[3]

The conventions of ornithological illustration, especially as developed by Gould from the 1830s to the 1860s, were not well-suited for depicting sexual selection: delineations of birds were generally taken from stuffed specimens and focused on plumage and structure, not mate choice. However, since Darwin was interested in how mate choice had brought about differences in plumage and structure, as well as the behavior for displaying them, he initially attempted to use traditional illustrations that depicted these differences, relying on his textual language to enable readers to "see" how sexual selection had produced them. Apparently dissatisfied by the limitations of this strategy, Darwin obtained several new illustrations for the second edition of the *Descent* that *did* depict sexual selection directly, as in

Fig. 51.   Polyplectron chinquis, male (from Brehm)

4.2 "*Polyplectron chinquis*, male (from Brehm)." Figure 51 in Charles Darwin, *The Descent of Man, and Selection in Relation to Sex*, vol. 2 (London: Murray, 1871), 90. Darwin had this illustration of the Assam peacock pheasant copied from A. E. Brehm's *Illustrirtes Thierleben* (1864–1869), but he replaced it in the second edition of *The Descent*. *Special Collections Library, University of Michigan.*

Fig. 51. Polyplectron chinquis, male (T. W. Wood).

the peacock pheasant engraving, with the male displaying before the
female. While Darwin had many reasons not to go to Gould for illustrations, one of the strongest, I will argue, is that Gould's illustrations
were dominated by motifs of monogamous domesticity and familial
harmony rather than the male-male competition, frenzied male sexual display, and female choice that Darwin emphasized. Although
Darwin's discussion of sexual selection in birds is sometimes read as

inscribing Victorian patriarchal notions about the sexes onto nature, it is Gould's vision of the avian world that accords more closely with prevailing cultural notions about gender roles, and Darwin's accounts and illustrations were directed heavily against this vision. While Gould's own contradictions and concessions about the bower's role in courtship enabled Darwin to appropriate Gould's words and deploy them against Gould's illustration, for the second edition Darwin commissioned several new illustrations that depicted sexual selection more directly. Yet even these illustrations did not free Darwin from professional and popular resistance to the notion that female choice could drive evolutionary change.

Sexual Selection in Birds

Darwin's treatment of sexual selection in birds is saturated with culturally bound notions about gender and sexuality. Indeed, for Darwin, the strong element of female choice among birds brings their mating habits into closer accord with those of "civilized" humans than does the courtship behavior of most mammals. As feminist critics have pointed out, Darwin's comments about women and about sexual selection in humans are to a considerable extent the result of first applying Victorian bourgeois values to birds. The interest of female birds in bright colors and exotic ornamentation, these critics argue, becomes a sign of vanity, superficiality, and irrationality. Elaborate male display is a function of the female's muted sexuality, which needs to be aroused by the more ardent male. The female's selective role is comparatively constrained—she waits passively for the male to approach her, and the mating process results in her entry into her ordained domestic sphere. When Darwin turns to humans, these values are re-discovered and re-confirmed, but as facts of nature rather than constructions of culture.[4]

While Darwin's depiction of courtship among birds frequently reflects such patriarchal notions, his spectacular lack of success in convincing his contemporaries—including fellow evolutionists—about the truth of sexual selection suggests that the gender plots of the *Descent* were multiple and frequently disruptive of bourgeois notions of gender roles.[5] In many species, Darwin notes, female birds choose the exotic, posturing, self-absorbed dandy rather than the sober, industrious provider. The need to satisfy female preferences also can lead males into absurd behavior. Sometimes this absurdity takes on a more sinister cast, with the male's courtship shown to be a cocktail of violence and sexual passion. In extreme cases like the peacock's, sexual selection can shackle the male with unwieldy physical attributes. Crucially, Darwin's ascription of considerable choice and an aesthetic sensibility to females was resisted strenuously. Alfred Russel Wallace's view that the male's color and ornament were the norm, with the female's drabness conferred by natural selection for protection during incubation, was accepted much more widely. The female response to male ornament, finery, and beauty, for Wallace and others, was passive and programmed, physiological rather than active and rational. They argued that female birds simply do not have an aesthetic sense, and even if they did, it would not be sufficiently precise to discriminate subtle differences in color and shading. Male coloration and "antics," moreover, were merely the result of what Wallace called "the superior energy and vitality in the male."[6]

Darwin was certainly no John Stuart Mill when it came to advocacy for women's political and economic rights—and in the *Descent* he criticized Mill's argument in the recently published *Subjection of Women* (1869) that the supposed intellectual superiority of males was the result of education and social norms rather than any inherent difference in the sexes' respective mental capacities.[7] Appearing at a time of ongoing agitation for women's suffrage, and in the immediate aftermath of the founding of Girton College, Cambridge, and the passage of the first Married Women's Property Act, the *Descent* was not mistaken by contemporaries as a feminist treatise. Yet by drawing attention to mate selection, and by giving females such prominent roles in it, Darwin troubled gender waters as much as he calmed them. And it was John Gould's illustrations of the avian world against which he was working, to a considerable degree.

John Gould and Ornithological Illustration

Gould and Darwin had known each other for years. Gould and his wife Elizabeth had described and drawn the bird specimens, including those from the Galapagos, for the third part of Darwin's *Zoology of the Voyage of the H.M.S. Beagle* (1838–1841). While preparing the *Descent*, Darwin sought Gould's assistance on a number of ornithological questions and relied on Gould's *Handbook of the Birds of Australia* (1865) for information on Australian species. Gould, however, was no supporter of Darwin's theories. The 1861 *Introduction* to his stunningly illustrated monograph on *Humming-birds* (1849–1861) quietly reasserted the fixity of species, while his magisterial *Birds of Great Britain* (1862–1873) provided clear if unpolemical images of an avian world in which neither natural nor sexual selection operated.[8] Gould's visual style had itself evolved, from static, background-free bird-on-a-branch figures in his early illustrated works to the elaborate scenes of peaceful avian nuclear families in *The Birds of Great Britain*. In these domestic family portraits, competition, courtship, and sexuality were avoided in favor of

4.4 "*Erythacus rubecula*" (European Robin). Hand-colored lithograph by John Gould and H. C. Richter from John Gould, *The Birds of Great Britain,* vol. 2 (London, 1862–1873), plate 48. Gould's plates from *The Birds of Great Britain* focused on domestic scenes like this, with parent birds feeding and protecting their nestlings.
Special Collections Library, University of Michigan.

ERYTHACUS RUBECULA.

depictions of the ornithological equivalent of the separate spheres. Females frequently were pictured on or near their nests, incubating, protecting, feeding, or simply hovering over their offspring (figure 4.4). Males often stood or perched to the side after having brought food. Whereas Gould's American contemporary, John James Audubon, frequently had represented violent intra- and interspecies competition and the capture of prey in his influential *Birds of America* (1827–1838), Gould limited and domesticated violence, mostly restricting it to the feeding of prey to young birds.

By the time Darwin published the *Descent,* illustrated bird books, from sumptuous folios with colored plates to moderately priced volumes full of wood engravings for popular audiences, had been appearing in droves for forty years, with Britain by far the leading producer.[9] Writing from London in 1835, Audubon complained that "Here there are at present three Works publishing on the Birds of Europe—one by Mr. Gould and the others by No one Knows who—at least I do not Know—Works on the Birds of *all the World* are innumerable—Cheap as dirt and more dirty than dirt."[10] Whatever the merits of the notoriously critical Audubon's assessment of the quality of these books, his comment on their quantity was exaggerated only slightly.

At the time of Audubon's remark, Gould was in the midst of both his *Birds of Europe* (1832–1837) and an illustrated monograph on toucans. Edward Lear, whose volume on parrots a few years earlier had received lavish praise, assisted with the drawings and taught lithography to Elizabeth. Gould had begun *The Birds of Europe* shortly before the completion of Prideaux John Selby's *Illustrations of British Ornithology* (1821–1834), with its splendid metal-plate etchings, and he was more than halfway through it when Henry Leonard Meyer's four-volume *Illustrations of British Birds* (1835–1841) and Thomas Campbell Eyton's *Rarer British Birds* (1836) appeared, the latter designed as a supplement to the much-loved *History of British Birds* (1797, 1804) of Thomas Bewick, whose accurate, lively wood engravings influenced bird illustrators throughout the nineteenth century. In 1837, the ornithologists William Yarrell and William Macgillivray each commenced a multi-volume *History of British Birds,* Yarrell's completed in 1843, Macgillivray's in 1852. Although the ornithological content of Macgillivray's book was regarded as superior (Darwin used it in the *Descent* as his primary source on British species), its poor illustrations hindered sales, and Yarrell's work quickly became the standard illustrated textbook. Selby was also in the midst of his collaborations with William Jardine on *Illustrations of Ornithology* (1825–43) and with Jardine and William Swainson on the fourteen volumes of birds for *The Naturalist's Library* (1833–43), the first inexpensive illustrated volumes of ornithology for middle-class readers. Widely read scientific popularizers such as Jane Loudon (1807–1858) and the Reverends F. O. Morris (1810–1893), C. A. Johns (1811–1874), and J. G. Wood (1827–1889) increasingly placed figures of birds before children and readers seeking more informal introductions to ornithology in both illustrated bird books and illustrated natural histories.[11]

As Ann Shelby Blum has demonstrated, by 1800 most popular natural history illustrations in Europe and America, and especially those of birds, combined the depiction of the animal in profile in the foreground with some gesture toward landscape in the background. This primary emphasis on the bird's external appearance, its structure and plumage, reflected the concerns of Linnaean taxonomy, while the inclusion of landscape in preference to the bird-on-a-branch reflected the insistence of the French naturalist Buffon on the classificatory importance of an animal's surroundings.[12] As a general rule, both sexes were depicted only when their plumage or ornamentation differed, and even in such cases it was often only the male who was delineated. The visual point was the male's appearance, not the interaction of male and female, for behavior played a comparatively small role in classification, and mating behavior almost none. Gould quickly adopted these conventions for *The Birds of Europe,* but with his next major undertaking, *The Birds of Australia* (1840–1848), he began to elaborate them in his distinctive ways.

Endowed with Europe's best collection of Australian species by virtue of the collecting efforts of his brothers-in-law, who had emigrated to Australia in 1827 and 1834, Gould decided in 1837 to visit the Australian colonies himself. He and Elizabeth set sail in the spring of 1838 and ultimately spent twenty months there. The first installment of *The Birds of Australia* appeared shortly after their return to England in 1840. While the book was one of Gould's least successful undertakings from a financial standpoint, it significantly enhanced his reputation as an ornithologist and illustrator, for it introduced many new species to Europe, a number of them exotic in behavior or appearance. Two visual aspects of *The Birds of Australia* attracted special attention: the accurate, detailed rendering of appropriate flora, and the lavish double-plate scenes of bower birds, a species unique to Australia and a source of fascination for their elaborately constructed and decorated bowers. These bower bird plates set the pattern for the domestic, familial motifs that increasingly would become the hallmarks of Gould's bird illustrations.

At the time of Gould's trip to Australia, little was known in Europe about these birds or the purpose of the bowers, for bower birds were extremely shy and inhabited thick brush. Since both sexes were known to congregate at the bowers in the spring, it was thought that the bowers were used in courtship, as the term "bower" implies. Yet it was unclear if this was in fact the case, and the possibility that the bowers were actually nests, or also served as nests, was a strong one. While in Australia, Gould was able to collect a number of bowers and observe the behavior of two species in particular, the spotted and satin bower bird. He quickly recognized the value of these bowers and of his accounts of

4.5 "Spotted Bower-Bird (*Chlamydera maculata*)." Hand-colored lithograph by John and Elizabeth Gould from *The Birds of Australia,* vol. 4 (London, 1840–1848), plate 8. This illustration, which originally appeared in Part 4 (September 1, 1841), was one of two spectacular double-plates of bower birds in *The Birds of Australia.* Darwin reproduced a wood-engraved copy of it, taken from A. E. Brehm's *Illustrirtes Thierleben* (1864–1869), for *The Descent of Man.* The plate is ambiguous as to whether the bower is a nest or a courtship spot. *Department of Special Collections, Spencer Research Library, University of Kansas Libraries.*

the birds' strange behavior for publicizing *The Birds of Australia.* Just one week after his return to England, Gould delivered a paper to the Zoological Society on the bowers, and he presented one of them to the British Museum. The extraordinary plates of these two species appeared in the fourth part of *The Birds of Australia* in September 1841 (figures 4.5 and 4.6). These double plates of birds in fully elaborated natural scenes, unprecedented in Gould's work, could not help but capture the attention of ornithologists and the general public. Hugh Strickland told Gould they were "truly pictorial and *Audubonic,*" a comment echoed in the *Annals of Natural History.*[13] Gould apparently also had oil paintings of these plates to display at the 1841 British Association meeting in Plymouth.[14] When, in 1849, the Zoological Society's pair of satin birds constructed a bower, visitors flocked to the Society's gardens, launching a new round of fascination with bower birds.[15] Gould's illustrations and accounts of the bower birds also circulated widely in the works of prolific scientific popularizers such as Loudon and Wood.[16] Publishing an illustration of a new species of bower bird in one of the supplemental installments to the work, Gould made clear how closely he was associated with these birds: "if any one circumstance . . . would tend to hand down the name of the author of the 'Birds of Australia' to posterity, it would be the discovery and the publication of the singular habits of the Bower-birds."[17]

Gould's treatment of the bower birds and their bowers reveals the extent to which he wished to present these birds as domestic,

blurring or erasing almost any suggestion of sexuality and courtship. In his initial presentation to the Zoological Society, Gould
stated unequivocally that the bowers "are used by the birds as a
playing-house, or 'run,' . . . and are used by the males to attract the
females."[18] Yet he was considerably less assertive, and even contradictory, about the bowers' role in courtship in the descriptions accompanying the plates in *The Birds of Australia* itself. "For what
purpose these curious bowers are made," he wrote, "is not yet, perhaps, fully understood." They are clearly not nests, he insisted, but
it is "highly probable" that the birds use them "at the period of incubation." It is similarly likely that they serve as gathering places "at
the pairing time," although Gould uses the terms "playing-
grounds" and "halls of assembly" to describe the way "many individuals of both sexes . . . run through and around the bower in a
sportive and playful manner."[19]

4.6 "Satin Bower-Bird (*Ptilonorhynchus holosericeus*)." Hand-colored lithograph by
John and Elizabeth Gould from *The Birds of Australia*, vol. 4 (London, 1840–1848),
plate 10. This plate, which also originally appeared in Part 4 (September 1, 1841), was
the other of Gould's spectacular double-plates of bower birds in *The Birds of Australia*. It presents the bower unambiguously as a nest in a domestic scene.
Department of Special Collections, Spencer Research Library, University of Kansas Libraries.

The plates reinforce the association of the bowers with nests and downplay their use in mating ritual, offering highly domestic scenes in which courtship and sexuality are largely erased in favor of husband/wife or family portraits. In his discussion of the spotted bower bird, Gould stresses that in his experience a bower "formed the rendez-vous of many individuals" and that he observed only males racing through the avenue-like run; the plate, however, depicts a single pair, with what is apparently the female inside the bower. While the plate certainly can be read as the male courting the female, the female's positioning within the bower invokes the iconography of nests, with the solicitous male attending to his mate's needs. The plate of the satin bower bird is even more domestic. At the center is a female seated in the bower, its sides encircling her. The larger, darker male perches just outside the bower. On the ground nearby are two juvenile males. The one in the right foreground is younger, for its plumage closely resembles the female's, while the one to the left is in the process of acquiring the black feathers of the adult. This scene's visual logic works at many levels. The female is enshrined in a position suggestive of incubation in what is made to look unquestionably like a nest rather than a "playing-ground" or "hall of assembly." The male stands placidly to the side rather than running frenetically about, and his size and position cast him as the female's protector. We see not many birds but a single family, with not one but two offspring, and of different ages.

In the years that followed, as evidence of the role of the bower in mating increased, Gould simultaneously acknowledged this evidence and sought to mute it. Both his *Introduction* (1848) and *Handbook* to *The Birds of Australia* included an account of the satin bower bird by a Sydney man who stated that the bowers are "built for the express purpose of courting the female in" and who emphasized the male's extraordinary sexual energy: "the male will chase the female all over, then go to the bower, pick up a gay feather or a large leaf, utter a curious kind of note, set all his feathers erect, run round the bower and become so excited that his eyes appear ready to start from his head." The male's behavior is neither innocently flirtatious nor vaguely civilized, but simultaneously ridiculous and menacing. Yet against this Gould sets his own circuitous, euphemistic, and vaguely chivalric language, affirming in the *Handbook* that the bowers "are places of resort for both sexes of these birds at that season of the year when nature prompts them to reproduce their kind. Here the males meet and contend with each other for the favours of the females, and here also the latter assemble and coquet with the males." The bowers are "merely sporting-places," says Gould, the "merely" curiously reducing them, against the grain of his own text, to insignificance. The

Handbook's account of the spotted bower-bird makes no reference to mating at all.[20]

Gould's emphasis on domestic, familial motifs in his plates of the bower birds, as well as his subsequent reluctance to endorse fully the increasing evidence of the bower's role in courtship and mating, suggest the extent of his commitment to a vision of the avian world in which gender roles were structured along lines remarkably similar to those prevailing among the Victorian middle classes. The influence of this vision was at or near its height when Darwin began work on the *Descent*, for Gould had been driving it home in his plates for *The Birds of Great Britain*, his most popular work, for the better part of a decade. Ornithological illustration, especially as developed by Gould, was thus not very congenial for the purposes to which Darwin needed to put it in the *Descent*. Nonetheless, Darwin initially was content to work within existing visual conventions, and he was able to exploit one of Gould's bower bird plates for his own purposes. But for the second edition of the *Descent*, Darwin sought bird images that would better illustrate his own theories and highlight his rather different conceptions of gender and gender relations.

Picturing Sexual Selection

Half of the bird illustrations in the first edition of the *Descent* depict a single bird or a pair against a landscape background, while the other half consist of individual feathers. With one exception, Darwin's birds were engraved in fairly detailed static profile, with foreground foliage and/or background landscape represented in a much sketchier fashion, thus following the conventions of popular ornithological illustration as epitomized in England by Bewick and Gould. That Darwin chose to illustrate birds with such static figures, however, seems rather surprising. If natural selection was by its very nature impossible to capture directly, the static bird in profile, even in a highly detailed and appropriate landscape, hardly did justice to Darwinism's emphasis on the dynamic relationships among individuals, species, and the natural surroundings. By the time of the *Descent*, moreover, Darwin was familiar with examples of bird illustration that depicted action, violence, and competition, particularly in the work of Joseph Wolf. An accomplished animal artist whose specialty was birds, Wolf drew for the Zoological Society and was commissioned by numerous ornithologists, including Gould, for whom he drew many of the birds of prey in *The Birds of Great Britain*. His *Zoological Sketches* appeared between 1861 and 1867, and Darwin engaged him in 1871 to draw the Niger ape for *The Expression of the Emotions in Man and Animals*.

Although Darwin would illustrate the *Descent* with some of the birds most closely associated with Gould—hummingbirds, birds of paradise, grouse, bower birds—and although he would come to understand the display of the male Argus pheasant through a Gould drawing, he selected *Illustrirtes Thierleben* (1864–1869), the popular work of the German naturalist A. E. Brehm, as the source for his bird figures. The selection of Brehm over Gould also seems surprising. Despite their disagreement about natural selection, Gould and Darwin remained on good terms, and Gould sometimes allowed his plates to be copied. But having already approved the use of other Brehm illustrations for the Russian translation of *The Variation of Animals and Plants Under Domestication*, Darwin was able to obtain Brehm's woodblocks from Brehm's German publisher and thus reproduce them directly rather than having them copied. It was cheaper and easier to print Brehm's birds directly than to commission wood engravings based on Gould's lithographic plates.[21] Darwin may well have had an additional reason to utilize Brehm's illustrations, namely, that Brehm was a supporter and popularizer of Darwin's theories.

Brehm's illustrations of mammals often depicted dramatic and violent confrontation and thus reflected the competitive world of natural selection. His more traditional bird illustrations, however, were hardly ideal for representing either natural or sexual selection. The single (usually male) bird in static profile captured neither competition nor courtship. While Brehm's illustrations were at least not saturated with the domestic motifs so prevalent in Gould's work of the 1850s and 1860s, they illustrated neither male competition nor male-female courtship. Their illustrative value for Darwin was thus mainly limited to depicting the product rather than the process of sexual selection. He chose some of the avian world's most exotically colored and ornamented males—the umbrella bird of South America, with its elaborate top-knot and long ornamental vocal sac; the cock of the rock, with its brilliant orange plumage; the red bird of paradise and peacock pheasant (figure 4.2), with their elaborately colored and ornamented feathers—to emphasize the results of sexual selection.

Yet even in cases like the peacock pheasant, the illustration does not capture the male display before the female that Darwin's text emphasizes. Unlike the peacock, the peacock pheasant has a dully colored breast and ocelli (eye-spots) on its wing feathers as well as its tail. Darwin explains that the male thus does not display directly in front of the female, but instead stands a little to one side, expanding his wings as well as his tail, lowering the wing nearest to the female and raising the one on the opposite side. "In this attitude," writes

Darwin, "the ocelli over the whole body are exposed before the eyes of the admiring female in one grand bespangled expanse."[22] Darwin's text must do the work that his illustration cannot. The reader is urged implicitly to see the static illustration in dynamic and evolutionary terms; the description of male display and admiring female selection invites the reader simultaneously to envision this male engaging in courtship and to construct a narrative history in which he is the product of generations of such display and selection. The example of the peacock pheasant and the similar but even more striking one of the Argus pheasant are vital to Darwin, for they show both that the display of such elaborate but dully colored patterns serves a utilitarian purpose and that the females possess an extraordinary level of taste, refinement, and discrimination. Indeed, he develops this argument at length in the chapter that follows and illustrates it with seven figures of feathers from the peacock, the peacock pheasant, and the Argus pheasant. Yet he provides no representation of the act of display and selection itself.

Two illustrations of hummingbirds—the only bird illustrations in the *Descent* to contain both male and female—afforded a better opportunity for depicting the act of sexual selection, yet even these can only do so by suggestion. In both cases the emphasis is on the differences between male and female, male hummingbirds providing an example of the "wonderful extreme" to which sexual selection can be carried, for "[a]lmost every part of the plumage has been taken advantage of and modified."[23] The presence of a female underscores Darwin's point that "selection by the females" is the sole cause of the male's brilliant colors, elaborate ornaments, and highly developed tails. The iconography of the single pair, however, points to courtship not in process but completed. In the illustration of the white-booted racket-tail, the female perches just below the male, her head and eyes directed upward towards him, but not at his chief ornament, his extraordinary tail. In the illustration of the tufted coquette (figure 4.7), while the male is positioned in an attitude more suggestive of display, the rather static female is not looking directly at him, and the presence of the nest suggests selection has already occurred. Darwin subversively highlights his indebtedness to Gould—he notes that anyone who has seen Gould's "splendid volumes or his rich collection" will admit to the beauty of male hummingbirds, and he informs his readers that Gould himself has shown him the wonderful extremes of male modification—but he does not reproduce Gould's illustrations of hummingbirds, which did not provide visual examples of courtship. If Brehm's hummingbirds did not depict courtship either, at least they were taken from a naturalist sympathetic to Darwin's own views.

4.7 *"Lephornis ornatus, male and female (from Brehm)."* Figure 48 in Charles Darwin, *The Descent of Man, and Selection in Relation to Sex.* vol. 2 (London: Murray, 1871), 76. Darwin had this hummingbird illustration copied from A. E. Brehm's *Illustrirtes Thierleben* (1864–1869). This and another hummingbird illustration were the only bird illustrations in the first edition of the *Descent* to depict both sexes, but they have more in common visually with Gould's domestic scenes than with Darwinian sexual selection.
Special Collections Library, University of Michigan.

Neither Gould nor Brehm offered depictions of another prominent trait of male hummingbirds emphasized by Darwin, their violent competitiveness. However, Brehm did provide Darwin with an example of male competition. In the case of the ruff (*Machetes pugnax*)—its common name based on the male's elaborate and richly colored collar of feathers, its Latin name reflective of the male's "notorious" reputation for "extreme pugnacity"—a rough background sketch contains two males confronting each other, one with the ruff expanded, while two other birds, apparently females, look on.[24] Although Darwin states that the male's collar "probably serves in chief part as an ornament," he focuses on its use as a shield during the violent battles among males during the breeding season. Indeed, Darwin uses the ruff as one of his chief examples of violent male competition, noting that male ruffs "seem always ready to fight" but are especially aggressive during the spring and will "often kill each other"

when at close quarters. This is one of just two illustrations in the first edition of the *Descent* to even gesture at the use of the secondary sexual characteristic under discussion, but it hints only indirectly at the potential for the ruff to be deployed for charming a female.

The other illustration that attempted to depict sexual selection is that of the spotted bower bird, but in this case Brehm's drawing clearly is based on Gould's plate of the bird for *The Birds of Australia* (compare figures 4.1 and 4.5).[25] Whether he did so knowingly or not, Darwin was able in effect to set Gould's text against Gould's plate, exploiting Gould's admissions and inconsistencies in an effort to entice readers into seeing the gender traits and sexuality of these birds in radically different ways. Darwin found in Gould's books a wealth of evidence to support his own views on both natural and sexual selection, annotating his copy of Gould's *Handbook* extensively for the *Descent*.[26] In the text, he highlighted the very behavior of bower birds that Gould was reluctant to acknowledge: their extended "nuptial assemblages," the males' frenetic and even violent "antics," and the females' aesthetic preferences and active role in mate-selection. Darwin opens his discussion of bower birds by framing it in terms of natural selection. The various species of bower birds have inherited their instinct for bower building from a single progenitor species. This instinct, the most curious and striking example of male "love antics," is itself the product of sexual selection, of females preferring the males who have constructed the most beautifully decorated bowers. Where Gould minimizes or even suppresses the bower birds' courtship and mating, Darwin revels in it. Whatever tranquil domesticity or female coyness in courtship is evident in the plate is shattered by Darwin's text, as Darwin directs us to see a mutual and very sexual courtship scene rather than a nesting pair. The bowers are built "for the sole purpose of courtship," he says. These are not nests, for the nests are constructed in trees. In its Darwinian context, Gould's ambiguous plate can be read quite differently: We see either the male in the bower, attempting to entice the female, or the female in the bower already having been enticed. While Darwin has to rely on his textual language to emphasize the frenetic sexuality of the male, he makes this aspect of the male's behavior much more prominent than it is anywhere in Gould.

The illustrative additions and alterations made for the second edition of the *Descent*, however, suggest that Darwin felt the need for more and better visual representations of sexual selection. Even before the first edition reached booksellers early in 1871, Darwin regretted using Brehm's illustrations. Responding to P. L. Sclater, who apparently disparaged Brehm's work while checking the proofs of the bird chapters in the *Descent* for Darwin, Darwin wrote that "I wish with all my heart I had thought of consulting you about woodcuts, . . . but I thought Brehm's drawings fairly good enough for my purpose of popular illustration; & it saved me trouble; but I now much regret I did not get better drawings."[27] Darwin's characterization of his illustrative needs as "popular" presumably reflected his sense that he did not require a high degree of ornithological accuracy in his depictions of secondary sexual characteristics. But his desire for "better drawings" was primarily a desire for a different *kind* of drawing, one showing secondary sexual characteristics *in use*. And the desire was sufficiently intense that the search for better drawings began almost immediately, with the first edition barely in print and the second almost three years away.

Less than four months after Darwin's letter to Sclater, Darwin's publisher, John Murray, commissioned the zoological artist T. W. Wood, almost certainly at Darwin's behest but unquestionably with Darwin's approval, to re-draw several of Brehm's birds. Wood, who worked extensively for *The Field,* took a particular interest in the courtship of birds and the same spectacular instances of male display on which Darwin relied. In two letters to *The Field* in 1869 and 1870, Wood provided a female's-eye view of the male Argus pheasant's ornamented wing feathers, the second letter accompanied by a diagram illustrating the fall of light on the feathers. A more extended article on "The Courtship of Birds" for *The Student and Intellectual Observer* included discussions of the peacock, the Argus pheasant, and the prairie grouse and was accompanied by a color plate of the prairie grouse and an uncolored wood engraving with nine "male birds during courtship," including the peacock pheasant. Indeed, Wood already had initiated a correspondence with Darwin on the subject while Darwin was still at work on the *Descent,* sending him a copy of the second *Field* letter, directing his attention to the *Student* article and its illustrations, and offering to provide Darwin with an improved version of the woodblock from which the Argus pheasant diagram was printed.

Of the four Brehm illustrations replaced by Wood's drawings, three were fundamentally reconceived, and two of these depicted sexual selection in action. Wood asked Darwin for a copy of the *Descent* to assist him in his work, "as I should wish to know what characters were particularly pointed out in the text." His version of the prairie grouse thus showed the male with his vocal sacs expanded while two females and a male in the middle ground looked on, and his rendering of the peacock pheasant contained a male displaying before a (seemingly inattentive) female (figure 4.3). Each of these clearly was based on Wood's similar illustrations for *The Field.* In addition, Darwin paid Wood for a completely new illustration for the

4.8 "Side view of male
Argus pheasant, whilst displaying before the female.
Observed and sketched
from nature by Mr. T. W.
Wood." Figure 52 in Charles
Darwin, *The Descent of
Man,* 2nd ed. (New York:
Burt, 1874), 411. This wood
engraving by T. W. Wood
was commissioned by Dar-
win for the second edition
of the *Descent* to illustrate
his argument that the elaborate markings on the wing
feathers of the Argus pheasant are the product of sexual selection.
*Special Collections Library,
University of Michigan.*

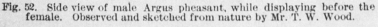

Fig. 52. Side view of male Argus pheasant, while displaying before the
female. Observed and sketched from nature by Mr. T. W. Wood.

second edition: a male Argus pheasant displaying his wing feathers
for an undepicted female (figure 4.8). This figure, too, was based on a
recent half-page engraving by Wood for *The Field* of two males displaying before two females. *Field* editor W. G. Tegetmeier called
Wood's illustration, the result of first-hand observations of the
Argus pheasants at the Zoological Gardens, "the first correct delinea-
tion of the display of the Argus pheasant that has been produced."[28]

These commissioned illustrations, however, did not fully solve Darwin's representational dilemmas. The public writings and private correspondence of Darwin and Wood on male display reveal that Wood concurred with Darwin about its proximate but not its ultimate cause. In the Duke of Argyll's popular rebuttal of Darwinism, *The Reign of Law* (1867), the ornament and brilliant plumage of male birds, especially species like hummingbirds and the Argus pheasant, simply could not be explained by natural selection. Speaking specifically of hummingbirds, and ignoring Darwin's suggestion in the *Origin* that these were the result of sexual selection, Argyll asserted that "A crest of topaz is no better in the struggle for existence than a crest of sapphire. A frill ending in spangles of the emerald is no better in the battle of life than a frill ending in the spangles of the ruby." Such color and ornament were thus a sign of the pleasure taken by the Creator in variety and beauty for their own sakes. Moreover, the Argus pheasant confirmed spectacularly the fundamental convergence of human and divine aesthetics, the wing feathers of the male providing the sole instance in all of nature "in which ornament takes the form of pictorial representation."[29] While Wood shared Argyll's sense that the ocelli of the Argus pheasant "present exactly the appearance of having been painted with consummate skill by an artist whose perfect knowledge of the laws of light and shade enable him so to deceive the eyes as to cause a flat surface to appear convex," he argued that the "sole purpose" of this elaborate ornamentation was to enable the male to "fascinat[e] his lady love." Male display generally, Wood asserted, "undoubtedly has for its object the winning of [the females'] favours." Yet such chivalric locutions reflected Wood's ambivalence about the extent of female choice and aesthetic refinement. Does the male exert an irresistible power over the female, or is he ultimately at the mercy of her individual tastes? Lacking direct observational evidence of Argus courtship, Wood is clearly more uneasy about the latter possibility than the former: It is, he writes, "very difficult to believe that these birds can appreciate such perfect beauty as they are gifted with." As "gifted with" suggests, Wood, like Argyll, ultimately saw the aesthetically perfect wing feathers of the male Argus, and the female attraction to them, as originating in an external power rather than a natural law. "[A]lthough I feel convinced of the truth of your theory of the origin of species," Wood wrote to Darwin, the perfect ornamentation of the male Argus "cannot be explained by it" and "seems to point to (& almost to prove) the existence of a great artistic power."[30]

Even with his commissioned drawing of sexual display, then, Darwin found himself having to rely on his text to steer his readers away from the postulation of a "great artistic power" behind the male Argus pheasant's ornamentation and the female Argus pheasant's aesthetic preferences. Despite his reliance on Wood's drawings and his use of Wood's observations, Darwin rejected, both privately and in the *Descent*, Wood's claim that the ocelli of the male Argus were perfect. Darwin clearly responded with skepticism to Wood's original letter and article on the ocelli, for Wood in turn replied that he was "greatly surprised and disappointed to find by your last letter that you cannot see the Argus as I and some others do."[31]

In the *Descent* itself, Darwin noted Wood's view that the shading of the ocelli is slightly different in different feathers, "in order to bring out their full effect, relatively to the incidence of light." But after "carefully examining" two mounted specimens with Gould, Darwin asserted that "I cannot perceive that this acme of perfection in the shading has been attained; nor can others to whom I have shewn these feathers recognize the fact."[32] Influenced by Wood's and Tegetmeier's observations of the Argus pheasants at the Zoological Gardens, Darwin softened his opposition in the second edition, accepting that the ocelli are shaded in such a way as to ensure that when displayed they always give the appearance of being illuminated from above. Nonetheless, Darwin continued to insist that in spite of their "artistic" appearance, the ocelli "are not illuminated from strictly the same point as they ought to be" and thus are not uniformly and absolutely perfect. What was at stake in this disagreement? From Darwin's perspective, a great deal: it is the *imperfection* of the ocelli that illustrates how sexual selection operates over time. "In order to discover how the ocelli have been developed," he wrote, "we cannot look to a long line of progenitors, nor to various closely-allied forms, for such do not now exist. But fortunately the several feathers on the wing suffice to give us a clue to the problem, and they demonstrate that a gradation is at least possible from a mere spot to a perfect ball-and-socket ocellus." What the eye was to the *Origin*, the eye-spots of the Argus pheasant were to the *Descent*. Indeed, Darwin insisted in the second edition, we have "no right to expect absolute perfection in a part rendered ornamental through sexual selection, any more than we have in a part modified through natural selection for real use." The wing feathers of the male Argus pheasant were not the completed work of a divine artist, but a still-evolving project involving untold generations of female Argus pheasants. "[N]o one who admits the agency of sexual selection," Darwin concluded, will deny that, over time, variations in a simple dark spot, if appealing to females, gradually could develop into "elliptic ornaments" and then into the ball-and-socket ocellus, and that this development could occur at different rates and achieve different levels of perfection on different areas of the wing feathers. Unfortunately for Darwin, most of his readers did *not* "admit the agency" of sexual selection, and certainly not the agency of selecting females.[33]

Illustrating sexual selection thus proved to be more difficult and problematic than Darwin initially assumed. With both the traditions of ornithological illustration and cultural notions of gender roles working against him, he originally was content to work within those constraints, relying on his textual language to shape the way that readers viewed his illustrations. He seems to have realized quickly, however, that the effectiveness of this strategy was limited. At its best, as in the case of Gould's bower birds, it could expose the tenuousness of such representations of desexualized domesticity. But Darwin came to see the need for more direct and unambiguous images of sexual selection, new images whose content correlated more closely with the language of this theory. Commissioning such illustrations, however, did not fully solve his difficulties. Depicting male display was not the same thing as depicting female choice, and it was female choice, and the aesthetic sensibility seemingly implied by it, that made Darwin's contemporaries uneasy. Darwin's illustrations required rather than replaced thousands of words, and those words still could not fully control the meaning of the illustrations. As had been the case with the textual language of natural selection in the *Origin,* the visual language of sexual selection in the *Descent* could not fix the nature and identity of the selector. In the earlier work, Darwin's analogy between natural and human or artificial selection, coupled with his occasionally vivid personifications of nature, had opened the door to an array of interpretations of natural selection as a process ranging from a Lamarckian striving of individual wills to the unfolding of a divinely superintended plan of life. With sexual selection, centrally concerned with the actual choices of individuals, the issue was not so much one of the individual or natural law versus God, but of males versus females. Birds were the main source of controversy over the theory because Darwin insisted that most female birds did the choosing. Selection of females by males seemed natural to Darwin's contemporaries; selection of males by females did not. He thus provided illustrations that enabled his readers to picture sexual selection, and he sought more effective ones for the second edition. Darwin's lack of success in gaining acceptance for sexual selection even with his improved illustrations, however, suggests the extent and continuing power of a domestic vision of gender in which the autonomy even of female birds was constrained radically.

Notes

1. Charles Darwin, *The Descent of Man, and Selection in Relation to Sex* (1871; Princeton: Princeton University Press, 1981), 2: 39.

2. *Ibid.,* 2: 112.

3. My thanks to Bernard Lightman and Ann Shteir for suggesting the conception of my analysis here as an "intervisual" one.

4. Gillian Beer, "Descent and Sexual Selection: Women in Narrative," *Darwin's Plots: Evolutionary Narrative in Darwin, George Eliot, and Nineteenth-Century Fiction,* 2nd ed. (Cambridge: Cambridge University Press, 2000), ch. 7; Jennifer E. Gerstel, "Sexual Selection and Mate Choice in Darwin, Eliot, Gaskell, and Hardy" (Ph.D. dissertation, University of Toronto, 2002); Rosemary Jann, "Darwin and the Anthropologists: Sexual Selection and Its Discontents," *Victorian Studies* 37 (1994): 287–306; Evelleen Richards, "Darwin and the Descent of Woman," in *The Wider Domain of Evolutionary Thought,* ed. David Oldroyd and Ian Langham (Dordrecht: Reidel, 1983), 57–111; Cynthia Eagle Russett, *Sexual Science: The Victorian Construction of Womanhood* (Cambridge, Mass.: Harvard University Press, 1989); Ruth Bernard Yeazell, *Fictions of Modesty: Women and Courtship in the English Novel* (Chicago: University of Chicago Press, 1991); and Yeazell, "Nature's Courtship Plot in Darwin and Ellis," *Yale Journal of Criticism* 2 (1989): 33–53.

5. On the reaction to sexual selection, see Helena Cronin, *The Ant and the Peacock: Altruism and Sexual Selection from Darwin to Today* (Cambridge: Cambridge University Press, 1991). For a critique of the limitations of modern feminist discussions of sexual selection, see Richard Kaye, *The Flirt's Tragedy: Desire Without End in Victorian and Edwardian Fiction* (Charlottesville: University Press of Virginia, 2002), ch. 2.

6. Alfred R. Wallace, "Humming-Birds," *Fraser's* 28 o.s./22 n.s. (1877): 784.

7. Darwin, *Descent,* 2: 328.

8. See my "John Gould, Charles Darwin, and the Picturing of Natural Selection," *The Book Collector* 50 (2001): 51–76.

9. Christine Jackson, *Wood Engravings of Birds* (London: Witherby, 1978), 34.

10. Audubon to John Bachman, April 20, 1835, *John James Audubon: Writings and Drawings,* ed. Christoph Irmscher (New York: Library of America, 1999), 832 (original emphasis).

11. Works like Loudon's *Entertaining Naturalist* (1843), Wood's *Illustrated Natural History* (1853), Morris's *History of British Birds* (1851–1857), and Johns's *Birds of the Wood and Field* (1859–1862) went through multiple editions and were reprinted frequently through the century. On the history of ornithological illustration, see Jackson, *Wood Engravings of Birds; Bird Illustrators: Some Artists in Early Lithography* (London: Witherby, 1975); *Bird Etchings: The Illustrators and Their Books, 1655–1855* (Ithaca: Cornell University Press, 1985); and *Prideaux John Selby: A Gentleman Naturalist* (Northumberland: Spredden, 1992). For ornithological illustration in the larger context of zoological and natural history illustration, see Ann Shelby Blum, *Picturing Nature: American Nineteenth-Century Zoological Illustration* (Princeton: Princeton University Press, 1993); S. Peter Dance, *The Art of Natural History* (1978; New York: Arch Cape Press, 1990); and David Knight,

Zoological Illustration: An Essay Towards a History of Printed Zoological Pictures (Folkestone: Dawson, 1977). On Gould, see Ann Datta, *John Gould in Australia* (Melbourne: Miegunyah Press, 1997); Lambourne, *John Gould— Bird Man* (Milton Keynes: Royal Society for Nature Conservation, 1987); Gordon C. Sauer, *John Gould, The Bird Man: A Chronology and Bibliography* (London: Sotheran, 1982); and Isabella Tree, *The Ruling Passion of John Gould* (New York: Grove Weidenfeld, 1991). On the popularizers, see Barbara T. Gates, *Kindred Nature: Victorian and Edwardian Women Embrace the Living World* (Chicago and London: University of Chicago Press, 1998); Bernard Lightman, "'The Voices of Nature': Popularizing Victorian Science," in *Victorian Science in Context,* ed. Bernard Lightman (Chicago: University of Chicago Press, 1997), 187–211; and Lightman, "The Story of Nature: Victorian Popularizers and Scientific Narrative," *Victorian Review* 25 (2000): 1–29.

12. Blum, *Picturing Nature,* 13–18.

13. Strickland to Gould, November 9, 1841; *John Gould the Bird Man: Correspondence,* ed. Gordon L. Sauer, 3 vols. to date (Mansfield Centre, Conn.: Maurizio Martino, 1998–), 2: 359 (original emphasis); "Gould's Birds of Australia," *Annals and Magazine of Natural History* 9 (1842): 338. While "Audubonic" for many naturalists meant "exaggerated," Stickland was clearly praising Gould, for he declared himself "much pleased" with the last two installments of the work.

14. Gould to Jardine, July 2, 1841; *Correspondence,* 2: 316.

15. Henry Scherren, *The Zoological Society of London: A Sketch of its Foundation and Development* (London: Cassell, 1905), 89.

16. Loudon obtained Gould's permission to reproduce his illustrations and descriptions of the satin bower bird for a new edition of her *Entertaining Naturalist,* a work widely used in schools. Wood's *New Illustrated Natural History* (1855) included extended extracts from Gould on the satin bower bird, with illustrations based on, if not copied from, *The Birds of Australia.* Loudon to Gould, November 9, 1842; *Correspondence,* 3: 127.

17. Gould, *Supplement* to *The Birds of Australia* (London: 1851–1869), plate 36 (Fawn-breasted bower-bird).

18. John Gould, "On the 'Bower' or Playing-House Constructed by the Satin-bird . . . ," *Proceedings of the Zoological Society of London* 8 (1840): 94.

19. John Gould, *The Birds of Australia,* 7 vols. (London, 1840–1848), vol. 4, plate 10.

20. Gould, *Handbook to The Birds of Australia,* 2 vols. (London, 1865), 1: 444, 448; Gould, *Introduction to The Birds of Australia* (London, 1848), pp. 56–57.

21. Darwin to V. O. Kovalevsky, June 3 and June 24 [1867]; Darwin to [Bibliogr. Inst. Hildburghausen?], June 8, 1868; *A Calendar of the Correspondence of Charles Darwin, 1821–1882,* eds. Frederick Burkhardt and Sydney Smith (New York: Garland, 1985), letters 5562, 5575, and 6235; Darwin to [Bibliogr. Inst. Hildburghausen?], [August to December 1868] (draft), Darwin Papers, Cambridge University Library, DAR 96:52. All quotations from unpublished material in the Darwin Papers are by permission of the Syndics of Cambridge University Library.

22. Darwin, *Descent*, 2: 90–91.

23. Ibid., 2: 78.

24. Ibid., 2: 41.

25. Both A. E. Brehm and his father, C. L. Brehm (1787–1864), also a famous ornithologist, were subscribers of Gould, but the bower bird is the only one of Brehm's illustrations used by Darwin to be taken from Gould. See Gordon C. Sauer, *John Gould the Bird Man: Associates and Subscribers* (Mansfield Centre, Conn.: Martino, 1995), 25.

26. Mario A. DiGregorio, ed., *Charles Darwin's Marginalia* (New York and London: Garland, 1990), 1: 337–40.

27. Darwin to Sclater, January 4 [1871], Zoological Society of London Library and Archives.

28. Murray to Darwin, May 10, 1871, DAR 171.398; Wood to Darwin, June 14, 1870 and April 24, 1871, DAR 181.147 and 89.22–23; Darwin to Robert Cooke, April 8, 1874, DAR 143.290. T.W. Wood, "Plumage of the Argus Pheasant and Bird of Paradise," *The Field* 34 (June 26, 1869): 538; "The 'Eyes' of the Argus Pheasant," *The Field* 35 (May 28, 1870): 457; "The Courtship of Birds," *The Student and Intellectual Observer* 5 (1870–1871): 113–25. W. G. Tegetmeier, "Display of the Argus Pheasant," *The Field* 43 (March 28, 1874): 296. Tegetmeier sent a copy of the article to Darwin. Darwin to Tegetmeier, April 5, 1874, DAR 148.65.

29. Duke of Argyll [George Douglas Campbell], *The Reign of Law*, 5th ed. (New York: Routledge, n.d.), 192, 234. The preface to this edition is dated January 1868.

30. Wood, "The Courtship of Birds," 123–24, 113. Wood to Darwin, June 14, 1870, DAR 181.147.

31. Wood to Darwin, [June? 1870], DAR 181. This letter is damaged and the date missing, but the *Calendar*'s conjecture about the date is almost certainly correct, as it clearly follows Wood's letter to Darwin on June 16, 1870, DAR 181.148.

32. Darwin, *Descent*, 2: 144n.

33. Charles Darwin, *The Descent of Man, and Selection in Relation to Sex*, 2nd ed. (1874; Amherst, N.Y.: Prometheus Books, 1998), 449, 456–57.

NATURE BY DESIGN

Masculinity and Animal Display in Nineteenth-Century America

Sally Gregory Kohlstedt

When taxidermist William Hornaday presented his "Orangs in a Treetop" (figure 5.1) to the American Museum of Natural History in the late 1880s, the New York exhibit was a sensation, covered by a two-page spread in the illustrated *Harper's Weekly* where a familiar social construction of the nature and behavior of these primates positioned a large male at center stage surrounded by females eating or caring for their young.[1] Hornaday's adventures in securing these orangutans in Borneo fit seamlessly into imperial narratives of exploration. In fact, his narratives were not striking in themselves, but public excitement and curiosity were heightened by the physicality of this three-dimensional tableau presented as both science and art.

Hornaday's account emphasized the physical prowess and intellectual expertise required to discover and acquire the specimens and thus effectively signaled the field scientist as having masculine authority. In highlighting sometimes aggressive male mounts and enhancing gender by posture and position within carefully designed animal groupings, museum taxidermists like Hornaday added not only to the excitement of capturing or killing their specimens but also to their own gender identity. This essay argues that in the early nineteenth century zoological field naturalists and taxidermists began to fashion their behavior in order to enhance themselves and their displays. While their gendered presentations were never singular or static, the persistence of maleness in zoological displays over the nineteenth century reflected and shaped ideas in public discourse about the masculinity—characterized by intellectual cunning as well as physical strength—of those who hunted, prepared, and displayed these animals.

When naturalists placed natural history objects behind glass and under human gaze in prominent museums, social and ideological as

GROUP OF ORANGS IN THE AMERICAN MUSEUM OF NATURAL HISTORY, CENTRAL PARK.

5.1 The American Museum of Natural History purchased this domestic scene of orangutans, prepared by William Hornaday, from Ward's Scientific Establishment. "Group of Orangs in Central Park," *Harper's Weekly* 24 (December 18, 1880): 809.

well as scientific and aesthetic categories influenced the organization of space and the presentation of specimens.[2] The visual vocabulary of eighteenth-century natural history illustration carried over into the display of physical objects in the early nineteenth century.[3] Painters based their drawings on prepared specimens, and the viewing public seemed to anticipate zoological configurations in museum displays that reflected illustrated natural history books. Audiences responded enthusiastically to the preparators, like Hornaday, who brought three-dimensional, life-like specimens into habitat groupings.

The fact that naturalists used gender as a subtle but standardized aspect of these displays makes it clear that sexual differences and similarities were part of discussions about the natural world, and that masculinity took the featured position.[4] Familiar themes and conventional presentations about nature proliferated in a variety of public exhibitions, newspapers, magazines, and lectures using lantern slides and other devices, as well as in more exclusive art. Public awareness of natural history, especially in cities, was influenced significantly by natural history museum exhibits.[5] Here, the manliness of those responsible for museum exhibition was made more emphatic by the relative absence of women who worked as curators and taxidermists.[6] The museum-employed male preparators gained unprecedented authority as they developed sophisticated projects and established common goals including the "authentic" representation of nature, education of the public, and sponsorship of exhibition expenses through paying visitors and patrons. Their lives and work interlocked as they emphasized both the technical skill and the aesthetic sensibility required, providing "artful nature," to borrow Barbara Stafford's term, in public exhibits.[7] One means of emphasizing the fierceness of wild animals was to highlight the courage, strength, and sense of adventure required by those who obtained them for display. The heroic posture of explorers reached its apogee with the wealthy big game hunters at the end of the century.

Increasing accessibility of materials and changing tastes of public audiences—both malleable and influential—meant, however, that neither the appearance of museum displays nor the themes they embodied could be static.[8] Even as work practices within museums became more professional, the authority gained from technical and artistic expertise enabled each generation of taxidermists to re-inscribe their own work and subjects with meaning that would resonate with patrons, audiences, and exhibits. These shifts were not without tension. Museum displays had overlapping goals involving documentation of natural objects and aesthetic presentation. The "ethos of the artist-naturalist" in the first half of the nineteenth century that emphasized an intimate relationship between observation and illustration did not always mesh easily with the closet naturalists' major goals of carefully preserving collections of natural objects, describing them in print, and then carefully preserving them as "type" specimens—evidence of the originality and significance of their work within a shared taxonomic enterprise.[9] As the size and purpose of exhibition changed, public displays became representational, and scientific research materials were put in storage, thus selecting certain specimens to stand in for entire species. And both the field and closet naturalists who engaged informally in nature studies, purchased illustrations, and visited museums, also sought, as Anne Secord reminds us, aesthetic stimulation, new knowledge, and simple pleasure.[10] In communication with public expectations, patron preferences, scientific intentions, and practical possibilities, museum display underwent striking transformation over the course of the nineteenth century, and in that process worked out themes about nature in which sex and gender played a prominent role.

Authority and Presentation in Peale's Philadelphia Museum

Charles Willson Peale's museum, a model among those in the young republic from the 1790s to the 1820s and reference point for later generations, featured its proprietor alongside specimens whose lives or positioning promoted a strong narrative (figure 5.2). The ambitious portrait painter adapted his early apprenticeship as a saddler and his

5.2 This classic self-portrait of Charles Willson Peale (1822), clearly marked as a gentleman, demonstrates the ideal-ized, probably retrospective organization of the museum, his work in both art and natural history, and his entrepre-neurial skill at cultivating a sense of importance and mystery around his holdings.
Courtesy of the Pennsylvania Academy of Fine Arts, Philadelphia. Gift of Sarah Harrison (The Joseph Harrison, Jr. Collection).

artistic skills to the preservation and display of natural history.[11] Having never seen a European museum himself, although well aware of European developments, Peale created his collection around individual specimens, reinforcing a printed genre of "life history" in which the life and capture of a particular animal was as important as the group to which it belonged.[12] By the turn of the century, his "cabinet of curiosities" held marvels and monstrosities (large mastodon bones and a two-headed calf) alongside ordered rows of minerals, mounted insects, shells, antlers, skeletons, fossils, and other elements of natural history.[13] Aesthetics were important, but so was the rational thinking that the objects might stimulate.[14] Peale's orderly museum indicated his intellectual mastery of these materials, signaled by his use of Linnaean nomenclature as well as his original and large exhibits like the reconstructed mastodon skeleton positioned tantalizingly beyond the viewer's gaze behind the curtain in his invitational self-portrait. Despite a significant twenty-five cent admission fee, the museum attracted local families as well as travelers who visited the short-term capital and major commercial center of Philadelphia, including the Marquis de Lafayette and Baron von Humboldt.[15] Peale turned such prominent visitors into advertising moments, aided by the prestigious specimens brought back by the heroic transcontinental explorers Meriwether Lewis and William Clark.[16]

Attractive displays were important in a museum funded by paid admissions, so the entrepreneurial Peale highlighted bird species whose males had dramatic and colorful plumage.[17] His life-like preparations could be theatrical, with individuals strikingly displayed on tree branches or grouped together in water-like settings, without attention to their real world compatibility or taxonomical relationships.[18] Leading American artist-naturalists such as Alexander Wilson, John Godman, and Peale's own son, Titian, as well as several women colorists including sisters Malvina and Helen Lawson, who brought black and white engravings into so-called "living color," used Peale's museum as an informal artists' studio. The familiar male blue jays, bright goldfinches, and Baltimore orioles as well as powerful eagles with talons open and peacocks with their variegated plumage were common both in published illustrations and on public display.[19]

Artist and preparator John James Audubon, perhaps inspired in part by Peale's Museum in the 1820s, developed a wonderful illustrative style that prefigured later wildlife illustration, using expert colorists for his elephant folio plates. Even more compelling, Audubon put his own active figure into an illustration to highlight the physical effort required to recover the detail on eagle behavior that he captured on paper (figure 5.3). As Bruce Hevly suggests, "The rhetoric of adventure was an important element in the culture of field science, one

5.3 John James Audubon's golden eagle illustration includes trapper and artist John James Audubon straddling the log in the lower corner and suggests the determination and bravery required in obtaining specimens. Golden Eagle (*Aquila chrysaetos*), 1833, by John James Audubon, watercolor, pastel, graphite, and selective glazing, 38 × 25 inches.
Collection of the New-York Historical Society, accession number 1867.17.181.

5.4 This turkey cock is positioned in the foreground with the hen gathering food in the rear. Drawn by Titian R. Peale and engraved by Alexander Lawson for Charles Lucian Bonaparte, *American Ornithology,* vol. 1 (Philadelphia: S. A. Mitchell, 1925–1931), plate 9.
Courtesy of the Owen H. Wangensteen Historical Library of Biology and Medicine, University of Minnesota, Minneapolis.

Wild Turkey. Male and Female.
Meleagris Gallopavo.

claiming reliable perception on the basis of authentic, rigorous, manly experience."[20] Audubon carefully recorded animal behavior in the field and often presented male and female pairs tending nests or posed in natural habitat.[21] Audubon's paintings varied greatly, but when a male and female were pictured together, the male was typically in the foreground and given a more active stance. Fellow artists, like Titian Peale, also tended to mount and illustrate pairs, but the two—male and female—typically did not have equivalent postures (figure 5.4). These juxtapositions, which would become apparent in animal mountings, were too consistent and deliberate not to have significance to the preparators who put the male into prominence and displayed the female as an essential but more docile and grounded figure.

Peale steadily improved techniques for mounting the skins of larger mammals, and experimented with natural settings by building a small thicket that he populated with stuffed frogs, toads, and water-fowl surrounded by fox, raccoon, deer, and other specimens.[22] Well-preserved skins and skeletons stretched over and around wooden frames and mounted in upright, if awkward postures, were more compelling than flat bear rugs or a shelf of skulls.[23] Travelling exhibits demonstrated the popularity of aggressive caged bears and imposing male elephants, and Peale's large and life-like mounts similarly drew more audience comment than his systematic displays of minerals, shells, and dried plants.[24] The artist turned naturalist prepared a lion with a full mane, a moose with a large rack, and even a bear—all apparently males, despite the ironic fact that such specimens are classed as mammals.[25] In the early republic, the American frontier, as it continuously receded beyond the Appalachian chain, became a symbol of the ways that men, in particular, faced challenges and highlighted their active roles in bringing nature under control.[26]

These displays and illustrations emphasized prevailing cultural norms of maleness. Powerful, even fierce posture, as well as vigor, size, and specifically male characteristics as the mane of the lion or the rack of the moose, heightened the theatrics of the human conquest of nature. Females usually were put on display when they were the only specimens available or when they had a particularly interesting story. Peale, for example, was fascinated by the North American elk and owned a female that he domesticated to a treadmill. When she died, he mounted her, noting in his lectures that she had been "good humored and affectionate."[27] Female and male qualities for Peale and his contemporaries constituted another way of seeing natural laws and order.[28] They thus articulated assumptions about the polarity and complementarity of masculinity and femininity even as they foregrounded male specimens and underscored the masculinity of those who captured and displayed them.[29]

Paying visitors seemed drawn to drama and size, and the mysterious mastodon provided both. The skeletal remains of the "Incognitum," which some thought might still be roaming in the Western wilds, proved difficult to mount, but was magnificent. Peale emphasized his own role in the exhumation of these bones, a major financial and technological undertaking, in an illustration linking his heroic enterprise with the oversized, excavated bones (figure 5.5).[30] A large painting portrays the *paterfamilias* overseeing a challenging moment when thunderstorms threatened to wash the soft banks into the pit where men were working to extract the bones, but bravery and persistence yielded a "tolerable compleat skeleton."[31] Descriptions of the mastodon did not overtly assign sex and gender, perhaps because those seemed less relevant in a possibly extinct species, but Peale put himself clearly in charge of the fate of its massive remains.

5.5 Peale exhumed two specimens from a pit along the Hudson River in a major financial and physical undertaking. The event is commemorated in this portrait that features family members in an idealized setting at the murky business of extracting the bones from a marl pit. Here the heroic task of discovery and excavation became another way to bring the exhibitor into the exhibit. Charles Willson Peale, *The Exhumation of the Mastodon*, 1805–1808. *Courtesy of the Maryland Historical Society, Baltimore, Maryland.*

Masculinity was featured on display in Peale's museum and those of his less well-known emulators in New York, Boston, and other major cities. The use of the male of the species was not just about biology— for example, the colorful plumage of male birds and the larger size of the male in some mammals—but related as well to impressions of male and female behavior. Cutting across simple biology was the possibility that species might be linked with gender, making the lion masculine and the hyena feminine. Size was used to imply maleness, although in most non-mammal species the female is, in fact, larger.[32] The hulking moose with its rack, the aggressive stance of a wolf, and the towering mastodon—all put nature into a wild state. Matched against such nature were the explorers who braved the wilderness to bring back these natural prizes. Peale, Audubon, and later preparators found ways to remind visitors that dangerous male animals heightened the need for human male athleticism and acumen.[33]

Acquisition practices dictated that most of the mounts were individual, and Peale's informative life histories about each of them reinforced ideas about the "nature" of animals.[34] Like many contemporaries, he had a complex understanding of the human-animal connection, in which there was an assumed "animal nature" that included apparent sensibilities toward others of the species as well as the dangers and fruits of the environment. Peale occasionally evoked human imagery to make a moral point, as with the "industrious" female elk. Approval for such animal narratives can be found in his visitors' book, suggesting that the tactile realities reminded visitors that the feathers, skins, and fossilized bones once belonged to living creatures that had a particular life history. But naturalists who concentrated on taxonomy challenged Peale's mode of presentation, and by mid-century opinion diverged about both who should frequent museums and what should be seen there.[35]

Limiting Public Influence in Mid-Century Scientific Collections

Peale's innovations, important as they had been for early Philadelphia naturalists, were criticized by a core group affiliated with the younger Philadelphia Academy of Natural Sciences. Concentrating on field work, research collections, and publications, these curators disparaged drama in public displays, particularly after the remnants of Peale's museum became part of P. T. Barnum's American Museum in New York City.[36] Among the more often cited diatribes was that of Elliott Coues, whose *Key to North American Birds* (1872) put the point clearly:

> Spread eagle styles of mounting, artificial rocks and flowers, etc., are entirely out of place in a collection of any scientific pretensions, or designed for popular instruction. Besides, they take up too much room. Artistic grouping of an extensive collection is usually out of the question; and when this is unattainable, half-way efforts in that direction should be abandoned in favor of severe simplicity. Birds look best on the whole in uniform rows, assorted according to size, as far as a natural classification allows. They are best set on the plainest stands, with circular base and a short cylindrical crossbar on a lightly turned upright. The stands should be painted dead-white, and be no larger than is necessary to secure support; a neat stiff paper label may be attached.[37]

Mid-century museums of learned societies, whose only visitors were pre-screened and admitted with a pass on designated afternoons when a (male) member of the Society was present to explain holdings to the uninitiated, were likely to hold glass-fronted, library-styled cases.[38] Arranged for systematics, rather than aesthetics, the museum labels for insects, mollusks, dried plants, birds and small mammals offered only scientific nomenclature of class, family, and geographic locality. Older mounts might remain but were obscured within the tightly spaced aisles where everything was on display as museums sought to move from the "marvelous to the commonplace."[39] The largely anonymous curators who toiled for hours to identify, prepare, and present ordinary as well as exotic species, provided densely packed, detailed presentations that appear to modern tastes to be highly cluttered and without much interpretation.

The technical orientation and concern for systematics also were evident in publications, and extant handbooks provide only subtle traces of gender presentation that may well have been part of the oral commentary given to visitors by curators.[40] Scientific reports of the widely distributed federal exploring expeditions and surveys of the American West suggest a distinctive interest.[41] Physical sex differences could be more explicit in these scientific illustrations, with sex-specific characteristics drawn to show distinctions between the male and female in highly technical works. Physicians and intellectuals were also deeply preoccupied with sex differences, echoing the prescriptive literature of mid-nineteenth century America.[42] At the same time, there was self-conscious public reticence about sexual matters, and it is possible that ideas of public modesty resulted in neutered specimens.[43]

Although not lavishly colored, and with greater attention to taxonomy and standard morphological features than those of Wilson, Audubon, and their contemporary naturalists, scientific volumes produced in Washington, D.C., were intended for targeted distribution to naturalists and politicians. The images helped reinforce the idea of the male of the species as the "norm," with the female of the species described in comparative terms. Certainly that is what the curator of Brown University's collections, J. W. P. Jenks, intended when he asked museum supplier Henry A. Ward to provide a mounted buffalo for display and specified a male because, he asserted, a male was most "typical."[44] Attention to sexual dimorphism became even more evident after Charles Darwin published *Origin of Species* (1859) and then *Descent of Man* (1871), and evolutionary naturalists concentrated their attention on the apparent physical and mental differences among humans as well.[45] Evolution seldom was found articulated explicitly in museum displays, although the rapid inclusion of anthropological holdings suggests how important the issue of human evolution was becoming.[46]

By the 1870s, museums turned back to a broad public, initially seeking to attract teachers and school children in the Boston Museum of Natural History and eventually in most major museums across North America. Further social change happened rapidly thereafter, with audiences moving from leisured attendees with refined manners to jostling crowds, including children, attracted by expanded visiting hours and days when no fees were charged (figure 5.6). As audiences became younger and more diverse, and patronage came from city and state funding as well as from wealthy private patrons, the displays became more consciously didactic. Museums took their place among other institutions providing informal public education and were expected to play a mediating role among social classes visibly divided by

economic dislocations and widespread social unrest in the last quarter of the century.[47] Renewed attention to the public aspects of the museum was buttressed by the "new museum idea" developed at the British Museum and the Smithsonian Institution in the 1880s. Particular functions of the museum were distinguished, with specimens designated for purposes of display and public education maintained in different locations from those for preservation and research. In practice, this meant that curators uncomfortable with special exhibits could retreat into workrooms, while the public saw and heard particular messages by staff hired to provide exhibits and education. While Peale had fulfilled a multiplicity of roles—collector, taxidermist, exhibitor, patron, and entrepreneur—these became more discrete areas of expertise, although continuing to overlap and intersect. What returned as the center of the public museum project was the vivid dimensionality that recalled both the earlier efforts of Peale and new capacities transported by European preparators.

Male Exhibitionism

Urban natural history museums relied on commercial enterprises as well as major expeditions to supply and frame exhibitions of the later nineteenth century, typically with support from wealthy merchant patrons and their political colleagues. The most successful museum supplier was Henry A. Ward's Scientific Establishment in Rochester, New York. After building up an inventory of minerals, casts of famous fossils, and skeletons, Ward responded to increasing demand for skillfully mounted skins by hiring skilled preparators from Europe. For a time in the 1870s and 1880s, Ward's preparation rooms offered the best apprenticeship opportunity for ambitious taxidermists in North America.[48] Among his successful hires was William T. Hornaday, a Midwesterner who had left Iowa Agricultural College and, shortly after his arrival at Ward's, proposed going on a collecting expedition for rare and highly sought specimens.[49] After proving his capabilities in Cuba and South America, Hornaday embarked on a trip to India and Southeast Asia, where he was determined to acquire, among other things, skins of orangutans in Borneo. Gorillas brought back from Africa to the United States and then to Europe by Paul du Chaillu had contributed to the intense discussion about the relationship of primates to humans, and Hornaday hoped to learn more about other primates.[50] Indeed, Hornaday's detailed records of his travels provided the careful measurements, behavioral descriptions, and environmental setting he would use when mounting specimens, and they became published accounts of his field adventures. His first-person narrative, like Audubon's small but significant self-portrait, presented wilderness adventures that made especially popular reading in the late nineteenth century.[51]

Returning to Rochester with boxes of specimens, including forty-two orangutan skins, Hornaday persuaded Ward to give him time to mount a group that he entitled "A Fight in the Tree Tops." Perhaps inspired by the popularity of a French mount of a lion attacking Arab Couriers, two mounted snarling orangs shared the stage at a meeting of the American Association for the Advancement of Science in Saratoga, New York, in 1879 as Hornaday presented a paper "On the Species of Bornean Orangs." His account emphasized challenging days battling through swamps and primeval forests while searching out specimens, and the fierceness of the primates was matched by the striking bravado of the explorer behind the podium. He took the two fighting male orangs that he had prepared to Saratoga, and the following year took his complete display to the Society of American Taxidermists meeting. Hornaday described the scene:

> The group in question represented a pair of immense and hideously ugly male orang utans fighting furiously while they hung suspended in the tree-tops. The father of an interesting family was evidently being assailed by a rival for the affection of the female orang utan, who, with a small infant clinging to her breast, had hastily quitted her nest of green branches and was seeking taller timber. The nest which she had just quitted was an accurate representation of the nest constructed by this great ape. In the middle of the group, and at the highest point, was another nest in the top of a sapling, on the edge of

which another interesting young orang utan—a production evidently of the previous year, was gazing down with wide-eyed wonder at the fracas going on below.[52]

His narrative focuses first on males, ugly and combative, while the female is moving away from the male competition and protecting herself and her infant—choices and behaviors are determined by sex in this narrative. In the full account of his travels, Hornaday made clear that he relied upon his indigenous Bornean guides but also was the ultimate authority when overseeing them. Thus, the taxidermist is integrated into the presentation, actively formulating the narrative while presenting critical data. Hornaday rightfully claimed that this display and the one he created for Albert Bickmore at the new American Museum of Natural History in New York City marked a significant shift in emphasis in museum exhibits, from singular and sometimes fanciful mounts to habitat groups presented with close attention to detail.[53]

The New York exhibit was different, however, in that the orangutans "at home" were less dramatic and were presented as a "whole life" scene drawn from observations in Borneo—although it is important to note that orangutans are solitary animals and would never have been in such close proximity. A report in *Harper's Weekly*, the oversized and well-illustrated "journal of civilization," described this scene (see figure 5.1):

> The central and most striking figure is a very large old male orang, with wide cheek callosities and very long hair, who is hanging by one hand and foot to a stout tree, and reaching stealthily out and down with his right hand to snatch a large durion from the foot of the old female who hangs to a tree on the left. She is quietly eating of a durion she holds in her free hand, quite unsuspicious of the stealthy attack being made from behind. Behind this female, high up in a small tree, is her baby, looking very much like a huge fat spider, hanging in precisely the position he had assumed when discovered in the forest. On the right of the group in the foreground is a young female orang lying on her back, fast asleep, upon a nest she has just built of green boughs broken off and piled crosswise on the top of a young sapling. Although fast asleep, she grasps the nearest large limbs as naturally as the feet of a sleeping bird grasp its perch. This is an exact reproduction of the nest constructed by the orang utans. Behind the "sleeping beauty," perched upon a large horizontal branch, sits another large male orang, eating another durion, while he watches the stealthy movement going on below. The entire group is to be regarded as a section cut out of the top of a Bornean forest, with animals, leafy trees, and all.[54]

The author of the *Harper's* essay went out of his way to note the large size of the male and to comment that "a full-grown male orang with his powerful arms and hands, his formidable canine teeth, and darkly scowling face is an object that never fails to inspire a timid person with dread."[55] The journalist concentrated much of his attention on the parallels to humans, suggesting that scientists were still seeking the "missing link." His observation that the Malayan term "orang outan" meant "jungle man" implicitly related to the imperial mission that also fascinated readers. The journalist's interpretation was explicit: "In the living animal we can see actions very similar to our own, and a perfect reflection of our own peculiar passions and emotions."[56] Thus the domesticated orangs could, in fact, be brought into the company of New Yorkers.[57]

Later, Hornaday would admit that the first group of mounted primates was "a trifle sensational." His published principles of group mounting recommended representing "everyday, peaceful home scenes" of animals that would "interest and direct" observers.[58] The tension around issues of authenticity, realism, artfulness, and didacticism were, inevitably, not resolvable but rather negotiable and influenced by individual curators and the audiences and administrators with whom they dealt. Even the wonderfully successful habitat groups that became popular after the turn of the century, with mounted specimens in wall niches, complete with painted backdrops to create the illusion of a natural scene and foregrounded naturalistic vegetation, typically placed animals in relative proximity not found in nature. The move toward domestic scenes may have been initiated by Albert Bickmore, director of the American Museum of Natural History, or by Robert Colgate who purchased the group for it, or even by the teachers bringing their classes to the museum. Hornaday offered a clue about his purposes, however, when he suggested in his handbook that taxidermists "suppress all tendency to the development of violent action on the part of your specimens. In a well-regulated museum no fighting is allowed."[59] Museum managers turned explicitly toward a promotion of social harmony and thus reacted against the radical materialism implicit in some explications of evolutionary theory.

Accuracy was important, and many taxidermists preferred to do their own field collecting so that they could describe thoroughly the habits, postures, and habitats of individuals at various life stages and thus compose genuinely representative creatures. However, the "scientific analysis" was focused narrowly on accurate detail in individual presentations (careful measurements of limbs and crania, for example) while the arrangement was clearly "artful." Hornaday presented the orangs, grey monkeys, and other wildlife through the lens of his personal experience. Over time, he shifted from hunter to preserver. Without apparent reflection on the irony, he "adopted" a small orang temporarily while in Borneo even as he systematically killed more than forty of the species. Later, when director of the New York Zoological Garden, however, his focus would turn to conservation. He became well known as a lecturer on extinction, a phenomenon he understood to be driven by the "greed, selfishness, and cruelty of 'civilized' man toward wild creatures." This turn problematizes his early career as naturalist-hunter but coincided with shifting public opinion.[60] Hornaday always had had a sense of wonder and respect for nature, echoing what Donald Worster has termed "romantic thinking," and the preparator included emotional elements in his presentations from the outset.[61] Perhaps it was for this reason that he offered the playful suggestion of the stealthy "theft" of a durian fruit from the complacent female orangutan. His personal authority, gendered masculine but with feelings, was never contested in his narratives.

Large family groups like Hornaday's famous bison, centered around the largest and most dramatic (male) specimens, originally were presented simply on a relatively flat landscape without any painted backing in a four-sided box (figure 5.7).[62] Smaller species allowed taxidermists to be particularly creative, adding more detail to the topography and providing a painted background. For example, Hornaday created an opossum display that represented a sectional view of a burrow along a stream; his interest in the unusual reproductive habits of the marsupial led him to another kind of narrative:

> In the foreground is an old mother opossum with several young ones riding on her back, clinging to her gray coat, while the head of another protrudes from her pouch. This represents the manner in which the opossum carries her young after they have reached a certain age. From a small branch hangs another opossum, suspended by its prehensile tale, sprawling in mid-air. This specimen is a female and shows the size and location of the wonderful marsupial pouch. Another individual is climbing up the trunk of the tree.[63]

There is little discussion of the male of the species, as Hornaday concentrates on breeding and nurturing habits, elements that sometimes displaced centralized male figures when taxidermists concentrated on unusual aspects of a species, in this case marsupial reproduction.

The larger mammal groups, however, nearly always followed a formula with a kind of "nuclear family" where a male adopts a protective stance, the female is a nurturer, and the young are playful and attractive. The gendered message was not lost on an approving Belgian naturalist touring American museums in the 1890s who reported his general impressions:

5.7 The bison started with the most important specimen, the largest male, and then Hornaday grouped the others to gain artistic effect, creating a foot scape with dirt and prairie grass from Montana. A sketch shows the early use of full glass cases, before painted backdrops became the norm. William T. Hornaday, *Taxidermy and Zoological Collecting* (New York: Scribner, 1929), plate 19.

PLATE XIX.

Drawn by C. B. Hudson.

GROUP OF AMERICAN BISON IN THE NATIONAL MUSEUM.—COLLECTED AND MOUNTED BY THE AUTHOR.

that which one specially admires in most of these museums and especially in Chicago, is the marvelous art shown in the formation of groups, in the choice of attitudes, in the intense expression of life and movement, the disposition of decorations which serve to give the illusion of reality . . . the male, female, and little ones are shown in their characteristic attitudes. The male, trusting in his strength, rules by his might the troop of which he is guardian. The female, with alert ear, appears fearful and anxious; the little ones careless, sleep, browse, and frolic in the midst of plants which are their native pasture and surrounded by other animals, especially birds, their friends and companions.[64]

These scenes of family and community life were replicated by another taxidermist trained at Ward's, Carl Akeley. His taxidermy in Milwaukee gained him a reputation for innovation in which he paid considerable attention to habitat as well as behavioral interactions. Artists prepared carefully detailed plant reproductions and, later, background paintings that enhanced the artistic taxidermy. The resulting exhibits were too tightly packed and too intense to be "real" but accomplished the goal of taking viewers into a natural site far from the cityscape outside the doors of the museums. Some scholars have identified this as "illusionism," and others suggest it is "extreme realism."[65] For Akeley, the displays were a condensed and intense representation of his own recollections of the nature he experienced. His best remembered taxidermy is African Hall at the

American Museum in New York, which featured large and impressive mounts in the early twentieth century. His mount of the Giant of Karisimbi, with its attention on this emblematic male ape, came to represent a version of egotistical manhood made famous through film icons like Tarzan and King Kong and the analysis of Donna Haraway (figure 5.8). Not always noted is the other, smaller figure in the foreground.[66] The white explorer in Africa is not explicit, but the fact of exoticism and imperial control play out in these exhibits as well.[67]

The rapid growth of public museums and the determination to bring an audience to them were paramount in establishing these habitat groups, particularly as patrons and taxidermists sought to influence a broader class of visitors. Sponsors in New York insisted that their museum be on a subway line, Milwaukee citizens paid a milage tax so that school children, indeed crowds of girls and boys, could attend without a fee, and the Smithsonian became a national attraction.[68] Hornaday, who as director of the New York Zoological Garden would initiate breeding programs for endangered species, was conscious of his influence on an audience. His goal was to have visitors acquire his own "feelings of admiration that often amount to genuine affection" for wild animals, reinforcing a growing concern for conservation among city dwellers and new immigrants to the United States.

5.8 Probably the best known of Akeley's displays, other than his elephants, is the gorilla group, the Giant of Karisimbi, at the American Museum of Natural History, which has a striking male with apparently another male and female observing his show of strength.
Image #: 330585, American Museum of Natural History Library.

5.9 The Dall Sheep exhibit at the James Ford Bell Museum, shot in Alaska by James Ford Bell, has a dramatic and detailed background with the sheep on a distinct promontory and guarded by the apparent head of the family.
Photograph courtesy of the Bell Museum of Natural History, University of Minnesota, Minneapolis.

Wealthy patrons, often men interested in big game hunting, certainly helped shape such exhibits. As the American West seemed tamed, Africa and South Asia provided for a different imperial adventure. Hornaday, and later Akeley, wrote of their explorations even as they led in technical taxidermy in the interiors of urban museums. Their examples were followed not so much by other taxidermists as by the wealthy sportsmen (and a few sportswomen) who captured the drama of the big game hunt quite literally and sustained it through museum exhibitions that recapitulated their exploits and bounty.[69] Theodore Roosevelt has become a kind of caricature of these individuals, but many large and small museums (such as the American Museum in New York, Bell Museum in Minneapolis, and Museum of Vertebrate Zoology at Berkeley) relied on such wealthy hunter patrons to provide specimens and financial support for the building and maintenance of large exhibits.[70]

The habitat dioramas were works of art as well as science, giving play to human imagination and intuition as well as acculturated observation; the domestic interpretation was not challenged (figure 5.9). Adding females and "young" (male and female) to exhibits turned out to have other advantages. Younger specimens typically had more vivid and still undamaged fur, and they readily engaged children and adult observers. The female of the species still might be in the background but she was likely to be engaged in the fundamental (read "instinctual") routines of gathering food, tending the nest, or nurturing her young. The imposed "body language" of the male and female typically placed the male in a dominant position, typically upright and assertive, often looking directly out through the glass panes on the museum visitors. The female of the species was essential to reproduction, as suggested by larger groups, but, in the generation before systematic studies of animal behavior, was presented as subordinate.

The assumptions about gendered roles in nature persisted through the scientific preoccupation with systematics and morphology and into the beginning of behavior analysis and ethology.

Conclusions

During the nineteenth century, natural history museums inscribed displays with masculinity, an elusive but nonetheless resonant set of cultural concepts. Professional taxidermists, almost exclusively men, viewed and presented their fieldwork and even zoological preparations as enterprises requiring vigor, strength, and courage. Their out-of-door adventures and intellectual authority transmitted these themes and inscribed them in public exhibitions. Taxidermists thus directed their audiences' gaze to the large and powerful male mammals, heightening the masculine strength of their captors. Even without physical features designating sex, maleness was translated through posture, relative position within a group, and other signifiers of strength and power, especially towering size. Many habitat groups reflected a formula in which a male could be identified by a readiness pose, and occasionally a fighting stance, suggesting a capacity for defensive if not aggressive action in a competitive world where survival could not be taken for granted.

Peale's use of the "life history" format in his presentations privileged male specimens. There were few female mounts, and the taxidermists, like illustrators, presented females as a kind of smaller, less distinct counterpart in paired species. There is little evidence of emphasis on sex differences, although Peale's sensibility about animal nature led him to project gendered qualities on some of his subjects. Primarily the male remained, as from ancient times, the expression of the standard (or "typical," as Brown University's curator suggested) of the species.

Representing nature in a visual and even tactile way was the explicit intention, but presenters understood that each design was more than simple representation, and they posed specimens with deliberation. Artist-naturalists continued to emphasize an intimate relationship between personal observation in the field and subsequent illustration.[71] Narratives that revealed capture and thus dominance inevitably preserved a certain distance between the observing human and the representative of nature under scrutiny. Although evolutionary thinking challenged older distinctions and helps explain the fascination with primate displays that proliferated by the turn of the century, the distance between "man" and "beast" seldom was obscured.

Throughout the nineteenth century, natural history museum curators and taxidermists trained visitors to look at animals in three dimensions through particular lenses. Museum professionals sharpened the focus and reoriented objects in relation to their own scientific and personal interests even as they responded to audience preferences. Exhibits were to function like textbooks, showing the visitors what to see and how to connect that information in the tableau and with their lives. In the choice of exhibits, museums privileged specific kinds of specimens and artifacts from zoology, botany, and even human society. They reflected the interests of the naturalists who oversaw acquisitions, managed them, and provided supplementary information in which the masculine had center stage. Masculinity was persistent as a text but unstable in detail. Further analysis remains to be done on just how the masculinizing tendencies influenced the anthropology exhibits in these museums, leading to an emphasis, for example, on comparative narratives or on the choices of material culture, such as weapons of island and coastal peoples, that became prevalent in museums of the late nineteenth century.[72]

By the early twentieth century, the influence of museums as key interpreters of nature's progeny became more constrained, as zoological parks, urban nature centers, and national and state parks provided alternative opportunities to observe living animals.[73] Zoological parks continued many of the characteristics of museums in their early caged exhibits and often put "families" on display.[74] In the 1920s, films produced by museums as well as commercial enterprises captured animal experiences in the wild within frameworks similar to those of museum displays; here, as well, gender themes would be well worth pursuing further.[75] Museums found that habitat groups were (and would remain) the most popular aspect of natural history museums, even as scripts and the representations changed with regard to behavior and habitat. As the concept of "life zones" became more prominent in the thinking of naturalists, backgrounds suggesting climate, altitude, and other geographical features became more "accurate" and developed with specific often extraordinary features, such as promontories.[76]

Museums in North America expressed the assumptions of their staff and responded to expectations of audience and patrons. While naturalists concentrated on individual specimens and the taxonomic relationships among them in the early part of the nineteenth century, their successors tended to emphasize species relationships and geographical distribution.[77] Proprietors and administrators also learned by experience that museum exhibits with rows of like specimens that so interested those in taxonomic work did not attract large audiences. Well-mounted habitat groups provided an important alternative, allowing the research specimens (and their curators) to remain in secure and non-public facilities while providing more highly focused and aesthetically attractive displays for visitors. Didactic goals shifted somewhat away from scientific information and toward behavioral and social meaning. Weaving through these reinterpretations and renovated presentations was the ubiquitous thread of masculine intellectual and physical prowess, enhanced by the potentially wild side of untamed nature that also was gendered masculine through connections drawn among the hunt, collection, taxidermy, and display of animals.

Ironies abound in museum history as we contemplate the animals killed in the name of preservation and the objectifying of individual specimens even as preparators and visitors often identified closely with their behaviors. Museums by their very functions of preservation and presentation designed a nature interpreted through and yet in tension with human experience. The men who organized and filled the museums projected their experience into exhibits, thus making personal virtues into public norms of masculine behavior.[78] It will be important to investigate further how this masculinity that was strong and even sufficiently violent to deal with the challenges of wilderness related to implied family responsibility. Masculinity reflected a complex set of characteristics, and in the museums, at least, the male posture of guarded alertness suggested a potential for violence while situated in the domestic, even placid, setting of habitat groups.[79] Nature designed for museums configured maleness in ways that re-inscribed prescriptions for human behavior, and the animal displays highlighted the role of the male of the species with a high degree of confidence. Simultaneously, the wilderness backdrop reminded visitors that, whatever common characteristics existed between humans and other animals, the males of these animal species also were distinct from civilized men.

Acknowledgments

Thanks to Nancy Tomes for insightful comments on a very different version of this paper at a Berkshire Conference on the History of Women; to colleagues at Minnesota, especially Margot Iverson, Donald Opitz, Piers Hale, Stephen Groening, Paul Brinkman, Juliet Burba, Mary Anne Andrei, Georgina Hoptroff, and Amy Fisher; to my commentator, Annette Burfoot, as well as the audience at York University, and particularly to our editors, Bernie Lightman and Rusty Shteir, for their persistent, perceptive, and always friendly suggestions. Early support for this research came from NSF Grant #9123719.

Notes

1. "Group of Orangs in Central Park," *Harper's Weekly* 24 (December 18, 1880): 809–10.

2. For historiography of museums, see Ronald Rainger, "Recent Books on the History of Museums," *Biology and Philosophy* 10 (1995): 235–48; and Sally Gregory Kohlstedt, "Museums: Revisiting Sites in the History of the Natural Sciences," *Journal of the History of Biology* 28 (1995): 151–66. Other useful sources on museum history include Charlotte M. Porter, "The Natural History Museum," in *The Museum: A Reference Guide,* ed. Michael Steven Shapiro (Westport, N.Y.: Greenwood Press, 1990), 1–29; and Tony Bennett, *The Birth of the Museum: History, Theory, Politics* (London: Routledge, 1995). An important book on the international spread of museums is Susan Sheets-Pyenson, *Cathedrals of Science: The Development of Colonial Natural History Museums during the Late Nineteenth Century* (Kingston: McGill-Queens University Press, 1988).

3. On the intersection of collections, illustrations, and printed descriptions, see Paula Findlen, *Possessing Nature: Museums, Collecting, and Scientific Culture in Early Modern Italy* (Berkeley: University of California Press, 1994).

4. The classic account is Joan W. Scott, "Gender: A Useful Category of Historical Analysis," *The American Historical Review* 91, no. 5 (December 1986): 1053–75. On masculinity, see Harry Brod, ed., *The Making of Masculinities: The Men's Studies* (Boston: Allen and Urwin, 1987); Mark C. Carnes and Clyde Griffen, *Meanings for Manhood: Constructions of Masculinity in Victorian America* (Chicago: University of Chicago Press, 1990); David D. Gilmore, *Manhood in the Making: Cultural Concepts of Masculinity* (New Haven: Yale University Press, 1990); Gail Bederman, *Manliness and Civilization: A Cultural History of Gender and Race in the United States 1880–1917* (Chicago: University of Chicago Press, 1995); and Michael Kimmel, *Manhood in America: A Cultural History* (New York: The Free Press, 1996).

5. A classic account of popular displays, including those in natural history museums, is Richard D. Altick, *The Shows of London: A Panoramic History of the Exhibitions, 1600–1862* (Cambridge: Belknap Press, 1978). On North America, see David Brett Mizelle, " 'To the Curious': The Cultural Work of Exhibitions of Exotic and Performing Animals in the Early American Republic" (Ph.D. dissertation, University of Minnesota, 2000).

6. A few intrepid women worked privately, and the most notable are discussed in Maxine Benson, *Martha Maxwell: Rocky Mountain Naturalist* (Lincoln: University of Nebraska Press, 1986); and Margaret Rossiter, *Women Scientists in America: Struggles and Strategies to 1940* (Baltimore: Johns Hopkins University Press, 1982), 57–59. Others are referenced in private correspondence: Mrs. Drexler worked on contract, as cited in Allan A. Burton to S. F. Baird, April 17, 1874, Baird MSS, RU 52, Smithsonian Institution [SI], Washington, D.C.; and Jared P. Kirkland indicated that his sister prepared bird skins for his display for Northwestern University, Kirkland to Baird, June 16, 1858, Baird MSS, RU 7002, SI. Such assistance in preparation and decoration for taxidermy was encouraged in the occupational handbook, *Ladies' Manual of Art: or Profit and Pastime: A Self-Teacher in All Branches of Decorative Art* (Chicago: Donohue, Henneberry, and Co., 1890).

7. Barbara Maria Stafford, *Artful Science: Enlightenment Entertainment and the Eclipse of Visual Education* (Cambridge, Mass.: MIT Press, 1994).

8. These business enterprises are discussed in Sally Gregory Kohlstedt, "Henry A. Ward: The Merchant Naturalist and American Museum Development," *Journal of the Society for the Bibliography of Natural History* 9 (1980): 647–61, and Mark Barrow, "The Specimen Dealer: Entrepreneurial Natural History in America's Gilded Age," *Journal of the History of Biology* 33 (2000): 493–534.

9. Several books focus particularly on the natural sciences, including Ann Shelby Blum's *Picturing Nature: American Nineteenth-Century Zoological Illustrations* (Princeton: Princeton University Press, 1993); see page 342 for the quoted phrase. A growing literature explores key figures who were involved in the development of systematics in the nineteenth century; see, e.g., Peter F. Stevens, *The Development of Biological Systematics: Antoine-Laurent de Jussieu, Nature, and the Natural System* (New York: Columbia University Press, 1994). Discipline by discipline, details of taxonomy were puzzled out over the century; see, e.g., W. Conner Sorensen, *Brethren of the Net: American Entomology, 1840–1880* (Tuscaloosa: University of Alabama Press, 1995).

10. Anne Secord, "Botany on a Plate: The Pleasure and Power of Pictures in Promoting Early Nineteenth Century Scientific Knowledge," *Isis* 93 (2002): 28–57.

11. Peale's diaries, volume 5 of *Selected Papers of Charles Willson Peale and His Family,* in five volumes, ed. Lillian B. Miller (New Haven: Yale University Press, 1983–2001; hereafter *Papers of CWP*), make clear his initiatives, as on page 235.

12. Margaret Welch, *The Book of Nature: Natural History in the United States, 1825–1875* (Boston: Northeastern University Press, 1998) focuses on this idea of "life history."

13. The term "cabinet of curiosities" was beginning to be used as one of derision toward ad hoc or eclectic collections; see Lorraine Daston and Katherine Park, *Wonders and the Order of Nature 1150–1750* (New York: Zone Books, 1998). During the nineteenth century, much of the interest in "curiosities of nature" moved to human exhibition, as discussed in Robert Bogdan, *Freak Show: Presenting Human Oddities for Amusement and Profit* (Chicago: University of Chicago Press, 1988).

14. Peale contrasted European practices with his own use of landscapes and more detailed labels in Peale, *Papers of CWP*, vol. 5, p. 309.

15. David Brigham, *Public Culture in the Early Republic: Peale's Museum and Its Audience* (Washington, D.C.: Smithsonian Institution Press, 1995); and Ellen Fernandez Sacco, "Spectacular Masculinities: The Museums of Peale, Baker, and Bowen in the Early Republic" (Ph.D. dissertation, University of California, Los Angeles, 1999). While the museums ostensibly were open to all, in point of fact the audiences were almost always white, and the local subscribers tended to live in neighborhoods with high social standing. Peale, *Papers of CWP*, vol. 5, 328 and 332.

16. The nationalist motives and projects of the Philadelphia naturalists are discussed in Charlotte M. Porter, *The Eagle's Nest: Natural History and American Ideas, 1812–1842* (Tuscaloosa: University of Alabama Press, 1986).

17. Paul Farber, "The Development of Taxidermy and the History of Ornithology," *Isis* 68 (1977): 550–66.

18. Toby Appel, "Science, Popular Culture, and Profit: Peale's Philadelphia Museum," *Journal of the Society for the Bibliography of Natural History* 9 (Winter 1980): 619–34. Peale also mounted specimens for private homes as in Peale, *Papers of CWP*, vol. 2, part 2, 827 and 895.

19. For published examples, see Ann Shelby Blum, *Picturing Nature;* and S. Peter Dance, *The Art of Natural History: Animal Illustrators and Their Work* (New York: Arch Cape Press, 1978).

20. Bruce Hevly, "The Heroic Science of Glacier Motion," *Osiris* 11 (1996): 67- 86.

21. John James Audubon, *The Birds of America* (1827–1838), also the widely available and reprinted Royal Octavo edition (San Diego: Thunder Bay Press, 1994).

22. Peale's scene was described by contemporary Manassah Cutler in 1787 and recounted in Peale, *Papers of CWP*, vol. 5, 221.

23. *Papers of CWP*, vol. 5, 235.

24. Ann Shelby Blum suggests that size was a marker for class but does not elaborate on this point in *Picturing Nature*, 6; see also William T. Alderson, ed., *Mermaids, Mummies, and Mastodons: The Emergence of the American Museum* (Washington, D.C.: American Association of Museums, 1992).

25. On how this system and nomenclature were also significantly gendered, see the early chapters of Londa Schiebinger, *Nature's Body: Gender in the Making of Modern Science* (Boston: Beacon Press, 1993).

26. Particularly useful early discussion of the masculine themes in literature about the American West is found in Annette Kolodny, *The Lay of the Land: Metaphor as Experience and History in American Life and Letters* (Chapel Hill: University of North Carolina Press, 1975).

27. Cited in Charles Coleman Sellers, *Mr. Peale's Museum: Charles Willson Peale and the First Popular Museum of Natural Science and Art* (New York: W.W. Norton, 1980), 104.

28. David Brigham examines the emphasis on social harmony in Peale's displays of animals in "'Ask the Beasts, and They Shall Teach Thee':' The Human Lessons of Charles Willson Peale's Natural History Displays," in *Art and Science in America: Issues of Representation*, ed. Amy R. W. Meyers (San Marino: Huntington Library Press, 1998), 10–34.

29. Considerable attention to masculinity and femininity as polarities in the prescriptive literature of this period helped shape the history of women in science, but more recent scholarship is less persuaded of sharp distinctions. Useful on this topic is Mary Kelley, *Private Woman, Public Stage: Literary Domesticity in Nineteenth-Century America* (Oxford: Oxford University Press, 1984).

30. Alderson, *Mummies, Mermaids, and Mastodons*, 21.

31. The event is detailed in chapter five of Sellers, *Mr. Peale's Museum;* quotation, 138.

32. While males are often thought of as large and powerful, in fact males of most species are generally smaller, except among mammals. See Stephen

J. Gould, *The Flamingo's Smile: Reflections in Natural History* (London: W.W. Norton, 1985), 59; and Bettyann Kevles, *Females of the Species: Sex and Survival in the Animal Kingdom* (Cambridge: Harvard University Press, 1986).

33. The masculine in science is discussed in Robert Nye, "Medicine and Science as Masculine 'Fields of Honor,'" *Osiris* 12 (1997), 60–79; and Naomi Oreskes, "Objectivity or Heroism? On the Invisibility of Women in Science," *Osiris* 11 (1996), 87–113. Donna Haraway provided the most often cited account about gender in the exhibits of Carl Akeley, especially the great silver back Giant of Karisimbi in the diorama of Carl Akeley in "Teddy-Bear Patriarchy: Taxidermy in the Garden of Eden, 1908–1936," in Donna Haraway, *Primate Visions: Gender, Race, and Nature in the World of Modern Science* (New York: Routledge, 1989). See the full diorama in figure 5.8.

34. Mizelle in "'To the Curious'" argues that a significant part of the interest in performing acts and museum displays was intense interest in human as well as animal behavior.

35. On this debate, see Joel Orosz, *Curators and Culture: The Museum Movement in America, 1740–1870* (Tuscaloosa: University of Alabama Press, 1990). Amusements were thought to take museums down a dangerous path to entertainments like that discussed in Andrea Stulman Dennett, *Weird and Wonderful: The Dime Museum in America* (New York: New York University Press, 1997).

36. Barnum's American Museum in New York unfortunately was destroyed by fire and with it many of Peale's specimens. Neil Harris, *Humbug: The Art of P. T. Barnum* (Boston: Little, Brown, and Co., 1973).

37. Elliott Coues, *Key to North American Birds,* 2nd ed. (Boston: Estes and Lauriat, 1884), 44, as quoted in Frederick A. Lucas, "Akeley as a Taxidermist and Groups in the Field Museum and Elsewhere," *Natural History* 2 (1927): 144–45.

38. During this period, only a few women were members of the natural history societies and even those women never read papers or served as officers or as curators of the collections. Rossiter, *Women Scientists in America,* 75–79.

39. Giuseppe Olmi, "From the Marvelous to the Commonplace: Notes on Natural History Museums," in *Non-verbal Communication in Science Prior to 1900,* ed. Renato G. Mazzolini (Firenze: Olschki, 1993), 235–78.

40. In the tightly controlled museum of natural history societies, visitors were admitted by ticket and accompanied by society members. Alpheus Hyatt at the Boston Society of Natural History initiated presentations for selected teachers, thanks largely to the initiative of Lucretia Crocker; see James T. Edward, ed., *Notable American Women, 1607–1950: A Biographical Dictionary,* vol. I (Cambridge: Harvard University Press, 1971), 407–409.

41. Philip J. Pauly, *Biologists and the Promise of American Life from Meriwether Lewis to Alfred Kinsey* (Princeton: Princeton University Press, 2000).

42. On the illustration of male and female, see Blum, *Picturing Nature,* 170; and on gender in the period, see Carroll Smith-Rosenberg, *Disorderly Conduct: Visions of Gender in Victorian America* (New York: Oxford University Press, 1986).

43. Museum lore suggests that nineteenth-century mounts may have been neutered, but evidence is hard to find. At the same time, a gorilla mounted for the American Museum retained its genitalia in a line drawing in Ward's *Natural Science Bulletin* (April 14, 1882); Georgina Hoptroff kindly brought this illustration to my attention. Even in the mid-twentieth century, the Smithsonian Institution, at the last minute, did neuter a bull elephant prepared for display in the rotunda of the Museum of Natural History. See oral history with taxidermist Watson Mondell Perrygo, 1906–1984, by Pamela Henson, Smithsonian Institution Archives.

44. J. W. P. Jenks to Ward, December 22, 1874, Ward Papers, University of Rochester Special Collections. The collection for Brown was also to have "bright colored birds" (December 14, 1871). The male as standard (or even universal) is not startling—the idea can be traced back to the Greeks and is discussed briefly in Rosemary Agonito, *History of Ideas on Women: A Sourcebook* (New York: Putnam, 1977).

45. Ludmilla Jordanova, *Sexual Visions, Images of Gender in Science and Medicine between the Eighteenth and Twentieth Centuries* (Madison: University of Wisconsin Press, 1989); and Sally Gregory Kohlstedt and Mark R. Jorgensen, "'The Irrepressible Woman Question': Women's Responses to Evolutionary Ideology," in *Disseminating Darwinism: The Role of Place, Race, and Religion,* ed. Ronald L. Numbers and John Stenhouse (Cambridge: Cambridge University Press, 1999), 267–93.

46. Direct discussion of evolution was rare, but assumptions were built into displays by the turn of the century, especially for anthropology. See Steven Conn, *Museums and American Intellectual Life, 1876–1926* (Chicago: University of Chicago Press, 1998).

47. Ronald Rainger, *An Agenda for Antiquity: Henry Fairfield Osborn and Vertebrate Paleontology at the American Museum of Natural History, 1890–1935* (Tuscaloosa: University of Alabama Press, 1991).

48. For a contemporary account, see William T. Hornaday, "Masterpieces of American Taxidermy," *Scribner's Magazine* 72 (July 1922): 3–16; and Frederic A. Lucas, *The Story of Museum Groups* (American Museum of Natural History, Guide Leaflet Series #53, 1921). On the efforts to organize taxidermists, see Mary Anne Andrei, "Breathing New Life into Stuffed Animals: The Society of American Taxidermists, 1880–1885," *Collections* 1 (Fall 2004): 149–95.

49. The best account of Hornaday's early years remains James A. Dolph, "Bringing Wildlife to Millions: William Temple Hornaday. The Early Years, 1854–1896" (Ph.D. dissertation, University of Massachusetts, 1975). Akeley's own accounts are found in *Adventures in the African Jungle* (New York: Dodd, Mead and Co., 1930), and *In Brightest Africa* (Garden City, N.Y.: Garden City Publishing Co., [1923]).

50. Stuart McCook, "'It May Be Truth, But It Is Not Evidence': Paul du Chaillu and the Legitimation of Evidence in the Field Sciences," in *Science in the Field,* ed. Henricka Kuklick and Robert E. Kohler, *Osiris* 11 (1996): 177–200.

51. Steven Allison-Bunnell specifically links the dioramas to this movement in his conference paper, "Forward to Nature: Natural History Dioramas and the Idea of Wilderness," American Society for Environmental

History, Tucson, Arizona, April 15–18, 1999. I thank Erik Moore for bringing this reference to my attention.

52. William T. Hornaday, *Taxidermy and Zoological Collecting: A Complete Handbook for the Amateur Taxidermist, Collector, Osteologist, Museum-Builder, Sportsman, and Traveller* (New York: Scribner's Sons, 1929 [1891]), 230.

53. The exhibit became one of a series of large mounts built by Hornaday. The best history of the development of habitat groups is Karen Wonders, *Habitat Dioramas: Illusions of Wilderness in Museums of Natural History* (Uppsala: Almqvist and Wiksell, 1993), but she does not discuss the gendered nature of these displays.

54. "Group of Orangs in Central Park," *Harper's Weekly* 24 (December 18, 1880): 809–10.

55. The author of the *Harper's Weekly* article, cited above, went out of his way to note that "the female is smaller, of a lighter brown color, and covered with short hair, which grows more evenly over the body and limbs." Ibid., 809.

56. Ibid., 809–10.

57. Gregg Mitman carries a theme of increasing domestication of all of nature that culminates in the television series of the 1950s in his *Reel Nature: America's Romance with Wildlife on Film* (Cambridge: Harvard University Press, 1999).

58. William T. Hornaday, *Taxidermy and Zoological Collecting,* 244.

59. Ibid., 244. Hornaday's advice was direct: "Let them be feeding, walking, climbing up, lying down, standing on the alert, playing with each other, or sleepily ruminating—in fact, anything but fighting, leaping, and running."

60. William T. Hornaday, *Our Vanishing Wild Life: Its Extermination and Preservation* (New York: New York Zoological Society, 1913), 8.

61. Donald Worster, *Nature's Economy: A History of Ecological Ideas* (Cambridge: Cambridge University Press, 1977), 301–303.

62. The bison marked a significant advance in model building, with a clay-covered hollow manikin that mimicked the form and motion better than older "stuffed" specimens, and Hornaday also sculpted facial detail with papier-mâché so that the results were remarkably lifelike. A good discussion of technique under Hornaday is found in the biography of his apprentice by Bill Sharp and Peggy Sullivan, *The Dashing Kansan: Lewis Lindsay Dyche: The Amazing Adventures of a Nineteenth-Century Naturalist and Explorer* (Kansas City, Missouri: Harrow Books, 1990), 33–42.

63. Hornaday, *Taxidermy and Zoological Collection,* 241.

64. This typescript account relating to the Field museum is in the Carl Akeley MSS, Rush Rhees Library, noted as a translation from Dr. H. LeBrun, *Les Musées d'Histoirie Naturellee aux Etats Unis.*

65. The debate goes on, as shown in Steven Allison-Bunnell, "Making Nature 'Real' Again: Natural History Exhibits and Public Rhetoric of Science at the Smithsonian in the Early 1960s," in *The Politics of Display: Museums, Science, Culture,* ed. Sharon MacDonald (London: Routledge, 1998): 77–97.

66. See, in particular, Haraway, *Primate Visions;* and Rainger, *Agenda for Antiquity.*

67. See Cyndy Hendershot, *The Animal Within: Masculinity and the Gothic* (Ann Arbor: University of Michigan Press, 1998), ch. 6.

68. Sally Gregory Kohlstedt, "International Exchange and National Style: A View of Natural History Museums in the United States, 1850–1900," in *Scientific Colonialism: A Cross-Cultural Comparison*, ed. Nathan Reingold and Marc Rothenberg (Washington, D.C.: Smithsonian Institution Press, 1987).

69. On the role of sportsmen and big game hunting, see John Reiger, *American Sportsmen and the Origins of Conservation* (Norman: University of Oklahoma, 1975); John M. MacKenzie, *The Empire of Nature: Hunting, Conservation, and British Imperialism* (New York: Manchester Univ. Press, 1988); and David Shi, *The Simple Life: Plain Living and High Thinking in American Culture* (New York: Oxford University Press, 1985). One of the few women who struck out independently was Annie Alexander, who collected in Alaska for the Museum of Vertebrate Zoology; see Barbara R. Stein, *On Her Own Terms: Annie Montague Alexander and the Rise of Science in the American West* (Berkeley: University of California Press, 2001).

70. The best-known example described his own exploits, namely, Theodore Roosevelt, *African Game Trails: An Account of the African Wanderings of an American Hunter-Naturalist* (New York: Scribner's Sons, 1910). James Ford Bell furnished his namesake museum with game that he was able to procure using a license that allowed hunting for museum specimens. Don Luce, Janet Pelley, and Kevin Williams, *The Making of the Bell Museum Dioramas* (Minneapolis: James Ford Bell Museum, n.d.).

71. Blum, *Picturing Nature*, 342.

72. Historical accounts of "native" peoples at the worlds' fairs typically do not comment much on gender, as, for example, Robert Rydell, *All the World's a Fair: Visions of Empire at American International Expositions, 1876–1916* (Chicago: University of Chicago Press, 1984); and Ivan Karp and Steven J. Lavine, *Exhibiting Cultures: The Poetics and Politics of Museum Display* (Washington, D.C.: Smithsonian Institution Press, 1991).

73. On the influence of parks, see Gregg Mitman, "When Nature 'is' the Zoo: Vision and Power in the Art and Science of Natural History," *Osiris* 11 (1996): 117–43.

74. American zoological development is discussed in R. J. Hoage and William A. Deiss, eds., *New Worlds, New Animals: From Menagerie to Zoological Park in the Nineteenth Century* (Baltimore: Johns Hopkins University Press, 1996); Elizabeth Hanson, *Animal Attractions: Nature on Display in American Zoos* (Princeton: Princeton University Press, 2002); and Vernon N. Kisling, Jr., *Zoo and Aquarium History: Ancient Animal Collections to Zoological Gardens* (Boca Raton, Fla.: CRC Press, 2001).

75. Mitman's *Reel Science* study of nature films provides good evidence about the structured stories presented by scientists as well as commercial producers, but he does not discuss gender implications in much detail.

76. Worster, *Nature's Economy*, 197, note 62; Mary Louise Pratt, *Imperial Eyes: Travel Writing and Transculturalism* (London: Routledge, 1992), 201–208.

77. Juan Ilerbaig, "Pride in Place: Fieldwork, Geography, and American Field Zoology, 1859–1920" (Ph.D. dissertation, University of Minnesota, 2002).

78. Richard Phillips, *Mapping Men and Empire: A Geography of Adventure* (London: Routledge, 1997), clearly demonstrates the connection between masculinity and the daring exploits of those who ventured into less-mapped regions. That such field identity did not necessarily fit well with the late nineteenth-century professional scientists' self-image is discussed in Michael Robinson, *The Coldest Crucible: Arctic Exploration and American Culture* (Chicago: University of Chicago Press, 2006). Similarly, Ruth Oldenziel, *Making Technology Masculine: Men, Women, and Modern Machines in America, 1870–1930* (Amsterdam: Amsterdam University Press, 1999), 123–24, argues that engineering tales of this period linked male conquest with the domestication of nature—sexual, female, and wild.

79. The anxiety and uncertainty that surrounded prescriptive norms of successful, civilized, positivist masculinity are examined in Hendershot, *The Animal Within.*

GENDER AND GENRE IN VICTORIAN SCIENTIFIC PHOTOGRAPHY

Jennifer Tucker

In the mid-1860s, a popular London photographic magazine published a series of anonymously written articles on the unique "privileges and trials" of wives of amateur photographers. One writer, commenting on the privileges, explained that marriage to an amateur photographer had made her a "scientific woman." As such, she has a "peep now and then into a dark closet, very close and smelly, where a dim gaslight trembles over a bath in which prints are washed after due chemical treatments, and, if quiet . . . she is allowed to look at the dripping negatives, held up before the glimmering gas-jet, and to exercise all her feminine sagacity in guessing that a beautiful negative has been secured!" "If very careful," she was allowed to carry the plates to their resting places, and "see them drain and dry." As she shared in the "glory of perfecting *negatives,* and producing *prints,*" she stated, she counted herself a "votary of science," and triumphantly asserted that "women's rights"—at least in the department of photographic science—were "respected and secured."[1]

In another letter published about a year later, on October 11, 1867, however, a second writer (also anonymous) detailed the "trials" of marriage to an amateur photographer, claiming it made middle-class women's traditional domestic roles even more difficult. At home, she explained, china closets were converted into photographic dark rooms, nitrate of silver marked the porcelain dishes and ruined carpets, soiled shirts piled up in the laundry, the stench of chemicals filled the house, and the expense of camera and chemicals drew down the family's purse. In an age when middle-class social norms prescribed a well-ordered home as evidence of smoothly functioning gender roles, photography was "not some new phase of discovery," but "some new phase of annoyance."[2] The author of another letter made a similar point: "I thought, Mr. Editor, when I married that I gained a husband; but I find that I was mistaken—I only married a 'camera.'" "As a wife, as a helpmeet, we are invited into the fields." However, "We cannot be of any assistance; of course not, but as a special favour we are permitted to witness the triumphs of artistic skill!" When her husband was out of the house practicing photography, she never saw him, and, even when she was "allowed" to participate, she was given minor roles: "We must run for water, and wash plates and dry them, and at the same time stand as points in the views; be here, there, and everywhere, and abused if we betray weariness, or fail to divine our artist's somewhat confused ideas and undeveloped purposes."[3]

6.1 Depiction of a woman and young girl sitting and watching as a man and young boy photograph bird nests on the Isle of Wight. Colored lithograph, c. 1895. *Mary Evans Picture Library.*

Despite their divergence of opinion, these accounts resemble one another in the way they depict women's role in photography as confined to the margins. Although today we know little about the anonymous writers of these articles, their disagreement in the pages of a widely read photographic magazine over how to interpret women's circumscribed roles in photographic image production points to a matter that current accounts of nineteenth-century visual culture mostly obscure: the gendering of the division of labor in photographic practice. A lithograph from around 1895 depicts a conventional sexual division of labor in photography, showing a woman and young girl in the background, sitting and watching, as a man and young boy photograph bird nests (figure 6.1). The role of labor in the production of nineteenth-century photographs often is overlooked by historians because scientific photography made its claims to objectivity by denying that human agency is part of the process.[4] Many Victorian scientists themselves promoted the view that photographs "are free, so far as their outlines are concerned, from the deceptive, and therefore vitiating element of human agency."[5] As the British physician and amateur photographer W. Dougall wrote in 1882, "The great value of photography" lies in its capacity to give "a true and reliable representation of the cases"—in his example, cases of medical leprosy in the Andaman Islands, where he had worked—"and affords no room for the exaggeration or romancing which might naturally occur if the sketches were made only by hand."[6] Photography seemed to many to answer the call for a new kind of mechanical objectivity that eliminated judgment and interpretation in reporting and picturing scientific results.[7]

Victorian scientific institutions and their official publications often make the authority of scientific photography appear natural and self-explanatory, effectively discouraging inquiry into how certain scientific photographs and not others became powerful icons. This process is complicated further by the fact that photography itself was an ambiguous medium. Yet the study of the uses of photography in science demands an accounting of how ideologies of gender and class operated in the creation of the genre of scientific photography during the nineteenth century, when modern conceptions of scientific imaging and scientific objectivity came into being. To see this, an approach to the study of photographic truth in the natural sciences is required that considers both how individual photographs entered the scientific exchange system and how photography operated within ideas of historically specific legitimation, including the doctrine of "separate spheres" for men and women. Recent scholarship has begun to question the broadly uncritical assumption of photographic truth that used to dominate historical literature—and that, to a great degree, still does.[8] Yet despite growing appreciation among historians of the significance of emerging gender and sexual ideologies for Victorian science, little attention is paid to the significance of these forces in shaping the scientific authority of photography. This is especially true for scientific photography beyond the human sciences of medicine and anthropology, notably in the Victorian natural sciences of astronomy, biology, meteorology, geology, and natural history. If we are to understand the power that photographs—and especially scientific photographs—exercised in Victorian society, we must explore how scientific photography as a field of study was structured by gendered patterns of social authority, addressing not only the obvious and important question, "Where were the women?" but also the subtle processes whereby the authority of scientific photographs was established through asymmetries of gender and class.

Like the two dominant Victorian photographic genres, landscape and portrait photography, the genre of scientific photography was defined by standards, rules, and codes of subject matter and methods of practice.[9] But scientific photography differed from other types of photography both in how it was named and in how ideologies of gender worked within it. Few developments did more than photography to establish the public image of Victorian science as a middle-class masculine practice. Photography was discovered by mostly male inventors in the 1830s. Quickly harnessed to various research projects pursued by men of science, it took on an association with the power of objectivity often located in the emergent male-controlled professional natural sciences in the late nineteenth and early twentieth centuries. Scientific photography formulated a sense of what knowledge was and a new estimate of who could participate in making it. To understand science in the nineteenth century, therefore, it is important to consider how photography conveyed social meanings and images of gender and science to professional and lay audiences.

After briefly discussing the masculinization of scientific photography in the mid-nineteenth century through the intersecting forces of professionalization in photography and science, this chapter explores how gendered patterns of authority in scientific photography affected women's participation in photography as image-makers and consumers. European natural science from at least the 1400s put heavy emphasis on the production of visual images, and although women were excluded from most major scientific organizations and employment, they helped create the visual culture of science.[10] But in the nineteenth century, middle-class Victorian women faced a paradoxical situation in which, on the one hand, the field of photography allowed them options for artistic and scientific expression that they did not have in other pursuits, and yet on the other hand, they faced constraints in reproducing their photographic works as authentically scientific because of their gender. Paying attention to often overlooked genres such as spirit photography can tell us much about the presence of women photographers and about the history of science more generally. Examination of nineteenth-century discourses and material exchanges of photographs of scientific phenomena exposes prevalent concerns with gendered concepts of skill, judgment, and human agency in an age identified with the pursuit of mechanical objectivity.

Masculinity and the Social Order of Photographic Vision in the Sciences

Victorian photography, a new wonder of its age, conveyed an image of democracy; it introduced, declared one Victorian observer, a "new world" in which each practitioner was a scientific "experimentalist."[11] Even among the amateur population, practitioners came from increasingly diverse backgrounds, and included sculptors, architects, engineers, schoolmasters, astronomers, and physicists; it also, as we will see, included some women.[12] However, as Jeanne Moutoussamy-Ashe points out in her study of black women photographers, nineteenth-century photography was only a democratic medium "to the extent that those who used the process were free to express themselves."[13] The men and women who took up photography in Victorian England encountered a world of severe limits and asymmetries. This was especially true in science, where even middle-class white men and women who had the privilege of using photography for self-image making lacked the authority and training to make photographs that official institutions of Victorian science accepted as semblances of scientific knowledge. Although photography won praise as a new scientific tool, photography at mid-century was widely mistrusted. While historians are right to argue for the power of photography as a new standard of evidence, perhaps a Victorian photographer captured more accurately the disposition of nineteenth-century perceptions when he indicated that the status of photography was ironically never more uncertain than in the mid-nineteenth century. In 1874, in the midst of the celebrated courtroom trial of the Tichborne Claimant, in which the use of photographs contributed to the length of the trial, this photographer summed up the complexity of Victorian attitudes to photography in this way: "There is a certain anomaly in the public estimation of photography which is worth noting," he mused. "No art is so frequently treated with contempt and contumely," he observed, yet "none more blindly and unreasoningly admired and trusted."[14]

Many in Victorian England blamed the crisis of trust in photography at mid-century on the feminization of photographic consumption. Middle-class English women—who constituted a large number of photographic consumers—were blamed widely by male operators for what they saw as the rise of "bad taste" in photography. Photographs of sentimental subjects "are thought," said one photographer, "especially by women, 'pretty,' and 'interesting'; and the gross improbability of their composition goes for nothing." This photographer blamed Belgian artists, in particular, for preying on the ignorance and lack of artistic knowledge of English women—for example, with faked memorial photographs of the Royal Family after the Prince Consort's death (though one photographic expert pointed out that the alleged "faked" photographs were, in fact, studies from life).[15] Though none of these photographers evidently worked to admit women into knowledge of how the process actually worked, women were held responsible for stimulating photography that lacked veracity and artistic merit. Photographers particularly blamed the "young-lady portion of the public," for stimulating the desire for pictures such as "silly 'Christenings,' sentimental 'Weddings,' and namby-pamby 'Broken Vows.'"[16]

Public commentary on the lack of credibility of photographs tapped into a wider Victorian social discourse on the trials of masculinity. Angus McLaren has shown how Victorian men, deemed by middle-class society as untrustworthy, were differentiated as "cads," "bounders," and "rotters."[17] The emergence of itinerant operators at venues such as pleasure gardens and races began to link photographers in the middle-class public imagination with "despised occupations" such as travelling players and showmen.[18] As the historian of Victorian art Lynda Nead acutely observes, the mid-Victorian metropolis was an "indulgent host" to "new forms of visual and literary culture."[19] For critics "nostalgic for a slower and more containable world of high art," Nead writes, the commercial street culture of the 1850s and 1860s was an "assault on the senses."[20] It also was perceived as an assault on photography's progress and image of rationality. As one disgruntled photographer put it, "as one of a class which should be composed of men of education and refinement, there is no broad sign to the public eye to distinguish men [of reputation] from men who are an abomination to the profession"—such men as "show-men" and "bullies" who have "perforce turned photographers."[21]

Gendered images and racialized comparisons were used in characterizing the emergence of distrust in photography. Scientific photography at this time came under scrutiny in part because of the mystery of the darkroom as a "chamber of secrets," likened to Eastern opium dens.[22] Not only were photographic operators portrayed in the popular media as dangerously sexual men who preyed on innocent lady customers, they also were depicted as feminized "swells" who wore loose robes and red Moroccan slippers, aping the "eccentricities of genius" to impress their patrons.[23] Though some photographers denied the reality of photographic labor to support the objectivity that many claimed was necessary in photography, the mystery of the process had to be dispelled, as the best photographers were said to have no secrets. For example, a Mr. Kurtz, a photographer on Broadway in New York City, was according to the London-based *Photographic News* a "model photographer" in this sense: that he was a "skilful" manager of light, had "artistic feeling," and—most important—"has no secrets"; he was "willing to communicate all he knows to others," and "ever willing to receive instruction from others."[24]

Many photographers maintained that the field of photography required an infusion of rational scientific education. As one contemporary observed in 1867, a "whole army of professional photographers" had "sprung into existence, working with very various skill, and in very different social positions."[25] Another photographer remarked, "It is one of the singular facts in the history of photography that whilst thousands of persons are at this moment practicing it, with a greater or less amount of skill and success, as their sole reliance for an income, there is scarcely one to be found who has received any special education or training for its practice, or served any apprenticeship to it as a profession." There were "men who have blundered into the business for the sake of getting a livelihood in an easy kind of way," who acquired their knowledge from fellow operators, stock dealers, or chemists.[26] Professionalization worked differently in science and photography, but in both domains it was a strategy for keeping women and certain classes of men out, particularly those seen as rejecting or lacking the potential for a rational scientific education in photography.[27]

The photographic press is a valuable and widely overlooked resource for historians interested in the professionalization and cultural politics of Victorian scientific photography.[28] At a time when formal schools for photography did not exist, photographic journals—and the *Photographic News,* in particular—became crucial for criticism, education, and community bonding around fraternal ideals. Edited by photographic chemists William Crookes and G. Wharton Simpson, the *Photographic News* sought to democratize and elevate photography by instructing both amateurs and professionals at a time when most journals primarily addressed amateurs who belonged to exclusive photographic societies. Thousands of photographers turned to photographic journals like the *Photographic News,* the largest journal of its kind in the world, as a way to put photography onto a more scientific basis by sharing the results of experiments, exchanging advice, and publishing new formulas and discoveries.[29]

To improve the social status of photography, the editors of the *Photographic News* sought to regulate photographic practices informally, to induct a small group of amateur and professional photographers into a scientific education, and to evoke the social bonds and authority of rational manhood to unify the photographic community. To resolve the perceived crisis of credibility in photography, and to rescue photography from sloppy practice and poor taste in the selection of subjects, the magazine's staff and contributors declared that photographers must lay aside their differences of social status and temperament and be united as "gentlemen" and "brothers." As one photographer explained in the *Photographic News* in 1862, "[I]t is impossible to speak of the devotees" of photography *except* "as a fraternity, with the strongest bond of a common interest and sympathy." He declared that "every year" photography gained "earnest recruits" that aided the "perfection" of photography, adding that "such men are needed."[30] Brotherhood, they believed, would be the glue that held the photographic trade together. As one photographer explained in 1860, in photography, "men of the most diverse lives, habits, and stations are united, so that whoever enters their ranks finds himself in a kind of republic, where it needs but to be a photographer to be a brother."[31]

Promoters of photography also promoted masculinity as a solution to the crisis in photography, and recommended that amateur photographers look to men of science for examples of worthy photographic work being done. Photography's reformers praised men of science for their work on photography and their skills of making useful photographs. The Victorian astronomer Warren de la Rue was quoted, for example, saying that photographing the moon had been a laborious undertaking, requiring the full attention of one observer who had to pay attention to the condition of the chemicals so as always to be prepared for a fine night of observing. Although many portrayed him as a solitary investigator who worked alone, de la Rue actually recommended extended cooperation. As he stated, it required "many people working together to develop fully its resources."[32] This of course fit with the *Photographic News'* editorial agenda of harmonizing the work of various workers.

The *Photographic News* encouraged amateur photographers to imitate scientific experimentalists. As one writer put it: "Scientific technology may be mastered in a few hours, but a clear understanding of the ideas it is intended to convey can only be secured by a long and laborious exercise of the mind."[33] Entry into the field of photography demanded great skill and a highly exacting technique: what Victorian photographers came to describe as a "judging eye."[34] Scientific photography, editors urged repeatedly, required study not only of image making, but of scientific research as well. In 1865, the *Photographic News* gave an account of the astronomer Samuel Fry's lunar photography experiments, in which Fry explained that the light of the moon was so feeble that it would not produce an instantaneous picture and had to be exposed to the photographic plate for a long time, even with the most sensitive collodion available. As any change in the relative position of the moon, the telescope, and the negative would blur and destroy the image, it was necessary to have the telescope so mounted and moved that its axis continued to point to the same portion of the moon during the entire exposure. Success involved knowledge of the "very best" chemicals, the highest state of "cleanliness," and "perfect freedom from floating particles in the bath, collodion, or developer, and all three so suited to one another, as to work uniformly together."[35] *Photographic News* readers also learned that it took two years of hard labor before Lewis M. Rutherford obtained in 1865 what contemporaries described as the most perfect photograph of the moon ever taken up until then. During this time, to bring the focus into the proper position to produce a perfect image of the actinic rays, Rutherford even removed the object glass from the telescope and ground the lenses with his own hands, undertaking the arduous task to adapt the lens to the refrangibility of the actinic rays.[36]

Even men of science had to work at making their photographs appear trustworthy, however. Indeed, working at it was precisely the point, for it differentiated the manly "operators" from the effeminate "swells." The repercussions of unskillful practice could be seen, for example, in the case of the solar eclipse expedition to India. In London during the mid-1860s, after the failure of the English photographic expedition led by Major Tennant to record the solar eclipse in

India, Victorians were reminded that photography was an imperfect science and were told of the need for skilled men in scientific investigation. In a letter from India to the Royal Astronomer, George Airy, a shame-faced Tennant reported soon after the event that the expedition was a "failure": every plate had been underexposed, and all of them were covered with spots. The *Photographic News* journalist corrected him: it was not a "failure," it was a "disaster." It must have been a staff of men who "knew nothing of photography," or "we should not have heard of such puerile difficulties as spots from concentration of the silver solution," he exclaimed. The editorial staff of the *Photographic News* blamed the British government for sending inferior workers, and compared the British expedition unfavorably with a successful one by the Germans, led by Vogel and two other "*experienced photographers.*" By contrast, the Germans had tested the chemicals and collodion under different conditions, and—like a "military drill"—even had tried preliminary exposures before the event.[37] In this case and others like it, there was a tension between the rhetoric of scientific objectivity that evoked the image of the camera as a "black box" and the imperatives within the photographic and scientific community that emphasized the need for expert skills and judgment.

Ultimately, professionalizing photographers and scientists made it essential that entry to scientific photography depended on knowledge of the theories and practices particular to each field of scientific study. Scientific photography mirrored the developing specialization of the sciences. The "time is coming," predicted one photographic journalist in 1859, "when the various branches of photography will have to be subdivided." Eventually, none could adopt it as a profession "without studying also the subjects of that peculiar branch to which they intend to apply themselves"—botany, zoology, archaeology, and the like.[38] This prediction came true, with consequences for the sexual division of labor in photography. Over the second half of the nineteenth century, women increasingly were excluded from scientific institutions. In most cases, they were restricted from the training in scientific research methods that scientific photography increasingly required.

Women in the Culture of Scientific Photography

Despite the masculinization of photography, especially scientific photography, some women made, circulated, and consumed photographs within the scientific market. The question of how many women made photographs in the genre of scientific photography is not easy to answer. As Naomi Rosenblum points out in *A History of Women Photographers*, women's contributions have not been understood in the context of the medium's overall development. In fact, women are nearly invisible in photographic history, criticism, and theory, and even current anthologies include work by few women photographers or theorists.[39] This is in part because work by women photographers— even outside scientific institutions—is difficult to find. Photographic societies were mixed in their acceptance of women, and frequently women, reflecting the view of the era in which they lived, did not regard their images as important enough to inventory and save. Sometimes the disappearance of their work was caused by misfortune, such as fire or flooding. Work by women sometimes is indexed under men's names, as with Harriet Tytler, who with her husband Robert Christopher spent six months photographing sites devastated by fighting in the Indian Mutiny of 1858. Their work was praised as the "finest that had ever been laid before [the Photographic Society]," but as Rosenblum points out, Harriet's contribution was ignored by scholars, who indexed the image under Robert's name only.[40] Though more women than we know about yet probably were making portrait likenesses, landscapes, and photographs of scientific phenomena before the twentieth century, women seldom were seen with cameras in fields, forests, observatories, or laboratories, or on battlegrounds where, as Susan Sontag wrote, men with cameras (and guns) were testing the new medium as a way to authenticate reality and promote ideological positions.[41] Despite these obstacles, some women achieved scientific recognition for their photographs. Some women showed and published their work in some of the same places as their male contemporaries, such as private albums and magazines. Far fewer of their works are in evidence in official scientific venues of photographic display, such as specialist meetings, atlases, and specialist publications. Even with such an iconic and pioneering figure as Julia Margaret Cameron, it is relevant that Cameron's photographs of John Herschel and Charles Darwin (compared, for example, with her Hypatia pictures) do themselves reinforce the male lone genius vision of science.[42]

Before the 1880s, the cumbersome, heavy equipment required by the photographer discouraged many people of both sexes, but especially limited the interest of women. The bulky apparatus was only part of the problem. To be a photographer before the widespread use of gelatin dry plates in the 1870s and 1880s meant familiarity with the entire process of producing a print. This meant knowing how to make collodion, to coat, sensitize, and develop a plate, to construct the silver bath, and to print, tone, and fix the prints. Though some deemed photography, in the words of one photographer, as "peculiarly suited to the female capacity, requiring neat-handed skill rather than strength, and delicacy of taste rather than endurance," others saw it as a messy process unfitting of a middle-class woman.[43]

6.2 Engraving for a magazine of a well-dressed woman photographing two friends, 1899.
Mary Evans Picture Library.

Nineteenth-century magazine illustrators often showed how a "lady" photographer could both photograph and retain "feminine" characteristics (figure 6.2).

In England, several of the women who took an active interest in the new paper-negative process, or calotype, were friends and relations of its inventor, William Henry Fox Talbot.[44] Photography allowed some women options for artistic and scientific expression. For Anna Atkins, one of the best known of the early women photographers and a member of Talbot's circle, the photographic study of plants was not just a serious hobby; it also provided her with a measure of scientific recognition. Between 1843 and 1854, Atkins, the daughter of John Children, vice-president of the Botanical Society of London, compiled her *Cyanotypes of British and Foreign Flowering Plants and Ferns* (1854), and her *Photographs of British Algae* in twelve serial parts. Her albums consist of brilliant, cobalt blue photograms: cameraless photographs of plant specimens laid directly on paper treated with a light-sensitive cyanide solution (figure 6.3).[45]

The promotion of botany as a legitimate female pursuit opened up paths for women in photography. Flower subjects were thought by many Victorians to be "naturally" suitable for women, and amateur instruction manuals helped develop the botanical approach.[46] During the early 1850s, Celia Glaisher, who like Atkins was a botanical artist, inaugurated her photographic study of British ferns. Glaisher was married to the nationally renowned scientist James Glaisher, who was for a time the President of the Royal Photographic Society and the editor of its official publication, the *British Journal of Photography*. From 1852 to 1853, Celia Glaisher compiled her album, *The British Ferns Represented in a Series of Photographs from Nature by Mrs. Glaisher from Specimens Selected by Mr. Newman*. The album includes ten plates of photographs, each containing the specific botanical name given in Sir James E. Smith's *English Flora*, Charles C. Babington's *Manual of British Botany*, and Edward Newman's *History of British Ferns*. As Glaisher wrote in the preface, "The Process of Photography is admirably adapted to making faithful copies of Botanical Specimens, more especially to illustrating the graceful and beautiful class of Ferns: it possesses the advantage over all others hitherto employed of displaying, with incomparable exactness, the most minute characteristics: producing absolute *fac-similes* of the objects, perfect both in artistic effect and structural details." Glaisher's artistry is evident in how she arranged the plants physically on the page, with the fern specimens arranged on plates to conserve space, with their leaves displayed (figure 6.4).

Women's contacts through husbands and other family members and friends with men of science also helped create opportunities in

6.3 Anna Atkins, cyanotype, "*Bryposis plumos,*" *Photographs of British Algae,* vol. 3 (London, 1844).
Linnean Society of London.

photography that they otherwise might not have had. Jessie Smyth collaborated on scientific projects with her husband, the Scottish astronomer Charles Piazzi Smyth, who shared and encouraged her photographic interests. The "Museum Camera," which they used to make cloud photographs, was so-called because it was set up in a room used as a museum in the Smyth's house in Ripon, in the north of England. Like Jessie Smyth, Lady Mary Rosse, who won the award from the Photographic Society of Ireland for "best paper negative" in 1859, worked closely with her husband in photography. Rosse took up photography around 1853, at the age of forty, while pregnant with her eleventh child. The "Leviathan of Parsonstown," the great six-foot reflecting telescope that she and her husband built at the Rosse family seat in Birr Castle, in the center of Ireland, was one of Lady Rosse's favorite photographic subjects. Using the paper process for which she later received an award from the Photographic Society of Ireland, Rosse travelled widely and made many landscape photographs, only one of which is known to survive. A darkroom that she used to make her photographs still survives little altered at Birr Castle, complete with camera cases, negative boxes, and a treasure trove of negatives and bottles of early photographic chemicals, as shown in a recent photograph (figure 6.5).

6.4 Celia Glaisher, "Bree's Fern." In *The British Ferns Represented in a Series of Photographs from Nature by Mrs. Glaisher from Specimens Selected by Mr. Newman* (London, 1852–1853). *Linnean Society of London.*

6.5 Lady Mary Rosse's photographic darkroom at Birr Castle. David Davison, photographer. *Reproduced courtesy of Birr Castle, Dublin.*

The development of new kinds of cameras and the creation of field clubs opened up new opportunities for women to make photographs for use in science at the end of the century. The technological advances in photography from 1880 to 1910 had definitive and far-reaching implications for middle-class English women's expanded involvement in the medium. The introduction of dry plates during the 1880s, the invention of celluloid roll film, and the development of the hand-held camera changed and expanded the already burgeoning mass amateur market that was making photography accessible to thousands. They made the camera a practical, simple, and easily handled device for both amateurs and professionals. During these years, field clubs provided a context for scientific pursuits by women amateur photographers at a time when women who wanted to do scientific work were excluded from major scientific organizations, such as the Geological Society of London and the Linnean Society, both of which denied access to women until the early twentieth century. Clubs such as the Belfast Naturalists' Field Club, for example, established in 1863 as the first unofficial academy of the natural sciences in Ireland, sponsored numerous field outings to study natural history and archaeology.[47] In this context, photography began to provide a role in documenting women's scientific labor. A photograph of "Mme. Christen," née S. M. Thompson, for example, shows her sitting on a rock wearing a long dress and a hat, hammer in hand, in the act of doing geology at a field club outing (figure 6.6).

The Irish amateur naturalist Mary Andrews was among the new group of women amateurs who pursued an interest in British geological photography. Andrews was the youngest daughter of Thomas Andrews, a chemist and the vice-president of Queens College from 1846 to 1849.[48] The 1891 *British Association Report* lists several six- by four-inch photographs made by Andrews. In one photograph of a railway cutting at Green Island railway station, Andrews depicted a section of boulder clay, twenty feet visible. In another photograph, she recorded the remains of a windmill pump, which was later published under her name in *Geological Magazine*.[49] The variety of geological sites in Northern Ireland that she depicted suggest that she travelled widely by railroad and carriage in pursuit of these records.

On the one hand, the field of photography allowed women like Rosse and Andrews options for artistic and scientific expression that they might not otherwise have had in the late nineteenth century, when most scientific organizations closed their doors to women. As one commentator remarked, when women participated in photography, they experienced "a sense of power which borders on the

6.6 Photograph of amateur geologist Mme. Christen, seated with hammer, on an outing of the Belfast Naturalists' Field Club, c. 1895.
Collection, Ulster Museum, Belfast. Photograph reproduced with the kind permission of the Trustees of the National Museums & Galleries of Northern Ireland.

supernatural."[50] On the other hand, women who expressed their artistic and scientific visions through photography often had difficulty having their work accepted as "scientific" by the male scientific establishment. The case of spirit photography suggests how women could be both enabled and constrained by the emergent masculinizing norms of science and photography.

Victorian spirit photography was a subgenre of photography in which "spirits" materialized on photographic plates, often as veiled figures, but occasionally as geometric shapes or blurs. Nineteenth-century spiritualism was a movement based on the idea that the spirit survives after the death of the body and that those spirits can communicate with the living, usually through a human medium. The movement spread to Britain from the United States in the 1840s and flourished at the turn of the century. Spiritualism was both a way for the disenfranchised to access social power and for the socially privileged to reinforce dominant attitudes. Mediums frequently materialized as Africans, Indians, and Arabs, often furthering the idea of the racially exotic "other" (figure 6.7).[51]

Mediums were primarily women and women were thought by many to be required for spirit photography.[52] Through spirit photography, women who were disenfranchised by traditional restrictions on women's agency could transcend certain boundaries and access power through this gender-specific site. The autobiography of the spiritualist medium and artist Georgiana Houghton, *Chronicles of the Photographs of Spiritual Beings and Phenomena Invisible to the Material Eye,* published in London in 1882, offers a view of the paradoxical situation for women involved in spirit photography. Around 1872, Houghton, who was already well known in London because of the publicity surrounding her spiritualist drawings, announced the discovery of the first genuine photographs of spirits made in Britain. One of her early spirit photographs shows Houghton with two friends as if connected by a blur, which she identified as a spiritual presence (figure 6.8). This photograph suggested to Houghton the "great outpouring of spiritual gifts in these days, especially to women, of whom there was to be a linked chain—as if to work with one another."[53] Ultimately, she made more than two hundred and fifty visits to a local photographic studio for the purpose of spirit photography in north London between 1872 and 1874. The photographs that she made, in collaboration with the studio photographer Frederick A. Hudson, allegedly a non-spiritualist, became icons that caused a huge public sensation. Houghton did not take the pictures herself, but she directed the operations and filled the crucial function of medium. She draws our attention to her own role in directing the operations in Hudson's studio. In a typical photographic séance, Houghton generally stood close to the wall, about halfway between the sitter and the camera.[54] "I told Mr. Hudson that after he had uncapped the lens, he was to wait for me to say, 'Now,' before covering it again"; the spirits "judge best how long an exposure is needful."[55]

PLATE VI. (Page 34.)
From Untouched Negative.

6.7 Spirit photograph with medium, Sarah Power, shown seated, c. 1890. Her domestic servant Eliza stands behind her. The "spirit" is the white blur above Power's head. In Thomas Slaney Wilmot, *Twenty Photographs of the Risen Dead* (London: Midland Educational Co., 1894), plate VI, 34.
Harry Ransom Humanities Research Center, The University of Texas at Austin.

6.8 Spirit photograph showing Georgiana Houghton (seated) with two friends, joined by a "blur" that she interpreted as a symbol of the union of their friendship. In Georgiana Houghton, *Chronicles of the Photographs of Spiritual Beings and Phenomena Invisible to the Material Eye* (London: E.W. Allen, 1882), plate 4.28.

Houghton's ability to see spirits was vital to the success of the operation, for apparitions were mostly invisible to the sitters and Hudson. Houghton's theory of how spirit photographs were made was that spirits manifested themselves with help from the power "*naturally* issuing forth" from the medium and the sitter.[56] Like ordinary portrait photographers, spiritualists thought the sitter's attitude had an important bearing on the likeness. Houghton impressed on sitters that they must try to be in a "perfectly healthy state of mind and body" at their sittings "so that their atmosphere may be thoroughly receptive of the spirit-presence."[57]

Rather than simply being oppressed by the male scientists who came to investigate her practice, Houghton courted their participation as a way to expand the market for the photographs, from which she derived an income. Spirit photography gave Houghton a public platform for her spirit photography practice. Through her controversial practice, she met some of the leading celebrities of the day. Her spirit photographs became a topic of conversation among spiritualists, photographers, and others, throughout England, France, Germany, and the United States. For a time, charging more than a dozen pounds per spirit photograph, she made enough money doing it to offset the expense—and, like other spirit photographers, she charged extra for scientific investigations.

However, though Houghton complied with demands from hostile investigators to scrutinize her practices—partly, as I have suggested, out of the desire to fuel the publicity for her work—she also expressed resentment of these intrusions. Houghton gives this account of one scientific "test": "I may here venture to suggest, that scientific men are very exacting, and have no kind of compunction as to the labour and fatigue that their fancies may entail."[58] Despite occasional irritation, she and Hudson expressed their willingness to comply with all scientific tests "however incongruous they might seem." She added, "all this preparation in a glass-house, on an intensely hot day in July, was decidedly a trial to Mr. Hudson and myself (neither of us young)." "Reaching up with chairs and stools to pin those tapes to the upper part of the screen; measuring, marking, etc., so as to make them equidistant; hammering nails where we could manage them; and trying various contrivances to make the arrangements perfect; were none of them occupations to leave us in the calm, placid state that mediumship demands."[59] According to Houghton, tests by scientists ruined the aesthetic quality of her pictures. For example, after one test in which a "scientific gentlemen" recommended taping Houghton in a grid so that she "stood as it were in a kind of prison," she complained: "Of course as a picture it will be very unsightly, with the double array of crossing lines from the scratched glass and the tapes."[60] Though she lamented that scientific tests often led to failure from an aesthetic point of view, however, Houghton shared scientists' view that spirit photographs should be judged by non-artistic criteria. For her, they were not just pictures: they were "valuable as marvellous evidence of spirit powers."[61] Most of the photographs would have only "the slightest interest" for any one as pictures," she explained, yet, like scientific experiments, "each manifestation is a step towards that which is yet to come."[62]

Spirit photography reflects the opportunities and constraints placed on women in Victorian science more generally. Though spirit photography offered women some access to scientific culture, it proved to be a tenuous access point from which women worked, for it both challenged and reinforced gendered properties of skill and agency. Gender roles were not transcended spatially, as the entry of women into spirit photography did not significantly disrupt Victorian principles of the alignment of men with the public sphere and women with the private, domestic, and spiritual realm. Though women who were involved with spirit photography encountered the crisis of trust that many Victorians associated both with the female photographic consumer and with spiritualism, spirit photography still flourished as a feminine pursuit within the broader realm of Victorian scientific image production.

Conclusion

Victorian scientific photographs of stars, bacteria, and even ghostly ancestors can tell us much about the gendered structure of scientific authority in Victorian England and the history of science more generally. Gendered properties of skill and agency were as significant in nineteenth-century collective sciences as they were in the eighteenth century, though Victorian discourses of photographic professionalism and democratization often obscured them.[63] Not long after photography's emergence in the mid-nineteenth century, women were entering the scene, but often in peripheral ways. Women were kept at the margins of scientific photography in part because many photographers blamed the feminization of photography for stimulating "bad taste." One response was to rescue photography by unifying (male) photographers in the spirit of fraternity. This return to "photographic masculinity"—one that hardened sexual boundaries that may have started to blur in the 1850s as women began to participate more in the practice—also entailed a turn to scientific photography as exemplary labor. By the late nineteenth century, entry into the new field of scientific photography required study not only of photography, but also of scientific research—a background few women had or could obtain. The formal principles of the genre of scientific photography thus evolved in relation to political principles that governed the recognition of science in the first place.[64]

Much more work is needed on scientific photography, but this much is already clear: Victorian scientific photography was a genre that was defined not just by its subject matter (plants, stars, lightning flashes, and animals) but by its production, circulation, and consumption in a system of signification governed by men of science, a system in which women rarely participated as full members and which they never controlled. Photographs made for scientific research purposes became visible as scientific objects, not merely through their placement in a system of scientific exchange, but as material demonstrations of masculine scientific skills and knowledge. Examination of the gendered processes involved in the naturalization of scientific photography suggests, moreover, that the cultural boundaries and meanings of scientific photography were as complex and contested as Victorian science itself.

Acknowledgments

The research for this essay was supported in part by a fellowship from the Center for Humanities at Wesleyan University. I thank the Wesleyan undergraduate students in my Technologies of Photographic Memory seminar for their ideas and responses, two anonymous referees, and the editors of this volume, Bernard Lightman and Ann Shteir, for their careful readings of drafts and extremely useful suggestions.

Notes

1. "The Privileges of the Wife of an Amateur Photographer," *Photographic News* (April 27, 1866): 199–200.

2. "The Trials of the Wife of an Amateur Photographer," *Photographic News* (October 11, 1867): 490.

3. "The Trials of the Wife of an Amateur Photographer," *Photographic News* (June 9, 1865), 271–72.

4. As Lorraine Daston and Peter Galison explain, the nineteenth century is identified as an age of scientific objectivity, in which a new conception of scientific photography as a practice that eliminated the eye and visual expertise of the artist—thus guaranteeing the objectivity of the image—first came into being. Lorraine Daston and Peter Galison, "The Image of Objectivity," *Representations* 40 (1992): 81–128.

5. "The 'Quarterly Review' on Photography," *Photographic News* (October 28, 1864): 519–20.

6. W. Dougall, "Photography as a Handmaiden to the Sciences, and a Recreation," *Photographic News* (June 23, 1882): 359.

7. On mechanical objectivity, see Daston and Galison, "The Image of Objectivity."

8. For critical scholarship on photographic truth that challenges the predominant model of photography as a medium with a fixed meaning or authority, see esp. Elizabeth Edwards, *Raw Histories: Photographs, Anthropology and Museums* (Oxford and New York: Berg, 2001); Jennifer Green-Lewis, *Framing the Victorians: Photography and the Culture of Realism* (Ithaca: Cornell University Press, 1996); Deborah Poole, *Vision, Race and Modernity: A*

Visual Economy of the Andean Image World (Princeton: Princeton University Press, 1997); Alan Sekula, "The Body and the Archive," in *The Context of Meaning: Critical Histories of Photography,* ed. R. Bolton (Cambridge, Mass.: MIT Press, 1989); John Tagg, *The Burden of Representation* (London: Macmillan, 1988); and Jennifer Tucker, "Photography as Witness, Detective and Impostor: Visual Representation in Victorian Science," in *Victorian Science in Context,* ed. Bernard Lightman (Chicago: University of Chicago Press, 1997).

9. Two excellent introductions to the body of works understood as "scientific" photographs are Jon Darius, *Beyond Vision* (Oxford: Oxford University Press, 1984); and Ann Thomas, ed., *Beauty of Another Order: Photography in Science* (New Haven: Yale University Press, 1997). In addition to these works, which encompass the diversity of scientific photography, biographies of individual photographers often illuminate their place in a wider scientific and technological context. See esp. Marta Braun, *Picturing Time: The Work of Etienne-Jules Marey* (Chicago: University of Chicago Press, 1992); Larry J. Schaaf, *The Photographic Art of William Henry Fox Talbot* (Princeton: Princeton University Press, 2000); and Rebecca Solnit, *River of Shadows: Eadweard Muybridge and the Technological Wild West* (New York: Viking Press, 2003). Certain subdisciplines of the history of science, especially the history of the human sciences of medicine and anthropology, approach the history and theory of photography as a crucial agent in the formation of scientific disciplines. See esp. Edwards, *Raw Histories;* Christopher Pinney, *Camera Indica: The Social Life of Indian Photographs* (Chicago: University of Chicago Press, 1997); and James Ryan, *Picturing Empire: Photography and the Visualization of the British Empire* (Chicago: University of Chicago Press, 1997).

10. A body of scholarship is starting to emerge that explores work by women in the visual culture of science. See, e.g., Barbara T. Gates, *Kindred Nature: Victorian and Edwardian Women Embrace the Living World* (Chicago: University of Chicago Press, 1998); and Ann B. Shteir, *Cultivating Women, Cultivating Science: Flora's Daughters and Botany in England, 1760–1860* (Baltimore: Johns Hopkins University Press, 1996).

11. M. A. Belloc, "The Future of Photography," *Photographic News* (September 17, 1858): 13.

12. Robert Hunt, "Photography Considered in Relation to its Educational and Practical Value," *Photographic News* (July 29, 1859): 243.

13. Jeanne Moutoussamy-Ashe, *Viewfinders: Black Women Photographers* (New York: Dodd, Mead, 1986), 7. Laura Wexler notes that in the nineteenth century this freedom of expression was "limited and asymmetrical." Wexler, *Tender Violence: Domestic Visions in an Age of U.S. Imperialism* (Chapel Hill: University of North Carolina Press, 2000), 1.

14. "Identification by Photography," *Photographic News* (September 26, 1874): 462–63.

15. "Photography and Bad Taste," *Photographic News* (April 10, 1863): 175.

16. "Questionable Subjects for Photography," *Photographic News* (November 26, 1858), 135–36.

17. Angus McLaren, *The Trials of Masculinity: Policing Sexual Boundaries, 1870–1930* (Chicago: University of Chicago Press, 1997).

18. A. E. Linkman, "The Itinerant Photographer in Britain 1850–1880," *History of Photography* 14 (January–March 1990): 60.

19. Lynda Nead, *Victorian Babylon: People, Streets and Images in Nineteenth-Century London* (New Haven: Yale University Press, 2000), 151.

20. Ibid.

21. "Prices and Merit, The Rank of Photographers," *Photographic News* (April 15, 1864): 190.

22. See, for example, "Photographic Dens and 'Doorsmen,'" *Photographic News* (August 16, 1861): 389. Originally printed in the *Daily Telegraph*.

23. John E. Cussans, "Photographs of Photographers," *Photographic News* (January 6, 1865): 6–7. Possibly there were concerns about scientific photography in relation to obscenity laws. See Edwards, *Raw Histories*, 154, n.28. I discovered a reference to the case of Henry Evans, trapped by plainclothes policemen for "obscene" photographs, actually made for the Ethnological Society, in "Prosecutions of Photographers," *Photographic News* (1870): 493.

24. Anonymous, "Visits to Noteworthy Studios," *Photographic News* (September 10, 1869): 434.

25. Anonymous, "The 'Quarterly Review' on Photography," *Photographic News* (October 28, 1864): 519.

26. "Prices and Merit, The Rank of Photographers," *Photographic News* (April 15, 1864): 190.

27. Professionalization was a common strategy for keeping women out of various domains, including science and photography. Many Victorians held that the Darwinian definition of "feminine" nature was essentially incommensurate with the "masculine" pursuit of science. See Evelleen Richards, "Redrawing the Boundaries: Darwinian Science and Victorian Women Intellectuals," in *Victorian Science in Context*, 119–42.

28. As Elizabeth Edwards points out, "Despite, or perhaps because of, the ubiquity of photography by the late nineteenth century, there is relatively little commentary on it, on specific images or practices, when compared with the huge body of material in collections and archives" (Edwards, *Raw Histories*, 34).

29. "Photographic Schools," *Photographic News* (October 5, 1860): 265.

30. "Preface," *Photographic News* (January 3, 1862): 2.

31. "The Cost of a Patent," *Photographic News* (November 2, 1860): 313.

32. "Celestial Photography," *Photographic News* (June 29, 1860): 98–99.

33. "Jotting for January," *Photographic News* (January 15, 1864): 29.

34. Lake Price, "On Composition and Chiaroscuro," *Photographic News* (March 23, 1860): 367.

35. Samuel Fry, "Lunar Photography," *Photographic News* (January 11, 1861): 17.

36. "Photographing the Moon," *Photographic News* (October 13, 1865): 486.

37. "Failure of Photographing the Eclipse in India," *Photographic News* (October 23, 1868): 507–508.

38. "Photography and Medical Science," *Photographic News* (November 4, 1859): 97.

39. As Naomi Rosenblum points out, just four women are among the ninety-six individuals included in Mike Weaver, ed. *The Art of Photography, 1839–1989* (New Haven: Yale University Press, 1989). There are also imbalances in acquisitions, exhibitions, and in the commercial market, where collectors are more eager to collect men's work, and prices are inequitable. Work by men on average yielded about fifty to sixty percent more than that by women in 1989. See Naomi Rosenblum, *A History of Women Photographers* (London: Abbeville Press, 1994), 7.

40. Rosenblum, *A History of Women Photographers,* 40.

41. Susan Sontag, *On Photography* (New York: Farrar, Straus and Giroux, 1977), esp. pages 14–20.

42. I thank an anonymous reviewer for pointing out this example and suggesting its significance. On Cameron's role in the creation of a Victorian visual portrait of genius, see, for example, the recent exhibition held at the National Portrait Gallery, *Julia Margaret Cameron: Nineteenth-Century Photographer of Genius* (London: National Portrait Gallery, 2003). For scholarship on the Hypatia pictures and Cameron's place in a longer history of women photographers, see, for example, Sylvia Wolf, *Julia Margaret Cameron's Women* (Chicago: Art Institute of Chicago, 1998).

43. Anonymous, "Employment of Women in Photography," *Photographic News* (January 25, 1867): 37–38.

44. Rosenblum, *A History of Women Photographers,* 40.

45. On Atkins, see esp. Carol Armstrong, *Scenes in a Library: Reading the Photograph in the Book, 1843–1875* (Cambridge, Mass.: MIT Press, 1998); Ann Bermingham, *Learning to Draw: Studies in the Cultural History of a Polite and Useful Art* (New Haven: Yale University Press, 2000): esp. pages 213–14; and Gates, *Kindred Nature.*

46. See Clarissa Campbell Orr, "Introduction," *Women in the Victorian Art World* (Manchester: Manchester University Press, 1995), 13.

47. See Arthur Deane, "The Belfast Natural History and Philosophical Society , 1821–1921." Unpublished manuscript on deposit in Ulster Museum, Geology Department (Belfast, 1924).

48. Today, many of Mary Andrews's original photographs for the British Association survive in the holdings of British Association photographs in the Geology Department at Ulster Museum. I extend warm thanks to Kenneth James for showing me this material.

49. See, for example, her photograph of an old pump used to remove water from a quarry, in Mary K. Andrews, "The Old Pump, Cultra, Co. Down," reproduced in W. W. Watts, "Notes on British Geological Photographs," *Geological Magazine* (1897): opp. 62.

50. Andrew Glendinning, "Dorchagraphy as a Social Rage," *Borderland* 4 (1897): 29–30; 30. Elizabeth Rigby (later Lady Eastlake) made a similar claim years earlier. See Rosenblum, *A History of Women Photographers,* 52.

51. See Logie Barrow, *Independent Spirits: Spiritualism and English Plebeians, 1850–1910* (London: Routledge, 1986); Judith R. Walkowitz, *City of*

Dreadful Delight: Narratives of Sexual Danger in Late-Victorian London (Chicago: University of Chicago Press, 1992); and Alison Winter, *Mesmerized: Powers of Mind in Victorian Britain* (Chicago: University of Chicago Press, 1998).

52. See esp. Joy Dixon, *Divine Feminine: Theosophy and Feminism in England* (Baltimore: Johns Hopkins University Press, 2001); and Alex Owen, *The Darkened Room: Women, Power, and Spiritualism in Late-Victorian England* (Philadelphia: University of Pennsylvania, 1990).

53. Georgiana Houghton, *Chronicles of the Photographs of Spiritual Beings and Phenomena Invisible to the Material Eye* (London: E. W. Allen, 1882), 78.

54. Ibid., 92.

55. Ibid., 146.

56. Ibid., 22.

57. Ibid., 142.

58. Ibid., 53.

59. Ibid., 52.

60. Ibid.

61. Ibid., 31.

62. Ibid.

63. Philosophers of the seventeenth and eighteenth centuries carefully weighted observation reports by the skill and integrity of the observer. See Lorraine Daston, "Objectivity and the Escape from Perspective" (1992), reprinted in *Science Studies Reader,* ed. Mario Biagioli (New York: Routledge, 1999), 110–23.

64. Jennifer Tucker, *Nature Exposed: Photography and Science in Victorian Britain* (Baltimore: Johns Hopkins University Press, 2005).

Chapter 7

SCRAPBOOK SCIENCE

Composite Caricatures in Late Georgian England

James A. Secord

An intriguing genre of caricature prints shows naturalists, scholars, tradespeople, and natural philosophers composed of the objects with which they deal: a physiognomist made of faces, an apothecary made of drugs, a mineralogist made of minerals, a conchologist made of shells.[1] Take, for example, *A Lady of Scientific Habits* (figure 7.1). Her whole body, even her face, is made of books, most with titles punning parts of the body ("Walker's Tracts" for the feet, "Craniology" for the head, and so forth). She is an author, carrying a scroll and a sheaf of pens for writing. Or take the *Entomologist* (figure 7.2), whose body and clothes are made of insects, from beetle boots to grasshopper hat. His arms are caterpillars, his legs the wings of moths and dragonflies: the species could be identified from scientific works. Only his face is identifiably human.

Such images have an immediate appeal and a clear relevance to gender. The collecting nets and foppish insect clothes have subverted the entomologist's masculinity; the bookish lady has mannish "scientific habits." He is all curves and flounces; she is all straight lines. The messages seem obvious, and such prints often are assumed to express stereotypes that have persisted for centuries. As a result, such "composite" or "emblematic" portraits (as they usually are called) often are reproduced but rarely analyzed. They are brought together as a coherent genre extending back to Mannerist paintings of the sixteenth century, continuing in the eighteenth century with depictions of tradespeople made from their tools, and revived in the twentieth century by the Surrealists. Such images almost never are discussed outside their appearance in high art, being seen as part of the unchanging domain of the "popular print." The examples in large national collections were almost all purchased during the twentieth century. Historians, reproducing the preferences of print curators and collectors, have had little to say about why they appeared and how they were used.

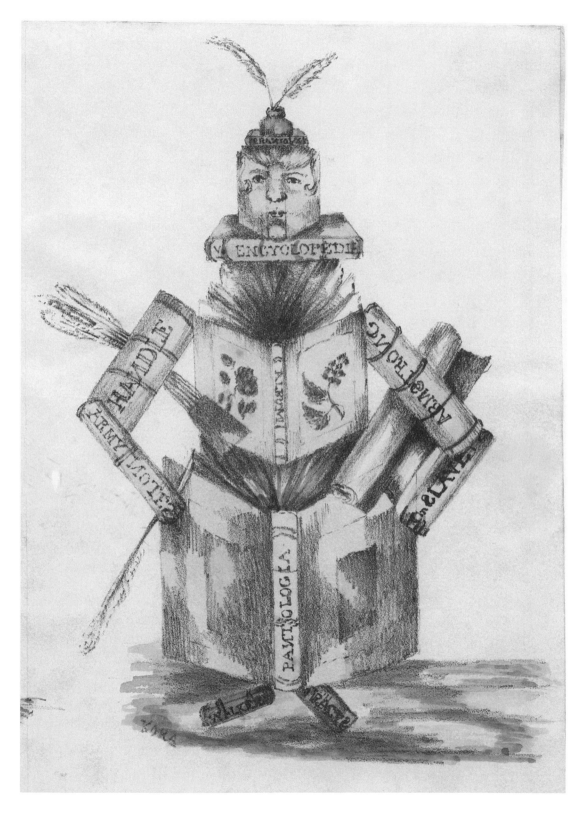

7.1 *A Lady of Scientific Habits.* Early nineteenth-century lithograph, signed KORA.
Author's collection.

7.2 *The Entomologist.* Drawn by G. Spratt, lithographed by G. E. Madeley, published by Charles Tilt, 1830. *Author's collection.*

Visual materials of this kind can open up new ways of understanding knowledge in relation to gender. After surveying the genre of composites from the Renaissance to the present, this chapter will focus on the decade leading up to the first Reform Act in England. The years before 1832 witnessed a remarkable flowering of composite caricatures, including many relating to science and medicine. This was a critical period for changes in the image of those engaged in pursuing knowledge, and it is also often taken as a turning point in the history of caricature, as the bawdy humor of the Regency gave way to mild drolleries and puns.[2] I will explore issues of gender in relation to production—reconstructing some of the principal series of prints and showing the practical work that went into making them—and also will tackle the more difficult question of how they were viewed and used. The results point to major forms of participation by women in science that have not been recognized previously.

The Arcimboldo Effect?

Everyone knows the celebrated pictures by the sixteenth-century Mannerist painter Giuseppe Arcimboldo (1537–1593), showing faces made out of fruits, flowers, vegetables, flames, birds, books, and tree branches. They appear on book jackets, posters, calendars, and birthday cards, and are hung in restaurants, shops, and dormitory rooms.[3] But this familiarity is recent. Up until the late nineteenth century, Arcimboldo makes only brief appearances in art histories, and his pictures rarely were reproduced. It was through his rediscovery by the Surrealists in the 1920s that Arcimboldo came to the wider attention of the art world, and his works gained the attention of a mass public only through the cannibalizing of Surrealist themes in twentieth-century advertising. In 1987, a large exhibition was held at the Palazzo Grassi in Venice, with a sumptuous catalogue published on both sides of the Atlantic. Entitled *The Arcimboldo Effect,* this featured spectacular illustrations from works identified as part of an Arcimboldo tradition.[4] But both illustrations and texts leapt from the sixteenth to the twentieth centuries.

Analogous works from intervening centuries sometimes are mentioned, and more often reproduced, but they have not been studied with anything like the care that has been devoted to many other kinds of images. Curators distinguish them as "popular prints"—as opposed to works of high art, especially by the old masters. As Sheila O'Connoll, organizer of a major exhibition at the British Museum, has remarked, the study of the cheap prints, although produced in huge numbers, scarcely has begun.[5] The problems and opportunities are similar to those presented in history of science by the study of so-called "popular science."[6] In both cases, as in studies of folk art and knowledge more generally, it is all too easy to assume that seemingly stable cultural forms reflect the unchanging needs of human nature.

What we can see, looking over the long term, are at least five categories of composite image:

- Composite images were in the first instance courtly wonders, with a role akin to theatrical spectacles or Galileo's telescope within the Medician court. They represented the overflowing fecundity and power of creation, and by implication that of their commissioning patrons. Arcimboldo worked in the courts of Maximilian II and Rudolf II in Prague, and his various series of paintings were made in their service and celebration. The paintings involved wit, defined not in the later sense of a joke, but as the "faculty that seeks out and realizes the hidden resemblances between things." Many of their details are tied symbolically to the imperial politics of the Habsburg court.[7]

- The dissemination of knowledge of Arcimboldo's paintings has not been much examined. During the seventeenth century, composite images continued to emerge from the culture of courtly festivals, notably the theatrical pageants of Louis XIV in France. Nicolas de l'Armessin issued nearly one hundred illustrations of the astrologer, physician, surgeon, printer, and so forth.[8] These focus on dress, so that the face and body are often recognizably human. During the eighteenth century, illustrations of trade costumes became a staple of printsellers, and composite transformations enjoyed sales as a curious offshoot among antiquarians and the virtuosi.[9] Composites also become significant within the British tradition of satirical prints, as is evident in their use in William Hogarth's *Some of ye Principal Inhabitants of ye Moon* (1724), in which the court, episcopacy, and law are composed of emblematic objects.[10]

- The third kind of composites is the subject of this chapter. As already noted, composites gained new prominence and meaning in the 1820s and early 1830s — less part of a systematic tradition of collecting by antiquarians, although that was still relevant, and instead within a new comic genre of "whims and oddities"; a form of humor familiar from journals such as *La caricature* in France and the early issues of *Punch* in England.

- Composite images gained a new currency in the context of the development of psychology and psychoanalysis early in the twentieth century. My impression, based on limited evidence, is that the number of composites declined from the 1840s onward, with a handful of examples known from the later nineteenth century. The twentieth-century revival had its roots in the Freudian psychology, as used on the one hand by the Surrealists and the other hand by modern advertisers. As part of a more general rejection of bourgeois cultural forms, the Surrealists claimed antecedents in Arcimboldo's paintings rather than in the bourgeois comic traditions of the nineteenth century.

- In the past quarter century, composite figures have become icons of postmodernity, as shown by Roland Barthes's *Arcimboldo* (1978) and Donna Haraway's use of Lynn Randolph's painting of the hybrid coyote/woman *Cyborg*.[11] Such images have been employed widely in characterizing the breakdown of distinctions between nature and culture, human and nonhuman, past and present, object and subject.

Each of these uses has produced a corresponding history, engendering an interpretation of potential visual precedents. In this way, a variety of unconnected images have been linked together as unproblematic expressions of (say) comic punning, inner psychology, or playful postmodernism. We find them intriguing today, but for reasons that have nothing to do with their appeal in earlier periods. Their generic constancy is only apparent. My aim is to locate the most neglected and least canonical of these images—those from the early nineteenth century—in a situated context of use.

The View from the Print Shop

In late Georgian London, the best place to see each week's new graphic production was the long side window of Charles Tilt's print shop on Fleet Street, which displayed a host of single sheet lithographs—fashion prints, landscapes, portraits, animals, flowers, and caricatures. Trade was brisk, and Tilt controlled a large proportion of the metropolitan lithographic trade, especially imports from the continent.[12]

What sorts of prints would a passerby have seen? Prints of trades continued to sell well, and composites parodied them as they had done in the eighteenth century. One series of hand-colored copper engravings, from an unknown publisher but probably dating from around 1800, included a greengrocer, brushmaker, tinker, poulterer, knife-grinder, old clothes-seller, and Italian peddler.[13] Among other publishers, Samuel Fores and Thomas Tegg had issued occasional items of this kind.[14] Orlando Hodgson sold a florist made of flowers and wearing a tulip dress as the work of Francesco Bartolozzi, perhaps the most famous engraver of his generation. Hodgson also produced a full-figure set of composites in copperplate around this time, including a *Leader of the Band* made from drums, violins, and other musical instruments.[15] Such prints, which typically showed composite bodies with human faces, drew not only on illustrations of trades but also on fashion plates and depictions of costume, both of which were growing in popularity.

Novelties were appearing in the shop windows as well: in the 1820s, the face also sometimes began to be made up of objects. This was part of a general shift in humor toward puns, puzzles, and visual conundrums, rather than any revival of interest in Arcimboldo's paintings. The printseller William Bernard Cooke of Soho Square in London issued mathematical personifications and other "whims" from the manuscript papers of the recently deceased caricaturist Henry Bunbury, with comic lines composed by the poet Thomas Hood. Cooke and Hood then joined forces a year later to produce the first really successful series of composites in Britain. These featured head and shoulders portraits drawn by various artists and accompanied by more of Hood's verses. The *Geometrician* is described as a

Friend of the Young Idea, in plane Geometry,—
He teaches it to shoot,—by Trigger-nometry![16]

Various artists provided drawings for at least eight of these characters, including an artist, grocer, blacksmith, dairy-maid, barber, chemist, cooper, and geometrician, as well as a *Man of Metal* by George Cruikshank. The prints were not inexpensive: Cooke charged 1 shilling apiece for colored copies, or 3s. 6d. for four. Only in later reissues (including four-to-a-sheet lithographed versions) did they become cheaper.

Hood became comic Britain's poet laureate for the next two decades, and his role in designing these composites is evident from his correspondence. In 1829, he sent (the appropriately named) Cooke "a recipe for making a cheesemonger," with ingredients ranging from a "glo'ster cheese for the face" to eggs for eyes and a "cheese-cutter for brows & nose."[17] Had this been issued, an artist would have worked Hood's accompanying sketch into a finished engraving. Hood was aware that combining diverse elements to make a single body had potential for comic comparison with the monster-making of the protagonist of Mary Shelley's famous novel. As one of his captions put it,

Frankenstein wanted to make man, & so, Sir,
He tried this first attempt upon a Grocer![18]

Such caricatures were "droll enough," as the *Literary Gazette* wrote in a review; "but we have had almost sufficient of such things."[19] Obviously, though, the buying public had not. For the next four or five years—around the time of the agitation leading to the first Reform Bill of 1832—a large number of composites of all kinds were issued.

The most extensive series was distributed by Tilt, which is not surprising given the position of his shop in the trade. The set was engraved by the jobbing lithographer George Madeley of Wellington Street off the Strand and drawn on stone by the botanist and accoucheur George Spratt of London. Born around 1784, Spratt was a member of the Royal College of Surgeons and active in the Medico-Botanical Society of London.[20] He was known for his illustrations of botanical books, including a two-volume *Flora Medica* (1829–1830) and wall-charts of poisonous plants. At least sixteen composites in his series were issued in 1830 and 1831, and probably more. No complete set is known, and they are nowhere catalogued together, so they need to be found piecemeal in print and ephemera collections. An advertisement showed subjects ranging from a greengrocer to an antiquarian, and the price, at 1s. 6d. each, 18 shillings for the original thirteen.[21] Like most items of this kind, they were produced in small numbers as lithographs, each carefully hand colored. They apparently sold well, for further subjects (including a *Gamester* made out cricket bats, playing cards, and a chessboard) were added later.[22] Other London publishers copied the format, and firms in Boston and Baltimore issued sets of the most striking images for the burgeoning American print market.[23]

The subjects are extremely varied and notable for the number of women. These include those familiar from the natural history of trades (a fishwife made of fish, a crockery-seller made of pots) as well as an unusual predominance of women engaged in intellectual pursuits. The *Circulating Library* features a woman composed of books, including botanical volumes with illustrations of flowers. The *Conchologist* shows a woman made of rare and beautiful shells, collecting specimens for herself. The *Botanist* is a woman of flowers, holding a specimen illustrating the Linnaean sexual system of classification.[24] The *Connoisseur* pictures a woman made of paintings examining paintings (figure 7.3). Her purse is, comically, a painting of a woman; however, she is not a casual dilettante, but looks critically with her lens, and the range of her study extends from such traditional feminine subjects as flower-paintings and miniatures to heroic male portraiture and images of antiquities.

Partners in Production

So how did Spratt, a vitual unknown in the print trade, come to produce the most extensive series of composite caricatures of the nineteenth century? One possibility relates to his career as a man-midwife and his authorship of an innovative obstetrical atlas, which featured flaps that revealed further elements of female anatomy as well as the progress of a pregnancy. This appeared in several editions, including ones issued in the United States with additional material. In the preface, Spratt took a firm stand on the value of illustrated works in medicine. "It is a well established fact," he wrote, "that in most branches of science delineations faithfully executed, convey more impressively to the mind the objects to be attained than mere descriptions possibly can." This was particularly the case with the use of the forceps, Spratt believed, which most practitioners employed so infrequently that "many years may elapse before it is necessary even to look at them." Well-executed illustrations could jog the memory of early training.[25]

Spratt's position as a man-midwife and author of a leading obstetrical atlas might suggest a parallel between his activities as a caricaturist and the wider history of the medical treatment of women. In both cases, the female body could be viewed as object to be taken apart and examined piecemeal.[26] For example, the last plate of his

7.3 *The Connoisseur*. Drawn
by G. Spratt, lithographed by
G. E. Madeley, published by
Charles Tilt [c. 1830].
Mary Evans Picture Library.

atlas shows a full frontal view of the abdomen, with flaps that can be
pulled down to expose the uterus, and finally a pair of unborn twins.
In another characteristic plate, the flaps expose successive views of
the forceps in action, so that the instrument could appear as a natural part of the female anatomy (figure 7.4). Such images were significant elements in the attempt to replace traditional midwifery with
the tools of scientific medicine and male authority. Spratt's composites might be thought to promote a similar vision, in which the
human body has no substance other than a face and (occasionally) a
pair of hands. As with the female subjects depicted in the atlas, corporeal reality is constructed by the viewer. The "woman of mind" is,

quite literally, disembodied. In this way, the *Connoisseur, Conchologist,* or *Circulating Library* might be interpreted as an attack on the intellectual activities of women.

There are attractions to this analysis, in which Spratt becomes something of a Frankenstein himself; but I no longer believe that it helps in understanding the array of composite images issued over his signature. For one thing, it attributes too much to the artist's potential motivations and interests—when surely, as will be discussed in the next section, the main issue is why there was a market for the series in the first place. It assimilates the caricatures to the very different visual genre of a specialized medical reference work, making a connection that no contemporary (not even the pun-loving Hood) would have found compelling. Moreover, it focuses solely on iconography and ignores the practical context in which the images were made.

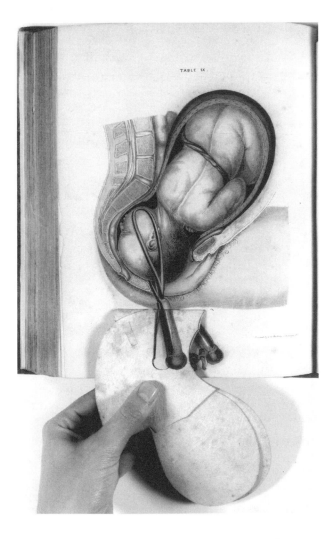

7.4 Illustration of forceps technique. Drawn by G. Spratt, lithographed by G. E. Madeley, from George Spratt, *Obstetric Tables* (London: John Churchill, 1833), tab. 9.
By permission of the Syndics of Cambridge University Library.

So we need to go back to the print world of late Georgian London. In this setting, the obvious starting point is that Spratt and Madeley collaborated not just on a series of caricatures, but on all of the medical and botanical works issued under Spratt's name. Several of these projects, such as a supplementary volume of William Woodville's *Medical Botany* (1832), involved dozens of plates in situations where quality of production in coloring could be a matter of life and death. In short, the crucial connection between the composites and Spratt's other works is not a vague iconographical parallel, but a working relationship exploiting the commercial possibilities of lithography. Spratt's knowledge as artist, naturalist, and medical man could combine with Madeley's practical expertise as a printer to the benefit of both. The result was a diverse range of works: medical atlases, botanical works, wall-charts, and separate prints.

More speculatively, there are signs that the creation of the composite caricatures was a family project, involving a substantial contribution from women. Spratt's wife grew up in the country and had a keen interest in nature. After her husband's death in the early 1840s, it appears that she and her daughter Julia set up a short-lived drawing school at Chester Terrace, Eaton Square.[27] In her only signed work (as Mrs George Spratt), *The Language of Birds* (1837), she wrote of the eloquence of "the feathered orators" and traced "a similitude between our best biped orators and those of the fields and groves." This small anthology of ornithological gems has gorgeous plates, which she designed and probably colored. Most important, the book mentions that she had "frequently assisted others in their endeavours to amuse or instruct the public" and had submitted "trifles" to the press on earlier occasions, though not under her own name.[28] For his part, George Spratt acknowledged that all coloring of plates in his medical works had been under his direct supervision, which makes a domestic operation likely.

Indications are, then, that we are dealing with a small family business in which husband and wife (and perhaps their children) were engaged to produce works to be printed at Madeley's lithographic press, and sold at his premises and those of Tilt and other publishers. Spratt's wife almost certainly would have been involved in coloring the composites, whose standard is unusually high, and probably in their design, given her artistic abilities and natural history interests. The project was built on the possibilities of drawing on stone, a relatively new technique that was both cheaper and more readily learned than the difficult process of engraving on metal. Skills in drawing and coloring, such as those possessed by Spratt's wife and daughter, were becoming more widely distributed in the early decades of the nineteenth century, and could be put to commercial use. The situation could be compared with that of the Sowerby family's natural history publishing business of the same period—on a small scale, the kind of enterprise that Leonore Davidoff and Catherine Hall traced in *Family Fortunes*.[29] The composite caricatures thus can be seen as the offshoot of a small domestic enterprise combining male and female labor, based on an established relationship with a specialist printer.

Figures in the Scrapbook

This leaves us with the question of why composite images became so widespread in the 1820s and early 1830s. To find an answer, we need to know more about who bought and enjoyed them; but here we come up against all the usual difficulties of finding out about the audiences for ephemeral visual material. This simply is not the kind of topic that tends to be mentioned in diaries, letters, or reviews. The problem is seemingly intractable, and for a while I feared that this chapter was going to be impossible to write.

A solution begins to emerge if we look not at reproductions, but at the originals, and not at their front sides, but at their backs. Virtually every example I have found, even in large public collections, is not in the pristine condition favored by print collectors, but shows signs of having been cut down and pasted into a scrapbook or album. This is the primary context in which these prints were used, and it is crucial to understanding them today. Thus the *Lady of Scientific Habits* (figure 7.1), a lithograph broadly similar to those produced by Spratt and Madeley, appears to have been placed in two albums at different times: the original paper is glued onto another sheet, which has spots of glue and remaining pieces of a different type of paper. These traces allow other evidence to fall into place. For example, the advertisement for Spratt and Madeley's series notes that the prints are "all neatly coloured, and adapted for the Scrap-Book, &c."[30]

Scrapbooks appear to have been most popular among women and girls, and could be objects of high status and considerable cost. The word "scrapbook" first came into use in the 1820s. Combining features of the commonplace book and the album of prints, the scrapbook served as an aesthetically pleasing female version of these older genres, uniting tasteful arrangement with a neat display of witty sayings, epigrams, curious facts, and visual surprises. As Thomas Hood wrote, scrapbooks were "theirs to insert bon-mots, riddles, anecdotes, caricatures, facetiae of all kinds."[31] The material could be clipped from newspapers, fashion magazines, or purpose-made sheets of material sold by publishers.[32] Such printed materials could be combined with original watercolors, drawings, and sayings, so that the ensemble reflected its owner's literary and artistic accomplishments. Friends, family, and visiting celebrities were asked to add some lines or a sketch, a practice ritually dreaded by poets and men of learning. The great aim was to compile an original anthology of genius and wit, a tangible memorial of wider networks of sociability.

The extraordinary popularity of scrapbooks is related to the rise of other domestic activities such as fancy work, which involved pasting scraps on wooden boxes, portable screens, and other objects. There was a growing market in ready-made blank albums. Leather or silk bound volumes, often of great beauty, were specially produced and sold at stationers and printsellers. One of them tells its story in Louisa Henrietta Sheridan's "The Adventures of an Album" (1831):

> I am not one of the ordinary class of common-place books of two-guinea value, to be found ready made and ready-faded at every repository of arts in the kingdom: no, I am an Exclusive, made in London for a lady who spared no expense to be considered one of the elite of a country-town. How much I was admired on my arrival!—and indeed I do not wonder at it, when I think of my splendid Burgundy-coloured binding richly gilt, and my pages of the purest white occasionally relieved by a tint of *coleur-de-rose,* which were preserved from the intrusive gaze of the unprivileged by a lock in the form of little-delicate hands.[33]

Such a book, as it grew under the careful attention of its owner, became an emblem of individual taste and intelligence, to be admired, enjoyed, and emulated by others.

The opening page was usually the most elaborate. In figure 7.5, published for the luxury market, a dozen women open their scrapbooks to invite contributions. The group is framed by the kind of prints and drawings that might be found inside: images of stock characters (a poacher, a rat-catcher); comic situations (a farmer's wife in a wheelbarrow captioned "Sleeping Beauty in the Wood"); together with flowers, fairy tales, and foreign costumes. At the bottom of the page, a tiny boy with crutch, wooden leg, and hat in hand leads the female chorus. Beggars often featured on scrapbook title pages. Not only were they seen to be appropriately picturesque, but their presence also showed that well-bred ladies acknowledged their own tendency to pester for contributions. Genteel women had a leading role in charitable philanthropy, but in asking for donations themselves they could claim to be led by the deserving poor. Ironic reversals of this kind, like references in prints to poaching and other potentially disruptive activities by working people, were important in maintaining a sense of social stability.[34]

7.5 Opening page for scrapbook album, published by Rudolf Ackermann.
Trade Prints and Scraps 1, John Johnson Collection, The Bodleian Library, University of Oxford.

As with other domestic activities pursued primarily by women, the making of scrapbooks attracted satire. Charles Lamb mocked them as:

> Those books kept by modern young ladies for show,
> Of which their plain Grandmothers nothing do know,
> A medley of scraps, half verse and half prose,
> And some things not very like either—God knows.
> The first soft effusions of beaus and of belles,
> Of future Lord Byrons and sweet L. E. L.'s;
> Where wise folk and simple both equally join,
> And you write *your* nonsense that I may write mine.[35]

Contemporary depictions show albums being enjoyed by people of different ages, races, sexes, and classes—old men, girls, children, servants, even in one case a cat.[36] Scrapbooks could enhance conversation and help in avoiding awkward silences; they provided "subjects" for talk, without demanding extensive learning or pedantry. During the 1830s, however, scrapbooks lost much of their fashionable, aristocratic aura. Although they continued to be produced in large numbers, their use was increasingly associated with children and the commercial middle classes. Separately published composite caricatures dealing with learning more or less declined at the same time; they went out of style with the scrapbooks they were made to fill.

Fashionable Pursuits

Making and appreciating scrapbooks of the specific kind being discussed here demanded a sophisticated understanding of the grounding of Romantic literary culture in clipping, cutting, pasting, abridging, reviewing, and recycling. Scrapbook humor was polite, refined, "droll"—intended to raise a genteel smile rather than a laugh. It was based upon visual and verbal punning, with bits and pieces coming together in unexpected ways. In that sense, it was a humor that relied on the comic possibilities of the anthology, a favorite literary form of this period.[37] From the mid-1820s, the fashion for scrapbooks led publishers to produce annuals, a new kind of anthology that targeted the emerging Christmas market with pre-packaged medleys of pictures, portraits, poems, and stories.[38] These annuals in turn spawned parodies and "humorous" versions, most famously Thomas Hood's *Comic Annual* (1830–1842). These are packed with composite caricatures (figure 7.6).[39] Hood used the opportunity to reach a wider, regular, and more lucrative market with the same sort of images that had proved so popular as separate sheets. Examples ranged from a fan-shaped *Fanny* and a stony *Captain Rock* to "fancy

FANNY.

FANCY PORTRAIT—GALILEO.

FANCY PORTRAIT:—M. BRUNEL.

FANCY PORTRAIT, AUDUBON.

CAPTAIN ROCK.

7.6 Composites and fancy portraits from Thomas Hood, *Comic Annual* (London: Charles Tilt, 1830), facing pages 17, 46, 85; (London: Charles Tilt, 1831), facing page 174; (London: A. H. Baily, 1836), facing page 147.
Author's collection.

portraits" of celebrated individuals, including a telescope-eyed *Galileo,* bird-like *Audubon,* and tunnel-mouthed *Brunel.* Many of these images appear in the book as unpaginated plates without text on the other side, to facilitate their use in scrapbooks.[40]

Compared with the ribald caricatures of James Gillray and the early work of George Cruikshank, the humor in scrapbooks avoided sexual innuendo and divisive references to politics, religion, and class. The change in tone was part of a deeper transformation of attitudes associated with a feminized drawing room culture. Amazing to modern readers, even Hood's *Comic Annual* was seen as too risqué, which is how Louisa Henrietta Sheridan was able to justify starting up her competing *Comic Offering.*[41] The contexts in which mixed conversations could take place, and what could be said, were changing rapidly.

An important part of this shift in sensibility reflects the difficulties that many, especially in the middle classes, felt in judging character and status. The clothes a person wore, or how they acted in public, might bear little relation to who they actually were. The growing concern with mismatches between appearance and reality is evident in the popularity of composites, and is revealed most clearly in depictions of occupations and roles that were newly politicized—those involving women and the working classes in particular.[42]

The change in tone and audience is best seen in prints illustrating in different ways practitioners of the same trade. Compare the tailor published by Thomas Tegg in 1811 (figure 7.7), with the image lithographed by Madeley (figure 7.8) some twenty years later. The London tailoring trade throughout this period was divided into militant "Flints," who formed clubs to resist their masters and who derided unorganized workers as "Dungs." Tegg's *Flint*—made out of cloth, scissors, irons, and buttons—confronts the viewer with a menacing air. He stands defiant, feet apart, a provocatively exposed "bodkin" between his legs. Even the blades of his scissors are open rather than safely shut. Cucumbers, the tailor's cheap food during the slow summer season, spill from his pocket. His head is a cabbage, a reference to the term used for the offcuts and trimmings that tailors appropriated as a right of their trade.[43] The lack of a human face, combined with a sense of racial otherness, underlines the angry, alienated character of an exploited work force. This is a crude, quickly engraved print: a claim for the rights of masculine labor unlikely to have been displayed in the homes of the gentry.

Madeley's *Tailor* is very different. Although also made from the tools of his trade (and with the symbolic cabbage at the center of his body), the overall effect is delicately aesthetic—an impression enhanced by the quality of the hand-coloring and the subtle effects of

7.7 *A Flint*. Published by Thomas Tegg, 1811. *Science and Society Picture Library, Science Museum, London.*

lithography. The image, though not signed by Spratt, is similar in style and purpose. It raises the specter of assertive labor through the cabbage and the symbolic tools of the trade, only to tame the fear through humor. The same also might be said of *An Original Portrait of Captain Swing,* which showed a rick-burner made out of phosphorous matches, flames, and other implements of destruction. This lithograph was published late in 1830, around the time that rural laborers throughout the south of England were destroying the property of farmers who used threshing machines; the protesters signed their letters "Captain Swing." Neutralized in a funny print, the anonymous terror of rural protest could become a clever joke.[44]

Disputes about the character of labor are just as central to understanding the composite prints of naturalists and natural philosophers,
which poke fun at the obsessive pursuit of learning. The *Entomologist,
Mineralogist, Connoisseur,* and so forth comment on the relation
between mental and physical work. Especially when juxtaposed with
others in the Spratt series, such as the *Fruiterer* or *Greengrocer,* these
images assimilate intellectual labor into the history of trade: Men and
women of learning became craft workers whose knowledge and skill
is embodied physically. This can be seen in a mid-nineteenth-century
scrapbook page (figure 7.9), in which *China*—an orientalized
porcelain-seller—has been pasted next to a woman conchologist gathering sea shells. In contemporary usage, conchology was not an occasional or dilettantish activity, but a serious scientific pursuit. So just as

China is simultaneously an assemblage of commodities, a hawker of goods, and a racial type, so too has the *Conchologist*'s labor made her precisely what she is.

Nowhere is the message about intellectual work more evident than in the *Lady of Scientific Habits* (figure 7.1). Here the word "habits" has its full double meaning—both clothes, and things habitually done. This may have been an amateur production, as the backwards letters may suggest a lack of familiarity with lithographic technique; in any event, the effect is to heighten the sense of the incongruity.[45] The pun on "habits" was especially appropriate to such prints when viewed in the context of scrapbooks, which often featured hand-colored plates of the latest Paris and London styles from the *Lady's Magazine, La Belle Assemblée,* and similar periodicals. Through association with such images, the composites became comments on intellectual fashion. Thus Spratt's *Conchologist* has lost herself in her single-minded pursuit of beautiful shells, arranged to mimic the tight waist, large bonnet, and leg-o'-mutton sleeves that were popular at this time. As parodies of fashion, the composites targeted feminine men as well as women. Spratt's *Entomologist* (figure 7.2) exemplifies a commonplace satirical subject of the Regency, the overdressed dandy concerned only with appearances, subverting the normal boundaries of gender through excess. The point of a follower of fashion chasing unselfconsciously after scientific specimens would have been obvious. "For dandies as for women," as one commentator has noted, "to seem is to be."[46] For contemporary viewers, such figures were understood most easily as fops.

7.9 Scrapbook page with *China* (1830) and the *Conchologist* (1830), drawn by G. Spratt and lithographed by G. E. Madeley. *Author's collection.*

Were such images simply intended to ridicule feminine learning and female accomplishments? Were they the visual equivalents of misogynist satires on learned women and bluestockings? The answer is no. As already noted, individual artists and publishers were unlikely to be concerned with marginalizing learning or excluding women from cultivating natural history and natural philosophy. In commercial terms, if nothing else, this would have been counterproductive; it was in their interest to encourage as wide an audience as possible to become engaged in the pursuit of knowledge.

Considering the images from the perspective of use supports this view. Their popularity in scrapbooks suggests that women used these caricatures as a way of expressing their own, often ambiguous, attitudes toward learning. Certainly to include such pictures in an album was to assert some kind of interest in science. Part of the fun in sharing composite prints with others would have involved identifying the specific objects out of which the figures were assembled. They could examine the shells that made up the *Conchologist,* or the specimens in the print of the woman labeled *Fish.* Scrapbooks, which often included natural history prints and actual specimens, could become a first step in participating in scientific practice.[47]

Direct evidence of the appropriation of science through scrapbooks is apparent in figure 7.10, which shows a composition dominated by the *Entomologist* and *Mineralogist.* The success of such a page as a conversation piece depended not only on such ready-made bits of humor, but also upon its owner's skill in selecting, clipping, arranging, and pasting. The pictures are cut out with exquisite care, the finest details preserved. The whole is tastefully composed, with a good sense of balance among the different elements. We are used to thinking of such skills in relation to eighteenth-century illustrated natural history works; but the same concern with pleasing patterns and carefully planned assemblages can be found in the nineteenth century (and the twenty-first, for that matter) as well.[48]

In this case, the detail and precise coloring of the figures invites the viewer to identify specific natural history objects and tools. The entomologist uses special collecting nets to capture new creatures of the kind with which he is made. Similarly, the mineralogist is composed of quartz, mica, fluorite, malachite, mica, agate, coral, and fossil wood. He sits on a rocky landscape with mountains in the distance, and lights a pipe—which, appropriately, is a blowpipe used to analyze mineral specimens. Such an instrument was common enough not to be obscure, but specialized enough not to be obvious.[49] Anyone could laugh at the idea of a mineralogist made of minerals, but pleasure in a joke about a blowpipe depended on being at least a little bit of a mineralogist oneself.

7.10 The *Entomologist* and *Mineralogist* (1830), drawn by G. Spratt and lithographed by G. E. Madeley, on a scrapbook page with insects from contemporary natural history works. As in figure 7.9, the original impact of this composition depended upon its effective use of color.
Puzzle Pictures Folder, John Johnson Collection, The Bodleian Library, University of Oxford.

But the most striking feature of this page is the array of caterpillars, butterflies, and moths that surround the two composite naturalists. Taken from hand-colored scientific works, these not only fill out the design, but also comment on the nature of natural history itself. Both in the design of the caricatures and in their use in on this scrapbook page, the distinction between collector and collected is broken down in practice. By creating an image of this kind, a woman could assert an interest in knowledge, while distancing herself from any idea that she was consumed by a passion for only one subject. The entomologist and mineralogist become natural history specimens themselves, stuck like insects in her collection.

Knowledge in Pieces

Recovering the gendered meanings of visual materials from the past requires us to think first and foremost about how they were used. Seen from this perspective, the composite prints of the late Georgian era were not derivative versions of Arcimboldo's paintings, expressions of folk *mentalities,* or precursors of Surrealist fantasies; rather, they derived from an elite drawing room culture specific to the early decades of the nineteenth century. With their complex visual and verbal puns, the prints were open to a wide variety of readings, which is precisely why they were valued as spurs to social interaction.

In scrapbook albums, more than in any other cultural form of the late Georgian period, we can see women actively appropriating and commenting on the world around them. This was a place where they could engage, even if in a highly specific way, with the findings of natural history and natural philosophy. Today, the vast majority of scrapbooks that come on to the market are broken up and sold by dealers for individual prints, thereby destroying a key cultural form of the early nineteenth century. The founders of the outstanding collections of ephemera, such as John Johnson (whose collection is now in the Bodleian Library at Oxford), derived much of their early material by disaggregating women's scrapbooks. As always in the history of collecting, new forms of ordering, selling, and displaying obliterate traces of earlier ones.[50] Partly as a result, the significance of scrapbooks in the wider intellectual life of this period in Britain has yet to be recognized. As I have argued, they provided a vital opportunity for participation during a period before science became dominated by ideals of specialist expertise.

Once we recognize the significance of the scrapbook, it becomes possible to see just how unlikely it is that composite caricatures would have been produced or viewed as attacks on women's intellectual powers. As I have suggested, the opposite is more likely to have been the case. The composites, by mocking only the extreme manifestations of female learning, could be taken implicitly to validate its pursuit in moderation. Composites showing learned women, such as the *Connoisseur, Conchologist,* and *Lady of Scientific Habits,* do not appear to have been used to question the suitability of such activities for women, but rather the pursuit of science as a self-consuming vocation. Similar warnings about the dangers of the single-mindedness of learning are of course central to the message of *Frankenstein* and other writings by educated women. In an analogous way, statements of modest aims often preface works that display the most acute forms of learning and skill. As Spratt's wife said in the preface to her *Language of Birds,* "this is not a scientific work, but one intended solely for amusement."[51]

The ultimate joke was that the composites could be read self-referentially as parodies of an obsession with making scrapbooks. Like the volumes into which they were pasted, the caricatures were piecemeal assemblages, using juxtaposition, contrast, and variety to encourage those who saw them to interpret them in different ways. Again, this is most explicit in the case of the *Lady of Scientific Habits.* As anyone who pasted this print in her scrapbook would have recognized, the picture was an ironic comment on taking the activity too seriously, for at the center of the woman's body is a volume labeled "Album." Too earnest in her pursuits, the scientific lady has become the scrapbook that she keeps.

Acknowledgments

Many thanks to seminar groups at the universities of York (Toronto), Oxford, Leeds, Harvard, and Cambridge for comments on this essay, and to many friends for comments, suggestions, and additional examples. I am especially grateful to Katherine Anderson, Patricia Fara, Vera Keller, Julie Anne Lambert, Bernard Lightman, Anne Secord, Wendy Sheridan, and Ann Shteir.

Notes

1. The *Physiognomist* is in the Wellcome Iconographic Collection and the Science Museum Library (SCM-2002–611), and is reproduced in Alison Winter, *Mesmerized: Powers of Mind in Victorian Britain* (Chicago: University of Chicago Press, 1998), 30; copies of the *Itinerant Apothecary* are in the collections of the Whipple Museum of the History of Science and the Science Museum Library (SCM 1989–451/3). The other figures mentioned are discussed below.

2. For the history of caricature in England, see M. Dorothy George, *Hogarth to Cruikshank: Social Change in Graphic Satire* (London: Viking, 1987); Diana Donald, *The Age of Caricature: Satirical Prints in the Reign of George III* (New Haven: Yale University Press, 1996); and her *Followers of Fashion: Graphic Satires from the Georgian Period* (London: Hayward Gallery Publishing, 2002). On science, the best starting point is Ludmilla Jordanova, "Feminine Figures: Nature Display'd" in her *Nature Displayed: Gender, Science and Medicine, 1760–1820* (London: Longman, 1999), 21–47.

3. Werner Kriegeskorte, *Arcimboldo* (Köln: Benedict Taschen, 2000) offers a readily available introduction and bibliography.

4. *The Arcimboldo Effect: Transformations of the Face from the Sixteenth to the Twentieth Century* (London: Thames and Hudson, 1987). See also F. C. Legrand and F. Sluys, *Arcimboldo et les arcimboldesques* (Brussels: La Nefce Paris, 1955). For criticism of this position from an early modern perspective, see Thomas DaCosta Kaufmann, *The Mastery of Nature: Aspects of Art, Science, and Humanism in the Renaissance* (Princeton: Princeton University Press, 1993); I am grateful to Vera Keller for this reference.

5. Sheila O'Connell, *The Popular Print in England, 1550–1850* (London: British Museum Press, 1999), 6–7; also valuable is Diana Donald, *What is a Popular Print?* (Manchester: Whitworth Art Gallery, 2000).

6. For these issues, see Roger Cooter and Stephen Pumfrey, "Separate Spheres and Public Places: Reflections on the History of Science Popularization and Science in Popular Culture," *History of Science* 32 (1994): 237–67.

7. Kaufmann, *Mastery of Nature,* 128.

8. The complete series is illustrated in Nicolas de Larmessin, *Les costumes grotesques et les metiers,* ed. Henri Veyrier (Paris: Henri Veyrier, 1974).

9. See the catalogue for the exhibition in the Bodleian Library by Julie Anne Lambert, *A Nation of Shopkeepers: Trade Ephemera from 1654 to the*

1860s in the John Johnson Collection (Oxford: Bodleian Library, 2001), and the auction catalogue for *The Norman Blackburn Collection of Images of Trade and Industry* (London: Phillips, de Pury & Luxembourg, 2001).

10. M. Dorothy George, *Catalogue of Political and Personal Satires Preserved in the Department of Prints and Drawings in the British Museum* (London: British Museum, 1949), vol. 9, 72; one of the figures, a pregnant servant made of pots, is illustrated in O'Connell, *Popular Print,* 116.

11. Roland Barthes, *Arcimboldo* (Milan: Franco Maria Ricci, 1978); Donna J. Haraway, *Simians, Cyborgs, and Women: The Reinvention of Nature* (London: Free Association Books, 1991), plate 1.

12. Henry Vizetelly, *Glances back through Seventy Years: Autobiographical and other Reminiscences,* 2 vols. (London: Kegan Paul, 1893), 1: 108–10; for an illustration of the shop, see George Cruikshank, "March," in *The Comic Almanack, for 1835* (London: Charles Tilt, [1834]), facing page 9. On print shops generally, see Donald, *Age of Caricature,* 19–21.

13. This series is in Trades and Professions 3 (27), John Johnson Collection, Bodleian Library, University of Oxford, and can be viewed online through the Visual Arts Data Service (http://vads.ahds.ac.uk).

14. Good examples are in the Puzzle Pictures Folder, John Johnson Collection; the British Library (see George, *Catalogue,* vol. 9, 71–72); and the Science Museum Library.

15. Copies of the bandleader, carpenter, fruiterer, and gardener were on sale at Grosvenor Prints of London in June 2002; I have not found copies in public collections. Good examples of many of the prints issued by Cooke in their various states are in the Puzzle Pictures Folder of the John Johnson collection, which also has the Bartolozzi engraving.

16. The verses for the *Chymist* (made out of retorts, alembics, and other tools for making materia medica) are as follows: "A Chymist this—your shoulders do not shrug,—/ Why not—when Malthus proves mankind a Drug!" A copy of this print, and of the *Geometrician,* is in the Whipple Museum of the University of Cambridge.

17. T. Hood to W. B. Cooke, [summer 1829], in Peter F. Morgan, *The Letters of Thomas Hood* (Toronto: University of Toronto Press, 1973), 121.

18. Copy dated July 1, 1834 in the Puzzle Pictures Folder, John Johnson Collection, Bodleian Library, University of Oxford.

19. *Literary Gazette,* July 25, 1829, 491.

20. P. J. and R. V. Wallis, *Eighteenth Century Medics* (Newcastle Upon Tyne: Project for Historical Bibliography, 1988), 563. Spratt appears to have died after 1840, but biographical information about him is sparse.

21. Thomas Hood, *Comic Annual* (London: Charles Tilt, 1831), Advertisements, 8.

22. The *Gamester* can be found in the Puzzle Pictures Folder, John Johnson Collection.

23. These sets are in the Boston Athenaeum and the American Antiquarian Society respectively. They are described by Sally Pierce in *Early American Lithography: Images to 1830* (Boston: Boston Athenaeum, 1997), 85, and eight are produced in color on the cover.

24. Copies of these prints are available as follows: *Fish* (SCM 1989–451/1, Science Museum Library); *Crockery* (SCM-2002–612, Science Museum Library; and Puzzle Pictures Folder, John Johnson Collection); *Circulating Library* (SCM-451/3, Science Museum Library); *Conchologist* (SCM-2002–613, Science Museum Library). I have not seen an original of the *Botanist,* although a version copied in Baltimore can be seen in George Spratt, *Twelve Original Designs,* Baltimore 1831 (Y350 S767 T831, American Antiquarian Society Library).

25. George Spratt, *Obstetric Tables: Comprising Coloured Delineations on a Peculiar Plan, Intended to Illustrate Elementary and other Works on the Practice of Midwifery, Elucidating Particularly the Application of the Forceps, and Other Important Practical Points in Obstetric Science* (London: John Churchill, 1833), unpaginated preface. I am indebted for further details about the book to Roger Gaskell.

26. Ludmilla Jordanova, "Gender, Generation and Science: William Hunter's Obstetrical Atlas," in *William Hunter and the Eighteenth-Century Medical World,* ed. W. F. Bynum and Roy Porter (Cambridge: Cambridge University Press, 1985), 385–412.

27. A "Spratt Mrs. & Miss Julia" are listed as "teachers of drawing" in *Post Office Directory* (London: Frederic Kelly, 1846), 488.

28. Mrs. G. Spratt, *The Language of Birds: Comprising Poetic and Prose Illustrations of the Most Favourite Cage Birds. With Twelve Highly-coloured Plates* (London: Saunders and Otley, 1837), iii–iv, 2, 14–15. This book appeared as part of a series, though it was issued in small numbers as the only copy listed in a public collection is in the British Library; another issue with a title page from 1851 is at Kent State University.

29. Leonore Davidoff and Catherine Hall, *Family Fortunes: Men and Women of the English Middle Class, 1780–1850* (Chicago: University of Chicago Press, 1987).

30. Thomas Hood, *Comic Annual* (London: Charles Tilt, 1831), Advertisements, 8.

31. Thomas Hood, "The Scrape-book," *Comic Annual* (London: Charles Tilt, 1831), 164. Scrapbooks in Britain have been little studied, but the perspectives in Ann Bermingham, *Learning to Draw: Studies in the Cultural History of a Polite and Useful Art* (New Haven: Yale University Press, 2000) provide the essential starting points. The literature on American scrapbooks is more substantial, although the chronology it describes differs from that in Britain; see especially Ellen Gruber Garvey's "Scissorizing and Scrapbooks: Nineteenth Century Reading, Remaking and Recirculating" in *New Media: 1740–1915,* ed. Lisa Gitelman and Geoffrey B. Pingree (Cambridge, Mass.: MIT Press, 2003), 207–28; and the same author's "Dreaming in Commerce: Advertising Trade Card Scrapbooks," in *Acts of Possession: Collecting in America,* ed. Leah Dilworth (New Brunswick, New Jersey, 2003), 66–88; and also Todd S. Gernes, "Recasting the Culture of Ephemera," in *Popular Literacy: Studies in Cultural Practices and Poetics,* ed. John Trimbur (Pittsburgh: University of Pittsburgh Press, 2001), 107–27.

32. Bermingham, *Learning to Draw,* 145–64. See also Alistair Allen and Joan Hoverstadt, *The History of Printed Scraps* (London: New Cavendish Books, 1983).

33. Louisa Henrietta Sheridan, "The Adventures of an Album," in *The Comic Offering; Or Ladies' Melange of Literary Mirth* (London: Smith, Elder, 1831), 251–85, at 252.

34. John Barrell, *The Dark Side of the Landscape: The Rural Poor in English Painting, 1730–1840* (Cambridge: Cambridge University Press, 1980); Ann Bermingham, *Landscape and Ideology: The English Rustic Tradition, 1760–1860* (Berkeley and Los Angeles: University of California Press, 1986).

35. Quoted in Amy Cruse, *The Englishman and his Books in the Early Nineteenth Century* (London: G. G. Harrap, 1930), 283; part of a useful (but unfootnoted) chapter on "Drawing-room Books."

36. Henry Heath, *The Caricaturist's Scrap Book* (London: Charles Tilt, 1840), frontispiece.

37. On the anthology, see Leah Price, *The Anthology and the Rise of the Novel: From Richardson to George Eliot* (Cambridge: Cambridge University Press, 2000).

38. Although the centrality of annuals is now recognized in Romantic literary studies (Jerome McGann, "The Rationale of HyperText: Example D," http://jefferson.village.virginia.edu/public/jjm2f/rationale.html), they have yet to be explored in relation to the sciences.

39. There were soon imitators, including the *New Comic Annual* (1830–1835), and Louisa Henrietta Sheridan's *Comic Offering* (1831–1835), in which her autobiography of an album appeared.

40. For those who wanted more, an advertisement at the back of the *Comic Annual* gave the details of the series of "Implemental Characters"; see Morgan, *Letters,* 121n.

41. Louisa Henrietta Sheridan, "Preface," *Comic Offering,* v–viii.

42. Sean Shesgreen, *Images of the Outcast: The Urban Poor in the Cries of London* (Manchester: Manchester University Press, 2002).

43. John Rule, *The Experience of Labour in Eighteenth-Century Industry* (London: Croom Helm, 1981), 126.

44. George, *Catalogue,* vol. 11, 395–96.

45. Another print from the same series, with equally erratic lettering, shows a drunken woman made out of bottles rather than books: *A Lady Who Has Sacrificed Every Thing for Her Bottle and Glass,* author's collection.

46. Quoted in Margaret Beetham, *A Magazine of her Own? Domesticity and Desire in the Women's Magazine, 1800–1914* (London: Routledge, 1996), 31. On dandies, see also Donald, *Followers of Fashion,* 68–70.

47. For the role of visual pleasure in stimulating an interest in science, see Anne Secord, "Botany on a Plate: Pleasure and the Power of Pictures in Promoting Early Nineteenth-Century Scientific Knowledge," *Isis* 93 (2002): 28–57.

48. See the fascinating discussion in E. C. Spary, "Rococo Readings of the Book of Nature," in *Books and the Sciences in History,* ed. Marina Frasca-Spada and Nick Jardine (Cambridge: Cambridge University Press, 2000), 255–75.

49. The public distribution of mineralogical skills at this time, and the commercial possibilities they engendered, are discussed in Brian Dolan, "Pedagogy through Print: James Sowerby, John Mawe and the Problem of

Colour in Early Nineteenth-Century Natural History Illustration," *British Journal for the History of Science* 31 (1998): 275–304.

50. The great exception to this rule is the collection of just under three hundred scrapbooks at Manchester Metropolitan University, which includes many examples from the early nineteenth century. For a sampling, see Gaye Smith, *Sentimental Souvenirs: Victorian Scrap Albums from the Sir Harry Page Collection* (Manchester: Manchester Polytechnic Library, 1989).

51. Spratt, *Language of Birds,* 139.

THOSE WHO DREW AND THOSE WHO WROTE

Women and Victorian Popular Science Illustration

Barbara T. Gates

In general, information about illustrations in women's popular science texts is sparse. Few women popularizers worked for publishers with extensive archival records. Fewer still attempted autobiographies, or kept archives of their letters, or wished to make their correspondence public if they did. And rarely did any discuss illustration or pay tribute to their illustrators in prefaces explaining the nature of their work. Nevertheless, there are scattered records of the sort I have just mentioned. Australian naturalist Louisa Anne Meredith (1812–1895) wrote letters and diaries that refer specifically to her book-art. Eliza Brightwen (1830–1906)—who made popular her own menagerie and natural environs—kept a journal (later published as her autobiography) that occasionally discusses the illustrations she was executing. And Darwinian popularizer Arabella Buckley (1840–1929) often mentioned her illustrators in her prefaces.

Because of their relative accessibility and because their work represents different kinds of science popularization, these three women writer-illustrators and their books are the primary focus of this chapter. The body of the chapter will consider differing ways in which the three juggled pictorial images and written text. It also will suggest ways in which the combination of words and pictures aided in the spread of scientific knowledge and the furthering of these women's careers.

In science popularizations, illustrations serve multiple functions. They are meant to delight as well as instruct and consequently have numerous aesthetic as well as pedagogical purposes. Sometimes they are used simply as decoration and adornment, sometimes they are supplementary to an idea or reinforce it for the memory, and sometimes they help to explain a principle. Their sheer variety makes ready generalizations about popular science illustration difficult, while still further difficulty arises from anonymity in illustration. Most frequently, illustrators of popular scientific texts were not identified. Often title pages say something like "illustrated by nearly 500 engravings," as does Jane Loudon's 1850 edition of *The Entertaining Naturalist*. To muddy the waters still further, that particular title page goes on to say that the illustrations are "by Bewick, Harvey, Landells, Thompson, Whimper, Sly, and others."[1] When one turns to the individual engravings themselves for verification of who did what, disappointingly few bear an illustrator's name.

If we look at the work of Emily Gosse (1806–1857), who rendered beautiful artwork for the chromolithographs that graced science popularizations by her husband, Philip Gosse, it is possible to see one of the reasons for such anonymity. Writers such as Gosse were considered responsible for an entire scientific work, pictures as well as written text. Emily Gosse, a talented artist who was trained as a landscape painter by John Sell Cotman, was therefore represented in the Gosse scientific books without picture-credits. Plates in Gosse's handsomely illustrated *Aquarium* (1854), for example, read: "P. H. Gosse, delt.," identifying him as the artist who prepared the drawing that was the basis for the plate. This particular model of publishing—where written text is considered primary and image secondary or supportive—was dominant in scientific texts for most of the nineteenth century. It resulted in an underestimation of the import of pictures to writing, even when the pictures were so large or exceptionally beautiful that today they seem to be the dominant textual elements. This was true of high science as well as popular science like Gosse's.

In the chapter "Two Texts, Two Hands, Two Looks" from her *Artist as Critic*, Lorraine Kooistra points out that this type of model "others" the picture. It establishes a cultural paradigm in which the picture "has been made for someone by someone at a specific historical moment" and creates a textual struggle in which the picture becomes the weaker element.[2] In the early and middle Victorian decades, the time of the Gosses' work, this binary mirrors gender politics. There is, however, another common Victorian model, one in which the writer of a text is also its illustrator, as was William Makepeace Thackeray, for example, in his *Vanity Fair*. Continuing her analogies to gender roles, Kooistra dubs this model "cross-dressing." The term refers to the dual natures of the author/illustrator who wears one authorial hat, then dons another hat, that of the collaborative illustrator. This alternative model also describes the work of adroit, ambidextrous women popularizers such as children's writer and seaweed expert Margaret Gatty (1809–1873); botanist Anne Pratt (1806–1893);

and Louisa Anne Meredith (1812–1895), the first of the three women popularizers to be discussed here.[3]

Coloring the Exotic: Louisa Anne Meredith

Meredith not only serves as an example of how written text and picture might function in tandem when both are the work of one popularizer; her work also affords an opportunity to look at popular science illustration in the British colonies. Meredith began her career as a native Englishwoman, Louisa Twamley, illustrator and expert on British wildflowers. Under the name Twamley, she published *The Romance of Nature; or The Flower Seasons Illustrated* in 1836, *Flora's Gems* in 1837, and *Our Wildflowers Familiarly Described and Illustrated* in 1839 before setting out for Australia with her new husband. All of her books, from this early work of the 1830s through that of the 1880s and 1890s, were published in London for a predominantly British readership. The preface to her first Australian work, *Notes and Sketches of New South Wales during a Residence in that Colony from 1839–1844,* offers its subject by acknowledging that

> many persons at 'Home' are deeply interested in these distant colonies, as being the residence of dear friends and relatives, and that, as in the case of my own home-connections, they really understand very little of the general aspect of things here, I [therefore] believed that a few simple sketches from nature, however devoid of scientific lore, would be a welcome addition to the present small fund of information on common every-day topics relating to these antipodean climes.[4]

Meredith wrote five books about her second and longer-term home, all containing "sketches from nature" and greater or lesser amounts of "scientific lore." All, however, served to familiarize the reader/viewer with the flora and fauna of Australia. The books are of several sorts. *My Home in Tasmania* (1859) is a travel account with descriptions of the settlement, the settlers, and their ways—but also the ways of Tasmanian plants and animals. By contrast, two *Bush Friends* books, *Some of My Bush Friends in Tasmania* (1860) and *Last Series: Bush Friends in Tasmania,* written in 1891, when Meredith was seventy-nine, are brilliantly illustrated folios with elaborate prose and poetic descriptions of the plates. The second of these books was the only one of all her books for which Meredith could supervise the production of plates, since its publication coincided with Meredith's one trip back to England. Of this later series of *Bush Friends* she would say: "The plates are being excellently done by Brooks Day and Son—Day being the firm who executed the former volume so well and singular to relate—the brass die mould of the former book's binding has been recovered, and can be altered for the new one."[5] *Tasmanian Friends and Foes: Feathered, Furred, and Finned* (1880) is a science popularization for children, modeled on earlier popularizations that tell the stories of a family learning together about the wonders of the natural world. It too is illustrated, often with brilliant, if smaller, color plates. Her travel books established Meredith's popularity; the others gave fuller visual insights into Meredith's natural world.

Living as far afield as Tasmania could afford Meredith special entry into the realms of science writing and illustration. In selecting popularizations of natural history as her mode, Meredith made a choice that enabled her to gain recognition as both a writer and an illustrator, something that Emily Gosse, as illustrator only, could not achieve. As one of Meredith's characters in *Tasmanian Friends and Foes* says: "Careful scientific descriptions of all these creatures have been written by learned naturalists for learned people; the only ground on which there is room for our pens is the familiar every-day knowledge of little habits and peculiarities, which the greatest professors at home cannot always observe for themselves."[6] Louisa Meredith could collect and witness at first hand many "little" things. Her natural history had the distinct advantage of being based on living evidence directly in front of her own eyes, in contrast to the work of those scientists who never left the shores of the British isles.

Experts in all fields who might be inaccurate are subject to Meredith's corrections in all of her books. Even John Gould, who lived in Australia for a time and whose bird pictures Meredith greatly admired, is criticized. For example, when discussing Australian oyster-catchers, whose common Australian name was "red-bills," Meredith notes that

> the figures of my favourite red-bills, under the name of "oyster-catchers" in Gould's "Birds of Australia," are less faithful than most of his admirable plates; they are too heavy-looking, and represent the bills and feet as orange-coloured, instead of their real hue of pure brilliant coral-red.[7]

If Meredith's Tasmanian painter's eye purported to capture living things, Gould and his team of illustrators, she implies, often worked from dead skins. They also took no heed of native or common names of species, the names that would mean most to her readers. Here, with her several talents as writer and observer/illustrator, Meredith judges John Gould, the famous "bird man" and respected scientist, challenging both his words and his illustrator's palette.

Pointing out errors like John Gould's probable misreading of color gave further credibility to Meredith's own words and pictures, which were determinedly vivid and scrupulous renderings. For example, one can view Meredith's color plates and then marvel with the children in *Tasmanian Friends and Foes* at the "Wonderful creatures! . . . How splendid is that Scarlet Dragon shape, with blue, yellow, and purple markings! and dark red fins all down its tail, exactly like leaves of seaweed! Its head is something like a hippocampus, but so vivid in colour. And what a bright eye!" (figure 8.1).[8] In this section of *Tasmanian Friends and Foes,* Meredith took great care that her entertaining fictional story should provide scientific accuracy as well as entertainment. In the discussion of the Scarlet Dragon, a Mrs. Leslie introduces the beauties of the southern ocean to a set of youngsters, first bringing in a globe full of "fishy characters." Then, so as not to interrupt the raptures of Lina, the child who has exclaimed over the dragon's bright eye, Meredith moves to the bottom of this page full of dialogue to footnote the dragon's scientific name, *Phyllopteryx foliatus.* Nothing must distract the reader from Lina's enthusiasm as she unfolds multiple wrappings of kelp to expose the wonders of the sea. Yet should a reader want to learn scientific nomenclature as well, he or she can turn to Meredith's footnotes and her careful labels on the plate. Or, if readers prefer, they can simply continue with the story, where more rapture ensues as Lina continues: "that must be the jewel-fish that old Donald said I should find. He said it glittered and shone 'all manner o'colours,' as he pulled it up, 'like the Queen's crown in the Tower of London.'"[9] With reference here both to Australia and its creatures and the United Kingdom, to working classes and to middle-class children and adults, Meredith covers a multiplicity of possible audiences for her popular science writing by means of her fictional characters, her labels, and her footnotes.

At the same time, she glosses her written text with her picture and her picture with her written text. Meredith calls special attention to her rendering of the outrageous and stunning sea creatures when her narrator says: "Mrs. Leslie used all diligence in making accurate portraits of the fish, often complaining that no tints her palette could furnish were able to realise half their beauty. . . . The 'Superb Dragon' is very rare."[10] The natural-history artist, Meredith here suggests, is beholden alike to viewers and to a brilliant natural world beyond the human mind and paintbrush, and this is not always a comfortable situation. Being an artist in two media caused Meredith herself some unease, perhaps because she wanted most of all to be considered a writer, aware of the stigma that attached to women illustrators as second-class artists. After the reviews of *Some of My Bush Friends in Tasmania* appeared, she wrote to Sir Henry Parkes, a personal friend,

TASMANIAN FRIENDS AND FOES.

SUPERB DRAGON (PHYLLOPTERYX FOLIATUS)
OSTRACIAN (ARACANA AURITA)

8.1 Louisa Anne Meredith, "Superb Dragon and Ostracian," *Tasmanian Friends and Foes: Feathered, Furred, and Finned* (London: Marcus Ward, 1880), 196, plate VII.

"I feel very keenly the mischief I have done myself by being an artist. Because my books are illustrated by my own pencil they are reviewed as picture-books chiefly."[11]

Other discomforts arose because of Meredith's geographical distance from her publishers. The bulk of her work was corrected in England and not returned to her until after the final printing. This tormented Meredith, especially when she found the written text rife with misspellings or the lithographic text riddled with inaccuracies. She would have preferred to respond more directly to copyediting and to supervise the reproduction of her images. Her concern is evidenced by Meredith's insisting on sending some of her early sketches to one of the Dalziel brothers—the famous engravers for the Pre-Raphaelites in Moxon's edition of Alfred Lord Tennyson—in order to get something closer to what she had in mind. As she said, "a clever and judicious engraver can make a charming picture out of next to nothing—and . . . a dolt can render such a clumsy version of excellence, as to make it seem below mediocrity."[12] Distance also presented another drawback for Meredith. Written so far way from European and American centers of technology, Meredith's books did not evolve with the times. The large-format, colorfully illustrated books that Meredith produced in her early days were not radically different from her last books. Yet such books were expensive to reproduce and consequently to buy and not good choices for late-century popularizations at a time when prices were kept down in order to broaden the audience. Nevertheless, with her keen eye, rich palate, and desire for accuracy, Meredith was always drawn to color. Only her travel books, which appeared in cheaper, more popular editions, have multiple, small, black-and-white illustrations, not all of which were drawn by her.

Domestication in Black and White: Eliza Brightwen

Eliza Brightwen, on the other hand, always published in smaller, post-octavo formats with ample black-and-white drawings and photographs, some of which were rendered by her and some by others. The mass popular culture of the late nineteenth century, when Brightwen produced her first works and Meredith her last, evolved as photography made photo-reproduction available and re-educated the Victorian eye to black and white. Halftones (pictures gradated by tiny dots) and line blocks supplanted wood engravings, and cheaper papermaking and printing enabled the proliferation of weeklies, monthlies, and annuals that reached out to a wider audience. Late Victorian audiences came to expect something to look at as well as to read. They favored amply illustrated texts and multicolored covers, two embellishments that Brightwen's publisher, Fisher Unwin, was able to supply. Brightwen's work featured a style of visual representation that perfectly suited her domestic type of popular science writing. For Brightwen's books carried the reader not to Australia but to Brightwen's own large estate, The Grove, located outside London. And Brightwen's readers were treated to at least five main types of illustration: adornments, photographs, drawings of wild plants and animals in wild settings, drawings of wild plants and animals in domestic settings, and more conventionally scientific-types of illustration, such as magnified water droplets.

From childhood on, Brightwen had a deep interest in nature. She said of herself that the "early lessons of Natural History kept me constantly wondering and asking 'the reason why.'"[13] Brightwen also ran experiments, grew cultures, dissected specimens, and sketched and produced finished watercolors, all of which honed her already well-developed powers of visualization. In later life, she kept copious notes on the natural history of her environs at The Grove. And there, in her sixtieth year and for the first time, she began assembling her work for publication. The literary result was *Wild Nature Won by Kindness* (1890), an unqualified success, which made her one of the most popular natural history writers of her day. *Wild Nature* was followed by five other books including *More about Wild Nature* (1892); *Inmates of My House and Garden* (1895); and *Quiet Hours with Nature* (1904), all of which will be mentioned further here. During this more than ten-year period, Brightwen carried on a wide correspondence about natural history, much of which was generated by inquiries from her readers.

Fragments of Brightwen's autobiography, introduced by her nephew and Philip Gosse's son, writer Edmund Gosse, were published in 1909 under the title *Eliza Brightwen, the Life and Thoughts of a Naturalist*. From the book's journal-like entries, one learns that Brightwen did her illustrating in the interstices of her life. About a typical day in November of 1892, Brightwen muses: "Letters were written; I drew and cut out a number of animals for a friend who was making a baby's rug. Pot-pourri was made and magazines were sorted to go to the binder; two drawings were made for my studio; a drawing of a pitcher-plant was begun; fifteen poppy heads were gilded to make into pincushions for a bazaar."[14] In the same month, Brightwen was redrawing illustrations for the German edition of *Wild Nature Won by Kindness,* and in December she was tutoring a girl in natural history while entertaining a professor who was to give her more authoritative scientific information. Gosse tells us that she went on like this to the end—that eight days before her death she received a rare South African beetle and was sketching it, finishing other drawings, and outlining plans for a cage for the beetle.[15] I focus on Brightwen's domesticity because the illustrations for her books also focus on it. In large part, Eliza Brightwen's fame stemmed from the ways that she chose to popularize science through her domestic settings; the field of natural history was for her best demonstrated by the fields, ponds, and forests around her home and by the rare animals she kept inside it. Pictures of The Grove serve as frontispieces for many of her books, which are all adorned with small, decorative designs, some reminiscent of the fancy work that also occupied Brightwen's busy hours.

At the outset of this chapter, I suggested that illustrations for popular science texts could serve education through entertainment and that popularizations often were meant to delight as well as instruct. In reviewing Brightwen's work, it becomes apparent just how carefully this author worked to enhance instruction with entertainment and vice versa and what an important role illustration played in these enhancements. The stay-at-home-and-enjoy-yourself-as-you-learn agenda of Brightwen's writing sets a tone that lends itself to ease, and this is echoed in the books' pictures. We are meant to relax and be comfortable as we enter the Brightwen world, and we do so in part by witnessing it doubly—through words and pictures. Brightwen was canny. She knew that many readers learn not only through seeing but also through allurement, a subject that Anne Secord has discussed in terms of the botanical popularizations of the nineteenth century.[16] Brightwen's garden, her pets, and her surroundings were all depicted with allure, as attractive sources of pleasure and delight.

This may be seen best through Brightwen's self-illustrated *More About Wild Nature*. Here, from the very first page, one can find sketching intended to reinforce the domestic ambiance that is always carefully written into the Brightwen books. Moreover, the book equally well affords a look at the main types of Brightwen illustration that I

8.2 Eliza Brightwen, "Ichneumon Attacking Cobra," *More About Wild Nature* (London: T. Fisher Unwin, 1892), 22.

MUNGO.

8.3 Eliza Brightwen, "Mungo with Ball," *More About Wild Nature* (London: T. Fisher Unwin, 1892), 30.

have listed. In the table of contents, for example, there is a diminutive sketch of the chalet situated near a lake on Brightwen's property, one of the small adornments common to all Brightwen books. This is then complemented by a photograph of the house itself, placed between the table of contents and the first chapter of written text. Thus from the outset, we are planted on Brightwen's turf. Students of nature willing to learn with Eliza Brightwen need to enter her spaces in order to see wildness in the things that live at one's very doorstep. In *More About Wild Nature*, Brightwen also drew pictures of a number of the animals that roamed inside her home or lived in its conservatory. Many of these add touches of playfulness to the text. Take Mungo, for example, the pet mongoose, illustrated first as Brightwen imagines he must have been in the wild, in combat with a cobra (figure 8.2), and then as he frolics with a ball in Brightwen's house (figure 8.3). The second picture seems meant to show us how safe and entertaining it was for a once wild, now domesticated, Asian animal to live at The Grove. Unlike Meredith, who saw, illustrated, and described wild animals from her second homeland, Brightwen liked to colonize them in England. Throughout her writing, she tends toward an imperialistic attitude, exhibiting things foreign in familiar British settings in order to teach others about how docile (or impossible) these "other" beasts can be. Similarly, she domesticates non-living, exotic things—peacock plumes, for example, which she arranges into a fan-like shape and offers in one of the illustrations for her book. In addition to being a teacher of scientific facts, Brightwen showed Victorian women how to make beautiful or useful things from what she seems to have thought of as nature's storehouse. A final kind of illustration present in *More About Wild Nature* is best exemplified by "Water Insects," where the variety of insects represented and the drop of water at front and center—reminiscent of water under a microscope—function to lend the book the stamp of a science textbook.

Wild Nature Won by Kindness, published two years before *More About Wild Nature,* was illustrated both by Brightwen and by Francis Carruthers Gould (1844–1925), and can serve to show Brightwen working in tandem rather than alone. Gould was a well-known political illustrator for *Pall Mall* and *Westminster Gazette* who founded his own paper, *Picture Politics.* He was also a natural-history enthusiast with a special interest in ornithology. If we view one of Gould's drawings alongside one of Brightwen's—something possible to do with the pictures of Zöe, the nuthatch, that appeared on facing pages (figure 8.4)—we can see that Gould's work is less smooth, more "scratchy," with its penmarks clearly meant to be prominent (right-hand page, initialed "FCG"). This kind of roughness serves Gould well in his political cartoons, where it suggests a kind of studied haste and often represents people in a sketchy likeness to animals or birds. At first glance, it seems odd that Gould and Brightwen should both illustrate the same bird side-by-side for one short chapter, a duplication that had to be somewhat expensive. There is no written correspondence mentioning Gould as illustrator for Brightwen, nor any information that might suggest that Gould was long in the employ of Fisher Unwin, or that his illustration could not be discarded, or anything else that might explain this particular doubleness.

A closer look, however, suggests that there are two faces of Zöe. Brightwen emphasizes the bird's more natural, outdoor life in trees and Gould her home life at Brightwen's estate. Contrary to her usual emphases, Brightwen here de-domesticates an image. The nuthatch may have been won by kindness, the author seems to be suggesting— Brightwen having bought her from a dark, unpleasant bird shop— but she was, after all, meant to be a wild bird, not a caged one. As elsewhere in her writing, one of Brightwen's aims in this chapter is to deplore the caging of birds. Brightwen may have desired a second illustration to emphasize this disapproval. This of course returns control of both written text and picture to Brightwen herself, to some extent undermining the fame of Gould in the name of Brightwen's dual talents. But there is more to it than that. Brightwen's Zöe looks as though she could fly off under her own volition. In Gould's picture, she is hunkered in and tentative about escaping the cocoon-like structure she inhabits—a coconut provided for her in Brightwen's home conservatory and rendered in a characteristically scratchy Gould drawing that makes her seem uncomfortable. In the case of Zöe, Brightwen's interest in bird protection appears to have taken precedence over her need to represent domesticity. Brightwen no

ZOE. THE NUTHATCH.

E. BRIGHTWEN, DEL.

ZÖE, THE NUTHATCH.

ZÖE, THE NUTHATCH.

A VISIT to a bird-dealer's shop always awakens a deep feeling of pity in my mind as I look at the unhappy, flutter-little captives, and think of the breezy hill-sides and pleasant lanes from which they came, to be shut up in cages a few inches square, with but little light, a stifling atmosphere, strange diet, and no means of washing their ruffled feathers or stretching their wings in flight. Truly, they are in evil case, and no wonder so many die off within a few days of their capture! In some places they are better cared for than in

doubt wanted to show some of her readers how to tame wild birds, for this sold books in late Victorian times, but she also needed to remain true to the bird protectionists, for whom she would soon become a heroine.[17] A drawing attributed to Gould, not Brightwen, might enable Brightwen to skirt this difficult issue by distancing herself, if ever so little, from a caged, wild bird.

For the pictures for *Inmates of My House and Garden* (1895), Brightwen relied closely not on Carruthers Gould but on Theo Carreras, about whom little is known other than that he was a highly desirable illustrator of popular science books in late Victorian decades. According to the London *Times* obituary for Brightwen, when Carreras illustrated Brightwen's books, he worked under the author's direction.[18] In the preface to the self-illustrated *More About Wild Nature,* Brightwen acknowledges that Carreras helped re-draw several of her own rough sketches and earlier drawings. (She reproduced several of her childhood sketches in this book.) Certainly Carreras represented Brightwen with a degree of reverence, giving her the power of the pen in *Inmates of My House and Garden* and putting

8.4 Eliza Brightwen, "Zöe, the Nuthatch," *Wild Nature Won by Kindness* (London: T. Fisher Unwin, 1890), opposite page 87; and Carruthers Gould, "Zöe, the Nuthatch," *Wild Nature Won by Kindness* (London: T. Fisher Unwin, 1890), 87.

A "FAIRY" STORY.

I AM often envied as the possessor of one of the most charming bird-pets it is possible to imagine.

"Fairy" is a tiny whitethroat, a sleek, delicate, grey-coloured bird with a white breast, lovely in form, swift in flight, and of most engaging disposition.

I met with it in this wise. A plaintive little cheeping sound attracted my attention one morning at breakfast-time, and looking outside the window, I saw a tiny, half-fledged bird sitting on the

59

her in special touch with wild things (figure 8.5). *Wild Nature Won by Kindness* might have seemed a different book with this smoother sort of illustration rather than Gould's harsher lines. The book might have appeared even more tender toward the natural world—its intent, after all. In *Inmates*, Carreras seems to caress Brightwen's written text, as in his illuminated letters for the openings of her chapters.

In the picture of the mantis (figure 8.6), Carreras's illumination serves a dual purpose: as illumination and scientific drawing, with the mantis appropriately perched on a plant but with one foot on a letter, pointing to Brightwen's writing. Science is here served not just by Carreras's faithful rendering but by Brightwen including the insect's name in both English and Latin. In Carreras's larger pictures—as for example the jerboa for Brightwen's *Quiet Hours with Nature*—the images are often equally elegant (see figure 8.7). There is a grace as well as charm about them that suits Brightwen's familiarly, often delicately written texts. With the jerboa, Brightwen deliberately glosses

THE PRAYING MANTIS.

(MANTIS ORATORIA.)

THE post has brought me some odd things from "foreign parts" in the course of the last few years, but never anything quite so strange and weird as a live specimen of the so-called "praying mantis," which reached me last winter.

This curious insect was sent from Mentone by

203

8.6 Theo Carreras, decorated letter for "The Praying Mantis," in *Inmates of My House and Garden* (London: T. Fisher Unwin, 1895), 203.

8.7 Theo Carreras, "Egyptian Jerboas," *Quiet Hours with Nature* (London: T. Fisher Unwin, [1904]), 11.

EGYPTIAN JERBOAS.

the picture rather than the more usual case of a picture glossing her text: "The drawing will show my readers the curious formation which enables this desert-dweller to play so many extraordinary pranks. Its long hind legs help it to leap with marvelous speed along the surface of the ground." But the picture also perfectly represents Brightwen's "softly furred tail, with its pretty black and white tip, an object of great solicitude to the jerboa."[19] In the Brightwen/Carreras partnership, word and image communicate fluidly.

With Brightwen's use of Carruthers Gould and Theo Carreras, artwork remains in the service of the written text, as it did in the case of the Gosses, although a woman writer now takes the lion's share of credit for both words and pictures. Nevertheless, with Carreras and Brightwen there is partnership of another sort. Carreras's renderings of Brightwen herself, whether feeding birds or writing her books, make her present to her text in a way she would not otherwise have been. She is not only the author and a commissioner of illustrations; she also becomes a central subject of her books. In Brightwen's day, readers wanted to see how authors looked as well as to read what they wrote. Publishers often had pictorial representations of their authors made—not just for frontispieces or title pages but as part of marketing strategies for promotional purposes. This seems to have been the case with Brightwen and her publisher, Fisher Unwin. Brightwen refers to such a picture in her correspondence with Fisher Unwin. There she thanks Unwin for the trouble he had taken over getting a good likeness of her and tells him of an admirer of her work who had requested to "'make [her] acquaintance by effigy' and begged a cabinet photo for himself."[20] But Carreras's illustrations are unusual, and of course perfectly suit the domestically oriented Brightwen texts. They are not full-face portraits but delicate renderings of Brightwen doing what she did best—writing, taming, and walking through her grounds. They capture the essence both of the Brightwen text and its author.

Educating the Eye: Arabella Buckley

A turn from Brightwen and earlier women popularizers to Arabella Buckley points toward the increasing stature of women popularizers. Buckley was Sir Charles Lyell's secretary and began a prolific career as science popularizer soon after his death, working to promote science education of all sorts—from the history of science, to Darwin's theories, to physical science. Although she was an able illustrator, only rarely did she illustrate her own writing, as in *The Fairy-land of Science* (1879), where she examines a line-drawing of her own and tells us "it is a sketch on the shores of Arbroath which I made some years ago" (figure 8.8). She goes on to say, "You will not find it difficult to picture to yourselves how the sea has eaten away these cliffs till some

Fig. 28.

Cliffs off Arbroath, showing the waste of the shore.

8.8 Arabella Buckley, "Cliffs off Arbroath, Showing the Waste of the Shore," *The Fairy-land of Science* (New York: D. Appleton & Co., 1888), 117.

of the strongest pieces which have resisted the waves stand out by themselves in the sea. That cave in the left-hand corner ends in a narrow dark passage from which you have come out on the other side of the rocks into another bay."[21] When Buckley glosses one of her own pictures, she loses some of the vitality that usually inflects her prose descriptions. As a rule, Buckley's written work is visual enough even without illustrations: "How do you enter the fairy-land of science?" Buckley asks. "There is but one way . . . you must open your eyes."[22] All of her writing, from start to finish (ending with *Eyes and No Eyes* in 1901–1924), moves toward enabling others to see.

The degree of visualization in Buckley's prose is beautifully suited for depicting the panoramic sweep that Buckley is most adept at rendering, lending a "you-are-there" quality to her view of nature, something I have discussed elsewhere.[23] She offers nature as the spectacle of time—transforming, reforming, and destroying creatures as the "winners" in life's race evolve and are classified throughout her two books on evolution, *Life and Her Children* (1881) and *Winners in Life's Race* (1883). Her writing in these books can be both dioramic and panoramic. It can paint detailed, static word pictures that allow the gaze to sink deeply, to penetrate a thing or a scene. Or it can be dynamic, sweeping our imaginative gaze along, seeming to move us horizontally through time or space:

> There the huge buffaloes come down in troops out of the forest to drink, while the great hippopotamuses leave their watery bed to feed on the rough grass of the swamps. Not far off, a herd of zebras comes galloping by to drink lower down in the river, startling the large antelopes feeding quietly in the soft green pasture above, for they know that this is the hour when the lions are abroad and will fall upon any straggler with tooth and nail, and they would not be far behind in seizing upon any weak or wounded animal.[24]

One hardly needs illustrations for this sort of graphic description. Buckley would have had to wait for twentieth-century filmmakers to get her moving panoramas right.

Yet Buckley and her publishers, like Brightwen and hers, did turn to the multitalented Carreras when they desired an illustrator for Buckley's texts. In him they found an artist who could work hand-in-glove with Buckley as she tried to revitalize long-gone animals in *Winners in Life's Race*. Carreras's pictures help transmit Buckley's style, not just her message. His work for Buckley forces us to pry into the past as though we were looking through a peep hole or attending one of the peep shows so common on Victorian streets. When Carreras represents the forests harboring the milk-givers, we peer into layers of time and find a verbal diorama by Buckley illuminated.

Take, for example, figure 8.9, where Carreras represents these words of Buckley:

> There . . .among the palms, screw-pines, and tree-ferns, which flour-
> ished in Europe and North America in those warmer times, were
> beasts larger than oxen, with teeth partly like the tapir, partly like the
> bear, and feet like the elephant, which may have been both animal and
> vegetable feeders. With them were the true vegetarians, which could
> be called neither rhinoceroses, horses, nor tapirs, but had some re-
> semblance to each.[25]

8.9 Theo Carreras, "The Pioneers of the Army of Milkgivers," *Winners in Life's Race* (New York: Appleton & Co., 1883), 209.

As in his work with Brightwen, so in his images for Buckley's work, Carreras has a way of keying in to his writers' prose, both complementing and recreating their form and meaning. This art was not lost on Buckley's reviewers. *The American Naturalist* (January 1884) found "the wood-cuts . . . by Mr. Carreras" to be "geological restorations of unusual excellence" and reproduced a number of them in the review, suggesting how much they added to an already fine text.[26]

Characteristically, Buckley acknowledged her illustrators in her prefaces. Nevertheless, when she thanked the illustrator, she also pointed out her own hand in the matter:

> The geological restorations given as picture-headings (some of which are here attempted, I believe, for the first time) have been most carefully considered, though the exact forms of such strange and extinct animals must necessarily be somewhat conjectural. My thanks are due to the artist, Mr. Carreras, jun., for the patience and care with which he has followed my instructions regarding them, and also to Mr. Smit for his masterly execution of the frontispiece.[27]

If Carreras catches the kind of picturing that Buckley produces in her writing, she tells us that this was her doing. By following "her instructions" here, Carreras worked for Buckley, not the other way around. Similarly, in the preface to her 1890 book, *Through Magic Glasses,* Buckley thanks Carreras, who supervised the illustrations for this text, for making "my task easier by the skill and patience he has exercised under the difficulties incidental to receiving instructions from a distance."[28] In citing these two passages from her prefaces, I am not suggesting that Buckley's texts present a great moment for women's professionalism in late Victorian times. Nor did illustrators and their illustrations gain prominence vis-à-vis authors and their words through such references, despite the prevalence of illustrations in popular science books. Again, what is evidenced here is simply a reversal of male and female roles—female writer, male illustrator— that nevertheless continues the practice of subverting picture to text that we saw at mid-century. All the same, Buckley's prefaces reveal a growing authority of women in popular science writing at the end of the nineteenth century. It was possible for Buckley to have full command over her text without having to illustrate it, as did Meredith.

Arabella Buckley's work also illuminates another of the points with which I began and the one that most bears repeating at the end of this chapter. Popularizing science is always about educating. That is its still-underestimated contribution to the Victorian need to know, and Arabella Buckley always put education first. This is a hallmark of her literary endeavors: She wished to re-open and re-educate the eyes and ears of her audience of men, women, and children, convinced that seeing led to knowing as well as believing. Determined to address laity hungry for new information, she was willing to begin at the beginning with them—to help make a little-known universe both more legible and more visible. From her numerous references to young people, there is little doubt that Buckley was especially interested in promoting a new generation of scientists. She therefore did everything she possibly could—lecturing, teaching, and writing—to stimulate others' life-long interest in science. Most importantly for this chapter, she strove to present science as visually apprehensible. Despite her remarkable talents as a word painter, Buckley also well understood what pictorial illustration could do—in her time and for her audience. It made the popular science text even more popular.

Conclusions

To generalize from the work of just three late-Victorian women popularizers poses dangers, even if their work represents a variety of popular science texts—travel and natural history, the observation and domestication of animals, the fairy story, or the verbal diorama that accurately tells the story of science. Far more research needs to be done in this relatively unexplored territory in order to complete even a short history of women and Victorian popular science illustration. But I will here hazard several tentative conclusions about the inter-relationships of text and picture in nineteenth-century popular science and about the role of women in the continued subversion of picture to text. In most cases, there is no certainty as to who had the most influence over pictures. Ultimately, although writers and artists had some say-so in book production, publishers and their editors ruled, and publishers were interested above all in marketing their own line. Nevertheless, by the end of the nineteenth century, well-known women writers did not need to illustrate their own work in order to have influence over its pictures, as did earlier women writers like Pratt, Gatty, and colonists like Meredith. Brightwen and Buckley both held considerable command of the totality of their texts even without illustrating them themselves. Changes in the marketplace after the 1880s, when black-and-white pictures could be reproduced relatively cheaply, would benefit later writers who were of stature. Brightwen had achieved such status from her nearly instant popularity; her works went through multiple editions. This enabled her, in the 1890s and early twentieth century, to help Fisher Unwin choose other artists to illustrate her books, although, talent-wise, she clearly was able to illustrate them herself. (She kept executing watercolors as a leisure pastime up until her death.) And Buckley was already known in scientific circles through her connections with Sir Charles

Lyell and Charles Darwin. These women writers' accomplishments enabled each to disengage herself from the rigors of illustration and to confer with illustrators. Brightwen, Buckley, and to a lesser extent fiction-writers like Juliana Horatia Ewing (1841–1885)—the daughter of Margaret Gatty, whose work lies beyond the scope of this essay but who wrote about natural history in stories for children—offer models of possibilities for women popularizers in late-century Victorian and early Edwardian times. In those eras, the written text remained dominant over the picture in popular science books. But even without illustrating their own work, the late-century and turn-of-the-century women examined or mentioned here had increasing control over pictures as well as written texts.

Notes

1. Jane Loudon, *The Entertaining Naturalist: Being Popular Descriptions, Tales, and Anecdotes of More than Five Hundred Animals* (London: Henry G. Bohn, 1850).

2. Lorraine Kooistra, *The Artist as Critic: Bitextuality in Fin-de-Siecle Illustrated Books* (Aldershot: Scolar Press, 1995), 11.

3. Both Gatty and Pratt were exceedingly popular in their particular spheres. Among other books, Gatty wrote the famous *Parables from Nature* (1855–1871) that combined morality with science told in the form of short parables. These often linked human behavior to stories of the plant and animal kingdom. The book was reissued in multiple editions and continued in print into the twentieth century. Pratt wrote numerous books dealing with flora such as ferns and club mosses, grasses, and wildflowers, all published near the middle of the nineteenth century.

4. Louisa Anne Meredith, *Notes and Sketches of New South Wales during a Residence in that Colony from 1839–1844* (London: John Murray, 1844), vii.

5. Quoted in Vivienne Rae Ellis, *Louisa Anne Meredith: A Tigress in Exile* (Sandy Bay, Tasmania: Blubber Head Press, 1979), 195.

6. Meredith, *Tasmanian Friends and Foes: Feathered, Furred, and Finned* (London: Marcus Ward, 1880), 69.

7. Meredith, *My Home in Tasmania* (London: John Murray, 1852), 116.

8. Meredith, *Tasmanian Friends and Foes*, 247.

9. Ibid., 248.

10. Ibid., 249.

11. Ellis, *Louisa Anne Meredith*, 191.

12. Ibid.

13. Eliza Brightwen, *Eliza Brightwen, Naturalist and Philanthropist: An Autobiography,* ed. W. H. Chesson (New York: American Tract Society, 1909), 7.

14. Ibid., 104.

15. Ibid., 208.

16. Anne Secord, "Botany on a Plate: Pleasure and the Power of Pictures in Promoting Early Nineteenth-Century Scientific Knowledge," *Isis* 93 (2002): 28–57.

17. See my *Kindred Nature: Victorian and Edwardian Women Embrace the Living World* (Chicago: University of Chicago Press, 1998), ch. 4, and *In Nature's Name: An Anthology of Women's Writing and Illustration, 1780–1930* (Chicago: University of Chicago Press, 2002), 158–85.

18. *Times* (London), May 7, 1906, 6.

19. Eliza Brightwen, *Quiet Hours with Nature* (London: T. Fisher Unwin, 1904), 10.

20. Letter of November 9, undated as to year, from Eliza Brightwen to Fisher Unwin. Courtesy West Sussex Records Office. The letter is from the Cobden collection, document 370.

21. Arabella Buckley, *The Fairy-land of Science* (London: Edward Stanford, 1879), 118.

22. Ibid., 12.

23. Barbara T. Gates, "Revisioning Darwin with Sympathy: Arabella Buckley," in *Natural Eloquence,* ed. Barbara T. Gates and Ann B. Shteir, 164–76; and *Kindred Nature.*

24. Arabella Buckley, *Winners in Life's Race; or the Great Back-boned Family* (London: Edward Stanford, 1883), 275.

25. Ibid., 213.

26. *The American Naturalist* (January 1884): 50.

27. Buckley, *Winners in Life's Race,* vii.

28. Arabella Buckley, *Through Magic Glasses* (London: Edward Stanford, 1890), vii.

Chapter 9

DEPICTING NATURE, DEFINING ROLES

The Gender Politics of Victorian Illustration

Bernard Lightman

"I am afraid," naturalist Eliza Brightwen confessed in her book *Quiet Hours with Nature* (1904), "that many of my readers will think that it is nothing more than a fanciful idea that one can cultivate friendship with an insect."[1] Brightwen's popular science books, which appeared throughout the 1890s and into the first few years of the twentieth century, were filled with accounts of her success in taming bats, mice, birds, toads, moles, and even snails. Butterflies, beetles, bees, wasps, and spiders were no exception, and Brightwen claimed that at least one of each of these insects had become her willing pets at one time or another. For readers who yearned to enter into a closer relation with "wild nature," Brightwen divulged one of her secrets. "In my garden there is a little dell embowered by trees," she confessed, "where I often spend an hour or two before breakfast for the special purpose of enjoying the company of my pet wild creatures."[2] And thus we see her in a photograph from her 1904 book (figure 9.1). She sits on a wicker chair in a garden, in domestic clothing, with a book on her lap, gazing at a nearby bird with a gentle smile on her face.

Brightwen's presentation of herself "at work" in this photograph is indicative of the important role of visual images in the writings of female popularizers of science in the latter half of the nineteenth century. Brightwen is not pictured at work with the aid of scientific instruments in a laboratory, then among the most privileged sites of knowledge and a predominantly male space. Nor is she depicted doing fieldwork in some exotic location in the British Empire, in the manner of an eminent male scientific explorer. She does not even appear, as do other women of science in this period, in her study, close to her books or writing tools. If the text did not tell the reader that she was involved in "early morning nature study," for that is the title

9.1 Brightwen at work, studying nature in her garden. Eliza Brightwen, *Quiet Hours with Nature* (London: T. Fisher Unwin [1904]), 175.

of the essay in which the photograph appears, this might merely be a picture of a woman sitting in her garden.

Nevertheless, this visual image played a key role in the text. It helped to elicit in her readers some sense of the beauty of nature and contributed to Brightwen's attempt to create a mood of peace and tranquility appropriate for a book titled *Quiet Hours with Nature*. It also allowed Brightwen to move effortlessly into religious themes dear to her heart. "In the country," she wrote, "the sights and sounds are such as tend to helpful thoughts of the love and goodness of the Creator Who has blessed us with so much to make us happy, if only we will open our eyes and hearts to see and understand the works of His hands."[3] Moreover, Brightwen's status as naturalist was bolstered by this photograph, since her authority was derived from her ability to learn more about wild nature by entering into an intimate relationship with individual animals that frequented her garden. "Even in the smallest garden there are problems for the observant eye for which the greatest minds cannot furnish an answer," Brightwen declared in the preface to the book.[4] The photograph was offered as evidence that deeper insight into nature could be found in Brightwen's garden, as legitimate a site for discovering scientific truth as any laboratory.

In her use of photographs from her everyday life, Brightwen was by no means unusual among women writers who contributed to the explosion of popular science books in the latter half of the nineteenth century. Like Brightwen, they assigned important roles to visual images in shaping their books. Their visual images were part of new narrative forms for popularizing science that were emerging at that time. Some female popularizers included vivid illustrations to present science as a form of educational entertainment to the reading public. For others, the incorporation of visual images allowed them to offer a more compelling and persuasive case for the religious implications that they read into nature. Still others could bolster their reputation as authoritative writers in the scientific world by establishing their expertise as guides to reading visual images or as creators of new forms of visual mapping. These three uses, which I will refer to as ornamental, rhetorical, and authoritative, could appear side by side in one text, especially since all three are so closely related to each other. It is rare to find a text where at least one of these uses does not appear. While female popularizers also called upon visual images to explain complex scientific ideas, their use in this sense often was inextricable from the patterns that I analyze here. The ornamental, rhetorical, and authoritative uses of visual images were crucial to these female popularizers of science, struggling to define their role in a gendered scientific community dominated by male professional scientists who frowned upon the participation of women in science. An examination of the various ways in which visual images functioned within popular science texts produced by women in Britain in this period illuminates the complex relationship among science, gender, and visual images.

Women Science Writers and Visual Images in the Nineteenth Century

Though they did not form a distinct group working together to achieve common goals, Brightwen and her sisters in science can be seen as part of a female tradition within science writing. During the late eighteenth and early nineteenth century, as Barbara Gates and Ann Shteir have shown, women science writers often chose letters, dialogues, and conversations—known as the "familiar format"— for teaching science to young readers and women.[5] By the mid-nineteenth century, women had established themselves as popularizers of science in record numbers. They wrote about almost every area of science, adopting new narrative forms as a replacement for the conversation and the dialogue.[6] For the most part, visual images did not play a central role in the works of the important female popularizers of science during the early years of this tradition. From Sarah Trimmer's *An Easy Introduction to the Knowledge of Nature* (1780) through works by Margaret Bryan, Jane Marcet, and Priscilla Wakefield, most popular science books by women carried few illustrations if any. The vast majority of these illustrations were simple black-and-white drawings of experimental apparatus and scientific instruments.[7]

In the opening pages of her *Mechanism of the Heavens* (1831), a condensation and translation of Laplace's *Méchanique Céleste*, Mary Somerville commented on the absence of diagrams in the French work and stated that some illustrations "will be occasionally introduced for the convenience of the reader."[8] However the additions were limited, for the most part, to small, geometrical diagrams.[9]

From the middle of the nineteenth century on, women played an important role in the explosion of popular science works. The list of women who were involved is impressive. Rosina Zornlin (1795–1859) produced a series of books on physical geography and geology; Margaret Gatty (1809–1873) published the extremely popular *Parables of Nature* (1855) as well as a guide to seaweed hunting; Jane Loudon (1807–1858), Anne Pratt (1806–1893), Elizabeth Twining (1805–1889), and Lydia Becker (1827–1890) all explored the world of botany, while Mary Roberts (1788–1864), Elizabeth Kirby (1823–1873) and Mary Kirby (1817–1893) wrote in the area of natural history. Arabella Buckley (1840–1929), who had been Charles Lyell's secretary before turning to popular science writing, produced a series of works on evolutionary theory. Mary Ward (1827–1869) focused in her works on scientific instruments. At the end of the century, women's involvement in popular science writing was still going strong. Agnes Giberne (1845–1939) and Agnes Clerke (1842–1907) explored the heavens while Alice Bodington (1840–1897) contributed her *Studies in Evolution and Biology* (1890). Eliza Brightwen (1830–1906) published her popular works on natural history during the same period.

Beginning in the 1830s, advances in printing technology made diverse imagery widely available and affordable for the first time, and visual images came to play an important role in women's popularizations of science. The rise of illustrated weeklies like the *Penny Magazine* heralded the development of a new popular culture in England distinguished by its increasingly pictorial character.[10] In London, crowds were entertained by vast panoramas of entire cities or military battles and by other spectacles, some geared specifically toward science.[11] In order to reach a popular audience, women who engaged in popularizing science recognized that they would have to take advantage of the developing mass visual culture. They became more sophisticated than their predecessors in their use of visual images, consciously manipulating the images in their texts.

By contrast, male professional scientists did not always use visual images when trying to communicate to a popular audience. Anne Secord has shown that in the first half of the nineteenth century, the growing middle-class appetite for illustrated novels and weekly periodicals led to fears that pictures would have an adverse effect on the mental faculties of the reading audience. Many male scientists were reluctant to use illustrations, since they could appeal to the senses or the emotions and not to the rational faculties. The debate in 1838 concerning the use of plates in natural history books revolved around the question of whether or not they would merely foster a superficial appreciation of the beauties of nature.[12] Similar concerns later in the century may have led professional scientists to use visual images sparingly and to rely mostly on certain types of images such as diagrams, maps, and cross-sections. T. H. Huxley, to take a well-known representative of a professional scientist in the latter half of the century, used blackboard sketches as tools in his lectures to science students. The four volumes of his *Scientific Memoirs,* as Bodmer has pointed out, contained 128 plates, 38 identified as coming from Huxley's hand.[13] But these illustrations, mostly of bones and fossils, were intended for an audience of fellow professional scientists or would-be scientists. Like a good anatomist, Huxley presented detailed drawings that analyzed things into bits. Rarely did the whole animal or plant appear. Interestingly enough, his works intended for popular audiences are sparsely illustrated. Most volumes of the *Collected Essays* contained next to nothing in the way of illustrations, with the exception of *Man's Place in Nature,* which is well illustrated.[14] Huxley's longer popular works are curiously barren of images. The *Science Primers. Introductory* (1880), his introduction to a popular science series that he edited for Macmillan, did not include any illustrations. His "Six Lectures to Working Men," published in 1862 by R. Hardwicke as *On Our Knowledge of the Causes of the Phenomena of Organic Nature,* and then later in the *Collected Essays* in the *Darwiniana* volume, contain five fairly simple figures.[15] All in all, Huxley's use of images was largely utilitarian.

In the latter half of the nineteenth century, male and female popularizers of science all began to use visual images in a distinctive fashion, forging a new visual tradition for popular science. Female popularizers made important contributions to this development because visual images figured more prominently in their work than in the popular science of their male counterparts. Men who popularized science did not exploit all three uses of visual images, especially the authoritative. Other groups within science were engaged in creating a new visual tradition during the same period. Martin Rudwick argues that as geology emerged as a self-conscious new discipline with clearly defined intellectual goals and well-established institutional forms in the 1830s, male geologists began to incorporate more visual images in their work as well as different kinds of images in order to communicate more effectively to other members of the geological community.[16] Though popularizers of science did not create a self-conscious new discipline as did the male geologists in the latter half of the nineteenth century, they formed a part of a new cadre of professional writers who also drew on more and varied visual images to reach a rapidly growing popular audience rather than communicate only with each other.

Visual Images as Ornaments

The impact of the new visual culture on popular science is evident in the works of Mary Roberts, Margaret Gatty, the Kirby sisters, and Sarah Bowdich Lee. Roberts's career as popularizer spanned the 1820s to the 1850s, just when visual images began to circulate more widely. Her *Wonders of the Vegetable Kingdom* (1822) contained no illustrations and the only image in *The Conchologist's Companion* (1824) was the frontispiece. But in her later works she included more illustrations, and their role is largely ornamental or artistic. Her *Voices from the Woodlands* (1850) featured nineteen color illustrations of various trees. Roberts's images of trees convey little scientific information in the contemporary sense of the term. The ornamental value of Margaret Gatty's work was part of the appeal of her *British Sea-Weeds* (1863) as well. In his review of the book, Charles Kingsley lavishly praised the illustrations. What gave the book "a really sterling value," according to Kingsley, was Gatty's use of the unrivalled colored plates of William Harvey's *Phycologia Britannica*. "This fact alone," Kingsley declared, "makes the book invaluable to the sea-weed collector, and an ornament, as a work of art, for any drawing-room table."[17]

The ornamental use of visual images should not be dismissed as frivolous or unimportant, even though the term "ornamental" today has about it the connotation of unnecessary embellishment or decoration. For female popularizers of science of the latter half of the century, illustrations helped readers to visualize magnificent new worlds of nature that were strange and foreign to them, whether they were exotic animals from far-off continents, spectacular heavenly bodies, or even the amazing features of commonplace objects. Illustrations of the beauty of nature were essential for engaging the aesthetic sensibilities of the reader and for creating a mood of awe. Words alone did not suffice. Moreover, in the competitive world of publishing, it was an advantage to be entertaining, as well as instructive. Through the ornamental use of visual images, female popularizers could link their science to the emerging visual culture and avoid producing the dreary didactic tracts of earlier times.

The ornamental use of images also was related to a narrative form adopted by many popularizers of science at that time. After the middle of the century, what some scholars have referred to as the "narrative of natural history" replaced the old familiar format. Unlike the narrative developed by professional scientists, the narrative of natural history made science accessible to a popular audience by stressing the plant and the animal (not the activity of the scientist), the singular (rather than the typical), and the emotional response of the observer. Indebted to the natural history tradition, it drew heavily upon the use of anecdotes. The narrative of natural history emphasized the exotic, the beautiful, and the wonderful, and embedded scientific information in a compelling story, spiced with first-person recollections and observations.[18] The development of a rich visual dimension in popular science, which vividly illustrated the wonders of nature and helped in the dramatic presentation of stories, went hand in hand with the creation of this narrative of natural history by male and female popularizers of science alike. Though not to be found in every work of popular science in the latter half of the century, the ornamental use of images to enhance a narrative of natural history was widespread. Philip Henry Gosse was among those men who presented a wide variety of vivid illustrations intended to serve as ornaments.[19] But women popularizers tended to draw even more than their male counterparts on the ornamental aspect of the narrative of natural history.

The ornamental dimension of Victorian popular science texts by women is apparent in physical aspects of these books as elaborate visual objects in themselves. Female popularizers took advantage of the introduction of cloth bindings in the 1820s, which allowed for the use of elaborate ornamental designs in the decoration of book covers.[20] The design of these books created an overall effect of physical beauty. In this sense, the physical nature of the book mirrored the picture of nature that many female popularizers of science wished to convey to their audience. A related aspect of the ornamental use of visual images involved the widespread inclusion of color in the works of female popularizers of science, as compared to the rare appearance of color illustrations in books by professional scientists with their more utilitarian attitude toward the use of images. Color images could appear almost anywhere in popular science books by women. On the front of the book or as a frontispiece, they signaled the importance of images in helping the reader to visualize new worlds of nature. The color frontispiece to Elizabeth Twining's *The Plant World* (1866) depicted the cultivation of sugar cane, while Anne Pratt's *The Poisonous, Noxious, and Suspected Plants of Our Fields and Woods* (1857) boasted a color frontispiece of the Monk's Hood. A particularly dramatic increase in color illustrations can be found in the body of popular science books on botany that took the reader on a guided tour of important plant species. Twining's two-volume *Illustrations of the Natural Orders of Plants* (1849–1855), for example, was illustrated lavishly with 160 full-page color plates. Anne Pratt's *The Ferns of Great Britain* (1855) featured 41 full-page plates, an overwhelming number for a relatively small book of 164 pages.

But women who wrote popular works on botany were not the only ones to include a wide array of color images. In their books on birds, the Kirby sisters stressed the importance of their illustrations, especially in giving their readers access to exotic new animals that lived in strange new worlds (figure 9.2). "A mere description of the Birds would have failed to convey any idea of their loveliness," they declared in their preface to *Beautiful Birds,* "but the Colored Illustrations which

9.2 Mary and Elizabeth Kirby's *Humming Birds* (1874) featured a beautiful color image of two hummingbirds on the cover of the book. Mary and Elizabeth Kirby, *Humming Birds* (London: T. Nelson & Sons, 1874), front cover. *Courtesy of Louisiana State University Special Collections.*

embellish the work bring them before our eyes with life-like reality."[21] In some cases, when the exquisite beauty of a particular bird was overwhelming, words failed completely. Sun-Birds "change colour every moment," the Kirbys wrote, "and flash and sparkle in a manner not to be described."[22] Since readers likely were unfamiliar with the native habitat of tropical birds, the authors tried to paint a vivid verbal picture. In the opening chapter, they began with a description of the English forest and then juxtaposed it to the strange woods in hot countries, emphasizing the denseness of the vegetation and the profusion of animal and vegetable life. "Now and then," they declared, "the scene is like fairyland."[23] The lush verbal description and the colorful images are intended to paint for the reader a magical vision that nearly overwhelms the senses.

But the Kirbys did not present merely a series of beautiful, yet disconnected, images to their readers. They aimed to combine their images with a story told in first-person narrative form, in the best tradition of natural history. Rich, first-hand verbal descriptions of flora and fauna, coupled with their vivid, color illustrations, were designed to transport the reader to exotic locations so that they could be involved in a story-like adventure. After several pages of detailed description of a tropical forest, the Kirbys then addressed their readers directly, explaining that "I have brought you to this part of the world to show you a beautiful bird called the Trogon."[24] Earlier in the book in a chapter titled "A Scene in the Forest," which relates how natives hunt for the Bird of Paradise in a forest "alive with brilliant creatures," the Kirbys asked the reader to observe a particular tree, as if they were there. "Do you notice yonder tree," they inquire, "with great spreading boughs that grow from the top of the stem, and form a kind of leafy plateau?"[25] Narrating adventures in a you-are-there style was not unheard of in natural history and travel literature.[26] The exotic beauty of foreign creatures and lands was rendered more immediate through the use of ornamental images combined with a narrative style indebted to natural history.

The Rhetorical Uses of Visual Images

In her popularizing book about the microscopic world of sea creatures, *The Mighty Deep* (1901), the prolific writer Agnes Giberne singled out the minute diatom plant, describing it as one of the most amazing organisms in all creation. Though too small to be seen by the unaided human eye, they are so "marvellous in their make" that "perhaps in all the world no greater marvels are to be seen than these extraordinary minute vegetable cases."[27] The illustration accompanying her discussion emphasizes the intricate

9.3 Minute organisms in the sea as containing traces of the hand of God. Agnes Giberne, *The Mighty Deep and What We Know of It* (Philadelphia: J. B. Lippincott Company; London: C. Arthur Pearson, Ltd., 1902), facing page 154.

structural symmetry in diatom cases, and uses this image as proof of divine design (figure 9.3). Giberne's rhetorical use of visual images—the use of images to persuade readers to her point of view—was shared widely by female and male popularizers. Professional scientists also used illustrations to convince their audiences of the validity of their theories and the social, political, and religious

9.4 In the frontispiece to *World's Foundations,* titled "The Mer De Glace," two human figures at the right are dwarfed by the majestic mountains, their strength insignificant compared to the power of ice, one of the geological agents which shape Earth's crust over time. Agnes Giberne, *The World's Foundations or Geology for Beginners* (London: Seeley & Co., 1888), frontispiece.

ideals that these theories reinforced.[28] But the radically different agendas underlying the goals of professional scientists, mainly bound up with the attempt to secularize and professionalize science, led many of them to use illustrations to validate a different set of ideals. Some popularizers used visual images rhetorically as a vehicle for justifying British imperialism and the existence of the British Empire. Many others used images rhetorically to illustrate divine design in nature, ranging from the most powerful natural forces to the tiniest forms of life. During the second half of the century, many popularizers of science—male and female alike—provided their readers with a readily accessible natural theology, updated in light of current scientific developments and integrated into the narrative of natural history.[29] Important male popularizers such as J. G. Wood, Richard Proctor, and Philip Gosse were no different from their female counterparts in their use of visual images as integral to their presentation of a religious message.[30]

The divine wisdom behind powerful forces of nature was a common and important theme among women who popularized science. Giberne used illustrations rhetorically in popular science works ranging across a number of fields, including botany, geology, astronomy, meteorology, and oceanography. Many of the visual images in *The World's Foundations or Geology for Beginners* (1882) depict grand landscapes that reveal the powerful forces at work in nature and point to the presence of God throughout geological time (figure 9.4). Such images are meant to support the view that powerful geological forces, at work since the earliest ages of world history, have been used by God to fashion the surface of the globe. "By 'powers of Nature,'" Giberne affirmed, "I mean simply powers used by God in nature. For this 'Nature,' of which we hear so much, is but the handiwork of God, the Divine Architect."[31] Giberne also emphasized divine power in her works on astronomy by overwhelming the reader with the vastness of the universe. She began her *Sun, Moon, and Stars* (1880) with a description of the colossal size and power of the sun. The sun's incredible output of heat and light was illustrated in a visual image of the solar corona and red-flamed prominences during an eclipse.[32] Later, she moved on to the size of the universe and the almost unimaginable number of stars, which reveal to us the "unutterable might of God's power!"[33]

Other women who popularized science were enthralled by the proofs of design to be found in living beings. References to the wisdom, power, and goodness of God are scattered throughout Jane Loudon's heavily illustrated zoological work *The Entertaining Naturalist* (1843).[34] The illustration of the bizarre-looking "Flying Scorpion" is intended to teach the reader to admire the creative power of divine nature (figure 9.5). Loudon exclaims, "How admirable is Nature! how extensive her power, and how various the forms with which she has surrounded the united elements of animated matter!" Though both frightful and beautiful, the "Flying Scorpion," like the "wallowing whale" or the "unwieldy hippopotamus," demonstrates how Nature seems to have "exhausted all ideas, all conceptions, and not to have left a single figure untried."[35] Women popularizers also were fond of finding divine design in the tiniest of living organisms. Anne Pratt's treatment of the coralline-like Griffithsia in her *Chapters on the*

THE FLYING SCORPION.

9.5 Loudon finds the creative power of a designing God in the bodies of strange and marvellous forms of life. Jane Loudon, *The Entertaining Naturalist* (London: Henry G. Bohn, 1850), 373.

Common Things of the Sea-Side was fairly typical. When studied under the microscope, the Griffithsia displayed a beauty and regularity hidden from the naked eye. Revealed to the earnest inquirer, it "bid us search more deeply into the works of God, and to come with humility even to the lowliest weed of the rock, to ask a lesson of his skill and care."[36] Mary and Elizabeth Kirby focused in a number of their works on the microscopic world of insects. The beauty of caterpillar eggs, with their intricate patterns, "as if they had been carved," leads the Kirbys in their *Caterpillars, Butterflies, and Moths* to "admire them as the work of an Almighty hand," while butterfly wings viewed through the microscope reveal "lovely tints that so please the eye."[37] Whether they were dealing with the depiction of divine power in the forces of nature, the design in the bodies of organic beings, or the more intricate patterns in the microscopic world, women who popularized science did not hesitate to use images rhetorically in order to push for the religious message so essential to their agenda.

Illustrations and Scientific Authority

In the frontispiece to her *Microscope Teachings* (1864), Mary Ward presented readers with an illustration of the burnet moth (figure 9.6, #7). When the scales of this moth were put under the microscope (figure 9.6, #8) and viewed with a high magnifying power, they assumed a "strange and almost startling appearance." Even though the scales were extremely small—like the "finest dust or powder"—they were "marked with some dozen lines, clear and sharp as staves of music, and between them are rows of characters wonderfully resembling some old Babylonish inscription."[38] Ward's visual image portrayed these scales as if they were indecipherable hieroglyphics. Scientific instruments such as the microscope revealed that nature, at bottom, was composed of mysterious symbols that only a reliable guide could interpret for the reader. Ward offered herself as that guide. She used her illustrations to demonstrate the need for an experienced interpreter of nature and to confirm her ability to assume that role with authority.[39] Visual images could help women in the Victorian period shore up their cultural authority as popular science writers and interpreters of nature. This was especially important because their male contemporaries denied that women had the qualifications to speak on behalf of science whether as professional scientists, or even as popularizers of science.

To male scientists bent on professionalizing their discipline during the nineteenth century, women were considered to be doubly disqualified from participation in science. Not only were they more easily seduced by the lure of Christianity, but they also did not possess

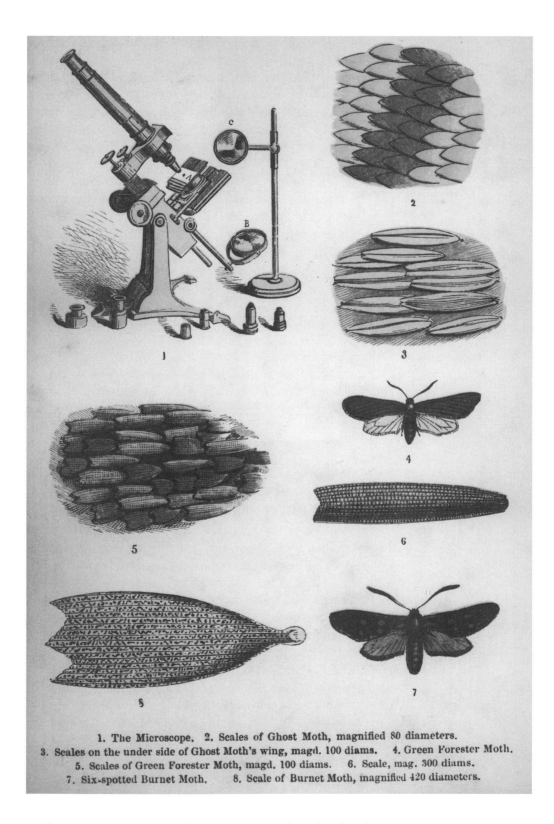

1. The Microscope. 2. Scales of Ghost Moth, magnified 80 diameters.
3. Scales on the under side of Ghost Moth's wing, magd. 100 diams. 4. Green Forester Moth.
5. Scales of Green Forester Moth, magd. 100 diams. 6. Scale, mag. 300 diams.
7. Six-spotted Burnet Moth. 8. Scale of Burnet Moth, magnified 420 diameters.

9.6 The microscope reveals mystifying inscriptions on the scales of moths. Mrs.
Ward, *Microscope Teachings* (London: Groombridge and Sons, 1864), frontispiece.

the required intellectual power to engage in genuine scientific research. They were considered to be "naturally" religious, emotional, and subjective. T. H. Huxley made it his special mission to drive women from professional scientific societies and from positions of importance in scientific institutions, and part of his strategy for bringing anthropology under Darwinian control in the late 1860s and early 1870s involved the reconstitution of the Ethnological Society into a "gentlemen's society."[40] Earlier, other male scientists, such as John Lindley, professor of botany at London University from 1829 to 1860, had redefined the intellectual focus of their disciplines in order to exclude women. Lindley's rejection of Linnaean botany was also a rejection of polite botany, previously identified with women, in favor of utilitarian botany. His attempt to envision a new kind of botanist, a new identity for the scientific practitioner, contributed to the creation of a masculine "culture of experts."[41] Excluded from universities until the end of the century, prevented from joining many scientific societies, faced with an intellectual redefinition of science that granted expertise to men alone, women in Britain in the latter half of the century were confronted by a multitude of obstacles when they claimed authority to assume the role of popularizer of science.

Popularization was a strategically important form of science writing for male professionalizers of the mid-Victorian period, and many of them were decidedly hostile to women working in this area. In the eyes of male professionals, the qualifications required to address a popular audience were no less rigorous than those needed to communicate with experts. The adoption of the role of popularizer constituted a claim to speak on behalf of science and amounted to an assertion that the individual possessed knowledge of complex scientific theories and the ability to interpret their larger significance for a lay audience. Recognizing that public support for science was essential to establish the cultural authority of the scientific elite and to free up funding for scientific institutions, professionals such as Huxley, Tyndall, and Herbert Spencer all tried their hand at writing popular works. They were major players in the two key publishing projects set up by professional scientists for a popular audience, and the absence of women in both projects is telling. The International Scientific Series was perhaps the most famous attempt at codifying and popularizing scientific knowledge in a systematic fashion to a wide reading audience. Appearing in the United States and five European countries in over 120 titles between 1871 and 1910, and written for the most part by professional scientists, the series stands as a monument to the efforts of professionals to control the public's understanding of modern science. Of the 350 authors who wrote for the International Scientific Series, none were women. An advisory committee composed of Huxley, Tyndall, and Spencer directed it in its early years in England. The popular science journal *Nature* had a similar cultural profile. One of the priorities of the astronomer Norman Lockyer in founding *Nature* in 1869 was to gain the support of the general public for the agenda of professional science. Lockyer counted on Huxley and his friends to help establish the journal and to provide stimulating pieces during the early years of the journal's existence. Though the journal was aimed at both professional scientists and a popular audience, the contributors were, with only a few exceptions, all male experts. In light of the hostility of male experts toward the participation of women in the popularization of science, the use of visual images to establish scientific authority was crucial to female writers, in some ways even more important for them than for their male counterparts engaged in popularizing science.

The relationship between illustrations and authority can be seen in the work of women involved in popularizing science who were gifted illustrators. Brightwen, Gatty, Loudon, Pratt, Twining, and Ward were among those who drew illustrations for their own works. Very few male popularizers possessed this skill. In her chapter in this volume, Barbara Gates argues that it became less necessary over the course of the nineteenth century for well-known women writers to illustrate their own work in order to control the visual dimensions of their texts. For some women, the illustrations that they drew or designed for their own books provided the opportunity to demonstrate their ability to reproduce nature faithfully, highlight their powers of observation, and showcase their expertise in operating scientific instruments. They also could claim to have made a contribution to science through the presentation of innovative visual images designed to improve traditional mapping techniques. Mary Ward, a highly regarded artist and painter, is a good example of a woman who used images in her popular science works to strengthen her own authority, as well as for ornamental and rhetorical purposes.[42] In addition to illustrating her own books, she contributed illustrations to some of Sir David Brewster's works, including the original drawings of Newton's and Lord Rosse's telescopes in Brewster's *Life of Newton*.[43] Family connections provided her with access to the world of science. William, the third Earl of Rosse, was her cousin, and while on frequent visits with him at Birr Castle in Ireland she met many of the eminent men of science and observed the construction of Rosse's colossal telescope, the "Leviathan of Parsontown." As a result of her interest in astronomy, she published *Telescope Teachings* (1859), which contained fifteen plates designed from her own drawings.

Ward presented many images drawn by her own hand in her *Microscope Teachings* as the products of careful observation undertaken by an expert who was well versed in the manipulation of scientific instruments. Her stated aim in this book was to "unite the provinces of the Guide Book and the Panorama" by including useful remarks for those who owned a microscope and by selecting "a few from the multitude of lovely scenes presented by the microscope in order to attract those readers who, unversed in microscopic marvels, might possibly feel repelled by a complete and lengthened treatise." Armed with a suitable instrument, the observer could be brought "face to face with the minuter parts of God's creation." "It is like visiting a rich, but hitherto undiscovered region," she insisted, which, when explored and studied, evoked a "new sense of the unfailing power and infinite wisdom of the Great Creator."[44] T. H. Huxley would have ruled out the possibility of seeing any trace of God while looking through the microscope. Huxley's training of students in his biological laboratory at South Kensington from 1871 was designed to maintain a strict discipline over what the students saw through the microscope. It was on the basis of Huxley's authority as scientist—he dictated the "instrumental stage-management and discourse-surveillance" used in the lab—that he could "generate an unequivocal 'authority of Nature' for trainee science teachers to follow in learning orthodox microscopy."[45] Whereas Huxley trained his students to see a secular nature, Ward, in her discussion of the microscope and through her use of illustrations, disciplined the senses of her readers so that they could discern a divine natural world.

Ward demonstrated her scientific versatility in *Microscope Teachings* by ranging across the fields of entomology, zoology, geology, and marine biology. Microscopic study, she claimed in one chapter, could add to knowledge of the vegetable world. In a later chapter, she declared that it afforded "a great deal of information to the geological inquirer" with regard to both the real nature of animal and vegetable remains and the composition of the strata themselves.[46] Expertise with the microscope allowed Ward to trespass on the domain of professional scientists in a variety of fields. Ward included chapters on insect wings, the scales of insects and fish, hairs and feathers, eyes, vegetable productions, organic remains, animalcules, and the circulation of the blood.

In some cases, Ward presented her observations and images as the results of her own original investigations. After giving instructions for viewing minute water animals, or animalcules, she informed the reader what discoveries she made using this method, listing all the different types of creatures that she encountered. In her chapter on the circulation of the blood, she discussed her sketches of

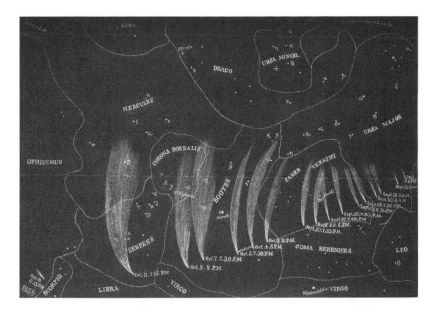

9.7 In a novel form of visual charting, Ward illustrated the path of Donati's comet during the time it was visible in the British Isles, showing the successive changes of its position, form, and apparent dimensions. Ward, *Telescope Teachings* (London: Groombridge and Sons, 1859), facing page 154.

the water-newt's circulation, which she began as her own experiment on July 2, 1853. "I figured everything which particularly struck me, adding written notes to each drawing," she wrote. "These I shall use in explaining the figures in Plate XVI." The images are not just designed to instruct her readers how to undertake microscopic examinations. They also dictate what they should see through the microscope. They are accompanied by thickly descriptive text, which specified the date the drawings were made, to underline their authenticity and accuracy.[47] Ward also enhanced her authority as a teacher of scientific truth by presenting innovative images intended to improve previous mapping techniques. In her chapter on comets in *Telescope Teachings,* Ward introduced a new mapping technique in her lengthy discussion of the unexpected arrival of Donati's comet in 1858. When it first became visible, Ward reported, she began to describe and track this comet in her diary. What followed was a detailed account of Ward's observations at various times, accompanied by vivid illustrations (figure 9.7).[48] Carefully moving back and forth between her images and the entries in her diary, she provided the reader with proof of her observational skills, her talent as illustrator, and her ability to produce original scientific work.

Visual images were used by many women popularizers as a means of establishing their expertise in their own domain. Only then could they claim to have the qualifications necessary to produce popular science for a general audience and to speak with authority on scientific matters. They could present themselves as experts in drawing scientific illustrations that faithfully represented nature and in interpreting images produced by scientific instruments.[49] They even could offer new types of visual images as improvements of traditional mapping techniques. In a time when T. H. Huxley and his allies were trying to force women out of scientific societies, it was of paramount importance for women engaged in writing popular science, like Ward, who worked to construct the narrative of natural history, to present in their works visual images that bolstered their authority as interpreters of nature.

The Power of Visual Images

In her *Rambles with Nature Students* (1899), Eliza Brightwen played with the relationship between image and text, at times employing a technique that emphasized the primacy of image. Pages seemingly were overgrown with illustrations of plants. A flax plant threatens to push the words right off the page.[50] A page of text is cut in half by the common blue butterfly, while another is choked by the flowers and buds of the wild succory (figure 9.8).[51] The image of the wild succory is so dominant that the text had to be chopped up into three distinct blocks of print. Since the text in all of these illustrations is placed in order to accommodate the images, we can only conclude that the unusual arrangement of text and image was done deliberately. Perhaps Brightwen's purpose was to illustrate vividly her point about worlds of nature that are hidden right underneath our nose. By magnifying plants to the extent that the reader could no longer avoid seeing them, so that even the words on the page were almost crowded out of the picture, she signaled to the reader that the text was meant to direct them to an immediate encounter with nature. Or, perhaps Brightwen's illustrations of plants growing wild on the page were intended as a reminder that books were made of the same materials as the plants being depicted. The book itself was organic—like everything else, it was a part of divine nature. Then again, Brightwen may have been trying to use her flowers to entangle readers, like the words on the page, so that they are held in rapt attention by the mesmerizing beauty and fascinating structure of the plant.[52] In all of these interpretations, illustrations highlight the importance of visual images for women who wrote popular science. They could be used in novel ways to reach a reading public with a voracious appetite for science and for visual images. The effective manipulation of visual images became an important part of the repertoire of many female popularizers of science, in the same way that the effective manipulation of language was essential for their success. Just as professional scientists prided themselves on their expertise in managing their experimental apparatus, so too these women could exhibit their scientific abilities through the presentation or drawing of illustrations.

One other characteristic of the teasel
is worthy of remark.   The bristly flower-
head expands its florets regularly.   First
a band of pale lilac will appear about
the middle ; when that withers a row
of florets above and then one below

will expand ;
but never
can we find
the handsome
flower-head all
expanded at
once.   It cau-
tiously opens a
little at a time
until the insects
have done their
work and all the
florets have been
fertilised.

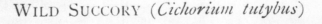

WILD SUCCORY (*Cichorium tutybus*)

Some plants seem to have a strong
preference for dry, dusty roadsides
and footpaths.   The plantain, for
instance, never flourishes more
vigorously than on a well-trodden

WILD SUCCORY.   path, and the wild succory is another

9.8 Plants grow wild on the pages of Brightwen's *Rambles with Nature Students*.
Eliza Brightwen, *Rambles with Nature Students* (London: The Religious Tract
Society, 1899), 125.

The ornamental, rhetorical, and authoritative use of visual images, as we have seen, was connected to the narrative form adopted by female popularizers of science. The narrative of natural history, with its emphasis on the unique and exotic (sometimes in the ordinary and everyday), was well served by the ornamental use of illustrations. The religious themes embedded in the narrative of natural history could be supported through the rhetorical use of illustrations. The continuing validity of natural history itself as a genre of scientific writing in an age of specialization and professionalization existed in a symbiotic relationship with the authoritative use of images. Visual technology and narrative form went hand in hand, mutually reinforcing each other. Since professional scientists pursued a different agenda, one that emphasized a study of the typical, a pursuit of the secular, and a rejection of natural history in exchange for specialized disciplines, the narrative form and visual images that they adopted could not help but be markedly distinct.

Elsewhere I have argued that the popularizers claimed, as did the professionals, to speak for a mute nature. For the popularizers, the voices of nature spoke to them of God's purpose and of his moral and natural laws.[53] Speaking on behalf of nature—representing nature—seems to have been the aim of almost all of those groups within science that were vying, to take a cue from Frank Turner, for cultural authority.[54] Turner and other scholars have concentrated for the most part on the contest between the gentlemen of science, in alliance with the aristocracy and the Anglican Church, and the scientific naturalists, who used evolutionary theory to justify the basis of an emerging middle class and industrial society. Recently, Crosbie Smith drew our attention to yet another group among scientists in that period, a circle of physicists that he labels the "North British Physicists," including Maxwell, Kelvin, and others, who constituted a distinct group from the gentlemen of science though often in sympathy with their aims.[55] The popularizers of science, both male and female, form yet another separate group within the scientific community, though they lacked the cohesiveness of the scientific naturalists or North British Physicists. Without any formal organizational ties of their own, popularizers were particularly vulnerable to the professionalization strategies of scientific naturalists, designed to exclude them from participation in the world of science. All of these groups were competing for cultural authority and using science, or at least their own definition of science, as a means towards that end. All claimed to speak authoritatively on behalf of nature, to "represent" nature, in effect, to be scientists. The representation of nature in the form of visual images therefore was caught up in the debate over who represents nature. Any attempt to represent nature in visual form was unavoidably a claim to possess knowledge and an assertion of scientific expertise. The generous use of visual images by women who popularized science was not only an affirmation of their agency, but was also part of their attempt to define their role as members of the scientific community.

Acknowledgments

I am indebted to a number of colleagues for their help in improving this essay. I learned a great deal from the members of the Gerstein Advanced Research Seminar at York University when the paper was first presented to them. I also would like to thank Jim Secord, Anne Secord, and Suzanne Le-May Sheffield for their helpful comments on earlier drafts. Without Ann Shteir's wise editorial comments, I would have been unable to reduce an impossibly long paper. Kay Neeley, Ruth Barton, and Michael Collie all supplied vital information.

Notes

1. Mrs. Brightwen, *Quiet Hours with Nature* (London: T. Fisher Unwin; New York: James Pott and Company, [1904]), 189.
    2. Ibid., 174.
    3. Ibid., 180.
    4. Ibid., x.
    5. Barbara T. Gates and Ann B. Shteir, eds., *Natural Eloquence: Women Reinscribe Science* (Madison: The University of Wisconsin Press, 1997), 8–9.
    6. Ibid., 12.
    7. Sarah Trimmer's *An Easy Introduction to the Knowledge of Nature* contained no illustrations. A frontispiece with a picture of Margaret Bryan and children, as well as sixteen black-and-white plates of planetary orbits, the moon, earth, and sun, a telescope, and trigonometry diagrams, were included in Margaret Bryan's *A Compendious System of Astronomy* (1797), while her *Lectures on Natural Philosophy* (1806) increased the number of illustrations to thirty-six black-and-white plates of scientific instruments, experimental apparatus, ships, magnets, the eye and lenses, planetary orbits, and geometric shapes, in addition to a frontispiece depicting the author. The illustrations in Jane Marcet's *Conversations on Chemistry* (1806), which included twelve illustrations, and her *Conversations on Natural Philosophy* (1819), with twenty-three plates, were primarily simple black and white drawings of experimental apparatus and scientific instruments. Priscilla Wakefield's *An Introduction to Botany* (1796) included eleven black-and-white plates at the back of the book. Later, probably in the sixth edition published in 1812, nine of the plates were colorized and placed at the front of the book. Her *Domestic Recreation* (1805) drew on six simple black-and-white illustrations of the microscope, sea anemones, and insects. An illustrator as

well as a popularizer, Sarah Bowdich Lee (1791–1856) was one of the few female popularizers of the period to use vivid illustrations extensively in her work. In her *Fresh Water Fishes of Great Britain Drawn and Described by Mrs. T. Edward Bowdich* (1828), she included forty-four beautiful color illustrations drawn by her own hand. See Barbara T. Gates, *Kindred Nature: Victorian and Edwardian Women Embrace the Living World* (Chicago and London: University of Chicago Press, 1998), 77–78.

8. Mrs. Somerville, *Mechanism of the Heavens* (London: John Murray, 1831), 3.

9. Similarly the illustrations in the first edition of her *On the Connexion of the Physical Sciences* (1834) were limited to some diagrams at the back of the book. Though a frontispiece depicting nebulae was added to the third edition (J. Murray, 1836), no illustrations appeared in the body of the text. Seventy-five small drawings, mostly geometrical, were placed in the notes at the back of the book, followed by four plates filled with small black-and-white patterns.

10. Patricia Anderson, *The Printed Image and the Transformation of Popular Culture, 1790–1860* (Oxford: Clarendon Press, 1991).

11. Bernard Lightman, "The Visual Theology of Victorian Popularizers of Science: From Reverent Eye to Chemical Retina," *Isis* 91 (2000): 654–55.

12. Anne Secord, "Botany on a Plate: Pleasure and the Power of Pictures in Promoting Early Nineteenth-Century Scientific Knowledge," *Isis* 93 (March 2002): 28–57.

13. George R. Bodmer, "The Technical Illustration of Thomas Henry Huxley," in *Thomas Henry Huxley's Place in Science and Letters: Centenary Essays,* ed. Alan P. Barr (Athens and London: University of Georgia Press, 1997), 281, 285.

14. James G. Paradis argues that in the second chapter of *Man's Place in Nature,* Huxley's use of images is quite unusual. Here "Huxley's illustrations take on a symbolic, iconographic significance, something that would never occur in a strictly technical work," though he refers to one chapter as a "visual boneyard." See James G. Paradis, *T. H. Huxley: Man's Place in Nature* (Lincoln and London: University of Nebraska Press, 1978), 129–30.

15. The one exception, Huxley's *Physiography* (1877), contained 122 illustrations and five colored plates, including diagrams, maps, scientific instruments, and even some depictions of natural phenomena such as volcanoes, geysers, and gorges.

16. Martin J. S. Rudwick, "The Emergence of a Visual Language for Geological Science 1760–1840," *History of Science* 14 (1976): 150.

17. [Charles Kingsley], "British Sea-Weeds," *The Reader* 2 (August 15, 1863): 162.

18. Bernard Lightman, "The Story of Nature: Victorian Popularizers and Scientific Narrative," *Victorian Review* 25 (Winter 2000): 1–29.

19. According to Jonathan Smith, Philip Gosse's books not only were illustrated copiously; these images also "were intimately connected to the visuality of the text, the culmination of a series of scopic acts." See Jonathan Smith, "Philip Gosse and the Varieties of Natural Theology," in *Reinventing*

Christianity, ed. Linda Woodhead (Aldershot: Ashgate, 2001), 255. Besides Gosse, John George Wood, Charles Alexander Johns, Francis Orpen Morris, and William Houghton all produced well-illustrated books.

20. Ruari McLean, *Victorian Book Design and Colour Printing* (London: Faber and Faber, 1963), 150–59. McLean has argued that the period between 1837 and 1890, the last era of hand-worked printing and illustration processes in commercial book production, was more exciting than "any other comparable period in the history of the world's printing." See Ibid., vii.

21. Mary and Elizabeth Kirby, *Beautiful Birds in Far-Off Lands: Their Haunts and Homes* (London: T. Nelson and Sons, 1872), v.

22. Ibid., 134.

23. Ibid., 13.

24. Ibid., 106.

25. Ibid., 21.

26. The naturalist Charles Waterton (1782–1865) used the technique in his *Wanderings in South America* (1825). An example of Waterton's use of the technique appears after his description of various South American animals and landscapes. Waterton advises his readers to "stop and look at this grand picture of vegetable nature," as if they were by his side. On the following page, he instructs his readers to "See that noble purple-heart before thee." Charles Waterton, *Wanderings in South America, the North-West of the United States, and the Antilles, in the Years 1812, 1816, 1820, and 1824,* 2nd ed. (London: B. Fellowes, 1828), 24–25.

27. Agnes Giberne, *The Mighty Deep and What We Know of It* (Philadelphia: J. B. Lippincott Company; London: C. Arthur Pearson, Ltd., 1902), 154–55.

28. For example, Darwin used photographs rhetorically to undermine natural theology. Phillip Prodger argues that Darwin's *The Expression of the Emotions* (1872) became one of the first photographically illustrated scientific treatises. But far from being scientifically factual, these photographs "formed part of a narrative strategy designed to advance his theoretical concerns" and to challenge Charles Bell's natural theological analysis of expression. See Phillip Prodger, "Illustration as Strategy in Charles Darwin's 'The Expression of the Emotions in Man and Animals,'" in *Inscribing Science: Scientific Texts and the Materiality of Communication,* ed. Timothy Lenoir (Stanford: Stanford University Press, 1998), 141.

29. Lightman, "The Story of Nature," 14–17.

30. Lightman, "The Visual Theology of Victorian Popularizers of Science," 657–71. Jonathan Smith has explored how Gosse's "representations of coastal marine life . . . were thus designed to illustrate both the Paleyan vision of organisms designed for their environments and Gosse's own typological readings." See Smith, "Philip Gosse and the Varieties of Natural Theology," 257.

31. Agnes Giberne, *The World's Foundations or Geology for Beginners* (London: Seeley & Co., 1888), 36.

32. Agnes Giberne, *Sun, Moon, and Stars: A Book for Beginners* (New York: Robert Carter and Brothers, n.d.), facing page 21.

33. Ibid., 125.

34. Divine design is detected in the decision not to place the immense elephant among the carnivorous beasts, in the large pouch allotted to the pelican for storing food, and in the checks that were put upon the fecund cabbage butterfly and the gnat. See Mrs. Loudon, *The Entertaining Naturalist* (London: Henry G. Bohn, 1850), 97, 330, 500, and 508.

35. Ibid., 373.

36. Anne Pratt, *Chapters on the Common Things of the Sea-Side* (London: Society for Promoting Christian Knowledge, 1850), 153.

37. Mary and Elizabeth Kirby, *Caterpillars, Butterflies, and Moths* (London: Jarrold and Sons, [1861]), 11–12, 129.

38. Hon. Mrs. Ward, *Microscope Teachings* (London: Groombridge and Sons, 1864), 50–51.

39. Simon Schaffer has pointed to the use of representations to establish scientific authority, but his focus is on practicing scientists rather than popularizers. See his "The Leviathan of Parsontown: Literary Technology and Scientific Representation," in *Inscribing Science: Scientific Texts and the Materiality of Communication,* ed. Timothy Lenoir and Hans Ulrich Gumbrecht (Stanford: Stanford University Press, 1998), 182–84.

40. Evelleen Richards, "Huxley and Woman's Place in Science," in *History, Humanity and Evolution,* ed. James Moore (Cambridge: Cambridge University Press, 1989), 253–84.

41. Ann B. Shteir, *Cultivating Women, Cultivating Science: Flora's Daughters and Botany in England 1760 to 1860* (Baltimore: The Johns Hopkins University Press, 1996), 156–58; Ann B. Shteir, "Gender and 'Modern' Botany in Victorian England," *Osiris* 12 (1997): 29–38.

42. According to Owen Harry, the attractive covers of her books, which were illuminated with gold-embossed lettering and figures set against green, red, and blue cloth, together with her lovely colored illustrations, ensured a steady stream of buyers. Indeed, Ward's books must have been highly valued for their aesthetic qualities: Two of them were put on display in the book section of the International Exhibition at the Crystal Palace, Sydenham, in 1862. See Owen G. Harry, "The Hon. Mrs Ward and 'A Windfall for the Microscope', of 1856 and 1864," *Annals of Science* 41 (1984): 471.

43. Owen Harry, "Mary Ward," in *Some People and Places in Irish Science and Technology,* ed. Charles Mollan, William Davis, and Brendan Finucane (Dublin: Royal Irish Academy, 1985), 52.

44. Hon. Mrs. Ward, *Microscope Teachings,* viii–ix.

45. Graeme Gooday, "'Nature' in the Laboratory: Domestication and Discipline with the Microscope in Victorian Life Science," *British Journal for the History of Science* 24 (1991): 339, 310.

46. Ward, *Microscope Teachings,* 103, 118.

47. Ibid., 209, 207.

48. Mary Ward, *Telescope Teachings,* facing pages 142 and 152.

49. Elsewhere I have discussed Agnes Clerke and her goal of bringing the extraordinary results of astrophotography before the eyes of the public. But this involved teaching the reading public how to understand new visual

images derived from an instrument only recently introduced into the practice of astronomical science, the camera. Among the first to present astronomical photos as book illustrations, she established her reputation on the basis of her expertise in interpreting these images for her audience and associated her work with the respected names of the astronomers who had contributed them. See Lightman, "Visual Theology of Victorian Popularizers of Science," 671–79.

50. Eliza Brightwen, *Rambles with Nature Students* (London: The Religious Tract Society, 1899), 107.

51. Ibid., 138.

52. I am indebted to Suzanne Le-May Sheffield for this suggestion.

53. Bernard Lightman, "'The Voices of Nature': Popularizing Victorian Science," in *Victorian Science in Context,* ed. Bernard Lightman (Chicago and London: University of Chicago Press, 1987,) 207.

54. Frank M. Turner, *Contesting Cultural Authority: Essays in Victorian Intellectual Life* (Cambridge: Cambridge University Press, 1993).

55. Crosbie Smith, *The Science of Energy: A Cultural History of Energy Physics in Victorian Britain* (Chicago: University of Chicago Press, 1998).

Chapter 10

GENDERED COLLABORATIONS

Marrying Art and Science

Suzanne Le-May Sheffield

The 1992 short story "Morpho Eugenia" by A. S. Byatt, adapted for the screen in 1996 as *Angels and Insects,* follows the growing attachment between two Victorians, William Adamson and Matilda Crompton, as they explore the natural world together, studying, writing, sketching, and painting. William and Matilda eventually fall in love. With William as writer and Matilda as artist, they produce a popular natural history work on ants that finances their united exploration of the Amazon.[1] While postmodern Byatt does not satisfy the reader with a marriage at the end of her tale, Andrea Barrett provides a marriage at the end of her 1998 novel *The Voyage of the Narwhal.* Alexandra, a talented illustrator and engraver, struggles for recognition in the male-dominated worlds of scientific art and scientific exploration. The conclusion of the novel finds her married to Erasmus, a nineteenth-century American scientific explorer and naturalist, traveling alongside him in the arctic regions. They are in harmony with one another and in harmony with the natural world.[2] In the case of both fictional couples, their relationships result in a superior scientific enterprise than that which might have been accomplished by either one alone. Matilda brings to William's more thorough scientific knowledge an understanding of the needs of a popular science audience, including illustrations for aesthetic interest and greater comprehension of the subject matter. Alexandra sees more in nature and sees differently from Erasmus, providing a more detailed and complex view of the natural world.

Both of these fictional works point to a contemporary hunger for accounts of male/female relationships that are productive, complementary, and harmonious. We must be careful, however, not to allow this modern romance with the past to color our historical interpretation of such real-life relationships. During the nineteenth century, women's artistic work for science, like their science practice more generally, could be anonymous, unpaid, and/or generally unrecognized publicly. Relationships of this kind between husband and wife were not often equal partnerships. Yet women did engage in scientific illustration. It was a natural extension for women to bring together their acquired skill in drawing with their interest in studying the natural world, painting, engraving and coloring plates for botanical works. Botany, as well as landscape and still-life art, were fields in which women most frequently worked, as they were socially acceptable female practices.[3] Nineteenth-century scientists understood botanical art to be an integral and central aspect of the botanical sciences in this period. Botanical art is not strictly a mechanical activity of dexterity with no thought, knowledge or creativity needed, but can be an active and interpretative contribution to science, integral to the development of ideas within botany and to the dissemination of those ideas both within the scientific community and to the general public.[4] Botanical art conducted within the context of marriage enabled women to make an important contribution to the scientific endeavor that they may not have made otherwise, drawing them into the center of scientific knowledge production.

Historians of gender and science have often noted the apparent present-day invisibility of women scientists from the past. Yet in our desire to recognize the work of such women, their artistic work for science often has been relegated to the background of any discussion about their scientific work.[5] Several biographies noting and describing women scientific illustrators and their work are beginning to uncover the extent of women's involvement in botanical art.[6] However, these studies of women's contribution to scientific illustration remain descriptive rather than analytical. Historians of science have been focusing their attention upon the relationship between art and science over the last decade rather than on that between artists and scientists. They are doing important work in analyzing and interpreting the impact of visual images upon scientific theory and in examining the broader consequences for interpretations of these images for scientists and the reading public.[7] Women illustrators for science need to be brought into the picture.[8]

The literature on marital collaboration in science, while acknowledging gender power imbalances, has tried to emphasize the importance of women's contribution in the collaborative process of scientific work, and stresses the variety of ways in which such collaborations could work themselves out.[9] Yet even in this context, artistic contributions by women to scientific endeavors are often marginalized. Women's illustration is often relegated to the peripheries of science in the secondary literature by scholars who overlook the importance of the interrelationship between art and science, and thus between artists and scientists, that was clearly acknowledged during the nineteenth century. Among recent publications, Pamela Henson's studies of Anna Botsford Comstock provide one of the few sources that examine such relationships from the perspective of gender.[10] In another publication, *Creative Couples in the Sciences* (1996), Janet Bell Garber's essay on the science/art relationship of John and Elizabeth Gould reveals the complex and multi-faced ways in which marriage partnerships could provide access to science for women.[11] Both Henson and Garber explore relationships that spotlight partnerships in art and science that are productive and unproblematic, much like Byatt's and Barrett's fictional relationships.

Marriage partnerships of art and science during the nineteenth century in England certainly could be productive and result in successful scientific works, but few were entirely equal working partnerships. While husband and wife could bring a range of artistic and scientific skills and talents to the partnership, the husband was far more likely to receive the majority of the public recognition and accolades for their joint work. How did women live inside their art and science marriages, and how is gender part of those stories? If we are aiming to reconstruct these circumstances, what resources are available and how can they be used? Three types of collaboration between art and science in marriage will be addressed in this chapter, moving along a spectrum from productive marriage partnerships of art and science, to those that are tenuous, and then to those that are parallel. By examining various working partnerships, we will see that marriage gave some women access to work in the visual culture of science that would have been difficult to attain otherwise. Given the paucity of written sources of information about the women under consideration here, their marriages and their work, visual materials offer us a rich resource for study. Through their art, the women discussed in this chapter attain a kind of visibility that they might otherwise not have.

Productive Partnerships in Art and Science: The Rudges and the Stebbings

Productive marriage partnerships in art and science do appear to have existed in life as well as in fiction. Such partnerships produced joint scientific work that recognized the importance of art to science, and drew on the scientific and artistic knowledge of both parties to accomplish the finished product. The positive recognition of their publications by the scientific community reflected in large part their successful partnerships in art and science. Living at opposite ends of the nineteenth century from one another, Anne Rudge and Mary Anne Stebbing found themselves, through marriage, becoming not only life partners but also work partners with their husbands. Both women contributed to their husbands' scientific endeavors by their artistic abilities and scientific knowledge. Their husbands' perception of their wives' roles in this work dictated, however, how these women would utilize and perceive their own skills and how history would remember their contributions.

Anne Nonaille (1763–1836) had been extremely well educated thanks to the efforts of her father. Besides a knowledge of languages and music, her "skill in drawing and etching was equal, if not superior, to her knowledge of music." By the time of her marriage to Edward Rudge (1763–1846), she had the ability to copy from nature "with fidelity and precision, both in landscape and natural history." Her husband had only to instruct her in the knowledge of botany and share with her his antiquarian studies to facilitate her ability to draw for his published works.[12] In the end, Anne Rudge was responsible for drawing fifty plates for her husband's *Plantarum Guianae* as well as numerous other botanical drawings for Edward's articles published in the *Transactions of the Linnean Society* in five different volumes between 1804 and 1808. Edward Rudge became an antiquarian and gentleman botanist with the assistance of other people, his wife included. The foundation of Rudge's botanical work was provided in part by his Oxford education, although he never took a degree. He also was inspired and encouraged by his uncle, Samuel Rudge, whose interest in botany had led to an impressive herbarium and library collection. Edward Rudge drew extensively on these resources for his own study of natural history and inherited them upon his uncle's death.[13] He was elected to the Linnean Society in 1802 and to the Royal Society in 1805, and was also on the Council of the Linnean Society. Rudge published his major work, *Plantarum Guianae*, between 1805 and 1807, but it was not the work of long, arduous personal collection. The collection of plants from which Rudge drew his information had been gathered by the French naturalist Joseph Martin (fl. 1796–1826) during six years in Guiana. The collection was captured by two British privateer ships and became the spoils of war. Rudge paid about £130 to £150 for half of the specimens when they were sold by Kew to provide prize money for the owners and crew of the ships.[14] Prior to purchasing these specimens and compiling the *Plantarum Guianae,* Rudge had the good fortune to have married Anne Nonaille, and she became responsible for producing the botanical drawings for his scientific work.

If the story Edward Rudge tells of his life via his published *Memoir* of Anne can be taken at face value, he and Anne formed a perfect scientific and artistic partnership. He wrote of her botanical work and illustration that the "magnified parts of fructification, so difficult to develop from dried specimens, are drawn with the utmost precision and accuracy, by which she obtained a perfect knowledge of the admirable and wonderful formation of flowers of the physiology of vegetation."[15] Unfortunately, no archival or published material remains in which Anne Rudge speaks for herself. Yet to some extent her artwork can speak for her.

Anne Rudge's botanical illustrations exhibit a consistent style and exacting detail in the sections on her plates, and these could only have come from intense personal study and interest. Her drawings are large, bold, clear, and precise (figure 10.1). Plants are reduced to their very essence in her art, with simple outlines that help clarify detail and complexity for the botanical reader. Yet her illustrations also communicate the character of the particular species, albeit not the individual plant. The clarity of her line drawings is somewhat reminiscent of the

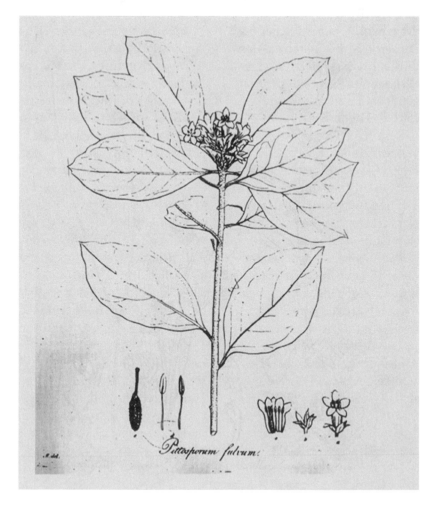

10.1 *Pittosporum fulvum* by Anne Rudge for Edward Rudge, "A Description of Several Species of Plants from New Holland," *Transactions of the Linnean Society of London* (1811): 298. *Courtesy of the Linnean Society of London.*

early herbals whose purpose was identification, yet her plates also include dissected sections paying close attention to the sexual parts of plants, indicating that she was familiar not only with the requirements of botanical illustration being established at this time, but also with Linnaean classification.[16] These features of her work have led the exacting botanical art critic William Stearn to write of Rudge's "wife's excellent plates."[17] Her work was held in such high esteem during her lifetime that Dr. G. F. W. Meyer, of Göttingen, who had published on the plants of Essequiboe, named a species of the genus Nymphaea, or water lily, after her.[18] Anne Rudge, as a woman botanical artist, likely would have been lost in obscurity if it had not been for the fact that her plates bear her name. Given the opinions that he puts forth in the *Memoir*, Edward Rudge likely encouraged or readily agreed to the publication of his wife's name on the plates. Her married life became one committed to the art and science of botany and Edward acknowledged the importance of her artistic renderings and botanical knowledge to their joint publications; he wrote a *Memoir* of her life and praised her artwork there. Her plates get the reader's attention in the *Plantarum Guianae*. In fact, without her illustrations, the *Plantarum Guianae* would have been nothing more than a list of botanical names. Together, the Rudges studied the plants of Guiana, while never having to leave British shores, and produced a "minor pioneer contribution" to their field.[19]

Unlike Anne Rudge, Mary Anne Saunders (1845?–1927) had been virtually born into science. She was the youngest daughter of William Wilson Saunders (1809–1879), banker for Lloyds and well-known for his work in entomology and interests in botany and horticulture. Family correspondence suggests that Saunders' children were involved continually and actively in gathering and identifying botanical specimens, sketching the same, and caring for the garden.[20] Like her father and her siblings, Mary Anne had learned to sketch early on and concentrated on honing these skills throughout her life. She met her husband through the Holmesdale Natural History Club, founded at Reigate in 1857 by her father. When Thomas Roscoe Rede Stebbing (1835–1926), her future husband, first met the Saunders family in 1863, he found the Saunders' residence to be "a very nest of naturalists."[21] Upon her marriage to Stebbing in 1867, Mary Anne presented him with a volume of watercolor sketches. The volume contains mostly orchids (one of her father's particular interests), which she had drawn herself, and had inscribed it "To my dear husband."[22] These are delicate, uncertain sketches, not particularly useful to the exacting botanical scientist; nevertheless, they are art that reflected Mary Anne's personal observation and her efforts to attain skill in botanical art. Mary Anne's aim as a young woman was to "illustrate

10.2 *Anemone nervosa* (Tunbridge Wells, April 5, 1880) by Mary Anne Stebbing, part of her work towards a British flora.
Holmesdale Natural History Club, Reigate.

the British flora by water-colour drawings" (figure 10.2).[23] Mary Anne Stebbing's art in this period was closer to that of an accomplished flower painter than to that of a botanical illustrator, paying more attention to the aesthetics of mood and color and the specific character of the individual specimen than to botanical detail.

Unfortunately, a fire in 1881 at Warberry House, Thomas and Mary Anne's home in Tunbridge Wells, caused her to lose a significant amount of her work and sketches.[24] Although she began again, it seems as though Mary Anne branched out from her scheme of publishing a

British flora and began to study botany more intensely, including vegetable teratology and the study of plant seedlings.[25] She put her self-styled artistic training to good use in these new projects. In the 1880s and 1890s, her art style changed, becoming more exacting, bolder in line and color, more detailed. She began to include sections of plants on the page as well as text notes of locations, and, where relevant, the name of the person who had collected it for her. Such specimens clearly were being drawn from life and studied in-depth and were more akin to botanical illustration now than her earlier flower paintings. By 1926, an obituary notice of Thomas Stebbing in *Nature* referred to Mary Anne as "an accomplished botanist."[26]

So, unlike Anne Rudge, Mary Anne was a botanist and botanical artist in her own right, and her scientific knowledge and artistic acumen contributed to helping Thomas produce strict line drawings for his professional papers, which were akin to Anne Rudge's style of work in their clarity and precision (figure 10.3). Unlike Mary Anne, Thomas had come late to science. After studying at Oxford and being ordained a priest in 1859 by Bishop Samuel Wilberforce, he became an "ardent convert" to Darwinian science and then devoted the second half of his life to the study of Crustacea.[27] His support for Darwin's theory caused a rift between himself and his church, leading to "active opposition, the denial of a parish, and thousands of words of minor criticism."[28] Stebbing had not grown up in a scientific household, but had been propelled into the study of science by his original desire to refute Darwin. However, he had been captivated by the theory of evolution and devoted many of his papers and books, directly or indirectly, to helping the cause of Darwinian science and refuting Darwin's detractors.

After the fire, the Stebbings new home, Mount Ephraim Lodge at Tunbridge Wells, was expanded in an attempt to contain the family's bookshelves and natural specimens of lime and coral, among other things, which filled every room. Plants in various stages of growth lived in a precarious bay window in the front room, cabinets of curiosities abounded, and Crustacea often found a home in the Stebbings' bathtub.[29] On their golden wedding anniversary in 1917, the *Kent and Sussex Courier* reported that the couple was spending at least part of the day working together on a drawing:

> Mr. Stebbing and his devoted wife spent part of his golden wedding day in completing a beautiful drawing of a section of the structure of a prawn as dissected under the microscope. With meticulous accuracy and skillful pencil, Mr. Stebbing devoted the most interesting anniversary of his life to a drawing which will be reproduced in the Proceedings of the Durban Museum.[30]

10.3 *Exhyalella Natalensis*, plate XI, for T. R. R. Stebbing, "Some Crustacea of Natal," *Annals of the Durban Museum*, vol. II, part 2, July 30, 1918.
Reproduced by permission of Durban Museum Novitates.

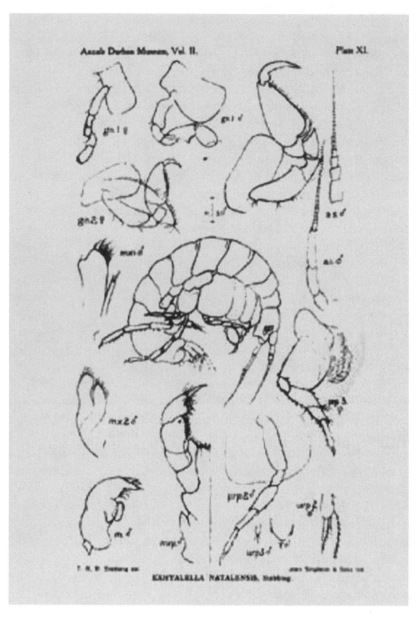

In 1926, upon the death of Mr. Stebbing, the *Courier* recollected how the couple had spent their golden wedding anniversary, this time noting in addition that Mary Anne, "who shared his scientific attainments, was assisting him in the classification of the specimens . . ." Both scientists, both artists, they worked together in "serene tranquility."[31]

Thomas Roscoe Rede Stebbing was as certain as Edward Rudge of the importance of his wife to his scientific endeavors. However, he also recognized that Mary Anne was a botanist and artist in her own right. In the privacy of their home, Thomas supported Mary Anne in her pursuit of her own interests and talents in botany. In public, however, the increasing press of professionalization in science by the end of the nineteenth century led Thomas Stebbing to publish all of his 242 articles and notes in his name alone.[32] Nevertheless, in 1905, as a result of her own studies, Mary Anne Stebbing was invited to become one of the first women members of the Linnean Society although she would never publish anything in her own name. Thomas Stebbing had no little hand in this turn of events. As a member of the Linnean Society himself, he pushed hard for women's acceptance as members. He believed women ought to read and study and have access to materials to do so.[33] Mary Anne had dedicated her life to studying plants in various respects. Moreover, her husband's voluminous publications were due as much to her dedication to art and to science as they were to his.

A family photograph of the couple reflects their quiet companionship of later life, surrounded by their much-loved books, their knees just touching one another's. While an equal partner in a scientific and artistic sense, Mary Anne remained an invisible partner in Stebbing's published books and articles and never published in her own right. As a woman working at the end of the nineteenth and beginning of the twentieth century, it would have been easier for her to request a share of the limelight than it would have been for Anne Rudge at the beginning of the nineteenth century. Anecdotal family lore suggests that Mary Anne and Thomas lived and worked as one.[34] Yet the distinctions between their scientific interests led them to claim authorship only in their respective fields.

Working for the greater good of science and their husbands' reputations called for self-sacrifice on the part of Anne Rudge and Mary Anne Stebbing. Equally, though, Edward Rudge and Thomas Stebbing recognized the importance of their wives' contribution to their scientific work and the importance of illustration to communicating their scientific ideas. Each made a point of recognizing his wife's contribution publicly, knowing that he was fortunate indeed to have her unpaid, skilled work to hand. Anne Rudge and Mary Anne Stebbing, in their turn, had found a route to science publication through art, via marriage.

A Tenuous Partnership in Art and Science: Mary and Dawson Turner

Unlike the work circumstances for Anne Rudge and Mary Anne Stebbing, Mary Turner's marriage did not provide a seamless entry into a harmonious partnership of art and science. During her lifetime, Mary Turner (1774–1850) established a strong reputation as an artist.

In 1825, she compiled one hundred portrait etchings that she had copied from medals, pictures, and sketches. She exhibited her knowledge and understanding of art in another work, *Outlines in Lithography*, published privately in 1840, of which one hundred copies were printed. These works were a culmination of her study of art over a thirty-year period, which included travels to the continent and within Britain, and endless drawing and etching at home and abroad. In their turn, her daughters were trained similarly. Mary and her daughters brought their skills to the assistance of Dawson Turner's antiquarian efforts, producing over two thousand drawings and etchings.[35] Dawson Turner (1775–1858) participated in his family's artistic interests by making significant art purchases from well-known contemporary painters and art dealers. The Turners were partners in art, constantly working, learning, and thinking about art together.

While Turner's wife and daughters were involved closely as artists in his antiquarian work, they participated only in limited ways in his extensive scientific endeavors. His scientific work was conducted largely in the first two decades of the marriage, when his daughters were babies and his wife was still honing her artistic abilities. Despite Anne Rudge's favorable comparison to Mary Turner by the contemporary botanist Dr. G. F. W. Meyer of Göttingen, Dawson Turner was largely unable to turn to his wife for botanical assistance. Turner, a Yarmouth banker, art collector and patron, antiquarian, and contemporary of Rudge's, was also a central figure in botanical circles, a "leading cryptogamist," and Fellow of the Linnean Society, the Imperial Academy, the Society of Antiquaries, and the Royal Society among others. Working with such prominent scientific figures as Sir Joseph Banks, Lewis Weston Dillwyn, and James Sowerby, Turner also published some of his own papers.[36] His most important botanical works were his *Synopsis of the British Fuci* (1802) and his four-volume work *Fuci* (1808–1819).

Although Dawson Turner sketched for his own botanical records, he did not have the time, or perhaps the skill, to draw for his publications, yet he was well aware that the success of his botanical work depended to a large extent on producing good illustrations.[37] Unable to turn to his family work force in this instance as their skills did not include botanical illustration, he sought out artists to stand in their stead. Turner welcomed correspondence from many quarters. The Irish botanist and illustrator Ellen Hutchins (1785–1815), was one of Dawson's favorite botanical correspondents. Unfortunately, Ellen Hutchins was often ill and when she was well much of her time was taken up with nursing family members. Despite her great skill, Turner had to look elsewhere for artists. A Mr. Mason, about whom not much is known, was responsible for the illustrations in Turner's

Synopsis of the British Fuci.[38] More significantly, Turner was indebted primarily to William Hooker for the majority of the plates in his *Fuci; or, Coloured Figures and Descriptions of the Plants Referred by Botanists to the Genus Fucus*.

Although it seemed that Turner could make do without his wife's assistance in drawing botanical illustrations, he nevertheless attempted to educate and train his wife and children in botany. Ellen Jane, the namesake of Ellen Hutchins, was herself personally interested in botanical study. One daughter collected shells,[39] and another daughter, Maria, who became the wife of William Hooker, was to become "a natural historian in her own right."[40] Mary Turner, Dawson's wife, appears to have been coached in botany and botanical illustration as well. In 1800, she privately published a work entitled *Drawings of Submersed Algae; with the addition of a couple of Norfolk Fungi of peculiar variety*. Authors for this work are listed as Mrs. Dawson Turner, Mrs. Simpson, and Mr. Mason but individual illustrations are not signed, so it is impossible to tell which artist drew which illustration. The specimens of algae are naively drawn and colored and are not particularly good examples of botanical art, hence they probably would not have served any detailed scientific purpose. Nor do they have any aesthetic appeal. Mrs. Turner and Mrs. Simpson likely were the primary artists, as Mr. Mason's 1802 work for Turner's *Synopsis* was of higher quality. Try as she might, it would seem that Mrs. Turner could not reach the artistic heights in botany that she later reached in portraiture and copying. Nevertheless, Mary Turner was a devoted wife and came to her husband's assistance when he needed her. Several plates of the *Fuci* were drawn by Mary (figure 10.4). She drew one plate for volume 2, one plate for volume 4, and ten plates for volume 3. By 1811, practice had enabled her to contribute botanicals to her husband's *magnum opus* alongside Hutchins and Hooker, albeit not with the same degree of skill. In a pinch, it would seem, Mary Turner's botanical art would do. As Turner found himself constantly hounding Hutchins and Hooker for their work, he on occasion turned to his wife as a last resort.

Dawson Turner appreciated his wife's talents, and in the preface to her *Outlines of Lithography* praised Mary's "perception, and the admiration, and the love of whatever is beautiful in nature or in art."[41] Yet nowhere did he pour upon Mary the kind of praise he reserved for Ellen Hutchins, to whom he felt he owed a great botanical debt and with whom he shared a mutual love of science. In a letter to Hutchins in 1811 he wrote, "in this [drawing] as in every other respect, I *must* be your inferior, I must."[42] He noted to her on another occasion that "I know no female in the world whom I shd so earnestly wish a child of mine to emulate."[43] He publicly bemoaned Hutchins's

death, writing at some length in the last page of volume 4 of his *Fuci*
that "few, if any, except myself, can appreciate her many amiable
qualities; her liberality, her pleasure in communicating knowledge,
her delight in being useful, the rapture she felt in tracing the works of
the divine hand, and the union in her of those virtues which embellish and improve mankind."

Mary Turner felt inadequate in light of her husband's accomplishments. She wrote to him, "I think I should join with those who
congratulate you on yr successful accomplishment of many things,
rather than echo your lamination [*sic*] at having done so little. At
least my powers are never commensurate with your endeavours &

inclinations & I suppose you do more by yrself than with me to drag forward."[44] In 1818, she commented specifically with reference to drawing that her own "slowness mortifies me exceedingly."[45] On several occasions, she noted that her abilities in various fields paled in comparison with his, forgetting that during this time she had given birth to at least twelve children. Mary Turner and her daughters, even as adults, went out of their way to please Dawson Turner through their artistic and scientific accomplishments, but none of them felt they lived up to his great expectations for them.

While all the factors necessary for a marriage of art and science were present in the Turner family, as they had been in the Rudge and Stebbing families, a harmonious, productive, and therefore successful partnership did not exist between Mary and Dawson Turner. The timing was off. Art and botany co-existed at the Turners' Bank House and were interwoven from time to time, but only by force of necessity. Turner might well have used his wife's illustrations more extensively, but recognized the need for exceptional illustrations to make his work credible. While Turner did find botanical illustrators beyond his home, lack of familial skill and interest created added burdens for him in his botanical work. Still, Dawson Turner encouraged his wife to share his scientific interests, opening science to her and all of their children. He benefitted from the support his family provided to his social scientific network and welcomed their ability to come to his artistic aid in moments of need. They, in turn, were offered routes to bring both science and art into their lives. Despite this awkward partnership of art and science, the Turners were aware of the usefulness of connecting the two disciplines within marriage, and they did attempt to create a productive partnership.

A Parallel Partnership in Art and Science: John Claudius Loudon and Jane Webb Loudon

Anne Rudge, Mary Anne Stebbing, and Mary Turner were, from the perspective of the public realm, largely invisible scientific and artistic partners. But not all women of their time remained invisible when utilizing their artistic and scientific knowledge in support of their husbands' scientific work. John Claudius Loudon and Jane Webb Loudon both worked in the horticultural realm, both held a belief in the need to promote specific gardening aesthetics and thus in the importance of illustrations in horticultural texts. Yet both of the Loudons published their own individual scientific works. They assisted one another informally in their writing endeavors, but looked to outsiders rather than to each other for illustrations. The Loudons' partnership in art and science was enforced by financial need, ironically a result of the huge expense incurred by John Loudon for botanical illustrations.[46] Living parallel working lives, each contributed to the family coffers by producing scientific texts that reflected joint interests. They drew upon each other for assistance in many ways but paid a high price for John's need to hire numerous artists. Perhaps Jane was uninterested in such artistic work, forcing John to seek paid artistic assistance, or perhaps Jane was not able to attain the level of artistic skill he demanded for his publications.

In 1830, at the age of twenty-three, Jane married John Loudon, forty-seven years of age, and well-established as a foremost authority in horticulture. He had toured European gardens, published numerous works, and edited several magazines including *The Gardeners' Magazine*. Loudon had gained a strong reputation in scientific circles.[47] He had been a member of the Linnean Society since about 1803. Sir Joseph Banks had introduced him to the scientific world and became his friend and supporter along with James Sowerby. Once married, Jane initially was embarrassed by her ignorance of botany, as all those who surrounded her in her husband's home were immersed in the subject. So, under John's guidance, she struggled to catch up with his life-time of learning, eventually succeeding in becoming well-versed in botany and horticulture herself, in part by acting as his amanuensis and also by attending the botanical lectures of John Lindley.[48] Jane's home education, together with her literary and artistic talent, aided her in these endeavors, but initially she had no botanical knowledge or interest whatsoever, although she enjoyed sketching and writing and had an appreciation for the natural world. She learned the Latin names of plants, and how to handle them, plant them, and care for them. Because John's right arm had been amputated, Jane wrote all his works for him by dictation, the two staying up in the library until the small hours of the morning.[49] Once educated to the task, Jane took on much writing and gardening work to assist her husband.

Jane also accompanied John on eight extensive tours through English gardens, contributing to the assessment of the gardens that they viewed and then reviewed in *The Gardener's Magazine*. The Loudons brought art to science in a three-dimensional way through their practice and promulgation of gardening. At this time, gardening was changing to recognize the importance of botany and as a result new aesthetic ideals were being introduced.[50] For the Loudons, their canvas was the garden, their mission to teach others how to bring civilized "art" to the science and nature of garden landscaping, from aristocratic estates to country cottage gardens.

John Loudon's personal interest in art led him to study and theorize about the relationship between art and science in a garden. He preferred to plant trees standing apart from one another rather than clumped in masses, so that all their features might be shown to best effect and identified. By placing botanical labels with trees, he hoped to interest the passerby in his particular passion for trees and to promote the planting of botanically interesting gardens and parks. For Loudon, gardening was a matter of context and "each element has an organic relationship to the other elements and to the whole." A particular site dictated a particular need. Vistas of space should be appreciated, not cluttered. He grouped all these beliefs under the heading "gardenesque," a variation on the eighteenth-century picturesque landscape.[51]

Jane Loudon was more interested in floriculture, which she noted was "pre-eminently a woman's department."[52] This interest was reflected in her published works. Loudon took much personal pleasure in "florists'" flowers.[53] In 1838, she published her illustrated *Ladies' Flower-Garden,* the first in a series of eight volumes that would feature hardy annuals, hardy biennials, hardy bulbs, corms and tubers, herbaceous perennials, garden roses, hardy shrubs, and greenhouse and hothouse plants. The vibrantly colored lithographic plates, emphasizing the flower in full bloom, indicated to the reader the specific appearance of the flowers they planted. Jane's plates provided a visual guide to the correct appearance of the readers' flowers, while her text provided the "how to" guide to success. But she also was interested in promoting the artistry of flower-garden design, noting in her *Instructions in Gardening for Ladies* (1840) that "the principal beauty of a flower-garden consists . . . in the evidence it affords of the art that has been employed in forming it."[54] The Loudons believed that gardening was both an art and a skill, and that botanical knowledge was important to this.

John seemed happy and proud of his wife's labors as a writer, a cultivator of aesthetically pleasing gardens, and an instructor of the same. Reviewing her *Botany for Ladies* and *The Ladies' Companion to the Flower-Garden* in *The Gardener's Magazine,* he noted "Both these works we are more proud of than any of our own," calling the *Botany for Ladies* "the best introduction to the natural system of botany for grown-up persons, amateurs, male or female, that has yet appeared."[55] Gardens could be places of freedom and expression for women.[56] The Loudons encouraged women in this occupation as John had encouraged Jane from the early days of their marriage.

While at home, after working with John on his writing and often staying up half the night, Jane would then return after breakfast to her own table, and work on her own publications. Jane originally took up writing in her own name due to the financial difficulties besetting the family. John Loudon had published his *magnum opus,* the *Arboretum Britannicus*, in 1838, a work still used as a reference today, but in doing so he incurred considerable debt. Adhering to his usual high standards, he found the work needed to be bigger and to contain more illustrations than he had originally planned. He had been working on this project since at least 1833, hiring seven artists full-time to make drawings from nature. Upon completion, Loudon found himself in debt for £10,000, and this was reduced to £1,200 by the time of his death by the sale of other works.[57] Between 1838 and John Loudon's death in 1843, Jane put pen to paper, writing and drawing in a frenzied attempt to get published and reduce their debt. Social niceties, polite discourse, and perhaps pride too, all dissipated under intense financial strain, and she often wrote in indignation and outrage to her publisher, the Murrays, when they kept her waiting for a response to an inquiry about the possibility of writing another book or waiting for payment she expected to receive for a publication. The intense financial pressure had not abated at the time of John Loudon's death in 1843. As a result, Jane was forced to continue to write and publish until her own death in 1858. At this point, Jane's personal correspondence reveals a sense of resentment toward her husband for leaving her and their daughter in strained circumstances. For example, she appealed in a letter to Mrs. Peel (wife of the Prime Minister, Robert Peel) in 1846 for a pension to protect her daughter in case of her own death, as she was already "labouring under a disease of the heart"; she commented that she was the widow of J. C. Loudon "who ruined himself by publishing on his own account a work on the trees and shrubs of Great Britain."[58] The wolf was always at the Loudons' door.

The brightly colored lithographs of Jane Loudon's own published works, for which she is probably best known today, have long been referred to as "Mrs. Loudon's flowers." Yet Jane herself avoided drawing and engraving as much as she could. She had learned to draw as a young woman, and encouraged the same skill in her daughter, Agnes.[59] Yet, as has been seen, she did not assist John Claudius Loudon artistically even though he was always in desperate need of illustrators and engravers. After the publication of the *Arboretum*, though, he engaged his two sisters, whom he supported financially in the other half of the Bayswater house, to do wood engravings for him.[60] At this point, the Loudons may have believed that Jane's time was better spent on writing money-making publications. Jane attested to having at least overseen the drawings for her first publication, *Instructions in Gardening for Ladies* (1840). She noted that "The engravings have been made here from drawings of specimens previously prepared, and I can therefore vouch for their accuracy."[61] It is not clear that she drew these small sketches herself. By the time she was working on a new edition of her long-established book *The Entertaining Naturalist* in 1843, Jane re-used the engravings already paired with the original text.[62] The plates for her *British Wild Flowers* were drawn by Noel Humphreys, who was known for his reproduction of illuminated manuscripts as religious gift books but was also a naturalist who drew flowers and insects beautifully.[63] An artist who had been responsible for the plates in *The Floral Cabinet* supervised the drawing from nature onto zinc for the eight volumes of Jane Loudon's *Ladies' Flower-Garden*.[64] Moreover, she remarked in several letters to her publisher that the Misses or Miss Loudon could or would be responsible for the illustrations in her work.[65]

Jane and John Loudon's scientific partnership was founded largely on the basis of financial necessity and on the fact of John Loudon's poor health. Both published books in their own names, hired their own artists, composed their own works, and had their own individual publishing contracts. Yet they shared a mutual love of botany, horticulture, and landscape gardening, bringing their complementary ideal for the Victorian garden aesthetic to the reading public. Twenty years apart in age, they found mutual satisfaction in working side by side for the same cause, each recognizing the importance of art to their scientific endeavors, firmly believing that art sold science, and that the science of horticulture was in part an artistic pursuit. But the Loudons' lives and health suffered for the cause. The fact that John was unable to make use of Jane's unpaid artistic assistance resulted in a heavy financial burden for the Loudon family that haunted and shamed them both until the end of their lives.

Conclusion

When women were first admitted as members of the Linnean Society, Frank Crisp, then the treasurer, commissioned a painting for £300 from James Sant R.A. to commemorate this important event. In his painting, Sant positioned Mary Anne Stebbing prominently and centrally in the foreground (figure 10.5). Crisp's wife, also one of the new members, was positioned shaking hands with the president in the background. In a letter to B. D. Jackson, general secretary of the Linnean, in 1905, Crisp wrote: "Naturally if I pay £300 for a picture, I should prefer that another 'Fellow's' wife should not be the selected figure!" This was followed by a telegraph of May 22, 1905: "we must surely have at the table a lady fellow who has done something[,] not one without a record[.] glad to assist artistic licence but that would be going too far."[66] Clearly, Crisp did not believe that Mary Anne Stebbing deserved any public recognition, whether for the invisible work on her husband's scientific publications, or for her own independent

10.5 *Admission of Lady Fellows,* by James Sant R.A. (1906), as originally painted with Mary Anne Stebbing in the foreground and her husband leaning on a table behind her.
Courtesy of the Linnean Society of London.

but unpublished work. Some periodicals used the occasion to poke fun at the admission of women to the Linnean Society. While one paper declared that Sant had "made the most of a not over-interesting subject," *The Daily Mirror* advised not missing a glimpse of the picture as it would "make you laugh," and *The World* "thought the picture was rendered somewhat comic by the figure [of Mary Anne Stebbing] in blue plush in the foreground."[67] This incident led Crisp to withhold the painting until his death in 1919, when Lady Crisp presented it to the Society. By that time, however, the painting had been altered. Both Stebbings had been painted out and Mary Anne Stebbing was replaced by an empty chair. The original painting still keeps the Stebbings in the shadows, invisible under the overcoat of paint (figure 10.6).

As was once the case for women scientists generally, women scientific illustrators have been painted out of history. The subject of visual images generally has been overlooked by historians of science until quite recently, which helps to explain the absence of studies about women's scientific art and the gendered relationships that existed between artists and scientists. Historians need to peel back the layers to make visible once more the primacy of women illustrators in Victorian science and the extent to which their role as scientific illustrators involved and indeed invited women into the scientific milieu. Other partnerships of art and science can be seen in the marriages of John and Emily Gould, Philip and Emily Gosse, Maria Emma and J. E. Gray, and Charlotte and Sir Roderick Impey Murchison. But marriage partnerships were not the only way that women could enter science via illustration. Daughters are part of this history, including the eleven daughters of the ornithologist Robert Bowdler Sharpe, who drew for their father and his friends; Charlotte and Ellen Sowerby, who were descendents of James and George Edward Sowerby, and who were both women of talent in botanical art; and Anna Atkins, who drew two hundred illustrations for the translation by her father, John George Children, of Lamarck's *Genera of Shells* (1823). Much work remains to be done regarding women illustrators who worked for science magazines and scientific institutions, one notable example being Mrs. Augusta Innes Baker Withers, who drew for the *Pomological Magazine, The Floral Cabinet,* and the *Transactions of the Horticultural Society*. In Ireland, Lydia Shakleton was employed by the Keeper of the Botanic Gardens, Glasnevin, to paint specimens there. Furthermore, there were women who worked for individual scientists to whom they were unrelated, such as Mrs. Griffiths who drew for George Shaw, and Sarah Drake who drew for John Lindley, Dr. Hamilton, and James Bateman. Of course, many women illustrated their own work, such as Sarah Wallis Bowdich Lee, Mrs. Hugh (Jemima) Blackburn, and Anne Pratt. Some women writers employed in their turn other women to illustrate their written works for them; the Kirby sisters, for example, employed Emily Bolingbroke in this capacity.

Innumerable nineteenth-century scientists recognized the importance of art to science, and were well aware of the role that women played in helping to bring the two disciplines together. Historians need to study the vagaries of the relationships formed between artists and scientists to better understand the relationship between science and art and women's role in science. The role of the contextualist historian of science should be to consider a history of

10.6 *Admission of Lady Fellows,* by James Sant R.A. (1906). Original overpainted by an unknown artist, removing the Stebbings and replacing them with a chair. *Courtesy of the Linnean Society of London.*

science that marries examinations of visual and literary texts with the lives and works, motivations and aspirations of those who produced them. Only in this way will Mary Anne Stebbing and other women like her become more than fictional characters in a modern-day novel and be able to stand in the foreground of their lives, as visible and prominent members of the Victorian scientific community.

Notes

1. A. S. Byatt, "Morpho Eugenia," in *Angels and Insects* (London: Vintage, 1992), 3–160.

2. Andrea Barrett, *The Voyage of the Narwhal: A Novel* (New York: W.W. Norton, 1998).

3. Ann B. Shteir, *Cultivating Women, Cultivating Science: Flora's Daughters and Botany in England, 1760–1860* (Baltimore: The Johns Hopkins University Press, 1996).

4. Gill Saunders, *Picturing Plants: An Analytical History of Botanical Illustration* (Berkeley: University of California Press, 1995), 8.

5. Exceptions to this general statement would be my own work on Marianne North in *Revealing New Worlds: Three Victorian Women Naturalists* (London and New York: Routledge, 2001), chs. 3 and 4; Natalie Zemon Davis's work on Maria Sibylla Merian in *Women on the Margins: Three Seventeenth-Century Lives* (Cambridge, Mass.: Harvard University Press, 1995), and Barbara Gates's brief section on "The Art and Science of Illustration" in her *Kindred Nature: Victorian and Edwardian Women Embrace the Living World* (Chicago: University of Chicago Press, 1998), 74–83.

6. See, e.g., Marcia Myers Bonta, "Maria Martin, Audubon's Sweetheart," in *Women in the Field: America's Pioneering Women Naturalists* (College Station: Texas A&M University Press, 1991), 9–17; Christine Jackson, "Richard Bowdler Sharpe and his ten daughters," *Archives of Natural History* 21 (1994): 261–69; Martina Kölbl-Ebert, "Mary Buckland (née Morland) 1797–1857," *Earth Sciences History* 16 (1997): 33–38; and Martina Kölbl-Ebert, "Charlotte Murchison (née Hugonin) 1788–1869," *Earth Sciences History* 16 (1997): 39–43. For all-encompassing biographical works, see Jack Kramer, *Women of Flowers: A Tribute to Victorian Women Illustrators* (New York: Stewart, Tabori & Chang, 1996).

7. For works on the Victorian period, see, for example, Bernard Lightman, "The Visual Theology of Victorian Popularizers of Science: From Reverent Eye to Chemical Retina," *Isis* 91 (2000): 651–80; Ann B. Shteir, "A Cultural History of Victorian Wax Flower Modelling," unpublished paper, 2000. See also the work of Jonathan Smith, "Eden under the Water: The Visual Natural Theology of Philip Gosse's Aquarium Books," presented at "Nineteenth-Century Religion and the Fragmentation of Culture in Europe and America," Lancaster, England, July 1997; and Martin Rudwick, *Scenes from Deep Time: Early Pictorial Representations of the Prehistoric World* (Chicago and London: University of Chicago Press, 1992).

8. Alex Soojung-Kim Pang, "Visual Representation and Post-Constructivist History of Science," *Historical Studies in the Physical and Biological Sciences* 28, no. 1 (1997): 164. There are two in-depth explorations of the relationships between artists and scientists but both studies include women only peripherally: Ann Shelby Blum, *Picturing Nature: American Nineteenth-Century Zoological Illustration* (Princeton: Princeton University Press, 1993); and James Hamilton, ed., *Fields of Influence: Conjunctions of Artists and Scientists, 1815–1860* (Birmingham: University of Birmingham Press, 2001).

9. Marilyn Bailey Ogilvie, "Marital Collaboration: An Approach to Science," in *Uneasy Careers and Intimate Lives: Women in Science, 1789–1979,* ed. Pnina G. Abir-Am and Dorinda Outram (New Brunswick: Rutgers University Press, 1987), 104–28; Helena M. Pycior, Nancy G. Slack, and Pnina G. Abir-Am, eds., *Creative Couples in the Sciences* (New Brunswick: Rutgers University Press, 1996); and Paul White, "Science at Home: The Space between Henrietta Heathorn and Thomas Huxley," *History of Science* 34 (1996): 33–56.

10. Pamela M. Henson, "'Through Books to Nature': Anna Botsford Comstock and the Nature Study Movement," in *Natural Eloquence: Women Reinscribe Science,* ed. Barbara T. Gates and Ann B. Shteir (Madison: University of Wisconsin Press, 1997), 116–46; and Pamela M. Henson, "The Comstocks of Cornell: A Marriage of Interests," in *Creative Couples in the Sciences,* 112–25.

11. Janet Bell Garber, "John and Elizabeth Gould: Ornithologists and Scientific Illustrators, 1829–1841," in *Creative Couples in the Sciences,* 87–97.

12. Edward Rudge, *Memoir* [of Mrs. Anne Rudge] (London: J. Mallett, 1836?), 1.

13. "A Botanical Library," *The [London] Times,* April 3–4, 1930, and an untitled article dated April 15, 1930; and "Edward Rudge," *Dictionary of National Biography,* ed. Sidney Lee (London: Smith, Elder, and Co., 1899), XLIX: 383–84.

14. W. T. Stearn and L. H. J. Williams, "'Martin's French Guiana Plants' and Rudge's 'Plantarum Guianae Rariorum Icones,'" *Bulletin de Jardin Botanique de l'État* 27 (1957): 244–45.

15. Rudge, *Memoir,* 1.

16. Botanical artists such as Georg Dionysius Ehret (1708–1770), although initially reluctant to include such sections, did so increasingly. Ehret worked on such dissections for his drawings under Linnaeus himself. Lys de Bray, *The Art of Botanical Illustration: The Classic Illustrators and their Achievements from 1500–1900* (Bromley, Kent: Christopher Helm Ltd., 1989), 114.

17. Stearn and Williams, "Martin's French Guiana Plants," 249.

18. Rudge, *Memoir,* 2.

19. Stearn and Williams, "Martin's French Guiana Plants," 249.

20. Saunders Family Correspondence. Bucks. Record Office, B34, 36, 37.

21. T. R. R. Stebbing, "An Autobiographical Sketch," *Transactions and Proceedings of the Torquay Natural History Society* 4 (1923): 1–5.

22. Orchids Volume I, Manuscript botanicals of Mary Anne Stebbing, Kew Library.

23. A. Lorrain Smith, "Mrs T. R. R. Stebbing," in *Proceedings of the Linnean Society* (1926–1927): 104.

24. Eric Mills, "Amphipods and Equipoise: A Study of T. R. R. Stebbing," *Connecticut Academy of Arts and Sciences Transactions* 44 (1972): 243.

25. Mary Anne Stebbing's original art at Kew attests to these newfound interests. Moreover, her "Form of Recommendation for a Fellow of the Linnean Society of London" in 1904 notes that Mary Anne Stebbing was "a lady attached to the study of Natural History, especially observation of seedling plants and vegetable teratology." Linnean Society of London, Loose Letters, Fellows Files.

26. "T. R. R. Stebbing," *Nature* (August 7, 1926).

27. Thomas Stebbing, as quoted in his obituary in the *Proceedings of the Royal Society,* Series B (101), 1926, xxx.

28. Mills, "Amphipods and Equipoise," 241, 254.

29. Personal correspondence from Rodney Stebbing to Eric Mills, August 21, 1969; from Margaret Clark to Eric Mills, undated but probably 1969; and W. P. D. Stebbing, "Reminiscences of the Rev. T. R. R. Stebbing," Address to the General Assembly, Congress at Tunbridge Wells; *The South Eastern Naturalist and Antiquary, being the Proceedings and Transactions, South Eastern Union Science Society* 51 (1946): 55.

30. "Golden Wedding of the Rev. T. R. R. and Mrs. Stebbing," *Kent and Sussex Courier,* 1917, 3.

31. "Death of Rev. T. R. R. Stebbing," *Kent and Sussex Courier,* Friday, July 16, 1926.

32. Eric L. Mills, "T. R. R. Stebbing: A Bibliography with Biographic Notes," *Biological Journal of the Linnean Society* 8, no. 1 (March 1976), 57.

33. Thomas R. R. Stebbing, Presidential Address to the Tunbridge Wells Natural History and Philosophical Society, October 20, 1893, 12.

34. I am indebted to Dr. Eric Mills for sharing with me his 1960s correspondence with various members of the Stebbing family.

35. For reference to the number of sketches see "Dawson Turner," *Dictionary of National Biography,* ed. Sidney Lee (London: Smith, Elder, and Co., 1899), LVII: 334; and Mea Allan, *The Hookers of Kew 1785–1911* (London: Michael Joseph, 1967), 33.

36. For example, "Descriptions of Four New British Lichens" and "Remarks Upon the Dillenian Herbarium," *Transactions of the Linnean Society of London* 7 (1804): 86–95, 101–16.

37. In letters to Ellen Hutchins, Dawson Turner often notes that he has sketched a specimen or that he is sending her a sketch he has completed. M. E. Mitchell, ed., *Early Observations on the Flora of Southwest Ireland: Selected Letters of Ellen Hutchins and Dawson Turner, 1807–1814* (Dublin: National Botanical Gardens, Glasnevin, 1999).

38. A note on the inside cover of the Natural History Museum's copy of the *Synopsis* reads: Regarding the *plates* bound into these volumes see: Hemsley, W. B. J. Bot. Lond. 31: 281, 1893. "In the Kew library are three small quarto volumes of coloured drawings of sea-weeds, with the following note, signed Dawson Turner, 1800, in the first volume: 'For the drawings contained in this

volume I am entirely indebted to the delicate pencil of Mr. Samuel Mason, of Yarmouth, a most indefatigable collector, as well as a most accurate observer of these plants.'"

39. Ellen Hutchins makes reference to this fact in a letter dated February 20, 1810, as she promises to send her some she has collected. Mitchell, *Early Observations,* 36–37.

40. Richard Drayton, *Nature's Government: Science, Imperial Britain, and the 'Improvement' of the World* (New Haven and London: Yale University Press, 2000), 144.

41. Mary Turner, *Outlines in Lithography from a Small Collection of Pictures* (Yarmouth, 1840). Preface by Dawson Turner.

42. Dawson Turner to Ellen Hutchins, March 8, 1811, in Mitchell, *Early Observations,* 46.

43. Dawson Turner to Ellen Hutchins, July 11, 1811, in ibid., 52.

44. Letter from Mary Turner to Dawson Turner. Undated. DT2/KK4/15, Dawson Turner Papers, Trinity College, Cambridge.

45. Letter from Mary Turner to Dawson Turner, Rouen, July 1, 1818. DT2/KK4/30, Dawson Turner Papers, Trinity College, Cambridge.

46. Taking up botanical art for financial reasons also can be seen in the context of the married lives of Elizabeth Blackwell (ca. 1700–1758) and Sarah Bowdich, later Sarah Lee (1791–1856). See Donald deB. Beaver, "Writing Natural History for Survival—1820–1856: The Case of Sarah Bowdich, later Sarah Lee," *Archives of Natural History* 26, no. 1 (1999): 19–31.

47. Jane Loudon, "A Short Account of the Life and Writings of John Claudius Loudon," in *Self-Instruction for Young Gardeners, Foresters, Bailiffs, Land-Stewards, and Farmers* (London: Longman, Brown, Green, and Longman, 1845). See also Melanie Louise Simo, *Loudon and the Landscape: From Country Seat to Metropolis, 1783–1843* (London: Yale University Press, 1988), 1, 5.

48. Geoffrey Taylor, *Some Nineteenth Century Gardeners* (London: Skeffington, 1951), 28.

49. Bea Howe, *Lady with Green Fingers: The Life of Jane Loudon* (London: Country Life Limited, 1961), 31, 33, 42–49.

50. A. J. Lustig, "Cultivating Knowledge in Nineteenth-Century English Gardens," *Science in Context* 13 (2000): 155–81.

51. Simo, *Loudon and the Landscape,* ch. 10.

52. Jane Loudon, *Instructions in Gardening for Ladies* (London: Murray, 1840), 244.

53. Howe, *Lady with Green Fingers,* 39–41.

54. Loudon, *Instructions in Gardening for Ladies,* 246.

55. As cited in Howe, *Lady with Green Fingers,* 81.

56. Jacqueline M. Labbe, "Cultivating One's Understanding: The Female Romantic Garden," in *Women's Writing* 4 , no. 1 (1997): 39.

57. Jane Loudon, "A Short Account of the Life and Writings of John Claudius Loudon."

58. Letter from Jane Loudon to "Madam" (likely Mrs. Peel), March 6, 1846. Add MS 40586f. 167, Peel Papers, British Library.

59. Howe, *Lady with Green Fingers,* 31, 99, 170.

60. Ibid., 55, 60, 62.

61. Jane Loudon, *Instructions in Gardening for Ladies*, vii.

62. Howe, *Lady with Green Fingers*, 82.

63. Ibid., 95; and Morna Daniels, *Victorian Book Illustration* (London: The British Library, 1988), 26.

64. Howe, *Lady with Green Fingers*, 64.

65. Letters to John Murray, publisher, October 27, 1838, October 6, 1839, November 9, 1838, February 3, 1842, September 29, 1843. This could be a reference to her daughter, or to her sisters-in-law. Given the laziness of Agnes Loudon described by Howe and based on Agnes's own journals, it is likelier that Jane relied on the help of her sisters-in-law, Jane and Mary Loudon, in this work.

66. Margot Walker, "Admission of Lady Fellows," *The Linnean: Newsletter* 1 (1984): 9–11.

67. Ibid., 9.

Part Three

THE TWENTIETH CENTURY AND BEYOND

Changes or Continuities?

⚘ *Chapter 11*

LOOKING FOR JEAN DOW

Narratives of Women and Missionary Medicine in Modern China

Margo S. Gewurtz

In 1927, Dr. Jean Dow, a Canadian medical missionary, died unexpectedly in Beijing following a short illness. She had served in China for over thirty years, and her friend Margaret Griffith, wife of the Honan Mission's Rev. John Griffith, compiled a memorial pamphlet to celebrate her life and work. One compelling photo in the pamphlet shows Dr. Dow at work in her clinic assisted by her Chinese co-workers (figure 11.1). All wear professional white uniforms. The scene appears quite conventional in its representation of gender, race, and medical science. It is anything but. The recovery of Dow's scientific career from the gaps, omissions, and conventions of the textual record requires an analysis of the visual record, primarily photographs. These photographs were preserved in archives or presented in printed form in missionary magazines, the memorial pamphlet, and other mission publications. The meaning of this and other like photos presented in this chapter constitutes a counter-narrative not only to conventional ways of representing the doctor and her co-workers but also to the metanarratives of women and missionary medicine in modern China. Read in conjunction with the texts, the visual images offer not only hidden narratives but also new meanings for the texts themselves.

Medical Science in the Service of God

We begin to look for Jean Dow in 1888 when the first party of seven Canadian Presbyterian missionaries set sail for China. Their intention was to secure Honan Province as the first mission field on the Chinese mainland of any Canadian church, following the start of their successful work in Taiwan a decade earlier. During tours and itineration and in the early stations, a prime attraction of the missionary presence was

11.1 Dr. Dow and Assistants. Margaret R. Griffith, *Jean Dow, A Beloved Physician* (Toronto: Literature Dept., Woman's Missionary Society, The United Church of Canada, [193?]), 9.
By permission of The United Church of Canada/Victoria University Archives, Toronto.

the offer of medical services. The original group of seven missionaries sent out in 1888 included two physicians, Drs. William McClure and J. Frazer Smith, and a nurse, Harriet Sutherland, sent by the Woman's Missionary Society (WMS) as their first foreign worker in China. After Sutherland married, Jennie Graham replaced her but left after one year because of ill health. Nurse Margaret I. MacIntosh, who became Dow's closest co-worker, arrived in 1889 and retired in 1927. The first woman doctor, Lucinda Graham, Jennie's sister, arrived in 1892 but died of typhus two years later while still mainly engaged in language study. Dr. Jean I. Dow arrived in 1895 and stayed until her death in 1927. She was the pioneer provider of medical services for women in the North Honan mission (figure 11.2).[1]

Medicine was an extremely effective access point for converts. Since the average stay for patients in clinics was ten days, they had plenty of time to listen to the preaching of the medical missionaries and to acquire tracts to take back to their homes. However, in the China field it was difficult to use medicine as a tool for evangelizing women. As in India, the sexes were segregated within the household, and even in a poor peasant society such as North Honan, strange males, especially foreigners, could not approach women. It was impossible for male doctors to treat females alone without a nurse present, and the ideal was to have female doctors to provide separate care for women and children.

One can see the evident priority given medical work as the avenue to reach women, as the Woman's Missionary Society did not send their first educational/evangelistic worker, Minnie Pyke, until 1896. The Foreign Mission Committee of the Woman's Missionary Society actively recruited nurses and doctors to serve in the China and India fields of the newly developing Canadian missions. These women went on to have exciting and rewarding careers, with responsibilities and opportunities often lacking in the home field. They became hospital superintendents, and created the nursing profession in China, as well as training women doctors, pharmacy, and clinic assistants. These female medical professionals had been recruited in the service of God, and embedded in narratives about them was the primacy of that vocation, not their scientific professionalism. The initial focus of the WMS was domestic or "home missions," and they had justified women's entry into public life and the professions to male church authorities and the public at large by emphasizing their special aptitude for work among women and children. The sex segregation of women in China and India enhanced this reasoning into a justification for a foreign calling. Thus the discourse of women and missionary medicine projected an image of "maternal feminism" wedded to devout faith that hid the more "masculine" qualities of scientific professionalism.[2]

The conventional narratives of "maternal feminism" and missionary medicine dominate both the textual and visual presentation of the career of Dr. Jean Dow. Dow herself left no diaries or personal papers. However, she regularly wrote letters to the WMS, and photographs that she either took herself or whose composition she authored often accompanied those letters. Neither the original photographs nor letters were kept, as was the usual practice of the WMS at the time. What did survive are some published and archival photos and the edited versions of the letters published in the WMS magazine. Since that magazine was intended for the home audience of women who raised the substantial

11.2 North Honan Staff, 1904. *Foreign Missionary Tidings* 22 (June 2, 1905), 25. *By permission of The United Church of Canada/Victoria University Archives, Toronto.*

sums to support the missionaries, it is not surprising that the texts Dow wrote as well as those produced after her untimely death contributed to the construction of her as a passionate evangelist for whom medical professionalism was always secondary to her true calling.

The evolving visual images of Dr. Dow and her Chinese Christian medical assistants analyzed in this chapter provide evidence of the paradoxes and complexities behind this simplistic narrative. The visual medium challenges the conventional message, and offers an alternate narrative. Considered as visual images of gender and science, rather than missionaries and converts, these visuals enable us both to reconsider the texts and to glimpse the hidden face of Jean Dow: a career woman whose Christianity brought Chinese women to careers in scientific medicine. She was devoted to improving medical standards in the mission, and she herself became a serious scientific researcher in the new field of microbiology through her work on the dread tropical disease Kala Azar.

Photographs of Jean Dow and her medical assistants at work in the women's hospital in Changte that were never published in her lifetime but only in the memorial pamphlet (e.g., figure 11.1) represent the fullest expression of this counter-narrative. The photographs show all these women in a professional setting as medical workers. While the text of the pamphlet conforms to the conventional narrative, the photographs do not. It is only by fitting these and other photographs to texts of the period that I have been able both to construct plausible details about their production and to see how visuals can artfully reinforce stereotypes or subvert them to reveal hidden narratives. The striking visual images of Dow and her assistants force us to re-examine issues surrounding women and missionary medicine: the relationship between Christian evangelism and medical science, between Western medical professionals and their Chinese assistants, between male and female medical missionaries, and between what is visible and what is hidden. The career of Jean Dow, her evolving relationship to her assistants, and the politics of medicine in her mission provide the focus to unravel this complex interplay of narratives and counter-narratives, of text and visuals.

Jean Dow: The Doctor as a Lady

Dr. Jean Isabel Dow was born in Fergus, Ontario, in 1870 and died on January 17, 1927, in Beijing.[3] A beautiful and precocious child, she entered high school at age ten intending to become a teacher. She did teacher training at the Model School in Mount Forest, and began teaching at the age of fifteen. As a teacher, she was both beloved and respected by pupils and her fellow teachers.[4] A deeply religious person, she harbored a secret wish to serve as a medical missionary, and

11.3 Dr. Jean Dow, pioneer doctor to North Honan, 1895. United Church of Canada/Victoria University Archives, 76.001P/1609. *By permission of The United Church of Canada/Victoria University Archives, Toronto.*

was admitted to the Toronto Medical College for Women from which she graduated in 1895 (figure 11.3). Upon graduation, she left for China to replace Dr. Lucinda Graham, who had died the year before. One of her teachers despaired that she had thrown away the promise of a brilliant career by "going out to that heathen country."[5] During her three years of language study, she assisted Dr. McClure at the Chuwang dispensary. The dispensary was then divided into men's and women's wards. Dow worked there until 1900, when the missionaries fled the Boxer upheaval and returned to Canada.[6] Upon their return in 1901, she moved to Changte city where the women's dispensary and small hospital were opened in 1904. Dow was hospital superintendent as well as sole physician until the arrival of Dr. Isabel McTavish in 1918.

From 1902 to 1904 when the new hospital opened, she primarily was engaged in evangelical and rural touring work. Margaret Griffith maintained that Dow later recalled that as "the happiest part of her missionary life."[7] But "her main life work in Honan," according to the same source, was at the Changte Hospital, and she died just after the new and much larger Women's Hospital was built there. During the terrible famine of 1920–1921, she did wonderful work in saving what were called the "famine babies," for which she and Dr. McTavish were awarded medals by the Chinese government. Dow furthered her medical education when on furloughs, at the School of Tropical Medicine in London, England in 1908, and later in obstetrics at a New York City hospital. For fourteen years, Jean Dow was the only woman physician in the Honan field. She did all the medical work as well as all the organization and administration, while training Chinese Christian assistants such as Mrs. Li Ming and Mrs. Jee, who became anesthetists. Dr. Percy Leslie, who was in charge of the Men's Hospital in Changte and covered for her when she took furlough, said that to have done all that "under pioneer conditions and with raw, untrained assistants" was "an achievement of no mean order."[8]

Most accounts of Dow's life and work written at the time of her premature death from an unnamed illness emphasize her physical beauty, womanly qualities, and deep religious commitment. In his eulogy, Dr. R. P. Mackay, the influential secretary of the Church's Foreign Missions Committee, did not speak of her medical work but stressed her Christian character, modesty, skill at learning Chinese, and above all her physical appearance and her "tender and sympathetic" heart:

> To begin with Dr. Dow was favoured in personal appearance. Whilst that is not an essential quality, yet a winsome face and graceful manner lie very near to the essentials. Dr. Dow was so endowed . . . Yet with all this attainment and assured appreciation, she could scarcely be induced to speak of her own work. When home on furlough she had a great story to tell, but could not be induced to tell it. She could speak but her words were always impersonal. The . . ."I" was ever lacking. She was heard to express the hope that the new Women's Hospital at Changte, which was her own life's work, might be opened before her return [from furlough] in order that she might not be in evidence.[9]

Mackay noted that she rarely would speak of herself or her own work. In letters to Margaret Griffith, her friends wrote that they learned more about her work after she died than they knew when she was alive.[10] Certainly, an unusual unpublished photo of Dow, Minnie Pyke, and Margaret MacIntosh found in the archives conveys Mackay's description of her (figure 11.4). It was taken in the garden of their home in the Changte mission compound. It is an entirely domestic scene that could have been taken anywhere in England or Canada. The location of each sitter in the group is not identified in the catalogue. Nevertheless, a comparison with other photographs from the same period (see figure 11.2) suggests that the seated figure gazing away from the camera is likely Dow, and MacIntosh is standing behind her with her hand resting on the back of the chair. Minnie Pyke has her back to the camera and is reaching for one of the roses growing in profusion in the garden. The style of dress would date this photo from the Edwardian period. In all likelihood, the photographer was Miss Minnie Robertson of the WMS, seen in figure 11.2, who visited Dr. Dow in August of 1904 and took great interest in the medical work in the dispensary.[11]

In arranging the subjects, the photographer has attempted to make the scene appear natural rather than formally posed. A similar effort to create a less formal grouping is seen in the photograph of the North Honan staff where Rev. Mitchell is turned and leaning at an angle to convey a relaxed attitude (see figure 11.2). Such naturalizing of group compositions was suggested in the guidelines for amateur photographers in the popular handbooks of the period. The composition of the group in the garden exactly follows that recommended in M. Carey Lea's *A Manual of Photography* (1871), a book whose subtitle states that it was "Intended as a textbook for beginners and a book of reference for advanced photographers."[12] Lea suggests the following arrangement for a group portrait:

> Thus, let *A, B, C,* be the heads of any group. *A B* will be the most important line, opposed and balanced by *A C.* But, also,

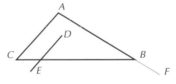

> some other line, *D E,* if introduced, will greatly support the line *A B* and balance the picture. And where the line *A B,* if continued, would terminate at *F,* on the ground or elsewhere, there should be some object for it to rest upon, as explained above.[13]

11.4 Missionaries at W.M.S. House, Changte (1904). United Church of Canada/ Victoria University Archives, 1999.001P/1686.
By permission of The United Church of Canada/Victoria University Archives, Toronto.

Dow and MacIntosh form line D/E and the flower bush provides the resting point for the line A/B of Pyke and MacIntosh. Only one figure is seated and all are in profile. The effect is more artful, and closer to nineteenth-century portraiture, than a mere grouping of the three standing in their garden. However, the photo appears more artificial than natural, and the effect is to isolate Pyke and emphasize the closeness of Dow and MacIntosh. Moreover, there is no gaze that would enable the viewer to connect with the scene, or enter into the interior life of the sitters. The result is a kind of self-effacement that corresponds to Dow's invisibility in the textual record.

The written texts emphasize only her role in maternal medicine, serving women and children and bringing them to the faith. The domesticity and femininity of the garden photograph encodes ladies, not professionals who happen to be ladies. That we have here a doctor, a nurse, and a teacher is entirely invisible. Contemporary narratives of women's professional work as missionary doctors had argued that it was "less injurious" to their femininity for women to enter this world when confined to treating women and children.[14] This photograph embodies that notion by presenting these women as ladies whose feminine qualities have been in no way undermined either by professional work or by the hardships of service in foreign lands.

The visual record of this complex narrative discourse was presented to a substantial home audience in the *Monthly Letter Leaflet*, later *Foreign Missionary Tidings*, the magazine of the Foreign Mission Committee of the Woman's Missionary Society, which by 1904 had a paid circulation of 19,350.[15] The *Leaflet* carried no photographs prior to 1892, when a photo first appeared of the Girls' Boarding School in Indore, Central India. But these were still rare and the photographic record really began in earnest in the spring of 1900. At that time, photographs often were reproduced as lithographs; the originals were not used because they did not turn out well.[16] But as the technology improved, both the quality and quantity increased. Since the home supporters paid salaries and infrastructure costs, the tendency overall was to favor pictures of the missionaries, buildings, and scenes of local color. The converts' names or stories did not, as one male missionary put it, "shine" as frequently, so that the locals rarely were identified. Scenes of medical work as such were seldom featured. The written narrative, emphasizing evangelical work, and the photographic narrative reinforced each other. Photos of female missionaries and their converts were a commonly highlighted genre in which only the female missionary was normally identified.[17] She typically would be placed at the center of the group and gaze away from the camera, unlike the others, who look front and center. The missionary, whom the readers either supported or had met on furlough, was always the central figure, set apart from the rest by dress, skin color, and gaze. Such a pose and gaze suggested an otherworldly spiritual attitude missing in the students.

"Muscular Christianity" and Male Medical Science

In narratives intended for the home audience that supported them, the male doctors also emphasized their religious work. However, their narratives and visual representations presented an heroic masculine image of modern science that was singularly lacking in similar representations about and by the women. A particularly interesting example of this type of discourse was the account of Dr. Frazer Smith in his 1935 autobiography, a work that is a form of quest narrative in which the "I" narrator exemplifies heroic "muscular Christianity" (figure 11.5).[18] The chapter of his memoir that dealt specifically with women converts focuses entirely on the medical work among women, with Smith as the central figure or hero. In his retelling of the life-threatening surgeries that he performed that brought women to Christianity, nurse Margaret MacIntosh, Dr. Lucinda Graham, and Bible woman Wu are given minor supporting roles. Smith notes only that, prior to Graham's arrival, the nurse and the Bible woman "proved a great help to me in my work," and he speaks fondly, and paternally, of "dear old Mrs. Wu." Lucinda Graham, whom he noted "had completed a very brilliant course in the Women's Medical College, Toronto," and had started a practice there before accepting the call to Honan, was engaged mainly in language study. Although a "splendid student" who made "rapid progress," her studies absorbed most of her time but "she was always ready to assist me whenever necessary."[19] The agency of all three women was diminished.

Smith's autobiography as well as his published letters at the time paid attention in great detail to scientific medical work. It was from one of his letters that I learned not only that the first convert was an opium addict, but also the details of Smith's method for treating addicts. While Smith firmly believed his medical science was in the service of God, nonetheless, his self-presentation is of heroic, masculine medicine. His is an androcentric as well as colonizing form of discourse. The male scientist/hero, with the aid of God, performs near miracles, quite beyond the reach of heathens or women. Indeed, his chapter on the early medical work for women is entitled "Two Miracles." Grateful patients then convert to the hero's religion, as he has asked no payment save that.

The sources written by and about women for a female audience — two published histories of the WMS (*The Story of Our Missions*, Toronto, 1915, and *The Planting of the Faith*, Toronto, 1921), their Annual

11.5 Dr. J. Frazer Smith, Dr. Dow on the right, and nurse Margaret MacIntosh on the left, [192?]. Smith is the dominant center while Dow gazes away from the camera. United Church of Canada/ Victoria University Archives, 94.014P/1.

By permission of The United Church of Canada/Victoria University Archives, Toronto.

Reports, and especially their monthly magazine with letters from the field—are texts whose underlying hermeneutic is the struggle to establish the importance and value of the role of women missionaries. Their marginalization is seen not only in narratives such as Smith's but even in their own writings. The WMS pre-war history relies on male sources and accounts and shows a marked deference to male authority. This account contained almost nothing about female converts although some of the stories about the male converts were included. The postwar history sought to situate the "power of Christianity and of Christian womanhood" in the "new day" brought on by the massive social changes of the postwar world that in China involved a more radical feminist movement. Unlike the earlier work, evangelism was here a very small part of a story that focused on social work, medicine, and the Christian home and family. The Social Gospel influence was quite evident. None of these texts presents women as medical scientists or challenges the dominant discursive link between medicine and "muscular Christianity."

The promotion before a home audience of women supporters of the importance of women's work for women within the larger mission cause resulted in an heroic discourse about women missionaries that marginalized female helpers and converts. Even when surrounded by Chinese women, only the Canadian women were identified in the photographs published in the *Leaflet*. In her study of Canadian women missionaries in India, Ruth Brouwer has included one of the few photographs that clearly names a female convert; the practice of not identifying the female converts shown in photographs was a commonplace for the WMS magazine.[20] By contrast, we have the photo of the Rev. Hood's staff in Hwaiking, North Honan, published in the *Tidings* in November 1902, in which all the Chinese males are identified by name and position. Hood described his Chinese teacher as "one of the most gentlemanly Chinese I ever met. Still a heathen."[21] The failure of WMS publications to "name" native female associates reflected the gender relations and assumptions of the time wherein male missionaries, male assistants, and male converts were given primacy. The *Leaflet/Tidings* incorporation of the male ethos can be seen best in the editors' refashioning of Dr. Dow's presentation of her female Christian medical assistants. Dow attempted to present these women as competent medical workers and her partners. Set against the dominant discourse of medicine as a tool to bring heathens to Christianity, we see in Dow's visuals and some of her writings a hidden narrative of Christianity bringing women to medicine, much as it had done for Dow herself.

The Chinese Christian Medical Assistants

In October of 1900, after the Boxer rebellion caused the Canadians to flee China, the *Foreign Missionary Tidings* published a photo in lieu of reports (figure 11.6). The caption reads:

> The above is a picture of the Woman's dispensary, and Chinese dispensary assistant at Ch'u Wang, Honan. Dr. Jean Dow speaks of the assistant as being a bright, intelligent woman. This room was doubtless looted with the rest of the Mission buildings.[22]

The unnamed dispensary assistant was Mrs. Han, identified by Dr. Dow in a letter a year earlier. In that letter, the "intelligent woman" was actually an unnamed recently deceased daughter of the Chai family. Dr. Dow recounted that Mrs. Han had been suspended from the Church for a year because she had given in to family pressure and accompanied her daughter's mother-in-law to a temple when the daughter's child was stricken with scarlet fever. Although she did not pray there as the other grandmother did, she was suspended nonetheless.[23] The editors not only misquoted Dow's letter but also did not bother to name Mrs. Han. Their focus was not Mrs. Han, but the carefully lined shelves of the dispensary that had been destroyed during the looting of the Mission compound. The photo undoubtedly accompanied Dow's original letter and was intended to display Mrs. Han, who is at its center and whose story is recounted in the letter. It was not published together with that letter but only later to illustrate a different story in which Mrs. Han played no part.

We cannot say who took the photograph. In light of the separation of the sexes in China at the time and of superstitions regarding photography, it must have been a woman, one whom Mrs. Han

11.6 Mrs. Han in the dispensary. *Foreign Missionary Tidings* 17, no. 6 (October 1900), 122.
By permission of The United Church of Canada/Victoria University Archives, Toronto.

trusted and admired. This strongly suggests that Dow herself was the photographer. The composition of the photograph of Mrs. Han is all the more interesting given that the conventions of late nineteenth-century Chinese commissioned portrait photography favored a "dignified frontality," that is, a full-length frontal pose and small props.[24] Virtually all groupings of converts, with or without missionaries, were arranged that way. Moreover, conventional Western genre images of Chinese types usually conveyed an attitude of "submissiveness."[25] Neither feature is present here. Wearing her fine clothes and embroidered bound-feet slippers, Mrs. Han is posed at an angle, though facing the camera as directly as possible. The photograph is intended to highlight her as the subject of Dr. Dow's letter, but the pose is not a domestic setting or grouping and there is no missionary. The angled pose allowed the photographer to capture as much as possible of the room, the dispensary itself. It is not so surprising that it was later used for a narrative about the dispensary. If Dr. Dow herself took the photo, then she was subtly presenting her assistant within a scientific setting, a pharmacy and treatment room with its neat rows of labeled bottles on the shelves. As we have seen, such a setting was the center of Dow's work for much of her career. Her dispensary has been identified erroneously in texts as the Chuwang women's hospital opened by Dr. William McClure, but this photo not only enables us to correct the error, it also makes claim to a different narrative, one that highlights a Chinese assistant.

The first photo in the *Tidings* that showcased a professional setting of medical work and nurses in uniform was of the Presbyterian Women's Hospital in Neemuch, Central India, published in September 1902. This was some years after Dow sent her photo of Mrs. Han to the magazine. Like the dispensary photo, this one emphasized equipment, as the caption and text identify the beds—the "Calgary cots" obviously bought by a WMS fund campaign—but not the "Native trained nurses [who] stand in attention."[26] This focus on the beds is found in several photos of the hospitals in India. Dr. Dow's highlighting of her dispensary assistant both in a text she hoped would be published and in a photograph is exceptional in this context.

Dow's written presentation of her assistant was within the convention of medicine in the service of God, for her narrative focus was on the woman's suspension from the Church. The professionalism of the setting comes from the photo, not the text. Dow had insisted that all her assistants be converts.[27] They were taught and trained so that they might train others. Dow's pride in them and her affection for them were evident. In her May 7, 1900, letter to the *Tidings*, her last before the Boxer upheaval of June that year, she noted that Mrs. Han was to be restored to full standing in the Church at the spring communion that Sunday. She reminded her readers of the reasons for Mrs. Han's suspension and concluded:

> She accepted the discipline in a becoming spirit and went on with her
> duties just as faithfully as before. It humbles one to think that again
> and again we people of exalted privileges are guilty of sins far more
> heinous in the sight of God than hers, though unnoted by any church
> session.[28]

The implied criticism of the actions of the Honan Presbytery in which women did not vote is quite striking, as is Dow's recognition of white privilege. Dow's success with training Chinese assistants and her high regard for their work at such an early date are as remarkable as they are unremarked upon in the literature.

Dow's confident foregrounding of her helper stands in sharp contrast to the attitudes of the male doctors. In a report in the *Tidings* of March 1911, Dr. Menzies at Hwaiking despaired of ever seeing nurses in China to train Chinese nurses. He described how he trained a Mrs. Bai as a medical assistant, nurse, and evangelist all in one, and how this training over the previous five years transformed her from "the laziest, dirtiest, woman who frequently came near us." He then went on to describe her excellent work and calls her "a constant miracle to us."[29] In a much more understated manner in a letter from early 1912, Jean Dow reported that she needed no trained help from home "unless it were a physician" as the "Chinese give wonderfully good service when trained." The timing of the letter strongly suggests that it may have been intended as a direct rebuttal to Menzies' letter of a year earlier. In her report, she names and describes the work of several of these women. Mrs. Li Ming, who came to the new women's hospital when it opened in Changte in 1904, was trained and became "an excellent anaesthetist." She had withdrawn from the staff the previous August, but her replacement, Mrs. Jee, was then being trained.[30] These women took their medical and evangelical work into the countryside on rural itineration, as Dow described in some detail. They were her partners in a caring medical service that performed God's work in Honan.

These women likely are the unnamed medical assistants who appeared in the photographs of the Changte hospital published in the memorial booklet for Dr. Dow (figure 11.7; see also figure 11.1). We do not know who took these photos or when, but it would make sense to assume that they were produced under Dow's guidance and accompanied her 1912 letter. This would accord with her earlier actions in sending the photo and letter about Mrs. Han. In the first image, Dow has her back to the camera. While she frames the photo and is at its center, she is not the focal "I." In both photos, the Chinese assistants were featured and, according to the conventions of photography desired by Chinese subjects, faced the camera directly. Both the doctor and her assistants wear a professional-looking white medical outfit, unlike Mrs. Han in the earlier setting. The carefully lined shelves are again highlighted.

The photographs clearly narrate a scene of a female Sino-Canadian medical partnership, a partnership of trained and skilled professionals in which the Westerner plays the leading role. Dow's letters obliquely critique the politics of gender relations in the mission. The letters about Mrs. Han critique the actions of the all-male Honan Presbytery while her later discussion of her "wonderfully good" assistants critiques Menzies' discourse. But it was really the photographs (figures 11.6, 11.1, and 11.7) that revealed Dow's counternarrative. The editors of the *Tidings* obscured this critique by not including the photographs with the letters as Dow had intended. In her memorial pamphlet, Margaret Griffith perpetuated conventional discourse by not naming the assistants that Dow had identified and chosen to foreground in the carefully posed visuals.

11.7 The Assistants. Margaret R. Griffith, *Jean Dow, A Beloved Physician* (Toronto: Literature Dept., Woman's Missionary Society, The United Church of Canada, [193?]), 42.
By permission of The United Church of Canada/Victoria University Archives, Toronto.

The religious dimension so central to the written narratives and to much of Dow's own reportage also was subverted by these photographs, where we see a hidden narrative of Jean Dow and her assistants as pioneering medical professionals for women. They are professionals who are women and Christians. Writing about Dow in the obituary in the April 1927 issue of the Mission's own magazine, *The Honan Messenger,* Minnie Shipley gave a moving account of the "Affection between her and her Chinese helpers" and their grief at her death.[31] Behind that story is the even more hidden one of Dr. Dow herself as a medical scientist working for a cure for the dread and fatal disease of Kala Azar.

Jean Dow and Kala Azar: The Lady as a Doctor

The paradox of Jean Dow's life was that while she was a devout and fervent evangelist who situated herself in the tradition of "women's work for women," over time she became a dedicated medical professional desirous of the best scientific standards. Her devotion to medical science only rarely was allowed into the textual narrative; however, it was presented in the visual narrative. I already have suggested that she may have used photographs to subvert the master narrative deemed appropriate for women medical missionaries and their Chinese assistants. While her letters to the *Leaflet/Tidings* emphasize the religious work, many give detailed statistics on medical work, such as this for June 15 to August 31: "we treated 547 patients giving in all 1,095 treatments. Operations happily were few—11 cases. Our quarters were too narrow for much more."[32] As only extracts from Dow's letters and reports were published and the originals no longer exist, we do not know where the balance of the narrative actually lay, but obviously the home audience was more interested in religious work than detailed medical reports.

The *Tidings* did publish an edited version of her 1908 furlough speech to the members of the WMS, an address described as "a review of the medical work, its aims, methods and fruits."[33] The aim was stated according to convention, namely, to use medicine to bring women to Christianity, and that is the narrative focus. The description of evangelical methods of work occupies about two-thirds of the text, and the role of the native assistants is only mentioned in the context of their being "all native Christians" and part of the "thorough Christian influence" evident in every aspect of the work.[34] Nonetheless, the medical work, in what Dow calls "our woman's hospital," encompasses about one-third of the text, and is worth quoting in its entirety:

> It is very humble in appearance, a row of native buildings. Work goes on native principles, that is, the women provide their own bedding, friends to wait on them, food, etc., latterly a small fee has been charged to prevent those coming from curiosity.
>
> There are just three small rooms for wards each holding two or three patients at a time, with the dispensary and chapel. It may be in the near future greater demands may be made in the way of developments, more modern appliances and methods of work involving greater expenditure. There are many points of equipment still lacking; but we have sufficient for great opportunities for service. No field gives a greater area for the young woman who is ambitious for a life of service. Our patients come from great distances, even 100 miles off . . .
>
> Today the hospital stands in a unique position and while first of all evangelistic, its outlook and aim is also educational.[35]

Dow's professional pride in "her" hospital and its medical-public health educational role is quite evident from these lines. Her desire to have the hospital meet modern standards is tempered by the financial realities. And the "young woman who is ambitious for a life of service" seems an apt self-description.

The discussion of Dow's medical work in Margaret Griffith's memorial pamphlet contains the disclaimer that "Medicine was her profession, Evangelism was her passion," so that the metanarrative is one of medicine as the subservient handmaid of evangelism.[36] Despite this, Griffith cannot displace her admiration for Dow's professionalism, and it is from her that we learn that in addition to being "a good all-round surgeon, she was particularly efficient in eye work of all kinds, life in interior China providing abundant opportunities for the exercise of her skill in this department."[37] Most importantly, Griffith is the sole source for presenting Dow as a scientist who pioneered in the study of Kala Azar. She states that:

> Dr. Dow was among the first to isolate the microscopic organism which causes the disease, and in subsequent years the Women's Hospital entered upon a new activity as methods of treating this scourge were introduced, necessitating repeated and prolonged courses of extravenous injections.[38]

Griffith then quoted at length Dr. Ernest Struthers's description of Dow's handling of a particularly difficult case in the autumn of 1926, when she went to Weihwei to care for the wife of one of the missionaries, and volunteered to help in the hospital during her stay. Most of the patients receiving treatment for Kala Azar were children, and one in particular was in a very serious condition. This boy had arrived with the disease in an advanced state, with little chance of recovery. Dow took over these cases and tried everything, but to no apparent avail. But she refused to give up, and "tried out additional methods, which had in some cases in her extensive experience with this disease proved of value." The boy began to improve, and, "to the amazement of all, was on the road to complete recovery before Dr. Dow returned to her own station." Struthers pointed out that Dow's approach involved risk, but that she had the "courage" to "tackle . . . what most would not attempt." Her "fearlessness" was "tempered with such good judgement that it was wonderful what she was able to achieve."[39] Griffith also noted that Dow was anxious to try new methods. In her last major operation, she successfully performed a method of controlling hemorrhage that she had seen during her furlough in New York in 1925. According to Griffith, she had hoped that the new hospital would "make possible more thorough and scientific work."[40]

This is an important counter-narrative of Dow, not just as a highly skilled practitioner, but also as a pioneer scientist—one of the first to isolate the organism that caused Kala Azar. The praise from Struthers is especially significant. Struthers went to North Honan immediately after graduation from the Medical School at the University of Toronto in 1912. He published his first article on this disease in the *Chinese Medical Journal* in 1924 and took a Diploma in Tropical Medicine and Hygiene in London in 1925, where he specialized in Kala Azar. But by 1924, Dr. Dow already had extensive experience in the study and treatment of this disease, and had gone to that same School of Tropical Medicine in London as early as 1908. Nowhere in his 1975 memoir did Struthers recall her or her work.[41]

Dow's achievements in the field of Kala Azar research and treatment are both impressive and nearly invisible. The chapter "In Search of Kala Azar" in a popular history of the research and treatment of malarial-type diseases focuses on India, so that little of the China work is included. Dr. William Leishman of the India Medical Service made the first accurate scientific diagnosis of Kala Azar in 1900 and Dr. Donovan of India developed the first test by extract from the spleen. Similar discoveries were made around the same time in China. By 1903, the organisms were recognized as being protozoan by nature, and given the name "Leishman-Donovan bodies." But no one actually knew what class of organism it was or how it was transmitted. In 1904, the organism was identified under the microscope as a parasite, but the method of transmission by sand flies took another thirty years to ascertain. Unless the manner of its transmission could be identified, the disease could not be controlled. Thus Dr. Dow was working on this problem from 1902 until her death in 1927 during the most exciting and important phase of discovery when microbiology was in its "infancy."[42]

Unlike Dr. Struthers, however, Jean Dow did not publish any of her work, either from modesty or overwork or in deference to her primary vocation of evangelism. The recovery of this aspect of her career reinforces the hidden narrative found in the visuals of a devout woman entirely committed to the advancement of scientific medicine. Missionary work in China provided her enormous scope for development as a professional and a scientist. From the image of the doctor as a lady in the garden with friends, she advanced to images of herself as the lady who was a doctor surrounded by her trusted Chinese assistants. A similar transformation is seen in her assistants, from Mrs. Han in traditional dress to white-coated workers in the dispensary. Over time, for her and for her Chinese assistants, scientific medicine moved to the center. While Christianity was always at the core of Dow's self-identity, medicine and science eventually came to define her life. Christianity had drawn her and her Chinese partners to medicine, a reversal of the dominant narrative of medicine as the subservient handmaiden of evangelism.

Visuals and the Hermeneutics of Recovery

The photographs analyzed here form a counter-discourse to narratives of women and missionary medicine. Whether they were intended consciously to do so raises a complex issue of interpretation. It is difficult to know who took most of the photographs or why, since the originals of the letters did not survive, and archival cataloguing often lacks valuable material on dating or provenance. If we know little about the production, we do know that the ladies of the WMS who edited the *Leaflet/Tidings* controlled the reproduction. They functioned within the accepted narratives of the missionary movement in Victorian and Edwardian Canada, and of women's place within that movement.[43] The photograph of the three women missionaries in their garden (figure 11.4) fits that so well as to reinforce my conjecture that Miss Robertson of the WMS took it during her 1904 visit. The editors' omissions and silences are revelatory. They assumed that their audience wished primarily to see and read about the missionaries whom they supported and the institutions they funded. Although the purpose of the enterprise was conversion, in this era they showed little interest in the names or lives of the actual converts. Medical work in particular was viewed instrumentally, as providing access to women and children and thus possibilities for conversion. Medical work as an enterprise carried out by professional women on behalf of other women did not figure in this hermeneutic. Reports and photographs recording that professional reality literally were edited out.

The most complex narrative was that concerning Jean Dow herself. Instead of the self-effacing, modest, and beautiful woman of the master narrative of her life, we find the woman who became a dedicated and "fearless" medical scientist and practitioner. What has been interpreted as modesty was actually, in my view, a deep sense of female collegiality in which the group was paramount. In defending her Chinese assistants, she voiced oblique criticisms of the male power hierarchy. The letter about Mrs. Han contains overt criticism of the Honan Presbytery in which women at that time had no voice. Her letter in praise of her Chinese assistants was in sharp contrast to the views of Menzies, McClure, and other male doctors in the mission, though it contains no obvious criticism. In each case, the photographs would have made a very compelling case for these critiques had they been published together with the letters.

The critique was presented most clearly in that seemingly conventional photo of Dr. Dow and her assistants (see figure 11.1). Unlike all the metanarratives of women and missionary medicine, the narrative of this image is of a collectivity of women working together as medical professionals. By foregrounding her Chinese co-workers and sitting with her back to the "eye" of the camera, Jean Dow presented herself not as an heroic "muscular Christian" doctor, nor even as doing "women's work for women" in the accepted sense. Rather, she is "prima inter pares," the first among equals in a team of professionals. It was as first among equals, and not as Mackay's self-effacing "I," that she expressed the hope of being absent for the opening of the new Women's Hospital in Changte so that the credit would not fall to her alone.[44] This image encapsulates a far-sighted conception of a Sino-Western partnership in medical science, one that is only now being fully realized.

I have summarized both the methodological and theoretical assumptions informing this work as the hermeneutics of recovery. In this study, I have confronted texts where women clearly were present and active but where their identity or the meanings of their presence and actions had to be recovered. It was through the interplay of texts and visuals that recovery became possible. In looking for Jean Dow, what I have really found is the power of visual images of gender and science to unlock a feminist hermeneutics of recovery.

Acknowledgments

I am grateful to Bernie Lightman and Rusty Shteir for their very valuable editorial guidance and comments on an earlier draft of this chapter, particularly regarding the interplay between text and visuals.

Notes

1. Jean Dow and Minnie Pyke are among the North Honan staff members shown in figure 11.2. Minnie Robertson, a member of the Women's Missionary Society visiting from Canada, appears in the photograph as well.

2. For a much more detailed discussion of this form of "maternal feminism," see Ruth Compton Brouwer, *New Women for God: Canadian Women and India Missions, 1876–1914* (Toronto: University of Toronto Press, 1990).

3. In this approach to the photographs and narrative of Dow, I am following Morantz-Sanchez's analysis of American women's entry into the medical profession that evolved from "the Doctor as a Lady" to "the Lady as a Doctor." See Regina Morantz-Sanchez, *Sympathy and Science: Women Physicians in American Medicine* (Chapel Hill: University of North Carolina Press, 2000), chs. 5 and 6.

4. Typescript dated January 17, 1927, in Personal File, United Church Archives.

5. Margaret Griffith, *Dr. Jean I. Dow, A Beloved Physician* (Toronto: United Church of Canada, Foreign Missions Committee, Woman's Missionary Society, n.d.), 19. Pamphlet in Personal File, United Church of Canada Archives.

6. The Boxer movement was a large-scale peasant uprising that swept across North China in the summer of 1900. Centered in Shantung, the movement was anti-foreign and anti-Christian. The name derives from the practice of "spirit boxing" that its adherents believed made them invulnerable to foreign bullets.

7. Griffith, *Dr. Jean I. Dow*, 32.

8. Ibid., 37.

9. Typescript, Personal File, United Church of Canada Archives.

10. Quoted in Griffith, *Dr. Jean I. Dow*, 53.

11. *Foreign Missionary Tidings* 21 (November 1904): 135. Publication of the Woman's Missionary Society in the United Church Archives, Victoria University at the University of Toronto. Hereafter *FMT*.

12. M. Carey Lea, *A Manual of Photography*, 2nd ed. (Philadelphia: Printed for the author, 1871). See also Alexander Black, *Photography Indoors and Out: A Book for Amateurs* (Boston: Houghton, Mifflin and Company, 1893).

13. Lea, *A Manual*, 249, figure 116.

14. Ruth Compton Brouwer analyzes the discourse around the notion of "a sphere less injurious" in *New Women for God*, 188–96.

15. *FMT* 22 (June 2, 1905): 32.

16. *FMT* 19 (September 5, 1902): 82.

17. The May 1900 photo of "Miss Duncan of Neemuch (India) with High-Caste Camp School" is a striking example of the genre. See *FMT* 17 (May 1, 1900): 5.

18. For a more detailed analysis of this discourse, see Margo S. Gewurtz, "'Their Names May Not Shine': Narrating Chinese Christian Converts," in *Canadian Missionaries, Indigenous Peoples: Representing Religion at Home and Abroad*, ed. Alvyn Austin and Jamie S. Scott (Toronto: University of Toronto Press, 2005), 134–51.

19. James Frazer Smith, *Life's Waking Part* (Toronto: United Church of Canada, 1937), 196–97.

20. Brouwer, *New Women for God*, photograph pages not numbered.

21. *FMT* 19 (November 7, 1902): 131.

22. Photo appeared in the *Leaflet*, now renamed *Foreign Missionary Tidings* 17, no. 6 (October 1900): 122.

23. Letter dated August 8, 1899, and published in the *FMT n.s.* 3, no. 7 (November 1899): 180–81.

24. See the section on portraits in Asia Society Galleries, *Picturing Hong Kong. Photography 1855–1910* (New York: George Braziller, 1997), 101–12 and specifically 101, 102, and 112 for "dignified frontality."

25. Ibid., 112.

26. *FMT* 19 (September 5, 1902): 82.

27. Griffith, *Dr. Jean I. Dow*, 43.

28. *FMT* 17 (September 5, 1900): 92.

29. *FMT* 27 (March 11, 1911): 174.

30. *FMT* 28 (April 12, 1912): 203–204.

31. *Honan Messenger* 13 (April 4, 1927): 2, in Dow's Personal File, United Church Archives, Toronto.

32. *FMT* 21 (February 10, 1905): 210. See also 22 (June 2, 1905): 29, which reports 1,135 patients treated.

33. *FMT* 26 (June 2, 1909): 231.

34. Ibid.

35. Ibid.

36. Griffith, *Dr. Jean I. Dow*, 42.

37. Ibid., 38.

38. Ibid., 37–38.

39. Ibid., 39.

40. Ibid., 40–41.

41. Dr. Ernest B. Struthers, *A Doctor Remembers* (Mississauga: Imperial Press, 1976).

42. For the history of research into Kala Azar, see Robert S. Desowitz, *The Malaria Capers* (New York: W.W. Norton, 1991), 44–59.

43. For a fuller discussion of the WMS in this period, see Brouwer, *New Women for God*, 21–52.

44. R. P. Mackay, Typescript, Dow Personal File, United Church of Canada Archives.

Chapter 12

IMAGES OF EXPERTISE

Women, Science, and the Politics of Representation

Lorraine Code

Captioned "Whistle Blower," the cover photograph of the November 16, 1998, issue of *Maclean's: Canada's Weekly Newsmagazine* features Dr. Nancy Olivieri, an eminent hematologist at the University of Toronto and Toronto's Hospital for Sick Children. It names her principled breaking of a confidentiality agreement with a pharmaceutical company whose product she had been testing as the catalyst for "a debate over money and morality . . . raging through the medical world" (figure 12.1). The photo positions its subject to glamorize and sexualize her, producing an incongruity between her overt professional self-presentation as a lab-coated doctor (albeit with stethoscope rakishly worn) and the tropes it mobilizes of the vamp, the defiant troublemaker, the woman who, as a whistle blower, steps out of line to become as much a part of the problem as of its solution. Because such incongruities permeate the early (1994–1998) press coverage, I am reading "the Olivieri case" through a feminist lens, to show how the attendant imagery invokes *gender* as an analytic category for understanding it.[1] My purpose is to highlight gender as an operative, if often silent, facet of the case by exposing a subtext, discernible in a sampling of photographs and beneath the surface of the rhetoric in various newspaper and magazine reports. Verbally and visually, the reports convey unspoken but legible gendered messages whose effects, often tacitly but sometimes more explicitly, are to divert attention from Olivieri's expertise and even to impugn her scientific-medical credibility. It is of course neither new nor startling for reporters, scientists, and others to evince sexism in depicting or discussing a successful woman. But the Olivieri affair is emblematic in showing how gender infuses public and professional responses to a female whistle blower, even when it is not named. Reading the imagery through a feminist lens and against these silences exposes underacknowledged modalities of social-structural

BRITISH COLUMBIA: Operation Salvage • CENTRAL AMERICA: The Horrors of Mitch

CANADA'S WEEKLY NEWSMAGAZINE

Maclean's

Whistle Blower

A top researcher warns that a drug she is testing could be dangerous. The drugmaker fights back. Now, a debate over money and morality is raging through the medical world.

Dr. Nancy Olivieri,
Hospital for
Sick Children

NOVEMBER 16, 1998 $3.95

46

6 20058 70001 3

http://www.macleans.ca

12.1 "Whistle Blower." *Maclean's*, November 16, 1998. Photograph by Peter Bregg.
Courtesy of Maclean's. *Reprinted with permission.*

power and privilege at play in the politics of knowledge, gender, science, responsibility, and expertise that shape these events. Photographs are particularly good sources in this regard for, unlike print, they cannot avoid displaying the players as embodied, thus gendered beings; they cannot keep gender out of the picture. The verbal and visual imagery, like images generally, functions as much to generate meaning as to transmit it.

The Olivieri Case

The outlines of the case are as follows: In *The New England Journal of Medicine* (NEJM) in 1994, Dr. Olivieri (then) of the Division of Haematology/Oncology at Toronto's Hospital for Sick Children (HSC) and Professor of Medicine at the University of Toronto, published a team-authored article, "Survival in Medically Treated Patients with Homozygous B-Thalassemia," reporting on "transfusion and iron-chelation therapy" (administered in a drug called deferiprone-L1) for patients (mainly children) with thalassemia major, a genetically transmitted disorder prevalent around the Mediterranean, in the Middle East and Southeast Asia, and in Canada among children of Chinese, Greek, and Italian parents. Characterized by red blood cell production abnormalities, thalassemia major (also called Mediterranean anemia) causes oxygen depletion in the body and, untreated, can cause death within a few years. Growth failure, bone deformities, and an enlarged liver and spleen are among its symptoms, evident within the first year of life. Before deferiprone was available, patients had required monthly blood transfusions, administered by connecting them to a drug infusion pump for up to twelve hours a day: its effects include a dangerous iron build-up. Because the procedure for clearing the iron is so onerous, many patients opted out of treatment in their teens, and many died in their twenties. Thus 1993 reports herald deferiprone as a "revolutionary new treatment," "an entire new way to treat these diseases" (that is, thalassemia and sickle-cell anemia),[2] citing testimony from parents relieved at taking their children off the intravenous pump, and children pleased with their new-found freedom.[3]

Just a year after the first NEJM article, Olivieri published concerns about deferiprone's long-term effects, having noted that, for some patients, it too could produce iron overload serious enough to cause heart, liver, and endocrine damage. In a 1995 letter to the NEJM, she cautions: "When new therapies are introduced, it is important to confirm promising initial findings . . . so that false hope and expectation on the part of patients . . . can be avoided."[4] And in 1998, a second team-authored article concludes:

deferiprone is not an effective means of iron-chelation therapy in patients with thalassemia major and may be associated with worsening of hepatic fibrosis, even in patients whose hepatic iron concentrations have stabilized or decreased. After a mean of 4.6 years of deferiprone therapy, body iron burden was at concentrations associated with a greatly increased risk of cardiac disease and early death . . . in 7 of 18 patients (39%).[5]

For Western scientists, philosophers of science, and an informed public alike, these events fit into received images of "normal science," following a trajectory from positive initial findings through cautionary warnings to (partial) refutation of a hypothesis in light of new evidence, with modifications of (putative) knowledge, and/or withdrawal of the drug as the result. Yet here the trajectory was blocked: what could and *should* have been uncontroversial epistemic and ethical decisions devolved into a contest of wills and interests, generating the "debate over money and morality" named in *Maclean's* cover story.

Deferiprone research had been financed by Apotex Inc., "one of Canada's most high-powered pharmaceutical firms";[6] both in 1993 and 1995, Olivieri had signed confidentiality agreements prohibiting disclosure of information about the drug trials without the company's written permission;[7] and Apotex was negotiating a large donation to the University of Toronto. Thus, making new evidence public, exposing the fallibility/corrigibility of the findings, cautioning parents and patients, and withdrawing the drug from circulation were not as easy as allegedly value-neutral empiricist epistemologies contend. When, despite a warning from the Research Ethics Board (REB) at the Hospital for Sick Children, Olivieri insisted on modifying consent forms to warn patients of the dangers, Apotex threatened legal action, and neither the hospital nor the university supported her. Nonetheless, she publicly "defied the confidentiality clause and the company's threats to sue, arranged for her own legal counsel, informed her patients and the [hospital's] REB, informed the federal government's Health Protection Branch, reported her research at a medical conference," and published the 1998 NEJM article.[8] In consequence, she was dismissed from her position as head of the hospital's hemoglobinopathy program. Although collegial and public pressure forced a review of the case; although a settlement was brokered by the Canadian Association of University Teachers (CAUT), and two of the world's other leading experts in blood disease testified to Olivieri's scientific integrity and worldwide eminence; and although early in 1999 she was reinstated, the story does not end there. Even a putative "ending" that Olivieri reports in October 2001 scarcely counts as a "resolution"; neither has justice unequivocally been done for Olivieri and her supporters, nor have issues concerning "money and morality," academic freedom, corporate sponsorship, and public trust been addressed.[9] Indeed, citing the Olivieri case, David Nathan and David Weatherall observe in an October 2002 NEJM article that such things are still happening, although "they generally take milder and less public forms."[10]

Despite her 1999 reinstatement, the university was slow to restore Olivieri's research space, laboratory access, and lab assistants; for months she and her supporters were subjected to vicious email attacks and anonymous letters calling them "pigs" and "unethical," and making damaging allegations about Olivieri's professional conduct. In a bizarre twist to the story, in January 2000, Dr. Gideon Koren, a colleague at the HSC, himself an authority on drug abuse in children, and respected for having established "Motherrisk"—a service that gathers evidence and dispenses advice on risks to fetuses and children from drugs, chemicals, and toxins ingested by their mothers—himself co-signer of the 1993 contract, and a co-author of the 1994 article, was exposed as the sender of the hate mail. His exposure surprised "a lot of people both inside and outside the hospital because of his stature and reputation as a top scientist and caring doctor."[11] Meanwhile, in 2001, Apotex was still promoting Koren's "scientific opinions regarding its controversial drug";[12] and attempting to license the drug in the United Kingdom and Europe without the expertise—indeed over the protests—of Olivieri and of Dr. Gary Brittenham, who resigned his co-chairmanship of the Italian research team following actions by Apotex which left "less experienced and less principled investigators . . . [to] continue . . . a year-long study, not designed in the first place to examine efficacy," as Olivieri describes it.[13] In 2004, Miriam Shuchman reports, doctors in the United Kingdom, Italy, India, and Taiwan continued to see deferiprone as an option for patients unwilling or unable to take the alternative, desferal. In Shuchman's view, deferiprone "owes its staying power to science."[14] But the question remains: does it?

Images and Implications

In the Western social imaginary, the operative image of laboratory science is of authoritative inquiry practiced by privileged, mainly white men, in enclosed communities sealed off from open public discourse by a language in which not even the highly educated, literate, and privileged nonscientific public can readily participate. The image masks the human—therefore fallible—provenance of scientific "discoveries" behind such impersonal, passive locutions as "it has been shown," or claims such as "the data show" and "science has proved," which transcend the specificities, and thus the responsibilities, of human agency. The aura of certainty that this discourse engenders creates a protected insularity for laboratory life, separating quests for "knowledge itself" from the social-political-ethical effects of its circulation and enactment, often dismissively labelled its "uses," which, in this rhetorical frame, are extraneous to science proper. Such assumptions may explain Olivieri's detractors' efforts to contain her story by labelling it "a scientific controversy," thereby situating it within procedures and rules that pose as self-justifying and thus as impersonal and apolitical. Olivieri observes: "Having created this fiction, they were able to express the desirability of 'not taking sides.'"[15] The strategy echoes what Evelyn Fox Keller calls an "unspoken agreement that privilege[s] questions of truth over questions of consequences . . . [and] demarcat[es] the internal dynamics of science from its social and political influences": a strategy adept, even in these days of the "science wars," at protecting a laboratory "club culture" from demands for public accountability routinely faced by more secular forms of knowing.[16] That such "external" factors would play a part in knowledge-production is neither a surprise nor a sin, but in shielding them from view, an institution of knowledge-production forfeits its responsibly authoritative status.

The metaphor of the *hortus conclusus* in medieval painting—the walled garden, isolated from the outside world, protected from unwanted (unwonted?) intruders by the stone wall surrounding it—captures how the laboratory figures in this imaginary.[17] Michèle Le Dœuff invokes a related image of philosophy's "islanded consciousness," elaborated from Kant's reference to the "territory of pure understanding" as "an island, enclosed by nature itself within unalterable limits."[18] Kant's first *Critique* endeavors to "prevent the understanding, which has at last applied itself to its proper, empirical employment, from wandering off elsewhere," leaving its rightful domain, Le Dœuff contends.[19] The aura of esotericism this discourse engenders preserves the insularity of laboratory life, separating quests for "knowledge itself" from their social-political-ethical consequences, and sustaining a mystique of secrecy in which a confidentiality agreement such as Olivieri signed would pass merely as a matter of course. These rhetorical images prefigure the "enclosed communities" of present-day laboratory science, where whistle blowers are vilified, pilloried, excommunicated from the ranks of those whose domain they threaten to unsettle. Residues of a chemistry-set image of the laboratory and a *tabula rasa* theory of mind, yielding a picture of white-coated (i.e., pure, politically innocent) practitioners engaged in solitary, value- and theory-neutral quests for truth, still tacitly shape secular visions of research. They underwrite an imaginary of scientific methodology as autonomous, internally justifying, and hence immune to the ethical-political critique of feminists and other Others.

The Olivieri case challenges these aspects of scientific self-presentation head on, showing why science's location as a *specifically populated* institution of knowledge-production cannot be ignored. It exposes some of the strategies that institutional authorities employ to shore up a cherished image of scientific purity and isolation, as laboratory science emerges into public discourse to address matters of confidentiality in conflict with principles of informed consent and academic freedom. Yet the mere fact that a high-profile *female* doctor is the main protagonist—and in some reports the victim—may not seem sufficient to represent the events, unequivocally, as effects of gender politics. Male whistle blowers face comparable sanctions from pharmaceutical sponsors and/or universities protecting their assets. Dr. Arpad Pusztai of the University of Aberdeen, whose contract was terminated when he spoke out about the risks of genetically modified foods, is among the best-known examples;[20] and Olivieri compares her experiences with threats directed at Dr. David Kern, formerly of Brown University, in response to his concerns about interstitial lung disease in workers at the industrial plant, Microfibers.[21] Nor are gender issues evident in reports of the professional harassment to which Dr. Ann Clark of the Plant Agriculture Department at the University of Guelph was subjected when she opposed the development and use of genetically modified seeds (but viewing her situation through a feminist lens might yield a different reading).[22] Yet whereas a 1998 U.S. Office of Research Integrity investigation concluded that the majority of whistle blowers on scientific misconduct were men in senior positions at their institution (and thus, by virtue of sex and seniority, not part of the most vulnerable research population), extensive research by Dr. Drummond Rennie, who "had dedicated himself to whistle-blowers in science" before becoming an Olivieri supporter, contests these conclusions. A former editor of the NEJM, then (during the Olivieri case) of the *Journal of the American Medical Association* (*JAMA*), he found that it is frequently young women who are "stuck in a corner," in positions of having to protest, and that too often "[t]he career of a young scientist who complained was left in tatters while senior figures who committed the wrong—or allowed it to happen—walked away unharmed."[23] Thus again, Olivieri's visible presence introduces the gender question into the politics of representation, especially when the press as a source of public knowledge is so active a participant in the unfolding, positioning, and judging of events.

In the affluent twenty-first-century Western world, public willingness to trust what "science has proved," and hence to entrust people's lives and well-being to medical science, rests, cautiously, on beliefs woven into the fabric of the received scientific-epistemic imaginary. Its rhetorical apparatus, in which the "science has proved" locution plays an emblematic part, is structured around tacit assumptions that accredited practitioners will adhere to received research standards and submit their results to established procedures of critical scrutiny. Professional codes of conduct are designed to safeguard such confidence, and the value of testimonial evidence is established routinely with reference to the credentials of the testifier. With knowledge remote from lay experience, accessible at first hand only to the initiated, giving or withholding trust rests on beliefs, nurtured in open democratic societies where free inquiry is said to flourish, that practitioners have conformed to the norms of "normal science" and that the participation of patrons, sponsors, and institutional guarantors of projects carried out under their aegis conforms to the requirements of professional *epistemic and moral* responsibility. Public outrage in the media and the academy when violations of such assumptions are revealed shows how tightly they are bound into this web of social expectations. Hence, as Daniel Jacobi and Bernard Schiele persuasively argue, photographic imagery "'socializes' newly acquired knowledge by integrating it into a system of familiar representations. . . . [It] *authenticates* the actors through whom knowledge comes about."[24] Such authentication, I am suggesting, is equivocal in Olivieri's case, owing precisely to the "familiar representations" that this visual and rhetorical imagery mobilizes.

Prior to the exposure of Apotex's role, the public credibility index of the deferiprone project was high, given the credentials of the research team, listed with their degrees—in effect, to confirm their conformity to these very norms—and reinforced by the articles' appearance in the *New England Journal of Medicine* with its proud policy of refusing to publish articles whose authors are financed by drug companies or have other vested interests. These are typical ingredients in maintaining public trust in research as both process and product. Indeed, Olivieri's public credibility remained high, on the whole, as "the case" unfolded because of her refusal to abide by the confidentiality clause, her commitment to her patients and to "the evidence," her ongoing readiness to make developments public despite high personal costs, and her resistance to allowing "the profit motive [to] take precedence over scientific rigour" or to "lose [her] objectivity."[25] But she did not become the hero she might have been, and the controversy was long and damaging. Even the CAUT's 540-page 2001 document, *The Olivieri Report,* which (in her words) "vindicates" her and "set[s] the record straight" about the egregious abuses she and her supporters experienced, leaves Olivieri pessimistic about prospects for resolving the issues of public responsibility and trust.[26]

To a feminist eye, some of the reports point, if obliquely, to gendered assumptions at the core of the abuses. First, well before Olivieri's dismissal, the hospital publicly debunked her claims that the administration was threatening to dismiss her. Second, a CBC television documentary full of "grave factual errors and innuendo" claimed that Olivieri was "not only an incompetent scientist but carries responsibility for the suffering and death of thousands of patients worldwide."[27] Third, a Toronto newspaper announced "Firm Axes Outspoken Scientist's Research: Woman Went Public with Concerns about Drug's Safety."[28] Fourth, a caller to *Maclean's* from inside the hospital "accused her of stealing money from her research grant, treating her patients unethically, and sleeping with some of the scientists who looked favourably on her research" while another, with links to Apotex, "stubbornly referred to the trained specialist as 'Miss Oliveria.'"[29] And fifth, the pediatrician-in-chief at the HSC claimed that patient care would be unaffected by Olivieri's removal from the research program: she would "have more time to care for her patients."[30] These remarks expose an unequivocally gendered subtext. Discrediting a woman's "take" on events is a well-known ploy in the politics of discourse. Just as "outspoken" is rarely a gender-neutral term, so too is labelling her a "woman" who went public rather than identifying her as a "doctor" or a "scientist."[31] Attributing a woman's success to her having slept her way to the top is a too-familiar strategy in the politics of gender, as is casually "forgetting" her name and title. Declaring that her time would be better spent with her patients trivializes Olivieri's scientific stature, relegating her to a caring position where she assuredly will "be better off." In gendered divisions of labels and labor, these are familiar scripts for designating woman's place in a man-made world and for cautioning her should she fail to know that place.

Do these items, then, establish a pivotal role for gender in the politics of knowledge and ethics of inquiry operative here? *Explicitly* gendered comments are sufficiently rare in the early press coverage of the Olivieri case that sceptics might discount them as mere slips of the pen, so perhaps not. But there are exceptions, telling enough to make the silences audible. For example, a reference to "the dysfunctional patriarchy in which she works—The Hospital for Sick Children"—describes it as "a place where senior scientists are scolded like schoolgirls and their concerns ignored";[32] a feminist columnist quotes one of Olivieri's male supporters at the University of Toronto as saying: "if she were a six foot two male football player, her concerns for her patients' well-being would not have been treated this way";[33] and the HSC's CEO Michael Strofolino refers to Olivieri as "this poor little innocent researcher"[34]—a comment unlikely to be made of a man.

Yet (partial) media silence notwithstanding, gender evidently plays a part in this case, located as it is in a scientific research climate where a sexualized politics of knowledge sustains hierarchies of credibility, epistemic authority, and trust in ways detrimental to open, democratic, epistemic negotiation. It is a research culture in which, as Sharon Traweek convincingly concludes, the image of female human beings held by male scientists "is that women are more passive, less aggressive than men. . . . The scientist is persistent, dominant, and aggressive, ultimately penetrating the corpus of secrets mysteriously concealed by a passive, albeit elusive nature. The female exists in these stories only as an object for a man to love, unveil, and know."[35] How, then, can she claim a place as a *scientist* in a territory shaped by such imagery?

Representations

Although the fact of a high-profile female doctor as protagonist—and sometime victim—cannot by itself catch the gendered tenor of these events, photographs offer a way of revisiting the Olivieri case to reread the silences around gender.[36] Their messages are as insistent as the whistle blower montage with which I began. Constrained by the very nature of the medium to show Olivieri as an embodied, thus gendered being, they *display* gender at work in ways unavailable to the verbal imagery of the print medium. Differently, but with effects continuous with those of the oblique rhetoric I cite, these photographs subtly inform, and work to confound, public evaluations of Olivieri's professional stature and of the value of her testimony, in a society better equipped to read stock representations of neutral, disembodied expertise and authority kept in circulation by images of male doctors and CEOs in which "the scientist (usually male) is shown in a medium shot . . . in his place of work (laboratory, office or library) . . . [holding] an object or device that helped him arrive at his discovery."[37] He is unequivocally a scientist.

Compare the typically feminine representation of Olivieri's professional demeanor in figure 12.2, showing her with a child, in a female-caring posture. In the larger montage from which this image is taken, her photo appears together with head-and-shoulders images of four men in suits—two of them her detractors, two her champions (captioned "The men in the middle")—and a full-length photo of the (also suited) president of the Hospital for Sick Children.[38] Contrasting sharply with the Olivieri image, the men stand against neutral backdrops that could be nowhere or anywhere. They are the dispassionate leading actors in the drama, exemplary autonomous men: men of reason, whose gendered positioning is itself

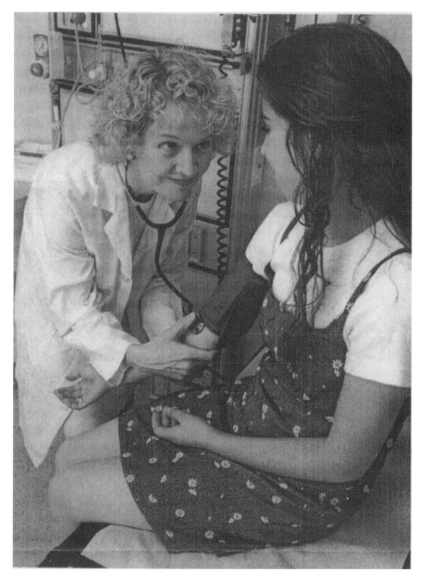

12.2 "Caring for her patients." *Globe and Mail*, November 2, 1998. Photograph by Tibor Kolley.
Reprinted with permission from The Globe and Mail.

neutralized, unmarked, while she bends forward in a strikingly subordinate position, leaning toward her patient and the camera. The montage recalls Traweek's comments about the "heroes of particle physics" identified in the margins of a 1971 physics textbook: "These scientific giants are shown from the waist up, alone in an office, or in a portrait pose which includes only their head and shoulders. The rhetoric of these images underlines the outward physical similarity of the men, their apparent social conformity . . . and their freedom from any particular social context."[39] Creating a further contrast, the provocatively defiant image of the bad girl—captioned "Courage

12.3 "Courage Under Fire." *Elm Street* (Holiday 1998) cover. Photograph by Derek Shapton, copyright Derek Shapton. *Reprinted with permission.*

HOLIDAY 1998 $2.95

Elm Street

FOR WOMEN

THE ULTIMATE SHOPAHOLIC

SORCERESS OF THE SKIN

HOLIDAY HORS D'OEUVRES

DRESSED TO PARTY

COURAGE under FIRE

Dr. Nancy Olivieri's stand against a drug company has rallied the forces of medicine

Under Fire"—recalls another set of stock of images, among which the taming of the shrew is a clear contender (figure 12.3). Like the images in figures 12.4 and 12.5, it offers an intriguing contrast with another head-and-shoulders photograph of Dr. Gideon Koren in which, looking at the photographer frankly and in a "normal" professional posture, his is the very image of the avuncular doctor everyone can trust: a kindly, misunderstood, physician whose blunder must be forgiven.[40] It was "the only way to express himself" against this out-of-control woman.[41] His body and clothing scarcely obtrude: He is the quintessentially thoughtful doctor who invites trust, a figure of appropriate professional modesty and detachment. Ironically, had *he* been depicted as the whistle blower in a pose as defiant as Olivieri's, it might not have touched his public image or his credibility either way. For although male whistle blowers are indeed at risk, there is a double standard at work here. For example, in 1999, the HSC made *public* allegations against "the quality of Olivieri's work"; yet in the same year, despite conclusive forensic evidence of misconduct against Koren produced by Olivieri and her colleagues, the hospital's board of trustees "urged them 'not to take any unilateral steps which might damage the reputation of one of your colleagues.' "[42] The effects of Olivieri's professional stature likewise should have been to protect *her* reputation, to destabilize standard stereotypes and establish their irrelevance. Yet reading the images through a feminist lens exposes systemically gendered features that generate asymmetrical evaluations of Koren's and Olivieri's actions. Viewed through the imaginary that holds stereotypes of masculinity, femininity, and science itself in place, Olivieri's credibility and trustworthiness have to be argued for, advocated with a degree of insistence that her professional stature should have rendered *hors de question*, while his credibility remains unchallenged.

The *Elm Street* photos (figures 12.3, 12.4, and 12.5), like the *Maclean's* cover photo (figure 12.1), might be read as self-consciously defiant, transgressing the scripts and expectations of docile, compliant femininity, countering the "blonde syndrome" to show a woman who need not downplay her femaleness to achieve professional stature: who can be classy, good-looking, assertive, *and* a rigorous research scientist. Olivieri is not without agency in the production of these photos; she authors herself, participates in crafting the images, acquiesces in the modes of address expected by *Elm Street*'s readers at that period in its history. She may have enacted such poses for these very purposes, by way of resisting those of the demure woman or the faceless professional. (Jacobi and Schiele observe that "science, through popularization, becomes a staged event; it uses the same strategies and borrows the same imagery as does theatre."[43]) Indeed, in a sceptical reading of the case in *MD Canada*, editor David Dehaas speculates that Olivieri, together with a communications consultant, orchestrated this "highly successful 'media blitz' . . . that put [her] . . . on the cover of *Elm Street* and *Maclean's* magazines and made hers a household name synonymous with 'academic freedom.' "[44] Even the lab-coat image (figure 12.4) is glamorized in a parody of those dispassionate stock figures of male scientists: despite the lab coat and the apparatus, she does not look, first of all, like a doctor. She is first a woman, then a doctor, as also in the fetching pose in figure 12.5. There Olivieri presents herself—or is presented—in the visual idiom of a

12.4 "Dr. Nancy Olivieri, scientist and clinician." *Elm Street* (Holiday 1998): 27. Photograph by Derek Shapton, copyright Derek Shapton.
Reprinted with permission.

fashion model or movie star, in her mock-assertive, come hither stance, posing as defiant, but unable to step outside the larger social imaginary where such emphasis on her body can work as readily to interrogate or mock her defiance as to celebrate it. Whether such effects were planned or are merely "natural" products of the hegemonic social imaginary, the stance, the lip gloss, and the earrings in these photos exploit a ready-made imagery over-determined in spite of itself to take its point of reference from the entrenched disciplinary apparatus of gender politics: an imagery that requires Olivieri to navigate across a narrow range of options. She has to defy, evade, refuse, ignore, exploit, or reconfirm stereotypes of acquiescent or of out-of-control femininity. Why would she not choose to do so in style?

It is instructive to read these displaced rhetorical stereotypes and photographs together with Londa Schiebinger's analysis of women scientists' efforts to achieve a credible professional image serious enough to present an authoritative demeanor and frank enough to avoid the dissembling that was one of the few options available to early women in Western science. Schiebinger's approach in *Has Feminism Changed Science?* is at once more cautious and more wide-ranging than earlier feminist science writings (such as Evelyn Fox Keller's *Reflections on Gender and Science*[45]), assuming neither a hard-edged, dichotomous imagery of masculinity and femininity nor fixed, unified gendered scientific "styles." Schiebinger examines structural-situational factors in the culture of science and the substance of diverse scientific practices in order to arrive at complex responses to her title question.

Analyzing an opposition between the dictates of femininity and Western ideals of science, Schiebinger traces its origins to the "privatization of the family and . . . professionalization of science" in the seventeenth and eighteenth centuries, when "[t]he private, caring woman emerged as a foil to the public, rational man," and science "came to be seen as decidedly masculine" (hence Olivieri would be "better off caring for her patients"). As more women entered professional science, in the early twentieth century, the persistent effects of this opposition turned "shedding the trappings of 'femininity'" into one of the prices a woman had to pay to be taken seriously as a scientist.[46] At the beginning of the twenty-first century, Schiebinger suggests, both scientists and non-scientists still assume precise alignments between science and masculinity and imagine "science" as naturally, appropriately populated by men.

So entrenched are residues of this history in the dominant social imaginary that it is scarcely surprising to find the Olivieri photographs delivering equivocal messages. Indeed, they work both *toward* defying intransigent gender norms, undermining sedimented stereotypical imaginings, and *against* a measured representation of Olivieri as a scientist worthy of respect. It is a notorious double bind: Women

12.5 "Not a personality debate?" *Elm Street* (Holiday 1998): 32. Photograph by Derek Shapton, copyright Derek Shapton.
Reprinted with permission.

who flout the norms of femininity are rarely commended, and women who conform to them are rarely taken seriously. Schiebinger recalls Martha Minow's "difference dilemma" according to which "calling attention to gender stereotypes can reinforce them and create friction where before there seemed to be none, but . . . ignoring gender differences can leave invisible power hierarchies in place."[47] Either way, the images insert a gendered dimension into this controversy as it plays into an overactive rumor mill exploiting gossip about Olivieri's personal life and character ("She's known to have a flaming temper"), and representing her as often as a scapegoat as an exemplary practitioner.[48] They divert attention toward her person, thus away from her research as the appropriate locus of inquiry, and away from issues of institutional accountability and corporate complicity in suppressing truths needing to be told. According to science's self-image as a project of constructing "a truth that is unanimously and collectively acknowledged" (citing Jacobi and Schiele), the practitioners "who formulate a small fragment of it are an anonymous element."[49] In defying this anonymity, the Olivieri photos expose the irony of the official claim that this is merely a "scientific controversy" in which the sex/gender or any other personal attributes of the scientist/knower would be insignificant.[50]

In the dominant Western scientific imaginary, a high-profile "outspoken" woman scientist remains an anomaly for whom everyday epistemic-moral discourse has no ready-made place. None of the available conceptual frames could have made space for gender to figure centrally in the case's unfolding, unless by naming it simplistically to enlist the mere fact of one woman's extraordinary success by entrenched criteria of "ordinariness" as evidence that the gender question has been resolved and ceased to be an issue because women have "made it" even into the upper echelons of science. But without addressing the question explicitly in its multiple inflections with power and privilege, the explanatory-analytic account is too slender, the choices too stark. They reduce to two: *Either* the case is a "scientific controversy" and gender by definition is irrelevant, and thus a new postfeminist era must be heralded and one successful woman suffices to establish the point; *or* Nancy Olivieri is just being difficult, a "troublemaker," living proof, after all, that women cannot do science-by-the-rules; so it is easy to contain her within a female/feminine domain, to downplay her expertise and blur the clarity of her professional profile.[51] In this "imagined community" forged around tacit understandings of what must and must not be said or shown—this community that coalesces around a set of common expectations and outrages to submit Olivieri to a trial by media—it is nothing less than disingenuous, a manifestation of false consciousness, to maintain silence about gender when "everyone knows" how anomalous a highly successful female scientist is, with so visible a public profile.[52] Hence the silences amount to a studied avoidance, a public posturing of a would-be enlightened postgender stance, enabled, in effect, by Olivieri's unimpugnable qualifications—her "brilliance" (to cite one of her supporters). Yet as public opinion and the CAUT inquiry begin to vindicate her, the images shift. Olivieri now appears in frankly professional head-and-shoulders poses (figure 12.6): innocent, without dissembling, and with nothing to hide.

12.6 "Dr. Olivieri vindicated." *CAUT Bulletin* 49, no. 1 (January 2002): A1. Photograph by Wayne Hiebert. *Courtesy of* The Ottawa Citizen. *Reprinted with permission.*

Had it been challenged, media neglect of the gender question might have been explained with an argument that the very category is obsolescent precisely because Olivieri—and others—have broken through outmoded barriers by doing what a woman must to succeed in a patriarchal world: become twice as good as most men, and on male territory. Thus, it would be ideologically excessive to raise the issue. But such a response would show only that the entrenched social-conceptual imaginary is not crafted sensitively enough to capture gender's ongoing effects as an oppressive mechanism—if more silently—even when a woman has achieved eminence in a world hitherto closed to members of her sex. The old tropes are right there, in the background: the gender stereotypes depicting and defending the legitimacy of a masculine, disinterested scientific expertise where a woman finds her place by assuming a feminine, caring posture, and where her defiance of the norms of femininity can be invoked to cast her as hysterical, out of control. Such tropes have been embedded in the Western imaginary since the birth of experimental science from the work of Robert Boyle, for whom, Elizabeth Potter writes, the "new man of science [must] be a chaste, modest heterosexual who desires yet eschews a sexually dangerous yet chaste and modest woman."[53] Women were excluded from the British Royal Society and from those "qualified to make knowledge by witnessing experiments and attesting to their validity."[54] There is scant evidence that such prohibitions have disappeared at the beginning of the twenty-first century.

Expertise, Credibility, and Trust

Significantly, from rereading through the silences to how the early press coverage *shows* gender, the matter of trust surfaces in a new register as the focus shifts to how Nancy Olivieri's public credibility—her trust*worthiness*—is unsettled, how it evolves into a contentious issue in the politics and ethics of knowledge. For the questions about public credibility and epistemic responsibility generated by the Apotex sponsorship and complicated by this verbal and visual imagery are entwined with issues about trust in knowledge and ethics. And while it is not essentially—though it may be quintessentially—feminist to name public openness, answerability, and trust as pivotal to an ethics of inquiry or to social-material-political analyses of institutions of knowledge-production, it is feminists who moved the question "whose knowledge are we talking about?" to center stage in epistemology, where it occupies a conceptual space close to Schiebinger's "has feminism changed science?" The epistemological question acquires a sharper edge when—as with Olivieri—it opens out to ask about the *provenance* and *ownership* of knowledge in an increasingly privatized research climate. It must ask about public access: about how a lay population of patients, parents, relatives, and other caregivers can "have" good enough knowledge to give adequately informed consent when knowledge becomes a commodity whose purchasers and beneficiaries guard it zealously against all challengers. Images contribute to the framing of such questions; and the imagery of the *hortus conclusus*, the closed—inaccessible—scientific community, is still operative. Within that protected space, the chemistry-set/*tabula rasa* image of (male) scientists engaged in solitary, value- and theory-neutral quests for truth is no longer plausible, despite its tenacity in the public imagination.

In the new corporate research climate, public trust and epistemic responsibility, both individual and collective, are integral to evaluations of scientific and other epistemic practices. This thought is not new, although questions about trust and trustworthiness faded from the epistemic imaginary when logical positivism heroically entered the scientific landscape with a method designed to eradicate an allegedly unreliable, naive, and potentially subjective reliance on trust that historically (according to Steven Shapin) previously had characterized communities of inquiry, both scientific and other, and not inevitably to their detriment.[55] The emergence of new forms of patronage in the present corporate research climate confers a particular urgency upon questions about responsibility and trust, as Apotex's policies show. Yet patronage in scientific research is not in itself deplorable. It has a long, often venerable history of fostering knowledge and creativity, even if neither its political innocence nor a disinterested commitment to pure inquiry can be taken for granted. Contrary to the positivistic imaginary of scientific insulation from the circumstances of its making, in the early twenty-first century the structures and effects of the institutions and forms of patronage that underwrite and enable laboratory research and the circulation/application of scientific knowledge again—as in Shapin's reading of seventeenth-century Britain—count among conditions that make knowledge possible. Such conditions shape research findings, block or promote lines of inquiry, and regulate patterns of circulation and application. It would overstate the case to claim that they *determine* scientific knowing as process or product, but would understate it to gloss over their constitutive effects. In other words, the structures of science as a public institution have undergone fundamental transformations since the industrial revolution and especially during the twentieth century, to reconfigure—re-imagine—patterns of accountability and redistribute responsibilities in ways that theorists of knowledge still have to think through. The persistent, intransigent, yet discredited, gender stereotypes embedded in everyday visual and verbal imagery of Western science and expertise show how much thinking remains to be done.

Prompted by these thoughts, I am adapting an insight of Cheshire Calhoun's to show how, within an instituted social imaginary, events like the Olivieri case generate *abnormal contexts*. These, for Calhoun, "arise at the frontiers of moral knowledge . . . when a subgroup of society . . . makes advances in moral knowledge faster than they can be disseminated to and assimilated by the general public and subgroups at special moral risk."[56] Calling the events abnormal casts them neither as singular nor isolated: it shows how they disrupt the settledness of the "normal," stretch the boundaries of fixed frames of reference. Olivieri's refusal to remain silent is not abnormal in the everyday discourse of knowledge and morality: in normal contexts, it would be a straightforward choice. Its abnormality is more epistemic than moral, for the resilience of the hegemonic social imaginary in sustaining a picture of normal science as a project of pure inquiry (despite evidence to the contrary) prevents the "general public" from assimilating revelations of scientific thralldom to the interests of its investors. It is hard for people educated to believe in direct correspondence between scientific-observational knowledge and "reality" to contemplate the dark underside of scientific practice that Olivieri exposes: to assimilate the complexity of negotiations instrumental to the production, validation, circulation, and now ownership of knowledge. My borrowing, then, reads these negotiations as counterparts of Calhoun's "frontiers," as sites where questions about epistemic responsibility and trust arise. A renewed philosophical focus on "the role of trust in knowledge" attests to their salience while confirming the ineluctable situatedness, in Donna Haraway's sense, of inquiry.[57] Situated knowers cannot perform the abdications of responsibility that positivism's value-neutral "god trick" would allow. They cannot remove themselves from view as distinctively embodied agents; nor is it possible, before the fact, to declare particularities of their embodiment irrelevant to their scientific practice. Abnormal moral contexts are, by definition, specifically situated even though the knowledge-production they foster may be more than locally valid.

In medicine throughout the affluent Western world, trust, both epistemic and moral, is constitutive of practices of giving and seeking informed consent: trust in the knowledge underpinning such transactions being responsibly sought, produced, and evaluated by established criteria of scientific trustworthiness; the information conveyed as neither concealing nor mystifying that knowledge; establishing openness and respect as a goal of physician-patient interactions. Physicians have also, judiciously, to know when to trust testimony in the professional literature and in collaborative practice, for responsible medical practice requires a reliable division of intellectual labor. Hence, writing of Apotex's efforts to suppress research findings, Dr. Miriam Kaufman remarks, "if drug companies can control research . . . we're sunk as clinicians."[58] Nancy Olivieri could not seek appropriately informed consent so long as she observed the confidentiality agreement; she could not earn or preserve her patients' trust. But the episode is framed within larger structural effects of the power-knowledge-privilege differential between doctor and patient, where the politics of knowledge often disempowers female patients and other marginalized Others in the consulting room and the hospital, and where specificities such as gender, race, and class structure clinical consultations so as to complicate seeking and offering informed consent.[59] Thus Olivieri's protest locates itself, by default if not by design, within values and styles of professional conduct that figure prominently in feminist inquiry. These are some of the structures of the politics of knowledge and trust that the visual images expose to view.

Perhaps paradoxically, feminists—and I among them—have argued that the question "Whose knowledge are we talking about?" confers a new salience upon *ad hominem*—in this case *ad feminam*—evidence.[60] So when "two of the world's other leading experts" testify to Olivieri's scientific eminence and professional integrity, their testimony enhances public support for her epistemic and moral stance. Their gender—male—enhances it further. *My* defense of her conclusions could not compete with the testimony of experts, whose credentials establish the credibility of their beliefs. Indeed, public presumptions in favor of affirming the truth or even the plausibility of knowledge claims often are generated by appeals to the character and credentials of the claimants, and reasonably so. They are strengthened or weakened by *ad hominem/ad feminam* imagery, both verbal and visual, that depicts conduct, character, and demeanor favorably or otherwise.

But such arguments lend themselves as readily to trust-destroying as to trust-enhancing purposes, as when media representations in the Olivieri case enter the *ad feminam* repertoire to deploy images whose effects are ambiguous as to whether they enhance or unsettle Olivieri's credibility. The contrast with Koren is again instructive: His reputation as a "top scientist and a caring doctor" is invoked to excuse his misconduct, thus to re-establish a credibility he might be thought to have forfeited. Olivieri's photos, and the rhetoric that often infuses the reports, by contrast, shift attention from her work's scientific merits to *her* unruliness. Such contrasts pose the gender question even when the answer is equivocal; they circumnavigate standard propositional analysis and orthodox verification-falsification to display credibility and trust as artifacts of rhetoric and imagery.

Clearly, my readings generate more questions than they answer. Those posed by corporate interests and pharmaceutical-company funding in science are about epistemic responsibility. They are about a cluster of factors that demand democratic public debate and collective rethinking of the very idea of responsible scientific and communicative practice.[61] Research institutions are not populated by the faceless, disembodied knowers that a positivist imaginary presupposes, but by diversely gendered, classed, raced, abled, aged practitioners whose embodied specificities and material-cultural situatedness participate in conferring or withholding credibility. Thus theorists have to address the negotiations integral to establishing or discrediting truths that are more urgently pertinent to human lives than the stripped-down examples that mainstream epistemologists serve up as paradigmatic knowledge, and to evaluate the part that verbal and visual images play in those negotiations. Such issues rarely figure in academic epistemology, but feminists and other Others investigating the politics of situated knowledges need to learn how to think about them, to recognize their epistemological significance.

In such inquiry, evaluations are more nuanced, less certain, more multifaceted than philosophers of science and epistemologists have hoped. Directing their attention to images, rhetoric, metaphors, styles of reasoning, for which the instituted scientific-epistemic imaginary has no place, makes for a more complex but, I suggest, a richer, more informative analysis. Establishing plausibility for new knowledge sufficient to underwrite responsible action becomes a matter of negotiation about what to count as evidence and why, how to read it, and whose readings warrant authoritative status. Gender-sensitive analysis enlarges the scope of inquiry while media imagery adds a layer of complexity to gender itself as an analytic category, refining and expanding its explanatory scope. The result may not be a never-ending story, but premature closure—a too-easy dismissal of the part gender plays—risks truncating the explanatory approaches capable of making all the difference.

Acknowledgments

My thanks to Susan Ehrlich, Bettina Bradbury, and Jenny Lloyd for insightful discussions of this project in its early stages, and to Kathy Davis for help in thinking through the issues about gender as an analytic category. Thanks to Rusty Shteir and Bernard Lightman for perceptive editorial comments on previous drafts of this paper, and to an anonymous reviewer for UPNE.

Notes

1. The concept of gender as an "analytic category" is from Joan Wallach Scott, "Gender: A Useful Category of Historical Analysis," in her *Gender and the Politics of History* (New York: Columbia University Press, 1988). Scott enlists gender as both "a constitutive element of social relationships based on perceived differences between the sexes, and . . . a primary way of signifying relationships of power" (p. 42).

2. Quotations from Lisa Priest, "Sick Kids Doctor Finds Anemia Drug," *The Toronto Star*, January 14, 1993, A3.

3. Miriam Shuchman, *The Drug Trial: Nancy Olivieri and the Science Scandal that Rocked the Hospital for Sick Children* (Toronto: Random House, 2005), presents detailed, and fluctuating, testimony from patients and their parents throughout her account of the case.

4. Nancy F. Olivieri, Letter to the Editor, *The New England Journal of Medicine* 333, no. 9 (1995): 1287–88.

5. Nancy F. Olivieri, M.D., Gary M. Brittenham, M.D., Christine E. McLaren, Ph.D., Douglas M. Templeton, Ph.D., Ross G. Cameron, M.D., Ph.D., Robert A. McClelland, Ph.D., Alastair D. Burt, M.D., and Kenneth A. Fleming, D. Phil., M.B., Ch.B., "Long-Term Safety and Effectiveness of Iron-Chelation Therapy with Deferiprone for Thalassemia Major," *The New England Journal of Medicine* 339, no. 7 (1998): 420–21.

6. Leslie Papp, "Firm Axes Outspoken Scientist's Research" (with the subheading "Woman Went Public with Concerns about Drug's Safety"), *The Toronto Star*, January 26, 1997, A2.

7. The 1993 contract with Apotex Inc., which Dr. Olivieri signed (with Dr. Gideon Koren), contained a "one-year, post-termination confidentiality clause"; the June 1995 contract Dr. Olivieri signed "had a three-year, post-termination confidentiality clause." Jon Thompson, Patricia Baird, and Jocelyn Downie, *The Olivieri Report: The Complete Text of the Report of the Independent Inquiry Commissioned by the Canadian Association of University Teachers* (Toronto: James Lorimer and Company Ltd., 2001), 24, 25.

8. Michael Valpy, "Salvage Group Tackles Sick Kids' Image Disaster," *The* (Toronto) *Globe and Mail*, November 2, 1998, A1, A9. Quotation from A9.

9. Nancy Olivieri, "Scientific Inquiry: The Fight's Just Starting," *The Globe and Mail*, October 31, 2001, A17.

10. David G. Nathan, M.D. and David J. Weatherall, M.D., "Academic Freedom in Clinical Research," *New England Journal of Medicine* 347, no. 17 (2002): 1370.

11. Krista Foss, "Sick Kids Doctor Breaks His Silence," *The Globe and Mail*, January 7, 2000, A2.

12. Olivieri, "Scientific Inquiry."

13. Nancy Olivieri, "When Money and Truth Collide," in *The Corporate Campus: Commercialization and the Dangers to Canada's Colleges and Universities*, ed. James L. Turk (Toronto: James Lorimer and Company Ltd., 2000), 54.

14. Shuchman, *The Drug Trial*, 363.

15. Olivieri, "When Money and Truth Collide," 53, 59.

16. Evelyn Fox Keller, *Secrets of Life, Secrets of Death: Essays on Language, Gender, and Science* (New York: Routledge, 1992), 84. On the "club culture" and "enclosed communities" of laboratory science, see Lynette Hunter, *Critiques of Knowing: Situated Textualities in Science, Computing and the Arts* (London: Routledge, 1999), 30, 104. See also Steven Shapin, *A Social History of Truth: Civility and Science in Seventeenth-Century England* (Chicago: The University of Chicago Press, 1994), especially ch. 1, and 104–107.

17. Kenneth Clark mentions the *hortus conclusus* in *Landscape into Art* (Middlesex: Penguin Books, 1949), 24, 29.

18. Michèle Le Dœuff, *The Philosophical Imaginary*, trans. Colin Gordon. (Stanford: Stanford University Press, 1989), 8. The quotation is from Immanuel Kant, *Critique of Pure Reason*, trans. Norman Kemp Smith (London: Macmillan, 1970), 257.

19. Le Dœuff, *Philosophical Imaginary*, 10, 11.

20. See for example Laurie Flynn and Michael Sean Gillard, "GM Food Scandal Puts Labour on Spot," *The* (Manchester) *Guardian Weekly*, February 21, 1999.

21. Olivieri, "When Money and Truth Collide," 58.

22. See E. Ann Clark, "Academia in the Service of Industry: The Ag Biotech Model," in *The Corporate Campus,* 69–86.

23. Cited in Shuchman, *The Drug Trial*, 214–17.

24. Daniel Jacobi and Bernard Schiele, "Scientific Imagery and Popularized Imagery: Differences and Similarities in the Photographic Portraits of Scientists," *Social Studies of Science* 19 (1989): 737 (emphasis added).

25. The phrases are from Krista Foss and Paul Taylor, "Volatile Mix Meant Trouble at Sick Kids," *The Globe and Mail*, August 22, 1998, A1, A4.

26. Thompson, Baird, and Downie, *The Olivieri Report;* Olivieri, "Scientific Inquiry."

27. Arthur Shafer, "Smear Tactics Unfair to Olivieri," *Toronto Star*, April 10, 2000, A17.

28. Papp, "Firm Axes Outspoken Scientist's Research."

29. Jane O'Hara, "Whistle Blower," *Maclean's: Canada's Weekly Newsmagazine,* November 16, 1998, 66.

30. Krista Foss and Paul Taylor, "Sick Kids Demotes Controversial MD," *The Globe and Mail*, January 8, 1999, A12.

31. A subsequent article refers to scientists (apparently male and female) who "have been outspoken in their support for Dr. Olivieri" (Krista Foss and Andrew Mitrovica, "Sick Kids Battle Turns Bizarre," *The Globe and Mail,* December 21, 1999, page 1), but my point holds.

32. Michael Valpy, "Science Friction," *Elm Street* 3, no. 3 (1998): 28.

33. Michele Landsberg, "U of T Should Back Demoted Doctor," *The* (Toronto) *Sunday Star*, January 17, 1999, A2.

34. O'Hara, "Whistle Blower," 66.

35. Sharon Traweek, *Beamtimes and Lifetimes: The World of High Energy Physicists* (Cambridge, Mass.: Harvard University Press, 1988), 103.

36. In listening to the silences, I follow Natalie Zemon Davis, who remarked of her work on *The Gift* (public lecture, Toronto, April 1999) that no matter how she read the evidence, she could discern no gendered implications. When a student recalled her insistence that gender is always an issue, if only for its invisibility, she re-examined the silences. See her *The Gift in Sixteenth-Century France* (Madison: University of Wisconsin Press, 2000), especially 75–79.

37. Jacobi and Schiele, "Scientific Imagery," 739.

38. See *The Globe and Mail*, November 2, 1998, A9. Efforts to obtain permission to reproduce these photographs were unsuccessful.

39. Traweek, *Beamtimes and Lifetimes*, 77. Her reference is to Eyvind H. Wichmann, *Quantum Physics* (New York: McGraw-Hill, 1971).

40. The *Elm Street* article, where these frankly female-feminine poses appear, praises Olivieri's courage under fire. It is one of only a few pieces to refer to her consistently as a scientist.

41. See *The Globe and Mail*, January 7, 2000, A2. It was not possible to obtain permission to reproduce this photograph.

42. Thompson, Baird, and Downie, "The Central Role of Dr. Koren in the L1 Controversy," section 5R in *The Olivieri Report*, 396.

43. Jacobi and Schiele, "Scientific Imagery and Popularized Imagery," 733.

44. David Dehaas, "Much Ado About Nothing," *MD Canada: Matters for the Medical Mind* 1, no. 2 (May/June 2003): 24.

45. Evelyn Fox Keller, *Reflections on Gender and Science* (New Haven: Yale University Press, 1985).

46. Londa Schiebinger, *Has Feminism Changed Science?* (Cambridge, Mass.: Harvard University Press, 1999), 72–80.

47. Ibid., 68.

48. O'Hara, "Whistle Blower," 66: said by a male caller who had not met her and offered no examples.

49. Jacobi and Schiele, "Scientific Imagery," 750.

50. I allude to the title of chapter 1, "Is the Sex of the Knower Epistemologically Significant?" of my *What Can She Know? Feminist Theory and the Construction of Knowledge* (Ithaca: Cornell University Press, 1991).

51. See Olivieri, "When Money and Truth Collide," 53.

52. The phrase "imagined community" is Benedict Anderson's; see his *Imagined Communities: Reflections on the Origin and Spread of Nationalism* (London: Verso, 1983, revised edition 1991).

53. Elizabeth Potter, *Gender and Boyle's Law of Gasses* (Bloomington: Indiana University Press, 2001), 4. Potter is not the first science studies scholar to address these sexualized features, but her way of presenting them is especially pertinent to my discussion here.

54. Ibid., 16.

55. See Steven Shapin, *A Social History of Truth: Civility and Science in Seventeenth-Century England* (Chicago: University of Chicago Press, 1994), esp. ch. 1. See Barbara J. Shapiro, *A Culture of Fact: England, 1550–1720* (Ithaca: Cornell University Press, 2000) for a provocative reading of the history of "factuality" that contests many of Shapin's conclusions.

56. Cheshire Calhoun, "Responsibility and Reproach," in *Feminism and Political Theory,* ed. Cass R. Sunstein (Chicago: University of Chicago Press, 1990), 250.

57. See John Hardwig, "The Role of Trust in Knowledge," *The Journal of Philosophy* 38, no. 12 (1991): 693–708; Bernard Barber, "Trust in Science," *Minerva* 25, nos. 1 and 2 (1987): 123–34; Naomi Scheman, "Epistemology Resuscitated: Objectivity As Trustworthiness," in *(En)gendering Rationalities,* ed. Nancy Tuana and Sandra Morgen (Albany: SUNY Press, 2001), 23–52; Donna J. Haraway, " 'Situated Knowledges': The Science Question in Feminism and the Privilege of Partial Perspective," in *Simians, Cyborgs, and Women: The Reinvention of Nature* (New York: Routledge, 1991), 183–201.

58. O'Hara, "Whistle Blower," 67.

59. See Lucy Candib, M.D., *Medicine and the Family: A Feminist Perspective* (New York: Basic Books, 1995); Kirsti Malterud, M.D., "Strategies for Empowering Women's Voices in the Medical Culture," *Health Care for Women International* 14 (1993): 365–73; and Susan Sherwin, *No Longer Patient: Feminist Ethics and Health Care* (Philadelphia: Temple University Press, 1992).

60. See my "Incredulity, 'Experientialism' and the Politics of Knowledge," in *Rhetorical Spaces: Essays on Gendered Locations* (New York: Routledge, 1995), 58–82.

61. See in this connection Lorraine Code, *Epistemic Responsibility* (Hanover, N.H.: University Press of New England, 1987). I develop this idea further, and that of an instituted epistemic imaginary, in my *Ecological Thinking: The Politics of Epistemic Location* (New York: Oxford University Press, 2006).

Chapter 13

MEN IN WHITE, WOMEN IN APRONS

Utopian Iconographies of TV Doctors

Janine Marchessault

O ver the past decade, the popular cultures of health and medicine have come to occupy a central place in Western democracies. The explosion of health cultures can be seen to correlate directly with cuts to public healthcare. The less access people have to healthcare, the greater the consumption of health culture. This places health firmly in the sphere of consumerism and a market that is seemingly without bounds as biomedical science enters its most spectacular and technologized period of discovery. Common purposes and biomedical knowledge, ethical issues and utopian aspirations, illness and death, are narrated through everyday stories that appear as news items or in popular culture. These are of universal interest and form a powerful cultural imaginary. They create, along with stories of war and atrocity, a common fabric that links us to one another through our bodies, our emotions, and particularly through our fears. They offer forms of comfort at a time when medicine is both more advanced technologically and more removed economically from many more people than ever before.

This chapter takes as its focus modern medical dramas—medicos—as these have developed since the fifties on American television. Given the massive growth of health media, there is a strong need to develop a media history of medical stories. In this chapter, I focus on the "Golden Age" of medical dramas from the early fifties to the early seventies where the principal visual and narrative conventions of the genre were developed. A central relationship in these dramas revolves around doctors and patients, often casting a utopian, even messianic, veil over the "men in white." Medicos grew out of the "woman's film," a studio genre of the postwar period that centered on the feminine sphere characterized by suffering and familial sacrifice.[1] This chapter argues that medical dramas are important mediators of gender relations, with the early examples of the genre casting doctors in an erotic paternalistic role designed to please a new demographic identified by television: the housewife. I seek to understand what these men in white offered the women viewers who made them popular. The idealized figure of the male doctor and the progressive disappearance of the female patient mark the historical trajectory suggested by this inquiry. The so-called universal assumptions about pain and healing that medical stories rely upon are tied integrally to articulations of gender within a sphere where ethics are central. This discussion is concerned with the way emotion and pain get played out on women's bedridden bodies and also the manner in which men are feminized though empathy, emotion, and pain.

Before examining TV doctors, let me briefly sketch an earlier visual regime of science in which illness was diagnosed not through a narration of symptoms but through an imaging of norms. This visualization enabled detection without the active participation of the patient. We might postulate that, just as the patient and the doctor disappeared from the diagnostic process into a technological regime of knowledge, they appeared in popular culture as melodramatic entities clothed in an excess of symptoms. Let us turn to the science through which this visual culture of medicine first appeared.

Men in Black

The prehistory of the cinema in the nineteenth century can be read through a drive to separate the popular culture of illusion from the empirical production of factual data. Nowhere is this better illustrated than in the early experiments with series photography and chronophotography carried out first by Eadweard Muybridge in the United States and subsequently by the physiologist Etienne-Jules Marey in France. The difference between the two men has been remarked upon.[2] Muybridge was the consummate travelling showman and "medicine man," utilizing science as a means to justify his erotic chronographs of veiled women, exotic animals, and deformed bodies. While his chronographs did help to uncover certain principles of human and animal locomotion, their pseudo-scientific appearance was more of a curiosity than anything else. New scientific images such as the early anatomy theaters were a form of entertainment disseminated to the public through illustrated lectures and through the great exhibitions in the United States and Europe.[3]

Muybridge's representations of bodies were filled with an excess of narrative detail that Marey aimed to eliminate. Marey, who was trained as a physician, was concerned to rectify the extreme inadequacies of the medical profession, which he saw as its dependence on symptomology.[4] Marey worked only with male bodies, athletes and acrobats, to define a human norm that would help to build a new physical education geared toward training soldiers and workers. Under the influence of Auguste Comte, Marey employed science to build a new society, to produce a Science of sciences and ultimately, a Body of bodies. His aim was to ascertain through this technology, the norm, the matrix; it was to uncover the fundamental economy of the body, the laws of its average.[5] This average body—like the Belgian social scientist Adolphe Quetelet's idea of "the average man"—fulfills the moral imperative of the Enlightenment aimed at leveling diversity through the rational processes of idealization and normalization.[6]

Marey's bodies were not only male but they also were rendered invisible, covered over with a black body suit whose lines functioned to transform bodies into graphs. Scientific progress is defined, according to Marey, by overcoming the "insufficiency of our senses," by creating "more powerful senses in order to detect the truth" that evades mere observation.[7] Here we ascertain the gendered nature of Marey's invisible norms, the male bodies that served to define standards by which illness could be detected or predicted. Here we also can detect the function of the female body as an alternate body that is emotional, subjective, narrated, and unscientific.

The photographic machine is imbued with the power of "rigorous observation," and a hierarchy of the invisible over the visible, of depth over surface, is set in place.[8] Through such an economy, which must conceal in order to reveal, we might begin to situate the impact of positive science and its anxieties on popular culture. As Freud's work illustrates so well, the female body comes to be associated with the uncertainty, ambiguity, emotion, and even perversion that constituted science's other.[9] The popular visual toys created to produce pleasurable illusions (thaumatrope, phenakistiscope, and zoetrope) that Marey utilized to create his scientific images, needed to be transformed in the practice of science into the new scientific instruments. Science should not use these technologies to reproduce the common-sense experience of visual reality (i.e., the illusion of reality). He maintained that chronophotography should seek to record what the eye cannot see.[10] Yet it is just as science defines itself in opposition to entertainment that popular culture comes to incorporate medical science's abstract images and invisibilities into some of its most enthusiastic and feminine fabulations. One way to study the binary and gendered ideologies of medical science as a cultural practice is to examine the rise of the medical drama with its iconographies of twentieth-century physicians who emerge as imagined figures able to read with complete certainty the graphing of a new objective science.

Film Blanc

Before the end of the nineteenth century, the portrayal of the physician in Western literature was more often than not negative. This is a reflection of the status of medicine before the industrial revolution and before the clear alignment of medicine with science. Indeed, Raymond Williams has pointed out that from the seventeenth century on, medicine and advertising were synonymous, and both were part of a "magic system" built on the quack's promise of the cure.[11] Just as advertising at the turn of the century would seek to distance itself from the quack, so organized medicine in the industrialized nations at exactly the same time would seek to consolidate and centralize the practice and professional status of medicine. It did so by distancing it from advertising, the trivialities of popular culture, and most especially commercial interests.[12]

"Internes Can't Take Money," the first Dr. Kildare magazine story conceived by pulp fiction writer Frederick Faust (AKA Max Brand) at the height of the Depression in 1936, was perhaps both a reflection of this early twentieth-century image of medicine and a reinforcement of it at a time when the financial interests of the profession became apparent. The American Medical Association had complained that Hollywood was producing propaganda films about socialized medicine. Films like *Arrowsmith* (John Ford, 1931), *A Man to Remember* (Garson Kanin, 1938), *Men in White* (Richard Boleslawki, 1934), *The Story of Louis Pasteur* (William Dieterle, 1935), *Dr. Monica* (William Keighley, 1935), *Of Human Bondage* (John Cromwell, 1934), *Internes Can't Take Money* (Alfred Santell, 1937), *The Citadel* (King Vidor, 1938), and MGM's Kildare series (Harold Bucquet, 1938–1941) to name a few, were seen to be part and parcel of Hollywood's critique of organized medicine. This was perfectly commensurate with Roosevelt's liberal social policies and the socialist context of America in the 1930s. The Dr. Kildare books, films, and radio series also later provided the utopian blueprint for the television doctor. Max Brand would describe Kildare as an "average American" who, in the tradition of the populist narratives of the Depression, was distinguished by an heroic self-sacrificing individualism that was anything but mediocre.[13]

The Kildare stories relied upon the cumulative effect of the conventions of the medical genre established in the previous century where many of the writers were physician/authors.[14] But Brand, having made a career writing wilderness tales, also drew on the conventions of the Western. The Kildare stories pitted the rugged individual against corrupt institutions and nature, pushing back the frontier between life and death by pursuing the utopian ideals of civilization within a large metropolitan hospital. As MGM developed the stories into a film series, these incarnated what I would describe as "film blanc" because they were antithetical to the moral ambiguity of the gangster genre and film noir that distinguished Warner Brothers' studio productions. Indeed, *Internes Can't Take Money*, the first Dr. Kildare film based upon Brand's character, incorporates both these tendencies. The story of an intern kidnapped by gangsters and forced to carry out a life-saving operation on a criminal was premised on a moral dilemma that has become a staple of the medico even today—the altruistic mission of the medical profession must be to save lives indiscriminately. The combination of both genres was clever and served to foreground the moral superiority of the medical profession. Kildare is a self-made man who gives life rather than takes it away; and he is also very close to his mother. The casting of Lew Ayres, who is small and feminine, as Kildare helped to articulate clear differences between the dark, masculine, and chaotic urban sphere of the gangster universe and the light, feminine and ethical sphere of the hospital populated by doctors and nurses (figure 13.1). All of the films opened with the same signature cityscape—Blair General Hospital in the center of a bustling New York City. The hospital emerges as a sanctified space for rest and healing. It appears as the heart of the city, opposed in many ways to its frenetic rhythms, movements, and capitalist goals.

Many of the patients that came to the hospital were victims of urban over-stimulations: heart attacks, car crashes, amnesia, blindness, and brain tumors. Lionel Barrymore as Dr. Gillespie inaugurates

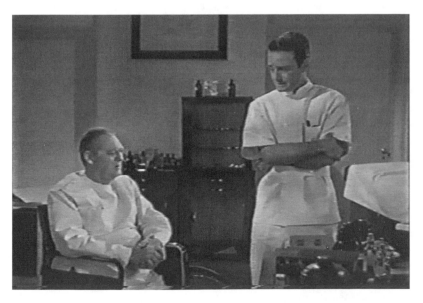

13.1 Dr. Gillespie (Lionel Barrymore) and Dr. Kildare (Lew Ayres) discussing a diagnosis in *Dr. Kildare's Wedding Day* (Metro-Goldwyn-Mayer, 1941).

another longstanding figure in the genre—the master sage and the doctor as patient, confined to a wheelchair, his legs "terribly crippled"—a state that is never explained. This reinforces the static quality of the hospital space where he lives, and the urgency involved in passing on all that he knows about diagnosis and medical research to the young Kildare. Dr. Gillespie also is dying of cancer and collapses regularly. Like Kildare, he is self-sacrificing, and while a relationship with Nurse Molly Bird (Alma Kruger) is intimated, he has devoted his life to his patients and to medical research. This is the path that is being prepared for Kildare, whose love interest is Nurse Mary Lamont (Laraine Day). She is willing to wait for Kildare and to sacrifice her own happiness for the sake of Kildare's medical practice. Kildare's celibacy is guaranteed in *Dr. Kildare's Wedding Day* (1941) when a car hits Mary Lamont a few days before their marriage. Kildare will never be the same but devotes himself even more rigorously to the selfless and disembodied caring of others.

In the Kildare films, we regularly find a class analysis, with the good but poor doctors sacrificing wealth and love for the people and for medical research. Most of the films include references to Kildare's salary (twenty dollars a month) as well as an offer to change it. In *Dr. Kildare's Secret* (1938), Dr. Gillespie believes that Kildare is leaving the hospital for more money: "What did you want to study medicine for? You'd have made a swell pawnbroker." The gangster world of crime is associated with wealthy doctors. The melodramatic narratives are premised on a moral universe of simple oppositions: men and women, life and death, right and wrong, altruism and self-interest. This is the defining feature of the melodrama as Peter Brooks has defined it. The emotional excesses and expressive oppositions that we find in the de-sacralized world of the nineteenth- century melodrama are intrinsic to its moral idiom:

> Melodrama is indeed, typically, not only a moralistic drama but the drama of morality: it strives to find, to articulate, to demonstrate, to "prove" the existence of a moral universe which, though put into question, masked by villainy and perversions of judgment, does exist and can be made to assert its presence and its categorical forces among men.[15]

While this "drama of morality" may appear premised on the secularity of science, Kildare is a Catholic doctor who does not act alone. As he and Gillespie often tell their patients, "it's the man upstairs who decides" or "everyday, miracles happen that no one can explain." Thus, in the Dr. Kildare films, the practice of medicine is a matter of talent, of technical skill, of advances in twentieth-century medicine, and most importantly of God's will.

Medicine was acted out regularly on attractive women patients who were almost always saved but sometimes were not, especially if they were engaged to Kildare. The role of the patient was one of surrender and of being saved. The doctors, however, were not virile and masculine. They were men who sought advice from their mothers or were physically frail. More often than not, Gillespie ended up confined to bed. Yet these doctors were men of advanced knowledge, with great medical skills and moral values, a conflation that the melodramatic narratives called forth.

The Kildare films were as popular as the elaborate Busby Berkeley musicals, another film genre produced by the Depression. Indeed, while almost directly opposed in style and tone, the two genres share a similar appeal. Film theorist Richard Dyer reads the musical as an "alternative to capitalism provided by capitalism."[16] I would argue that the success of the Dr. Kildare films might be found in the way these responded to real human needs and social inadequacies during the Depression. The films seemed to hearken back to the "magic system" when medicine was the cure. While the Kildare films were highly unrealistic, perhaps the young Dr. Kildare functioned to heal the nation by furnishing it with a utopian image of science and community, an alternative to medicine provided by a medicine that was kind, full of affect, and understanding. This is how the films could be critical of medicine and yet mythologize the individual doctor at the same time.

Unlike the Berkeley musical, the utopian image of medicine was not steeped in escapist fantasy. Taking on decidedly religious overtones, Dr. Kildare did not transcend the physical limits of nature as did the synchronized dancing women of the musical. Rather, Kildare extended them into the antiseptic space of modernity. Outside the law, history, and ideology, this is a liminal space—the emergency room or the operating table—where differences between people disappear at the border between life and death. Illness and disease as difference and dysfunction found their place in these early feminine narratives. Medical dramas about dysfunctional bodies, broken machines, and lost spirits can be read as allegories for a nation in crisis. It is precisely as an allegorical image that medicine finds its most mythologized, idealized, and ultimately comforting figuration, "the men in white." This is the image of medicine that was transposed to television in the postwar period.

Tele-Medicine

My interest in TV doctors was triggered several years ago by one of Marshall McLuhan's somewhat misdirected but nevertheless useful insights. Since the very beginning of television in the late forties, there has been a natural alliance between television and medicine. In

Understanding Media (1964), written at the high point of shows like *Dr. Kildare* (1961–1966) and *Ben Casey* (1961–1966), McLuhan maintained that doctor shows were a natural byproduct of television. Like the cool medium, the medico involves the viewer in depth by making the body the center of the drama. In fact, writes McLuhan, "in closed-circuit instruction in surgery, medical students from the first reported a strange effect—that they seemed not to be watching an operation, but performing it."[17] As McLuhan's formalist theory goes: the convulsive participation produced by television enhances corporeal anxiety, the doctor show is seen to soothe this anxiety while playing upon the tension between seriality and closure, life and death, doctor and patient. McLuhan goes on to note that, with very few exceptions, the portrayal of doctors and hospitals in the cinema focuses on the patient, illness and closure because the cinema encourages passive participation. His explanation for the difference between film and television portrayals is bound to the specifics of the medium and the way each determines a particular experience of spectatorship. According to his theory, television's low visual resolution encourages active participation and thus focuses not on the patient but on the doctor, who becomes the center in a narrative that is process-oriented and organized consistently around the never-ending business of healing illness. Thus it is no accident for McLuhan that the medico as a genre is born through television. Medicine and television share the same goal. Both have the power to overcome fragmentation and heal the global body. Television, like the physician is, according to what is perhaps McLuhan's most controversial assertion, a tactile medium. While the reader may argue that the physician is not a medium, McLuhan would contend that the physician, like any communication medium, is involved deeply in translating experience from one sphere to another.[18]

McLuhan's belief that medicine and television form a natural alliance finds support in what Joseph Turow in his very important study of TV doctors, *Playing Doctor* (1993), has described as "the tyranny" of the doctor formula on American television. This formula gives us some insight into the marketed omnipotence of both television and medicine as utopian institutions whose resources and boundaries are represented consistently as progressive and infinite. The coming together of medicine and television from the mid-fifties onward in the doctor show is a reflection of the commercial growth of both television and medicine during this period. Each needed the other: in medicine, television producers found a wellspring of drama and a documentary authenticity. Organized medicine in the United States needed to work on its public image in order to support a privatized healthcare system, and justify the exponential growth of healthcare expenditures from $12.7 billion in 1950 to $71.5 billion in 1970.[19] Moreover, the pharmaceutical industry from the late fifties onward recognized the importance of promotion, of being connected to the press, radio, and television to market drugs. By the late fifties, the twenty-two largest drug companies in North America spent more money (24 percent of total revenue) on promotion than on research and development (6 percent). The new market demographic for drug companies after the Second World War was women. Not only were more drugs prescribed for women than for men, but women were the primary purchasers of drugs for their families.[20] Two of the most successful promotional campaigns in the sixties were oral contraceptives and tranquilizers—the latter being prescribed for women twice as often as for men.[21] Thus, when television producers and medical organizations came together, there is little doubt that women were the target audience. It is important to bear in mind that the idealizations of the doctor formula served a complex intersection of market interests in the postwar era: the American Medical Association and its coalition of medical interest groups and pharmaceutical industries, television networks, sponsors, and women television viewers.

Medic

Although *City Hospital* (1952) was the first American network series built around doctors and a hospital, it is *Medic* (1954–1955) that truly would bring the genre to life on television. The universal drama of life is what the writer of *Dragnet*, James Moser, had in mind when he devised *Medic*, the first hit prime time medical drama, which aired in 1954 on NBC. Born in the context of cinema verité documentaries where the uncontrolled realities of life were beginning to find their way onto television, *Medic* was an anthology series whose realism sought to counteract the melodramatic feminine character of the Kildare films. Targeting the serious viewer, *Medic*'s highly publicized realism focused on the business of medicine rather than on human relations. Filmed on location in a county hospital, *Medic* was not live (although Moser had initially wanted it to be) but contained the stuff of life, real medicine.[22] Competing directly opposite the *I Love Lucy Show* (1951–1957), the staple stories for *Medic* revolved around gynecology and obstetrics and sometimes incorporated documentary images into the drama; a real birth opened the series (a pregnant woman with leukemia dies as she gives birth), and a real caesarean ended the show after a year and a half.

The new format that Moser introduced contained a great deal of medical information. Each episode was directed towards educating the public about one illness and its treatment, with a doctor (the actor Richard Boone) introducing the lesson to follow. In one episode, "With This Ring" (1952), an unwed mother comes to the hospital in labor with severe toxemia (figure 13.2). All is fine and she is given a lecture on the importance of prenatal care. The moral aspects of her situation have less to do with being unwed than with not having had a doctor supervise her pregnancy. What is fascinating about this episode is not that pregnancy was thoroughly medicalized, or that a woman's body was completely taken over and instrumentalized by the professional apparatus. These are of course important markers of this moment in the history of medicine. What is striking is the attempt to represent the patient's experience, point of view, and psychology. The birth scene in this episode highlights this aspect. While the mother lies on her back in stirrups surrounded by masked doctors and a highly realistic set with state-of-the-art medical instruments, the audience is treated to her hallucination: lights transform into a merry-go-round and laughter echoes an erotic escapade that no doubt led to the birth of her illegitimate child. The use of the merry-go-round is a particularly wonderful metaphor that brings together the cyclical nature of life and the intersection of birth, death, and infinity that Moser would explore some years later in his successful series *Ben Casey*.

Despite Moser's desire to move away from melodrama, *Medic* calls upon its most salient aspects. Each episode highlights the lives and experiences of patients, while doctors remain objective and distant (i.e., professional) (figure 13.3). This binary opposition between overwrought patients and cool medical professionals frames many episodes. This would be the difference between *Medic*'s doctors and

13.2 Patient subjectivity in "With This Ring." During labor, a woman remembers a romantic escapade. "With This Ring," 1952 episode of *Medic*.

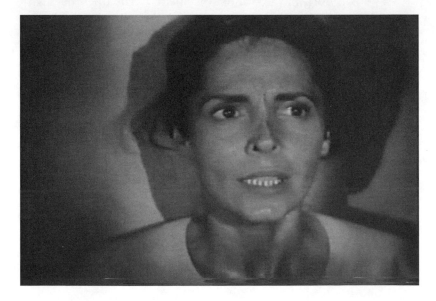

MGM's Dr. Kildare. In *Medic,* doctors often provide a reassuring and paternalistic narration of science and truth that is circumscribed by a modern morality of health and education so prevalent in the hygiene films of postwar America. As with the hygiene films, medicine and science provide the normative backdrop through which to evaluate and empathize with a patient. Indeed, patients' emotions are featured by recourse to the most excessive melodramatic conventions. In the episode "My Brother Joe" (1952), a mother and alcoholic father are unable to handle the emotional trauma of their child's accident. The older son is made to handle the family's ordeal as "Joe" lies comatose. The episode is divided between two spheres involving patients and doctors. On the one hand, the patient's universe is filled with chiaroscuro lighting, highly choreographed movements down dark hallways, and heavily framed encounters between family members (figure 13.4). On the other hand, the doctor's domain is clearly demarcated by uniformed doctors and a brightly lit realistic hospital setting filled with medical instruments and technologies. Each episode dramatizes the patient's anguish and, finally, gratitude to the "men in white" who center the plot with easy-to-understand pedagogical detail. The opposition between doctors and patients is clearly maintained and highly gendered. In "The Field of Neurology" (1952), the separation of the emotional and scientific spheres is undone by a nurse who gets involved emotionally with a young man suffering from epilepsy. A final encounter between them leads her to push him "out into the world," where, as Richard Boone explains, "with the help of medication he will lead a normal life." As with every episode, the final word goes to the doctor, whose discourse is measured and reassuring.

13.4 Family members discuss medical treatment in "My Brother Joe," *Medic*, 1952.

Very few black doctors and no women doctors as central characters were seen on *Medic*. Indeed, the show itself was shut down because of a controversial episode involving a black doctor choosing between life in the city or a return to rural roots. The Southern Network affiliates refused to run the episode, and sponsors began to pull out. In the history of the genre, black men and especially women are still few and far between, bringing a certain ontological depth to the "men in white" metonym—a point to which I shall return.

Medic's gynecological proclivity was said to be catering to the interests of the baby boom age, and was endorsed officially by the Los Angeles Medical Association. The association reviewed every script and, as Moser himself observed, the review process began to shape subtly the content of the show: very few deaths, no long-term illnesses, doctors always heroic, the latest medical technologies and drugs showcased, and an emphasis on gynecology and obstetrics as well as other highly specialized forms of medicine.[23] *Medic*'s authenticity and educational character depended on the involvement of a medical association, which in turn came to have a hand in defining the parameters of authenticity. At a time when reproduction was being thoroughly medicalized and marketed, but also at a time when the economic growth of the medical industries was fuelling a public distrust of organized medicine, the usefulness of television as a public relations vehicle was obvious.

Men in White

It is this interface between medicine and television that Joseph Turow argues would be an important determining influence on the medical genre during its formative years in the sixties. During this time, the authenticity and credibility of shows like *Dr. Kildare* and *Ben Casey*, which both began in 1961, and later the two most popular programs in the seventies, *Marcus Welby, M.D.* (1969–1976) and *Medical Center* (1969–1976), depended on receiving authorization from various medical associations that would appear in the credits. The American Medical Association had even formed its own special Advisory Committee on Television, Radio and Motion Pictures to ensure that the popular image of medicine was "accurate." This also ensured no negative portrayals of doctors.[24] Doctors during this Golden Age of medical narratives were shown as altruistic beings whose word was always the final one. Their interpretations of illnesses made sense of the chaos, pain, and suffering that patients were experiencing; they utilized a specialized language and referred to medical charts not accessible to the patients. They were messianic figures of knowledge. This image has remained remarkably consistent across a variety of media from television to pulp fiction, as Delese Wear and Brian Castellani have underlined:

> Even with significant contextual variables, the causation and motivation found in most medical plots could be traced to predictable images of how a doctor looked (male and white) and acted (benevolently authoritative, autonomous and paternalistic), what his social and economic status in the community was (high), and how his patients viewed him (deferentially). The plots also reflected how doctors enjoyed the benefits of extraordinary cultural legitimacy, extensive legal protections, legislatively based entitlements, and solo or group practices independent of corporations and business.[25]

Wear and Castellani have argued that this image from the Golden Age of medicos continues to have an influence on public expectations of medicine.

According to Turow, the result of television's mythologization of the doctor has been an image of the healthcare system in the United States that elides policy issues and is unable to address the limits of medical progress as well as the fee-for-service structure of physician-directed medicine in any significant manner.[26] Medicine generally is depicted as infinite, illness is always acute and cured through specialist medicine, and politics are reduced to rifts between doctors (sometimes nurses) and hospital administrators.

We should not underestimate the role that women played in shaping and in maintaining the sympathetic image of the doctor. Without a doubt, the eroticized image of medical culture was meant to appeal to women as the biggest consumers in the growing industry of both prescription and nonprescription drugs during the sixties.

The mythological image was materialized largely through *Dr. Kildare* and *Ben Casey,* programs which were compatible rather than competitive. Like the Hollywood Kildare, Richard Chamberlain was feminine, gentle, and compassionate. Casey, created by *Medic's* James Moser and played by Vincent Edwards, was surly, abrupt, and more overtly masculine. These images were profitable. The shows generated an entire pulp industry around hospitals and doctors, toys, games, clothes, comic strips, trading cards, and posters. Chamberlain and Edwards even posed together for publicity shots. The two programs were instrumental in solidifying the idealized image of the doctor. They were very different, but often dealt with similar themes. For example, in a 1962 episode of *Dr. Kildare* entitled "A Place Among the Monuments," the adulation of doctors is framed in terms of a larger moral issue. A young woman attempts suicide by means of barbiturates; her parents break into her New York apartment only to find her lifeless body on the couch. "We need a miracle," they cry. Enter the youthful intern Dr. James Kildare, who brings the woman back to life with a resuscitator. The Greek immigrant family refuses to see "The Doctor" as anything less than a saint, and Kildare, flattered by their reverence, does not seek to change their minds. The older and wiser Dr. Gillespie warns him against the egotistic fantasy of the doctor as god instead of healer. In the end, Dr. Kildare must face up to his own humanity as the episode concludes with a dramatic sacrifice: the young woman he has saved develops "complications" and dies suddenly. The girl's parents do not forgive Kildare for shattering their godly image of healers. But the audience does. As he stands beneath apple blossoms, an image of life's cyclical nature, he looks out to a future that always will be measured by the lesson of a death that he could not prevent, and perhaps was never meant to (figure 13.5). In this romantic image of nature, a spiritual sphere is beyond the control of doctors. Like the cinematic version, the *Dr. Kildare* television series produced a deeply moralistic universe in which medicine was practiced.

The mythologization of medicine was explored in a very similar way on *Ben Casey* the previous year in "A Certain Time, A Certain Darkness" (1961). Every episode of *Casey* opened with an omniscient male narrator who read out the meanings behind symbols drawn on a blackboard by a disembodied male hand: "Man," "Woman," "Birth," and "Infinity." In this particular episode, the last icon dissolves into a woman's face as she drives her car down a winding suburban road. Cubist paintings float across the road, her vision increasingly becomes blurred, and she drives into a truck. A metal pipe crashes through the windshield, knocking her unconscious. She is rushed to Casey's neurosurgery unit, and he discovers that she

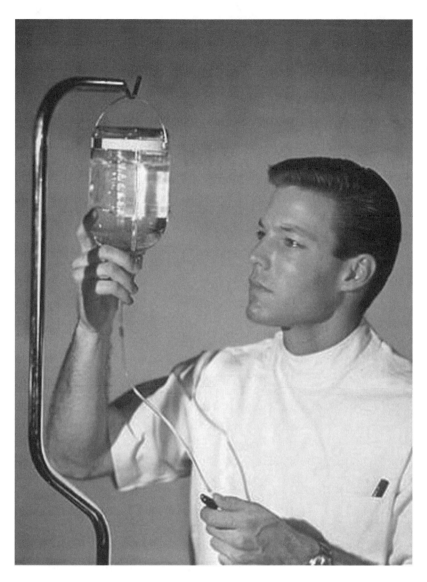

13.5 The transparent image of healing with Richard Chamberlain in "A Place Among the Monuments," *Dr. Kildare* (1961–1966).

is taking Phenobarbital to control her epilepsy (a common ailment on TV medicos of the fifties and sixties); the episode will revolve around self-acceptance. Her visions permeate the episode in marvelous psychedelic points of view that mark *Ben Casey* as a uniquely innovative and pedagogically underrated contribution to the genre (figure 13.6). The patient, an artist with overbearing parents who is pregnant and deserted, has great admiration for Casey, who is much wiser and more experienced than the young intern Kildare. He warns the young woman not to "mistake gratitude for love." But she cannot help herself. As with *Medic*, Moser allots a great deal of narrative space to patient subjectivity and the expression of emotion.

13.6 Patient subjectivity and cubist hallucinations in "A Certain Time, A Certain Darkness," *Ben Casey* (Bing Crosby Productions, 1961).

Indeed, both Kildare and Casey, like the original Dr. Kildare films, focus on patient psychology and human emotion as a means to express the complex modalities of pain and the ethical responsibilities of medical practice.

The mythologization accomplished by transforming actors into familiar characters that viewers encountered on a regular basis in a quotidian setting facilitated a psychic transference that Casey warns his patient against when she tells him "I feel like I know you." Mythologized doctors became real human beings through these programs, and it is this realism that has had an impact on ideological assumptions about doctors and medicine.[27] If we examine the trading cards of the TV doctors (figure 13.7), we note that we see them not only in their professional attire but also at leisure—eating lunch or out for an evening. This division between public and private, the representation of a private life for the stars/doctors, helps to support the confusion, as Chamberlain becomes Dr. Kildare and Edwards is Dr. Casey. Besides the erotic thrill of Kildare and Casey as glamour boys, what did these dramas offer the predominantly white middle-class women in lives of mobile privatization in American suburbs during the sixties and early seventies? In the midst of the women's liberation movement, growing divorce rates, the Vietnam War, exploding race relations, and civil rights, what did this romantic image of medicine provide?

Let me return to the metonym "men in white." We should not ignore the fact that American television entertainment of this period was shielded from the historical and political forces that were redefining the urban centers of North America.[28] These dramas, culminating

13.7 Vincent Edwards, *Ben Casey* trading cards (Bing Crosby Productions, 1962); Richard Chamberlain, *Dr. Kildare* trading cards (Metro-Goldwyn-Mayer, 1962).

with *Marcus Welby, M.D.*, regardless of where the hospitals or medical practices were located, were idealized suburban tales of family healing. Men in pairs populated these medical dramas: Kildare and Gillespie, Casey and Zorba, Marcus Welby and Steve Kirsh. This coupling serves to foreground the mediated aspects of diagnosis, the orality of medical knowledge passed down, and the humanistic dimension of the medical encounter. That is, they stressed patient psychology and point of view as an inherent aspect of the narration of pain. This empathetic dimension is something that modern medicine often is seen to lack.[29] An oft-cited characteristic of these ideal doctors, one that has become a cliché, is that TV doctors listened, they took the time. Marcus Welby only treated one and sometimes two patients per episode (figure 13.8). He made frequent house calls and became involved in his patient's lives.

Women did not figure prominently as medical staff in the medical dramas of the Golden Age. There were no wives in these medicos, and nurses had mostly minor roles. Women were cast as patients and as family members who had a central voice in these dramas, which also provided a narrative space for men to express feelings traditionally reserved for women. As Charlotte Brundson has pointed out: "The medical drama [from this period] colonizes the public masculine sphere, representing it from the point of view of the personal."[30] The medical dramas of this period were not only unrealistic but also directly opposite to what actually was going on in healthcare. The modernization of the image in Joe Gannon (Chad Everett), the heartthrob and heart specialist of *Medical Center* (1969–1976) came to stress less the medical detail and more the relationship to his patients; for this he was sometimes called unprofessional, but as he so often would put it, "I care, damn it" (figure 13.9).[31]

In her study *Doctoring the Media*, Anne Karpf has underlined that these doctors were "not the doctors we know, they are the ones we want." Kildare, Casey, Welby, and Gannon can be read as wish fulfillments; they were "the image of something better"[32]—not only doctors but also men. Furthermore, these humanizing dramas can be read as social allegories enacting masculine dramas of pain

13.8 Robert Young as Marcus Welby, M.D., the quintessential humanized doctor of the American medico in the seventies (Universal TV, 1970).

13.9 Chad Everett as Joe Gannon, who always got involved in the personal life of his patients, in *Medical Center* (Metro-Goldwyn-Mayer, 1969–1976).

and illness at a time when war and the civil rights movement, including the women's liberation movement, were fundamentally disturbing idealizations of a white patriarchal body politic in the fifties. Read as allegories, it is perhaps not surprising that the development of the genre sees those "men in white" become patients.

Conclusion: Doctor-Patient

It is the doctor-patient relationship, and the emphasis on the patient's personal psychology that would disappear in new doctor shows of the eighties and nineties, which stressed the uncontrolled reality of the medical environment. *M*A*S*H* (1972–1983) generally is referred to as an important turning point in the genre, as the doctors became patients, and patients along with the realities of war became the terminal illness for which there was no cure.[33] In shows like *St. Elsewhere* (1982–1988), in the nineties *ER* (1994–present), *Chicago Hope* (1994–2000), *L.A. Doctors* (1998–1999), and in more recent programs like *Scrubs* (2001–present), *House* (2003–present), and *Grey's Anatomy* (2004–present), the practice of medicine serves to foreground the troubled lives of doctors and sometimes other medical personnel. For Wear and Castellani, the rise of "dysfunctional narratives" measured by dysfunctional masculinities in medical fiction from the late seventies onward is a direct reflection of a healthcare system in crisis.[34]

In the second-generation doctor-centered dramas that feature an equal number of men and women as well as racial diversity in the medical profession, the narrative space that gave women a voice as patients has disappeared. The humanistic dimension of the early medicos, which were an intrinsic part of women's popular culture, has been lost in contemporary incarnations. I have argued that dramas gave women a voice while creating an awareness of bodies as affective and showing medicine as a practice integrally connected to an ethical framework. As much as these narratives were idealizations, they also were the only place in the popular media in North America where medicine and ethics were discussed openly on a regular basis and where empathy had a place in healthcare. Certainly, the sense of a shared social imaginary of good healthcare that the Golden Age of the medico was able to orchestrate is more difficult to imagine today.

Notes

1. Christine Gledhill, *Home Is Where the Heart Is: Studies in Melodrama and the Woman's Film* (London: British Film Institute, 1991).

2. Marta Braun, *Picturing Time: The Work of Etienne-Jules Marey* (Chicago: University of Chicago Press, 1992); and Linda Williams, "Film Body: An Implementation of Perversions," *Cine-Tracts* 12 (Winter 1981): 19–32.

3. C. W. Ceram, *Archeology of the Cinema* (New York: Harcourt, Brace and World, 1965).

4. Etienne-Jules Marey, *Physiologie médicale de la circulation du sang, basée sur l'étude graphique des movements du coeur et du pouls artériel, avec application aux maladies de l'appareil circulatoire* (Paris: Delahaye, 1863), 12.

5. Ibid., 22.

6. Adolphe Quetelet, *A Treatise on Man, and the Development of His Faculties* (Gainesville, Fla.: Scholars Facsimiles and Reprints, 1969).

7. Etienne-Jules Marey, *La méthode graphique dans les sciences experimentales* (Paris: G. Masson, 1985), ii.

8. Ibid., 66.

9. Sigmund Freud, "Three Essays on Sexuality: I. The Sexual Aberrations, II. Infantile Sexuality, III. The Transformations of Puberty," in *The Penguin Freud Library*, vol. 7., ed. and trans. James Strachey (London: Penguin Books, 1991).

10. Marey, *La méthode graphique*, 108.

11. Raymond Williams, "Advertising: The Magic System" (1962), in *The Cultural Studies Reader*, ed. S. During (London: Routledge, 1993), 320–36.

12. Kelly A. Cole, "'Men in White' on Television," in *Cultural Sutures: Medicine and Media*, ed. Lester D. Friedman (Durham, N.C.: Duke University Press, 2005), 97.

13. Quoted in Susan L. Zodin, "The Making of a Medical Man: Max Brand's Young Dr. Kildare," in *The Max Brand Companion*, ed. Jon Tuska et al. (Westport, Conn.: Greenwood Press, 1996), 118.

14. Cf. D. W. Smithers, *This Idle Trade: On Doctors Who Were Writers* (Tunbridge Wells, UK: Dragonfly Press, 1989).

15. Peter Brooks, *The Melodramatic Imagination* (New York: Columbia University Press, 1976), 21.

16. Richard Dyer, "Entertainment as Utopia," in *Only Entertainment* (London and New York: Routledge, 1992), 45.

17. Marshall McLuhan, *Understanding Media* (New York: McGraw Hill, 1964), 328.

18. For a more detailed explanation of McLuhan's notion of tactility and television, see Janine Marchessault, *Marshall McLuhan: Cosmic Media* (London: Sage Publications, 2005), 185–201.

19. Harry F. Dowling, *Medicine for Man: The Development, Regulation and Use of Prescription Drugs* (New York: Alfred A. Knopf, 1970), 123.

20. Andrew Chetley, *A Healthy Business? World Health and Pharmaceutical Industry* (London: Zed Books, 1990), 27–29.

21. Ibid.

22. Joseph Turow, *Playing Doctor: Television, Storytelling, and Medical Power* (New York: Oxford University Press, 1989), 37.

23. Ibid., 41, 156.

24. Ibid., 61.

25. Delese Wear and Brian Castellani, "Conflicting Plots and Narrative Dysfunction in Health Care," *Perspectives in Biology and Medicine* 42, no. 4 (Summer 1999): 547.

26. Turow, *Playing Doctor,* 78–79.

27. Throughout the history of medicos, actors who play doctors on television have been valuable spokespeople for pharmaceutical companies, governments, and health causes. It is this confusion that the American Medical Association (AMA) wanted to counteract with the creation of a Radio and Television review board of its own. Under pressure from the AMA, the National Association of Radio and Television Broadcasters amended the 1951 Television Code in 1957 to ban "men in white" actors from advertising. The ban insisted that if an actor was playing a doctor in a television advertisement, then the word "dramatization" needed to appear over the sequence. Cole, "Men in White," 103.

28. For an in-depth examination of the relation between American prime time television and the civil rights movement in the United States, see the excellent documentary *Color Adjustment/Signifyin' Works* (1991) by Marlon Riggs and Vivian Kleiman.

29. The opposition between science and empathy dates back to the new technologies of objective scientific imaging that Marey's contributions represent. It is the role of empathy in the practice of medicine that many medical professionals increasingly have been looking to understand as an inherent part of medicine. Cf. Lucy Fischer, "Big Boys Do Cry: Empathy in *The Doctor,*" in Friedman, *Cultural Sutures,* 149–65.

30. Charlotte Brundson, quoted in Anne Karpf, *Doctoring the Media: The Reporting of Health and Medicine* (London: Routledge, 1988)66–67.

31. McLaughlin studied the first twenty-five years of the TV medico and concluded that 95 percent of the programs featured doctors as "The necessary

outsider—one who can deal objectively with the facts at hand, interpret and shuffle them, and solve all kinds of problems." Doctors were best at solving personal problems, whether they were tensions between family members or self-acceptance. James McLaughlin, "The Doctor Shows," *Journal of Communication* 23, no. 3 (1975): 182–84.

32. Karpf, *Doctoring the Media*, 67.

33. The disappearance of the patient is something that is unique to the American medical dramas. Programs like *Side Effects* and *Little Miracles* in Canada, *Urgence* in Quebec, or *Casuality* in the United Kingdom continue to center dramatic narratives around patients rather than doctors. This demonstrates that medical dramas need to be studied in a national context.

34. Wear and Castellani, "Conflicting Plots," 547.

Chapter 14

THE FETAL VOYAGER

Women in Modern Medical Visual Discourse

Annette Burfoot

Each year, the European Society for Human Reproduction and Embryology (ESHRE), a reproductive medical association, meets to discuss and, in principle, share the latest developments in new reproductive technologies (NRTs) and their fast-growing spin-offs, prenatal screening and genetic engineering. ESHRE is the largest association of reproductive medical professionals and researchers in Europe and the second largest worldwide.[1] The annual conference, organized by the association, is aimed at a variety of medical professionals and researchers. These include doctors specializing in reproductive medicine (also called "assisted conception and assisted reproductive technologies," or ART), supporting medical staff, including genetic counselors and lab technicians who work with human embryos, and researchers in areas dispersed between the genetic engineering of human reproductive hormones (widely used in ART) and more basic science research, for example, micro-embryonic development. The design of the conference is typical of large medical conferences: small seminar sessions are interspersed with larger symposia, in this case sponsored by multinational pharmaceutical companies. Adjunct to the proceedings is a professional exposition demonstrating the latest in equipment, drugs, and so on, including visualizing and micromanipulation tools, hormone preparations for the control of the female menstrual cycle, sperm banks and sperm preparation equipment, and embryo preparation and storage technologies.

A poster distributed at the commercial fair of the 2000 annual meeting of ESHRE features "The Voyager": a backlit embryo of about two months, complete with connective tissue surrounding its crystalline sac, and set against a striking blue star field (figure 14.1). The image from the poster advertises reproductive technologies for the company IVF Science (IVF refers to "in vitro fertilization") and was freely available at the 2000 meeting of the ESHRE to conference

14.1 "The Voyager," free-floating human embryo, IVF Science ad, ESHRE Conference, Bologna, 2000.

participants ambling through the commercial exposition.[2] The radiant tissue and the embryonic heart at the center of the mouse-like fetus in the IVF ad speak to a medical mastery over the once-mysterious and inaccessible moment of conception. This mastery commonly is signaled by the presence of the newly constructed fetal being as autonomous but in the care of all that modern medical science can provide. The pregnant woman is not present. Throughout the conference, this lonely but courageous traveler appears again and again. It is in the logo for the entire conference—a backlit fetus/new-born clutching a quarter moon.[3] This is not the first time that this type of photo has been published. A similar image, commonly called "the star child" in film circles, was used to define the closing moments of the 1968 film *2001: A Space Odyssey*. The star child, in turn, draws directly from the world-famous, first-ever photos by Lennart Nilsson of a live fetus in utero published in *Life* magazine in 1965.[4] In the film, the star child signifies a great new beginning hardly imaginable—as do Nilsson's fetal photos and the new millennium voyager at the ESHRE conference. Now the space race is eclipsed by a biotechnological pursuit of new territories characterized by DNA code described by Sarah Franklin as "life itself."[5] Within this contemporary field of life sciences, all three fetal images above share the heavy symbolism of an entity produced through medical visual discourse that emphasizes replication over reproduction and tidies up the unruly effects of women's bodies in modern medical science that have been evident from its inception.

Since early modern medicine began representing the human form, the female body and its reproductive function, including the fetus, have figured prominently. Nilsson's photos of the fetal star child typically hidden by women's bodies were not the first visualizations of the human fetus. An examination of eighteenth-century Italian wax anatomical models that include fetal display demonstrates how this fascination with the fetus in modern medical visual discourse began. It also provides an important context to gender studies of contemporary medical visual culture surrounding new reproductive technologies and embryology. A critical examination of a selection of visual materials gathered at the annual meeting of the ESHRE held in 2000 is compared to examples of this early modern medical imaging. The powerful image of the fetus-as-voyager is evidence for problems within a medical visual discourse that replaces female procreativity with a potent fetal symbol. The image represents a shift from reproduction through women's bodies, exemplified by the eighteenth-century wax models, to a process of replication based on genetic and cellular components.

Science as Visual Discourse and Patriarchal Ideology

Recent considerations of science as visual discourse are significant here. In an interview discussing her concept of nature and culture, Donna Haraway describes how an interaction between a biological entity and science requires "an intimate relationship with the laboratory processes that bring the so-called natural object into our view."[6] She explains how the construction of an entity, in the case that she uses, a microorganism, is reliant on its representation or bringing to view by the scientific practices of collecting, imaging, naming, explaining, and applying value. She also speaks of how scientific discourse generates fetish objects through a process of "productive mislocation" whereby potent concepts such as life are aligned with powerful symbolic objects such as the DNA helix.[7] The effect of the mislocation is to render the image of the helix as a powerful symbol, or fetish object, on which we fixate. Continuing with this example, Haraway describes the master molecule gene discourse as an example of cognitive fetishism. By this she means the productive mislocation of the concept of a meta map or code for life with the DNA helix. It is argued here that the fetal voyager becomes a powerful fetish object in a long history of modern medical representation of human reproduction.

Contemporary feminist scholarship on the human body also provides several avenues for examining medical imagery as the site of gendered ideologies.[8] The considerable study of contemporary visualizations of the human body in medicine, as shown in the chapter by Naomi Adelson on the Visible Human Project in this volume, is particularly relevant.[9] Lisa Cartwright also examines this digital representation of a male and a female body, fully dissectible and available online, in terms of the history of medical anatomical representation, and concludes that this contemporary female representation is something of an innovation in a long line of male body forms presented as the human norm. In many ways, Cartwright's analysis updates Londa Schiebinger's work on early modern medical illustrations of skeletons.[10] Schiebinger concludes that sexual difference became of interest to the newly forming profession of modern medical science just as women began to make moves toward political emancipation in eighteenth- and nineteenth-century European society. Anatomical drawings, one of the mainstays of medical education, began including female skeletons to prove that sexual difference goes down to the bone, and effectively inscribed this as natural law (typically in terms of smaller brains and larger pelvises), from which political decisions and social norms were formed. These, in turn, were used to help deny women a place in much of public life and almost completely prevented their equal participation in (scientific) knowledge formation. Adelson, Cartwright, and Schiebinger provide important precedents for reading the visual discourse of medicine as socio-political practice, especially as related to the patriarchal stereotyping of women as physically and mentally inferior to men.

Also important is the work of Deanna Petherbridge and Ludmilla Jordanova, who like Schiebinger focus on early medical imaging and thus allow a more complete critique of modern science and the long effect of masculine mastery throughout. In the analysis of their exhibition "The Quick and the Dead" (1997–1998), Petherbridge and Jordanova reveal how women's bodies in early modern medical discourse are likened to clocks and the passage of time, especially the pregnant female form as the key signifier of human reproduction.[11] In an earlier study on the same theme, Jordanova notes how women's bodies increasingly become shown as dehumanized and literally truncated in favor of featuring the main attraction of the human generation event, namely, what the heavily pregnant uterus contains, the fetus.[12] Both Petherbridge and Jordanova note an oddly erotic effect in these historical presentations of women's bodies that are displayed immodestly for the first time as a framing device for the "well-developed *putti*," or fetuses that are featured prominently on their maternal bases.[13] They also point to the problematic representation of women's bodies as both horrible and sexually objectified. This dehumanization of the mother and the marginalization of maternity are replayed in the historical and contemporary reproductive scenes that are analyzed below. As we shall see, human reproduction that typically highlighted and at least included the mother is replaced by the replication of human gametes and genes where maternity is absented.

Although feminist considerations of new reproductive technologies vary, there is general agreement that they are problematic for female emancipation. From this generally critical position of new reproductive technologies (NRTs), I want to update the work of Schiebinger, Petherbridge, and Jordanova by bringing their analyses of historical medical discourse to bear upon those of NRTs and genetic engineering. Concurrently, I wish to extend reflections on contemporary corporality in scientific discourse, especially those by Cartwright and Haraway, back to the roots of modern science. The concept of cognitive fetishism is particularly central to the analysis that follows. It is used to chart the progress from the fetish of the female as mastery over reproduction in early modern medicine to the fetish of the fetus as the triumph of replication over reproduction in contemporary representations. The overall aim of this chapter is to provide a broader-based view of feminist implications of medical visual discourse than has been the case in the study of medical imaging of the human body. I argue that there is a gendered continuity in the medical visual discourse from the inception of modern medicine to the present, despite the varied and seemingly disparate images as demonstrated in the reading of the medical images at the ESHRE conference against the backdrop of eighteenth-century visual discourses of the female reproductive body.

As the fetal voyager signifies a progression, so it indicates something, or in this case, someone, left behind. When NRTs first broke onto the medical scene in the mid-1980s, women often were represented in the medical literature and commercial ads for NRTs as desperately infertile, an ideally "good" mother, and one grateful for the medical marvels that would make the realization of her heartfelt goal possible. Using Jordanova's terms, it is not the bodies of actual women that serve as the framing device of the *putti* as very young star, but instead it is feminine norms. An example at the 2000 ESHRE conference of this earlier type of representation was one of only a handful of images that featured women at all, and it still manages to erase maternity from the reproductive scene. The ad is for the hyperovulatory hormone Utrogestan, and it features the grateful and graceful white hands of the expectant young woman, her fingers forming a basket of sorts, waiting for the crystalline enveloped fetus to fall (figure 14.2).[14] The light that illuminates her fingers emanates from the fetus and its crystalline uterus without a body. The woman, presumably grateful with open hands, is given a baby; she does not give birth. A partial explanation for the shift away from depicting advances in NRTs with an idealized mother figure is that proponents of ART no longer need to justify this form of medical intervention to a skeptical public. This was not the case when the technologies first emerged in the early 1980s and typically were presented alongside images of desperate mothers and infertile couples, so as to counter public fears of a frankensteinian tampering with nature.

More commonly now, female reproductivity within ART is reduced and highly abstracted to what are considered the operational components of human creation, such as eggs, Fallopian tubes, umbilical cords, and uterine walls as the point of fetal attachment. This abstraction also signals a shift from human reproduction to replication. The fetus as early and autonomous life form appears as a self-propelled, walking egg in a brochure announcing an upcoming conference, "A Journey from Gamete to Newborn."[15] The walking egg is the logo for a rather bizarre journal by the same name: *The Walking Egg—The Gazette of the "Andrology in the Nineties."*[16] Various volumes of the journal were widely available at the 2000 ESHRE conference along with a free subscription for future volumes. The journal is aptly named ("andrology" literally means the study of the male human being) as its avant-garde illustrations almost completely eradicate or severely reduce women's reproductive role. The emphasis on the male reproductive role also resonates with Schiebinger and Cartwright's analyses of medical imaging of the body as normally

14.2 "Hands Reaching for Crystal Uterus with Baby," Utrogestan ad, ESHRE Conference, Bologna, 2000.

male, and becomes another significant moment in the erasure of a feminine starring role in reproduction. This publication is aimed at a more general audience than just medical professionals, but it serves the medical community as well; its articles are clearly written and accessible to an educated public and are also scientifically accurate and fairly complete. For example, one article in *The Walking Egg* that discusses the uses of umbilical cord blood features an image of three cords dangling: an umbilical cord, a modem cord, and an electrical cord (figure 14.3).[17] The woman's reproductive tissue—the umbilical cord—is playfully equated

14.3 "Cord Blood Bank,"
photo illustration by Koen
Vanmechelen, *The Walking
Egg* 26 (Summer 2001).
*With permission of Willem
Ombelet, Editor.*

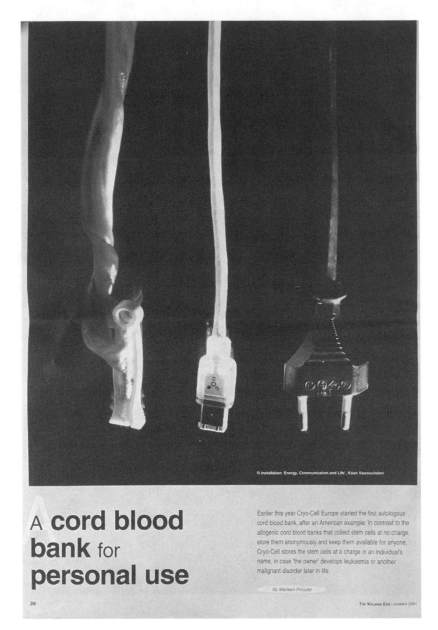

A **cord blood
bank** for
personal use

Earlier this year Cryo-Cell Europe started the first autologous
cord blood bank, after an American example. In contrast to the
allogenic cord blood banks that collect stem cells at no charge,
store them anonymously and keep them available for anyone,
Cryo-Cell stores the stem cells at a charge in an individual's
name, in case 'the owner' develops leukaemia or another
malignant disorder later in life.

By Marleen Finoulst

with electrical and communication cords that are essential for everyday life, and obviously abstracted from her body. Women are excluded from the image. Another potent and common example of abstracted reproduction or replication is that NRTs are now typically
represented with the highly magnified image of an actual human egg
being held by a glass micropipette on one side while a needle pene-
trates it on the other to deliver an individual sperm (figure 14.4).

One of the most literal and unusually graphic representations of the appropriation of female reproduction is found on the cover of the Autumn 2000 issue of *The Walking Egg* (figure 14.5). The tiny bloody hand grasping a surgically gloved finger immediately catches the eye. It takes a moment to realize that this hand is emerging from a surgical cut into a woman's pregnant womb. The handshake also seems to confirm a pact between the two principal characters, doctor and fetus; the woman is only a blood-filled backdrop.[18] This image signals a rising, usually masculine, mastery over reproduction that is obvious in an announcement found at the 2000 ESHRE conference about a Masters program in clinical embryology offered at the Danube University at Krems, Austria. The brochure features glowing sperm with the word "Master" in large letters printed over the swimmers. Despite the subject of the announcement of the Masters program, no eggs and no embryos are to be seen. An ad for the recent innovation in gynecological imaging, transvaginal hydro laparoscopy, provides one of the strongest and most common examples of this type of mastery (figure 14.6). It is typical in its illumination of the once-dark corridors of creation, as brightly colored (but not bloody)

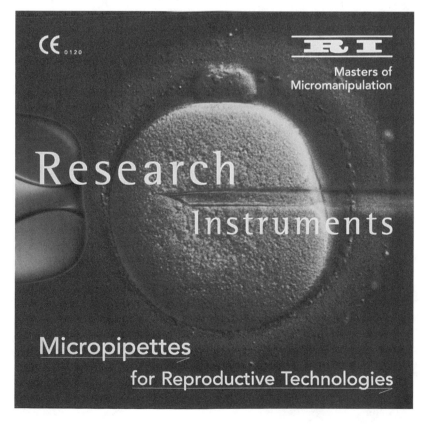

14.4 "Human Egg Penetrated by Micropipette Carrying a Human Sperm," Research Instruments ad, ESHRE Conference, Bologna, 2000.

and clear images of harvesting and implantation sites, ovaries, Fallopian tubes, and uterine walls, fill the ad. Centered in this illuminated tableaux is an image of two male medical professionals gazing at the screen that produces these images. One of them sits on an empty gynecological examining bed. The female body no longer appears even as a site of reproduction, while the signs of mastery over reproduction have become prominent and significant.

14.5 "The Fetal Handshake," cover design by Rudi van Beek, *The Walking Egg* 2, no. 3 (Autumn 2000).
With permission of Willem Ombelet, Editor.

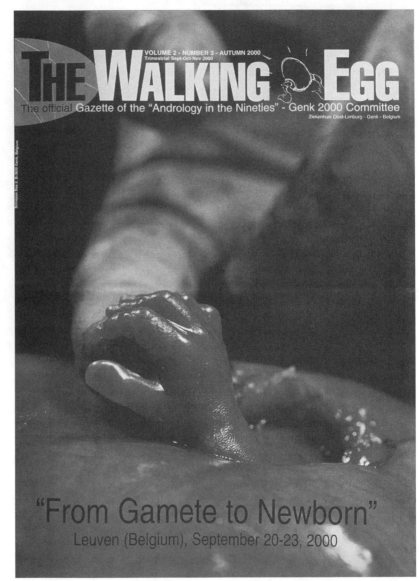

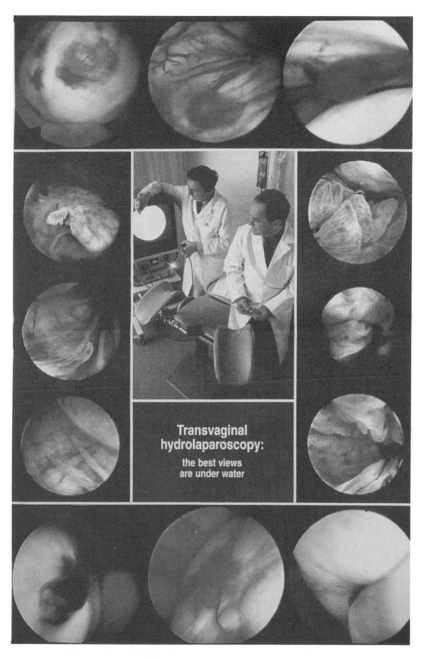

14.6 Images of female reproductive passages through transvaginal hydrolaparoscopy, ad, ESHRE Conference, Bologna, 2000.

Scientific Ordering and the Female Fetish

Although the technical signs within the images selected from the 2000 ESHRE conference speak to social advancement in terms of medical achievements, they form part of a long history of problematic representation of women by medicine that extends from the roots of modern science. An examination of eighteenth-century anatomical models, for example, illustrates how medical visual discourse mediates modern scientific principles especially in terms of the ordering of the natural world. This ordering served to control a fearful chaos in nature exemplified by female aspects of reproduction. But whereas contemporary medical visual discourse, as seen above, erases the female presence and introduces a new figure as emblematic of control over reproduction, earlier medical imaging attempted to tame nature-as-woman through sexual objectification.

Modern medical science has ordered the world since its inception in the 1700s through the process of bringing into view described by Haraway earlier: collecting, imaging, naming, explaining, and applying value. Paula Findlen draws attention to early modern science as collection and display in Italy in *Possessing Nature*.[19] She distinguishes between earlier eclectic collections of exotic finds and later catalogued displays of objects ordered according to the emerging Linnaean classification of nature. The former were typically the display of treasures of a curious gentleman-explorer and naturalist who delighted in the illumination of the strange and the fantastic. Ulisse Aldrovandi is one of the most notable Italian collectors, and his collection included a dragon reputedly found in the countryside surrounding his home in Bologna in 1572. The discovery and display of this fantastic creature served as a portent for the investment of Ugo Buoncampagni as Pope Gregory XIII.[20] Later catalogued displays were designed to serve a wider purpose of furthering knowledge, and included the innovation of empirical experimentation or the new rules of engagement with material from the natural world with the intent of improving upon the original.[21] Both the categorized display and the engagement with the materials displayed helped form a new natural law and the basis of modern natural science and experimental method. It is this newly ordered natural world that Schiebinger criticizes in terms of women's emancipation, the start of which coincides with the shift from eclectic collection to ordered display.

One of the more significant displays in the modern, scientific representation of human biology and reproduction is found at Museo La Specola, Florence, Italy. La Specola, the common name for the Imperiale Regio Museo di Fisica e Storia Naturale (The Imperial Royal Museum of Physics and Natural History), established in 1775 in Florence, Italy, houses one of the largest collections of eighteenth-century anatomical waxes.[22] In this stunning three-dimensional and life-like rendering of normal anatomy, the human body is ordered into an emerging modern medical logic throughout eight rooms filled with over two thousand wax models. The last room in the human biology section is the gynecological room, lined with life-sized wax replicas of women's truncated torsos as well as a dissectible life-sized female model with a five-month fetus inside. Each of the truncated torsos bears a heavily pregnant uterus, usually peeled back to reveal a fully formed fetus or, as in one case, twins. As with the two-dimensional truncated female torsos referred to by Jordanova earlier, women's bodies as modeled here serve as horrific and subjugated frames for the more important fetal *putti*. Just as Schiebinger concluded that representations of male and female skeletons of roughly the same period were highly gendered, these Florentine wax models also perpetuate gender stereotypes where the female form is simultaneously sexually objectified and rendered as Other to the male form.

The models of male bodies displayed at La Specola embody eighteenth-century traits of masculine intelligence and social stature. The life-sized figures are posed as lounging or standing in their display cabinets as they stare directly at the viewer mimicking the postures found in portraits of gentleman of this period (figure 14.7). In their display of the more intricate dissections of nerves, lymph glands, and so on, the anatomical models also serve as symbols of men of science. Although the dissections of these models are deep, they do not appear horrific. The models appear robotic and almost comical in their poses. In contrast, the female models, including but not limited to the gynecological models, sport skin and hair (figure 14.8). In addition to these sensual components, they are posed in a sexually appealing way: lying on their backs with heads tilted back, eyes and mouth slightly apart, and gazing into the distance as if in a sexual rapture. And as Petherbridge and Jordanova found, this erotic

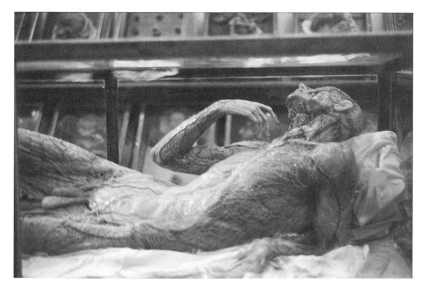

14.7 "The Skinned Man," male anatomical wax figure, La Specola, Florence, photo by Annette Burfoot. *With the photographer's permission.*

14.8 "The Doll," female anatomical wax figure, La Specola, Florence, photo by Annette Burfoot.
With the photographer's permission.

vision combines with the horrific.[23] The three full female bodies, complete with skin, plaited hair, and a vacuous gaze, are cut from clavicle to pubis with their guts pulled out from inside and draped over each side of the upper torso. In the adjoining gynecological room, female truncated uterine bases displaying well-developed fetuses carry obvious evidence of horrible dissection and amputation of the mother. This obvious violence to the body also is aligned with another typically astonishing site: the open view of female genitalia. Even today, such an open view of female genitalia draws reactions of surprise and disgust as visitors hurry by and avoid that part of the museum. The reaction to the initial display of the models in 1775 would have been even more pronounced, given the religious and other norms of especially female modesty at that time. And so the female body, which is aligned closely with the dangers and secrets of nature, is brought under control by an anatomical rendering that fetishizes the female form, violently sections it according to an emergent scientific logic, and exposes all its secrets, including the fetus.

These female wax anatomical models resonate with contemporary images of a male mastery over reproduction described above in terms of the materials from the ESHRE conference. Both sets of medical imagery of the body illustrate a control over the female role in reproduction by an emerging medical order. Where the representations differ, and this is important, is in the body selected as the fetish object of medical discourse. Early modern medical figurations of the human body contained subliminal fears of death and celebrated a new control of human life by featuring the female form. As we can see from the analysis of wax models above, this was achieved by simultaneously eroticizing female anatomy and cataloguing it in terms of the emergent logic of modern medical science. However, contemporary medical visions, especially in reproductive medicine, hold up the embryo as its new fetish object while completely erasing the female body. Today, medical visual discourse effaces women, displaces reproduction with replication, and transfers the generative principle to a fetal object, portent of a medical mastery over generation and life itself.

Replication: The New World and the Fetal Fetish

The replacement of women as holistic agents in reproduction with abstracted parts of human procreativity and an emphasis on an emergent genetic replication was evident at the 2000 ESHRE conference. It is also a part of a wider trend in contemporary biology. Once medical professionals and scientists could successfully manipulate human gametes at the point of conception (the key development in NRTs in the early 1980s), they could begin to screen for and manipulate genetic information at this earliest stage of human being. As we will see from the images gathered at the 2000 ESHRE conference below, both aspects of this trend contribute to the reduction of human life as malleable genetic code and render heterosexual intercourse dull and plodding in comparison to the bright promise of genetic replication.

The image of the voyager as fetus plays a significant role in this shift from reproduction to replication. It signals leaving behind one place for the discovery of another, and in this case the maternal as the origin of life is left in favor of something that holds out more hope and more promise. As an example, the ad for Gonal-F, a bio-engineered fertility hormone used to stimulate ovulation in women, features a smiling, white baby clutching a double helix. Again the baby is backlit, this time with a completely abstracted corona of villus-like tissue surrounding the baby's head. The combination of the haloed infant and the DNA helix signifies a miraculous new trend in assisted reproductive technology, genetic engineering. This element of discovery and promise also was evident at the opening plenary session of the 2000 ESHRE conference: The completion of the mapping of the human genome was announced to great applause and excited speculation on applications in ART. This great potential for life embedded in the image of the DNA spiral also resonates in the illustrations from a brochure announcing "A New-style Cutting Edge Web/Paper Journal: *Reproductive Biomedicine.*" The brochure foregrounds a very young embryo (about three weeks old) against colorful schematics of genetic formations. This shape of the genetic mass mirrors the embryonic form, with biochemical symbols replacing the villus halo. The engineered life form emerges as a replacement for the organic image and represents yet another level of abstraction from pregnancy and birth. An illustrated announcement for the new volume *An Atlas of Preimplantation Genetic Diagnosis* features on its cover a globe made up of patchwork images of microscopic globular organic objects glowing in different colors and patterns. The globe is set in a star field while a hazy spot with microorganisms floating within forms the background. The use of the term "atlas" alongside the visual merging of stellar and organic bodies points to the charting of a new territory that plays with boundaries of schematics and organism. But it is not the voyager who is mapping the way. This star child is only a symbol or mascot for masterful replication.

The voyager signals mastery and control with the DNA helix and genetic replication as key instruments—the baby is pictured above clutching the spiral like a toy. The new cataloguing of reproductive parts represents a part of our century's most potent collection: information on the genetic code, or what Haraway and Franklin discuss as "life itself," to characterize how master molecule gene discourse attempts to fix creation as a singular genetic component.[24] The nature of the "master" in this phrase calls for our attention. The ad for HTM Dimensions (which provides the means for examining sperm prior to use in ART) points to a new development in NRTs, the study of male infertility, and provides a new schematic that unabashedly illustrates a patriarchal matrix. The tails of the sperm surrounding the Earth form the lines of latitude and longitude and the global positioning system. To put it in a facile way— and also to reflect Aristotle's theory of reproduction, in which the male provides form and the female merely the matter—without the male component of reproduction we are lost![25]

In contrast to these global-positioning sperm, female gametes are presented as passive stellar orbs waiting to be discovered or as glowing spheres held ready for penetration with the material that will spark the replication process (see figure 14.4). An ad for a micromanipulator (a machine used to manipulate gametes and embryos) bears the heading, "As Precise as You Like."[26] This is one aspect of the deeply embedded notion of control in genetic discourse (to have, to read, to order the gene, is to control life itself). The masculine association with mastery is made clear in two other ads. The first is for a device designed to strip off the outer layer of the egg in preparation for penetration by the aspirating needle that delivers the sperm. The words, The Stripper™, appear in large print over a photo of a very sharp-looking needle-like device with the same name emblazoned along its side.[27] Here the erotic, in normative masculine terms of sexual desire and the striptease, elides with fine-tuned control of replication and thus provides another example of mastery in medical visual culture. The second ad is for an aspiration needle that is used to suck the eggs required for genetic engineering and research on embryos from ripe follicles within a woman's body.[28] The ad features the instrument, a fine and very long hollow needle attached to tubing and two plug-like ends, and a picture of the Mona Lisa smiling at the viewer. The needle takes the painting's title as a trademark. This use of classical aesthetics to valorize an object is hardly new and often features prominently in medical visual discourse. For example, announcements of professional congresses, especially in gynecology and obstetrics, are often filled with images of well-known paintings and sculptures, usually featuring female nudes. These images simultaneously lend cultural capital to the enterprise and provide a subtle and acceptable sexual titillation.

So it appears that the female body has returned as an object of the medical gaze, but this time she appears not to promote a newly ordered "natural" world as with the eighteenth-century wax anatomical models, but instead to sell the now highly profitable business of NRTs (keeping in mind that the ESHRE conference images are taken from ads). A harbinger of the fecund relationship between contemporary commercial interest and medicine was that patent law was enacted in 1474 in Venice just as personal collections of curiosities were becoming catalogued libraries of living beings. The stated principle supporting patenting is to encourage and protect those who can bring greater good to the society.[29] I am sure that if you asked any medical professional, pharmaceutical representative, or researcher at the 2000 ESHRE conference about the purpose of his work, he would reply that he is working for the greater good of society. In the name of human progress, ties between commercial interests and the images from the ESHRE conference analyzed here are likewise easily played down or obscured by claims of medical research.

The forward motion indicated by the term "voyager" advances the same principle. The commercial stakes are high in the business of ART, especially with the imminent prospect of prenatal human genetic engineering. This combines with an emerging visual discourse of reproductive science that, through a process of colonization, essentializes the female role in procreation to abstracted reproductive functional parts. This medical visual culture also effectively replaces reproduction with replication and women with a fetal mascot. As we saw earlier, objectification of women can be traced back to the inception of modern science and to some of the earliest examples of modern medical imaging. Whereas the eighteenth-century models form a visual discourse that brings the female body to order simultaneously as a sexed and catalogued object of a medical gaze, the recent medical objectification of women has shifted to the product of reproduction, the fetal voyager. It is as if the battle over chaotic nature articulated in eighteenth-century Florence has been won and the mystery of reproduction in women's bodies solved. Thus the voyager becomes the emblem of the triumph of replication over reproduction and of a burgeoning speculation in genetic engineering.

It is not the purpose of this chapter to argue that there is a proper representation of the female or even that femininity can be understood as a singular concept. The findings here are based on what is articulated by the visual discourse of ART within its social, political, and historical contexts. The images within this visual discourse reflect dominant views of gender. Yet other, resistant, and even militant readings and articulations are possible. Haraway's cyborg is a good example of a liberatory boundary figure between so-called nature and scientific discourse.[30] It would be interesting to investigate the eighteenth-century wax female models as early cyborgs, emancipate them from their socio-historical constraints, and return a sense of agency and even female-centered eroticism to women. Another image contemporaneous with those from the ESHRE conference explores this possibility and differs starkly from the dominant medical visual discourse of replication. The sculptor Ron Mueck has rendered a wax figure along the lines of the anatomical models used in early medical teachings at La Specola (figure 14.9).[31] The figure is of a woman and baby just after labor and birth. The hyperrealistic representation of the woman and baby's bodies, complete with sweaty hair, the evidence of amniotic fluid, and a still-attached umbilical

14.9 Ron Mueck, "Mother and Child after Birth," wax figure sculpture; shown at the James Cohan Gallery, New York City, June 2001, photo by Ann Shteir. *With the photographer's permission.*

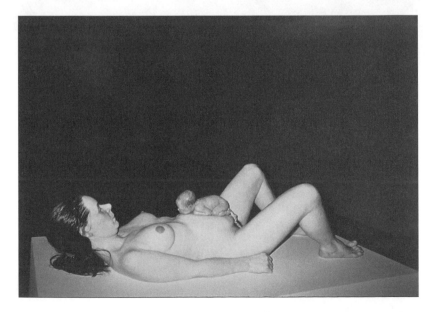

cord resists the visual dissection, appropriation, and objectification of women, pregnancy, and birth that we saw above. It also centers the female body in reproduction in a holistic and sensual manner that does not fetishize the star child but celebrates life herself.

Acknowledgments

My thanks go to Bernie Lightman and Rusty (Ann) Shteir for organizing such a stimulating and useful "laboratory" for nonscience academics at York University. A travel grant from Queen's University helped support the study at the ESHRE conference in Europe. A portion of a SSHRC grant for the York University seminar series enabled my participation there.

Notes

1. Dr. Robert Edwards was one of the Association's founders in 1985. Edwards and his partner Dr. Patrick Steptoe are claimed widely to be the first to succeed with in vitro fertilization in humans with the birth of Louise Joy Brown in the United Kingdom in 1979. By a 2001 count, ESHRE now has a membership of 4,342 practitioners and researchers in the field of reproductive medicine and science.

2. Annual Meeting of the European Society of Human Reproduction and Embryology (ESHRE), Bologna, Italy, June 25–28, 2000.

3. The increasing significance of the fetus also is present in an ad for "The Ultimate Embryo Freezer," where the womb is effectively reduced to a set of luggage.

4. See *Life*, April 1965 and August 1990. For more on the significance of fetal imagery, see Laury Oaks, "Smoke-Filled Wombs and Fragile Fetuses: The Social Politics of Fetal Representation," *Signs* 26, no. 1 (2000): 63–108; Carol Stabile, "Shooting the Mother: Fetal Photography and the Politics of Disappearance," *Camera Obscura* 29 (January 1992), 179–205; Sarah Franklin, "Fetal Fascinations: New Dimensions to the Medical-Scientific Construction of Fetal Personhood," in *Off-Centre: Feminism and Cultural Studies*, ed. Sarah Franklin, Celia Lury, and Jackie Stacey (New York: Harper-Collins, 1992): 190–205; and Rosalind Petchesky, "Foetal Images: The Power of Visual Culture in the Politics of Reproduction," in *Reproductive Technologies: Gender, Motherhood and Medicine,* ed. Michelle Stanworth (Minneapolis: University of Minnesota Press, 1987), 57–80.

5. Donna Haraway, *How Like a Leaf*, an interview with Thyrza Nichols Goodeve (New York: Routledge, 2000), 92; and Sarah Franklin, "Life Itself," paper delivered at the Centre for Cultural Values, Lancaster University, June 9, 1993.

6. Haraway, *How Like a Leaf*, 84.

7. "Fetish" is a term adopted from psychoanalysis, where it refers to the fixation on an object, typically for sexual gratification. Here it is used more

broadly to include the satisfaction of desire generally, including, for example, curiosity. Haraway, *How Like a Leaf*, 92–93.

8. In particular, studies of the body as represented in scientific and technological contexts are useful here. See, for example, Anne Balsamo, *Technologies of the Gendered Body: Reading Cyborg Women* (Durham and London: Duke University Press, 1996); and Paula Treichler, "Feminism, Medicine, and the Meaning of Childbirth," in *Body/Politics: Women and the Discourses of Science,* ed. Mary Jacobus, Evelyn Fox Keller, and Sally Shuttleworth (New York: Routledge, 1990), 113–38.

9. See also Lisa Cartwright, "A Cultural Anatomy of the Visible Human Project," in *The Visible Woman: Imaging Technologies, Gender and Science,* ed. Paula Treichler, Lisa Cartwright, and Constance Penley (New York: New York University Press, 1998), 21–43; and *Wild Science: Reading Feminism, Medicine and the Media*, ed. Janine Marchessault and Kim Sawchuk (New York: Routledge, 2000).

10. Londa Schiebinger, "Skeletons in the Closet: The First Illustrations of the Female Skeleton in Eighteenth-Century Anatomy," in *The Making of the Modern Body: Sexuality and Society in the Nineteenth Century,* ed. Catherine Gallagher and Thomas Laqueur (Berkeley: University of California Press, 1987), 42–82.

11. Deanna Petherbridge and Ludmilla Jordanova, *The Quick and the Dead: Artists and Anatomy* (London: Hayward Gallery and Berkeley: University of California Press, 1997), 104.

12. Ludmilla Jordanova, *Sexual Visions: Images of Gender in Science and Medicine between the Eighteenth and Twentieth Centuries* (Madison: University of Wisconsin Press, 1989).

13. Petherbridge and Jordanova, *The Quick and the Dead,* 86. *Putti* are the figures of male infants used in Renaissance art usually to highlight or frame the subject of a painting.

14. It is important to note that all the ads discussed here feature the ideal recipient of ART as white.

15. Leuven, Belgium, September 20–23, 2000.

16. This logo appears in figure 14.5, "The Fetal Handshake," which is analyzed below.

17. Marleen Finoulst, "A Cord Blood Bank for Personal Use," *The Walking Egg* 3, no. 1 (Summer 2001): 26–27.

18. The hand in the photo is of Dr. Joseph Bruner, Director of Fetal Diagnosis and Therapy at Vanderbilt University Medical Center in Nashville, Tennessee. He is performing surgery in utero to correct for spina bifida. During the procedure, Dr. Bruner was reported as saying that the moment his finger was grasped was the most emotional of his life.

19. Paula Findlen, *Possessing Nature: Museums, Collecting, and Scientific Culture in Early Modern Italy* (Berkeley: University of California Press, 1994).

20. Ibid., 17–24.

21. Some of the holdings of the Accademia del Cimento (1657–1667), a briefly constituted Florentine society of scientists wishing to experiment,

are found in Il Museo di Storia della Scienza, Florence. These items are chiefly physics experimentation instruments and viewing devices (telescopes and microscopes).

22. See *Encyclopaedia Anatomica: A Complete Collection of Anatomical Waxes* (Köln: Taschen, 1999).

23. Petherbridge and Jordanova, *The Quick and the Dead*, 86.

24. See, e.g., Lucinda Leeck, *The Atlas of Human Gametes and Conceptuses* (London: CRC Press/Parthenon, 1999); Haraway, *How Like a Leaf*, 92; and Franklin, "Life Itself."

25. Aristotle, "De Generatione Animalium," trans. Arthur Platt, in *The Basic Works of Aristotle*, ed. Richard McKeon (New York: Random House Books, 1941), 678.

26. "As Precise as You Like," Eppendorf ad, ESHRE Conference, Bologna, 2000.

27. The Stripper™, MidAtlantic Diagnostics Inc. ad, ESHRE Conference, Bologna, 2000.

28. "Mona Lisa Aspiration Needle," Gynotec ad, ESHRE Conference, Bologna, 2000.

29. Ruth Schwartz Cowan, *A Social History of American Technology* (Oxford: Oxford University Press, 1997).

30. Donna Haraway, "A Manifesto for Cyborgs: Science, Technology, and Socialist Feminism in the 1980s," in *The Gendered Cyborg*, ed. Gill Kirkup, Linda Janes, Kath Woodward, and Fiona Hovenden (New York: Routledge, 2000), 50–57.

31. Ron Mueck, "Mother and Child," shown at James Cohan Gallery, New York City, June 2001.

VISIBLE/HUMAN/PROJECT

Visibility and Invisibility at the Next Anatomical Frontier

Naomi Adelson

In 1986, the Board of Regents of the American National Library of Medicine (NLM) decided that a three-dimensional digital atlas of male and female anatomy and physiology was both necessary and technologically feasible. The electronic volumetric database and medical images library they envisioned would be as accessible as the two-dimensional text-based anatomical literature. The original goal for this project was to make the print and image libraries into a "single, unified resource for health information."[1] The three-dimensional digital imagery, to be available at relatively low cost primarily via high-speed computer networks, also would become central to the development of the latest medical technologies, including remote surgery, research models and simulators, and medical training and education. In 1989, the call went out for proposals to build a digital image library of a normal adult male and female that would include "digitized photographic images for cryosectioning, digital images derived from computerized tomography, and digital magnetic resonance images of cadavers."[2] The contract was awarded to a University of Colorado consortium of scientists and consultants. They, in turn, set the criteria for the needed cadavers. It took, NLM Project Director Michael Ackerman recounts, almost two years to find an appropriate male cadaver and six months more than that to find the right female cadaver. The two cadavers were transformed into the first virtual bodies and these digital data sets, now trademarked by the NLM, are known collectively as the Visible Human Project® (VHP®).

Bodies and machines have had a long metaphoric and literal relationship within both everyday and scientific discourse, providing an often taken-for-granted visual language for our contemporary social and scientific readings of the human body.[3] These readings are never neutral, however, despite the presence of a seemingly universal, quantifiable body. The Visible Human Project®, moving anatomical representations from the two-dimensional space of text to the three-dimensional virtual reality of the computer, is the latest incarnation in a long history of anatomical representation and its next frontier. The Visible Human Project® does not just connect anatomy with physiology and form with function, but joins human with machine and machine with human in a particularly specific amalgamation. In the Visible Human Project®, metaphor is usurped as flesh is transformed *into* machine and tissue quite literally becomes pixel. Machine, in this instance, materializes as (hu)man. Despite the sophisticated means by which the human body is represented, a far more static notion of that body—and one that is explicitly male—remains the contemporary standard of anatomical representation. Simultaneously fusing bodies with machines, the VHP® newly reconfigures the boundaries between the two, yet retains a far less innovative representational form of either men or women (figures 15.1 and 15.2).[4]

Issues of visibility, invisibility, and power long entrenched in our socio-medical world are reproduced in this biotechnology.[5] Biomedical knowledge is historically, socially, and culturally situated and hence produced, not discovered. Biomedicine, as a particular form of authoritative knowledge, powerfully permeates and mediates our fundamental perception of human bodies, naturalizing and normalizing these facts into that which constitutes what we see and perceive as *the* normal body.[6] From direct inspection (touch, auscultation) to mediated technologies such as radiography, ultrasound, and CT scan, the human body is never simply examined but constituted through visualization at the critical interval between perception and knowledge.[7] The Visible Human®, for example, is not an Ayurvedic or humeral body, replete as the latter are with complex patterns of flows and counterbalances. This "normal" body has been constituted wholly from within the historical trajectory of Western biomedicine and is presented as a natural phenomenon of bioscientific advancement in an age of virtual reality, trademarked human representations, biotechnological futures markets, and patented life forms. As we are now able to see into and through that naturalized and normalized body in ways that we could never have imagined just a few decades ago, we verify, in a tautological fashion, those constructed biomedical standards of human normalcy.

Human, as I have just used the term, refers to a homogenous entity, apparently void of any particular sex, age, or for that matter cultural or racial heritage.[8] Herein lies my central concern and the crux of this chapter: despite the technological sophistication in how we are able to see *humans*, we have come no further in our ability to envisage anything other than biomedical renderings, and hence interpretations, of male and female human anatomy. The VHP® is, ostensibly, a novel anatomical representation of male and female forms. Its novelty derives in part from how the bodies were constituted, in part from the technological sophistication that surrounds their creation as well as their visualization, and in part from the fact that they are the first-ever structural-anatomical representations. Yet the VHP® reproduces a traditional gendered representation of the body and in the process delimits how we see that body. As anthropologist Paul Rabinow summarized in his study of the social renderings of the new genetic technologies: "Older forms of cultural classification of bio-identity such as race, gender, and age have no more disappeared than medicalization or

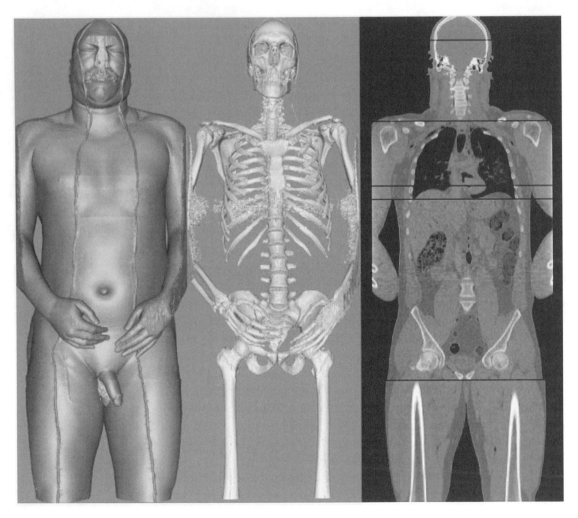

15.1 Composite Image, Visible Man™.
Courtesy of the National Library of Medicine. Image is derived from the National Library of Medicine's Visible Human Project and reproduced with permission of William Lorensen of General Electric.

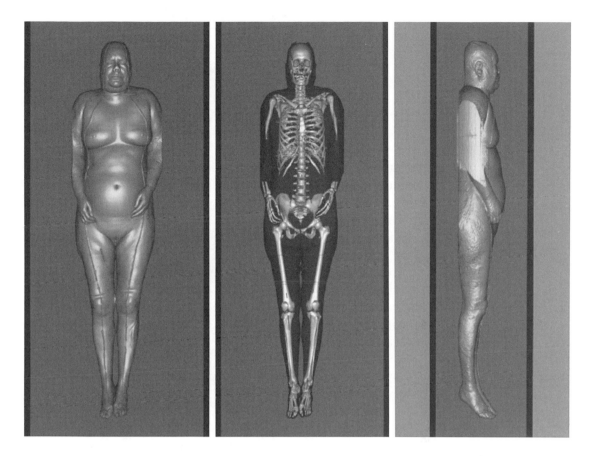

15.2 Composite Image, Visible Woman™.
Courtesy of the National Library of Medicine. Image is derived from the National Library of Medicine's Visible Human Project and reproduced with permission of William Lorensen of General Electric.

normalization have—although the meanings and the practices that constitute them certainly are changing." [9] Mediating between visuality and veracity (Visible), bodies and machines (Human), and technology and society (Project), the Visible Human Project® is one of the many contemporary biotechnologies (from sonography to genomics) that simultaneously re-constitute and entrench our knowledge of, as Rabinow says, "life itself." [10] In the process, our perception of what constitutes human remains rigidly intact and profoundly male.

The Visible Human Project®

"Wow, they can really put Humpty Dumpty back together again." "Looks like an anatomy class for the MTV generation." "But why did they do all that colorizing when they could have just created digital three-dimensional images without the original human body?" These comments and questions came from a group of graduate students who, with me, were viewing video images of the Visible Human®. I had typed the words "visible" and "human" into the dialogue box of Google®, a popular internet search engine, and within seconds received a sizable list of sites, promising a wealth of articles and images on the subject. Clicking onto one of the sites, we began to browse still and moving image libraries. With the Windows Media Player® program, we were able to access, almost instantaneously, three-dimensional digital representations of human tissue, organs, and systems. In other words, we were navigating—at the click of a mouse—through selected bits and pieces of the Visible Human®. The images that we perused on the "Marching Through the Visible Man" website, for example, included a dramatic rendering of the Visible Man's sinewy thighs, muscle richly colorized in claret red against the simplest blue backdrop (figure 15.3). As the thighs rhythmically rotated a full 360 degrees, we were offered the depth, dimensionality, and detail of thigh muscle, bone, and circulatory system. "Looks like a video game to me," remarked one of my graduate students. We all concurred. How these digital images were generated is a key feature of the story of the VHP®, rife as it is with comparisons to the biblical narrative of human beginnings and with the promise of a new measure of anatomical accuracy.

Creation myths, founded on the fundamentals of faith and sustained as guides to universal truths about the purpose and existence of human life, illuminate cultural values and transcendental truths. As Sarah Franklin has noted, the new genetic technologies are replete with similar creation metaphors as they are reconstituting, to an even greater degree, the conceptualization of "life itself."[11] Comparisons between Judaeo-Christian origin myths (and other origin myths of sacrifice and creation) and the VHP® are inevitable given that the developers informally named the first digital humans Adam and Eve. It is, however, a creation narrative for the twenty-first century, as these male and female corporeal bodies disintegrate millimeter by millimeter in order to reappear as eternal virtual configurations. The narrative that surrounds this couple is one of technological omniscience and a particular transcendental bodily truth.

The Visible Human® creation story is told by M. J. Ackerman, the scientific director of the VHP®, and details the transformation of the male cadaver into Visible Human®. Drawn from the "Visible Human Project® Fact Sheet," this wholly technical narrative of the rendering process establishes the bioscientific accuracy and technological precision of the project:

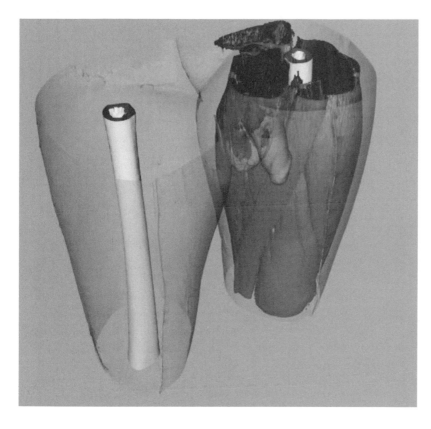

15.3 Marching Through the Visible Human™, three-dimensional thigh.
Courtesy of the National Library of Medicine. Image is derived from the National Library of Medicine's Visible Human Project and reproduced with permission of William Lorensen of General Electric.

[The male data set] consists of Magnetic Resonance Interferometry (MRI), Computerized Tomography (CT) and anatomical images. Axial MRI images of the head and neck and longitudinal sections of the rest of the body were obtained at 4mm intervals. The MRI images are 256 × 256 pixel resolution. Each pixel has 12 bits of grey tone resolution. The CT data consists of axial CT scans of the entire body taken at 1mm intervals at a resolution of 512 × 512 pixels where each pixel is made up of 12 bits of grey tone. The axial anatomical images are 2048 × 1216 pixels where each pixel is defined by 24 bits of color, about 7.5 megabytes. The anatomical cross-sections are also at 1mm intervals and coincide with the CT axial images. There are 1871 cross-sections for each mode, CT and anatomy. The complete male data set is 15 gigabytes in size.[12]

The body, belonging to Joseph Paul Jernigan, was, in fact, the third cadaver on which the team at the University of Colorado had performed this same procedure. They had experimented with various techniques of preparing and imaging bodies on a few cadavers and finally sent three full sets of scans to the NLM for review. Jernigan, despite a missing tooth, testicle, and appendix, ultimately was chosen to be the "visible man."

A second account of the same rendering process was written up in a *Life* magazine feature on Jernigan and the VHP®. The following excerpt from that article on Jernigan's transformation presents a far more mundane yet equally captivating accounting of Jernigan's journey from flesh into the "raw" data that would become the Visible Man®.

> The body was shipped air freight ($201.88) and unpacked within eight hours. At 5 feet 11 inches and 199 pounds, Jernigan had to be squeezed into the MRI machine; his elbows would not appear in the images. . . . To keep the body in the same position throughout the process, Spitzer ran rubber tubing along the cadaver, attaching it with Liquid Nails purchased at a local hardware store. . . . To make the cuts even, the tissue was frozen . . . at –94°F for two days. Once quartered, the body was positioned in blocks of gelatin, bought in one-pound cans from the school's cafeteria and colored blue with food dye. . . . [T]he slicing finally began. . . . "Everything broke," says Spitzer. "The computer that collected the pictures broke. The machine that stored them broke. All the cameras broke. The saw and mechanical devices broke. . . ." By the time they reached the head, it was summer, and with no air conditioning, the block was thawing too quickly. They limited cutting to six hours a day. In the end, it took nearly nine months to produce pictures of all 1,878 slices.[13]

This is not a creation story. It is a story of the everyday-ness of such things as cafeteria-purchased food dyes, hot summer days, and equipment mishaps, and offers a droll comparison to the official, technical, and highly authoritative account presented by Ackerman on the VHP® website. Ackerman's biotechnological creation story marks the body as specimen to be rendered into eternal digital form, whereas the *Life* version reflects the remarkably ordinary elements of that reformation. Taken together, these equally vivid but incongruent readings of the same process—and cadaver—are metaphoric nods to the range of complexities that otherwise disappear as a fleshy body is transformed into raw scientific data. In that transformation of human into digital data set, what becomes "visible" and what is left "invisible" constitutes, in other words, the parameters of the social, cultural, historical, and physical signifiers of the normative human body. It is, after all, the biotechnological creation story that is the official one; told and retold in the media representations of the VHP®, it alone remains the authoritative creation story.

With the rapid advance of computer technologies during the short span of time between the creation of the Visible Man® and the Visible Woman®, the task of creating the Visible Woman® was somewhat less complicated. The female cadaver still had to be frozen and segmented, but procedural and technological advances meant that the Visible Woman® could be milled and scanned at .33mm intervals. Given that the Visible Man® was milled and scanned at only 0.1mm, almost three times the number of images comprise the Visible Woman® (approximately five thousand in total).[14]

The two originary data sets, Adam and Eve, were rendered into three-dimensional human digital imagery by General Electric's (tellingly titled) Genesis Project. The Genesis Project's "Marching Through the Visible Man" website describes how they obtained the "fresh" data, that is, the digital images of the male (and female) cadaver. Then, on an Onyx Reality Engine 2 computer running Irix 5.3 and a variety of software tools that they refer to as the "Research Workstation" and adjusting for varying pixel dimensions and by applying the Marching Cubes algorithm, they were able to construct a three-dimensional full-body model from contiguous CT and MRI cross-sections.[15] The GE Genesis Project has produced a series of three-dimensional medical images (including the thigh described earlier), accessible via the internet from their Scientific Movie Library. One can, alternatively, opt to "Make Your Own Visible Woman" with their Visualization Toolkit, which will render a surface model of the Visible Woman®. There is no similar companion toolkit available for the Visible Man®. The VHP®, always intended to be the "raw," "fresh" data source for the creation of volumetric digital body applications, is now the basis for over one thousand separate medical imaging projects in forty countries, according to the director of the programme at the NLM.[16] This technology, in other words, is quickly becoming a fundamental digital resource for computer-mediated anatomy education.

Curious to know the degree to which digital technologies had been integrated into traditional medical school anatomy labs, a research assistant and I conducted a small telephone survey of anatomy professors at each of the fourteen medical schools in Canada in the summer of 2001.[17] I soon learned that all but one of the schools continue to use cadavers in their anatomy labs, either as a whole or in prosections, and that only five of the fourteen schools have attempted to use virtual systems in conjunction with the laboratory dissection. While there was some interest in the idea, and while some schools were developing their own anatomy computer programs, at the same time, there was concern about the loss of depth, dimensionality, and the relationships among anatomical structures in the virtual body. At the time, the University of Montreal was the only school in Canada that had made the switch to computer technologies and this mostly because of the high cost of maintaining an adequate anatomy lab. In 1996, they went without any means of dissection substitute and this was pedagogically disastrous. In the following year, they integrated four computer programs, intended to be used in a complementary manner.[18] Problems of depth and dimensionality and none of the qualities of a "real" dissection remained, however—perhaps because they were not yet using programs based on the Visible Human® dataset.[19] Despite this early slow start taken across Canada to introduce the digital cadaver into the anatomy lab, by 2003 virtual technologies based on the VHP® were becoming standard additions to medical curricula. Visible Productions™ (www.visiblep.com), for example, created a series of virtual realities, animated anatomical fly-throughs, and interactive multimedia for medical education based entirely upon the Visible Human® (and specifically the Visible Man®) dataset. As well, universities such as Stanford, Loyola (Chicago), Australia's Queensland University of Technology, Australia National University, and the Universities of Michigan and Syracuse developed digital anatomy labs and viewers based on the VHP®. In addition, at least fifteen separate viewing applications and twenty-one animation projects are now available through industry (e.g., Medical Multi-Media Systems; Anatomical Travelogue) and university medical schools in Europe, North America, Australia, and Asia (e.g., "3D Anatomy for Medical Students," McGill University, Montreal, Canada; "The Virtual Anatomy Explorer," University Clinic, Giessen, Germany).[20] As more and more medical schools internationally turn to digital biotechnologies they increasingly will view, study, and manipulate what is, I contend, a very rigid body.

Visible

"Images," says the scientific director of the VHP®, "are an important part of biomedical knowledge" and the goal of the VHP® is, first and foremost, to heighten the visual acuity of anatomical representation.[21] This project of visualization, however, is far from neutral, and it is for that reason that I now turn to exploring the relationship between the VHP®, the medical gaze, and the reproduction of that "rigid" human body.

Foucault's *The Birth of the Clinic* chronicles the rise of the body in anatomic study as the site of truth claims about the body, and the emerging clinical ordering of the body as the site of that knowledge production.[22] In his discussion of the "technique of the corpse," Foucault opened our eyes to the discursive construction of the body via the medical "gaze." Not simply an act of seeing or visualization, the multisensorial "gaze" constructs as it observes and, in that process, extends the authority of the clinic into the most intimate recesses of the human body. Thus, anatomical drawings serve to "subtract" the person/patient both from disease as well as from his or her body, with the concomitant growth in the power of that reductionistic method. As Samson succinctly states, "[m]edical knowledge that is the product of the clinical gaze establishes an authoritative 'truth' about the body and the person. And, as such, definitions and identifications that emerge from the observations of the physical body and its movements and behaviour produce power."[23] In other words, visualization technologies are historically tied to, and often indistinguishable from, social and political imperatives. From the first anatomical prints and engravings to the earliest microscope, stereoscope, daguerreotype, x-ray, and photograph and on to contemporary medical visualization methods, technologies of envisioning the body simultaneously have mediated, defined, and naturalized what constitutes knowledge of the body. This process is part of what gives the scientific profession authoritative control in matters relating to the definition and regulation of bodies in society.

In "The Body and the Archive," Alan Sekula traces the links between early photography, physiognomy, and phrenology and the deployment of a typology of deviance. The resulting images created our contemporary "scientific" standards of the deviant body. These standards, in turn, offered measurable parameters of the average, normal, socially stable body.[24] This kind of "scopic regime" effectively produces politically correct ways of seeing through an "ensemble of practices and discourses that establish the truth claims, typicality, and credibility of visual acts and objects."[25] Referencing Foucault's concept of the gaze, anthropologist Alan Feldman points to the "scopic regime" as a mechanics of power and, more explicitly, distinguishes the eye as the "sensory organ that can be socially appropriated to channel and materialize normative power in everyday life." Vision, for Feldman, is linked to cognition and to a higher ordering of interaction with the external world, whereby "[b]oth visual realism and the male gaze have in common the tendency to obscure the constructed origins of their perceptual apparatus and advance themselves as natural, unchanging and ahistorical."[26] In other words, what we see is mediated not only by the technologies of vision but also by the mechanics of a powerful, gendered gaze.

A Western or Euro-American history of the science of the body, and more specifically the history of the anatomy text, is not neutral on the subject of the meaning of the body. Indeed, to track the history of dissection and its record is to track a history of the shift in the relationship between the human body and the social meaning attached to it as both subject *and* object of study. Early European medical and religious beliefs precluded considerations of the body as the site of central pathological and thus observational concern. The scientific merits of direct bodily inspection grew through the Renaissance, however, with Andreas Vesalius's seven volume *De Humani Corporis Fabrica* (1543) emerging as the hallmark anatomical representation of its time. Vesalius's images (and treatise) on the human body are detailed and meticulous, yet reflect a Renaissance humanist's search (albeit through a resolute glance back to Hellenic and Roman times) for truth and a concomitant understanding of the relationship between man, his body, and the universe.[27] With the Enlightenment began the slow but systematic extrication of contemplative reflections on man's place in the universe from the practice of science. By the end of the nineteenth century, connections between the qualitative, philosophical, and more "rational" quantitative body all but fade away as the body increasingly is likened to a machine in both form and function. The science of medicine, equally reflected in its anatomical representations, was now based on dispassionate observation and experimentation to the exclusion of "faith, of philosophy, of emotion and of feeling."[28] Objective, dispassionate observation remains the *sine qua non* of scientific and biomedical method, practice, and representation. The medicalized body thus is a body removed from society, a quantifiable object of inquiry, and the locus of authoritative scientific knowledge.

The Visible Human®, or rather the visible digital volumetric data set, moves us from the nineteenth-century model of man as machine to the twenty-first-century machine as human. The VHP™, as Catherine Waldby writes, thus animates the central imperative of contemporary biomedical knowledge in that it "brings together capacities to render simultaneously the body as surface and depth, action and object, and in the process realizes a series of medicine's historical desires—for the body's visibility, for its standardization and for mastery over life processes through their simulation."[29] And while the medical gaze perpetuates a particular authoritative knowledge of the body, it is in projects such as the VHP® that a visually mediated "strategy of naturalization" achieves its success.[30] This visualization project defines for us not only *what* we see but also *how* we see (and not smell, touch, or hear), interpret, and hence understand the human body.

Human

How human is the Visible Human®? In other words, how can this "machine as human" now represent all humans, regardless of sex, age, or ethnic/racial identifications? Hovering oddly and perhaps even dangerously between life and death, this digital data set has become the gold standard of present day anatomo-physiological representation. From alive/human to corpse to specimen to "human" again, the Visible Human® is resurrected eternally in digital "reality" as a universalized human form. We must in this instance ask, as Linda

Hogle already has done in relation to other "life-technology forms": "how do we define and produce 'humanness' and what exactly is 'technological'?"[31]

The designation of Visible Human® suggests a conceit on the part of the project managers that arises out of a Western biomedical presumption of the universality of the human body. What, for example, constitutes the difference between male and female in the Visible Human™ and where does the Visible Woman® fit in all of this? Looking in particular at sex, there is a consistent pattern of representing human as male (and more specifically as Joseph Jernigan). Despite the fact that the Visible Woman®, or "Eve," was cryosectioned and imaged with greater precision than Adam, it is the Visible Man® that remains the gold standard in virtually all visualization projects arising out of the VHP®. The VHP®, while promoted as a fair representation of both the male and female anatomies, has hardly been able to live up to its own ideals. A quick search through the National Library of Medicine's VHP® website and linked sites indicates that there is a paucity of work on the Visible Woman®. I could only find, as mentioned earlier, a Visible Woman® Kit (not available in the Visible Man® version) and the Visible Woman® digital pelvis. *The New Atlas of Human Anatomy* is one of a growing number of text-based resources that rely exclusively on the original three-dimensional anatomical imagery of the VHP®. Touting itself as the "first anatomically exact and complete three dimensional, computer generated reconstruction of human anatomy," nearly all of the images in *New Atlas* are those of the Visible Man®. The Visible Woman® is represented only as reproductive organs and pelvis.[32]

Contrary to a history of disproportionate surveillance of the female body, we now are faced with a far *less visible* Visible Woman®. We might well breathe a sigh of collective historical relief that the Woman is considerably less visible than the Man.[33] For so long in the history of the biomedical sciences, women were viewed as the natural object of, and hence subservient to, the medical gaze. Although this history is complex and relates as much to social and cultural norms as it does to the politics of sex and gender, there remains a disproportionate degree of biomedical attention to what otherwise may be constituted as women's normal functions. Childbirth, menstruation, menopause, and female aging are all considered therapeutically manageable. The female body, in other words, is disproportionately medicalized and pathologized when normal, and typically visible only in contradistinction to a male norm. The Visible Woman® is similarly constituted as that which is not the Visible Man®. For example, why is there only a Visible Woman® Visualization Tool Kit? Barring any obvious answer (such as the higher technological status of the Visible

Woman®'s data set), I can only ask whether this is evidence of a gaze that can choose to recreate "Eve" at will. Has "Eve" been reduced to a digital doll that can be manipulated perpetually while "Adam" is eternally hard at work in the digital viewers and cyber-anatomy labs of the world's medical schools?

In life as in death (and digital re-birth), the woman who became the Visible Woman® was also "less visible" than the man who became the Visible Man®. Their individual stories bear repeating here as these more than likely have affected the degree of visibility accorded their digital depiction. Thanks to the efforts of a news reporter who matched the public records of state executions to the available facts about the Visible Man®, we know exactly who the Visible Man® was in life. Joseph Paul Jernigan was on death row when he signed his body over to science, awaiting his execution for the callous murder of the owner of the home from which he was attempting to steal a microwave oven. Jernigan was thirty-nine when he was executed for this senseless crime, and being relatively young and disease-free (albeit with no appendix, and missing one tooth and one testicle), fit the basic criteria for the Visible Human Project®.[34] A murderer in life, Jernigan was to be reborn as Visible Man® and the new Adam. Death seems to have accorded Jernigan (digital) immortality and, as at least one journalist noted, an odd sort of absolution in exchange for his final request.[35]

The Visible Woman® has been granted no similar status in her afterlife. Far less notorious in life, the Visible Woman® remains similarly unassuming in death and revitalization. The woman who was to become the Visible Woman® died suddenly of a heart attack at the age of fifty-nine, after which her husband willed her body to science. We never will know any more personal details of her life. Unlike a state prisoner whose rights and privileges are suspended in life and beyond, the woman's right to anonymity is preserved. With no particular identity and certainly none of Jernigan's notoriety, she is simply the Visible Woman®. Yet, the Visible Woman® has hardly been seen at all. Sardonically referred to as the "Internet Housewife," the digital Eve to Jernigan's Adam has been relegated to the virtual private sphere of predictably traditional female activity.[36] Only the reproductive organs and pelvic structure of the Visible Woman® merit regular attention. Thus, despite a higher degree of sophistication in processing (milling) and imaging the Visible Woman®, the universal anatomical standard is the Visible Man®. Despite all of the technology, we have come no further in advancing the notion that a male norm does not presume *the* norm or that women are different simply because of their reproductive functions.

There is an interrelated element of age differentiation. While the Visible Man® was deemed youthful at thirty-nine, digital Eve is postmenopausal, and hence old, at fifty-nine. At fifty-nine and postmenopausal, the Visible Woman®, it seems, cannot be representative of all women. Adding a premenopausal female (and the foetus, as proposed by the project developers) might complete the digital nuclear family, but what remains at issue is the reproduction of conventional standards in what is a highly innovative biotechnological advancement. Rather than creating space for alternative perspectives, medical technologies and cyborg visions have encoded in textual and visual imagery a much older and, at times, seemingly frozen incongruity between male and female.[37] In the process, male is constituted as Human; female, when present at all, remains Other.

Project

The Visible Human Project® is not simply a new model of anatomy; it is a visual language of the body. That visual language comes at a price, however, and this project has become an industry unto itself. Marketed and consumed as a specific kind of authoritative anatomical knowledge, the VHP® is the product of both public and private investments in research and development, always intended for use in both sectors. This human is copyrighted, after all; it is a manufactured good to be marketed in the vast economic arena of bioscience. The term "Project," in other words, is implicated in the larger social, cultural, and political networks of knowledge and power that already permeate the production, distribution, and consumption of biomedical technologies and biocapital.[38]

The VHP® has, *de facto*, become the most sophisticated model of anatomo-physiology available worldwide.[39] This digital imagery was manufactured with a number of highly sophisticated biotechnology ventures in mind and exclusively for those equipped with the right finances, technology, and skills to master the digital imagery and render it a human-facsimile. Anyone, ostensibly and after signing a licensing agreement, can purchase the VHP® dataset. Available on either 8 millimeter Exabyte or 4 millimeter DAT are six tapes of anatomical images (head, thorax, abdomen, pelvis, thighs, feet) and a separate seventh tape of the magnetic resonance and co-axial tomographic (CAT) images of the male dataset. Each tape can be purchased for a licensing fee of USD$150. Having paid these fees, the purchaser will gain access to the Visible Human Project® FTP site and instructions on how to download the purchased tape. Alternatively, the complete data sets of either the Visible Man® or the Visible

Woman® can be purchased for USD$1,000 in the United States, Canada, and Mexico (or for USD$2,000 elsewhere).[40] As mentioned earlier, there are currently fifteen separate international applications for viewing the Visible Human® dataset. These are generally free but require internet access and adequate computer capacity and memory for the applet viewers and other viewing technologies to run effectively (see, for example, the NPAC Visible Human Viewer, a Java applet viewer developed by Syracuse University).[41] Tools for use with the Visible Human® dataset can be significantly more expensive. While some tools (UltraVis or Microvision II) are free, others such as Surfdriver cost USD$299 for the basic package and USD$1,500 for a five-copy site licence. This particular tool, which offers a simple visualization for creating three-dimensional models, is available only with the male Visible Human® dataset. Other tools, such as Splatter, offer direct rendering of large datasets but are only for use on supercomputers.[42] These are profoundly sophisticated technologies at the cutting edge of three-dimensional imaging and simulation software. The market for these tools, as for the original dataset, is vast yet highly specific. Similarly, all of the projects based upon the VHP® are based either in university laboratories or the biotechnological industry.

As a biotechnology, the VHP® is the appropriate model human in an age of medicine that is so profoundly reliant on technological intervention. This is a technocrat's anatomo-physiology, wholly devoid of its innately human origins.[43] This Human and, more specifically, this Project does not exist outside of the realm of a profoundly "virtual" space that is ultimately contingent on one's material ability to "see."

The human body has been transformed through the VHP® into a system of interchangeable virtual bits and bytes. In that transformation process, the Visible Man® is constituted as the quintessential virtual human form: the Visible Human®. Much good, no doubt, will come from a novice surgeon being able to prepare in a virtual surgical setting before putting real scalpel to real patient or from allowing both surgeons and patients to visualize, in three-dimensional form, a tumor in one's brain or bowels, or to perform screening exams without the discomfort, time, and cost of any one of a variety of invasive procedures. I am not implying that there should be no technological advancement. Nevertheless, we must ask ourselves questions about the implications of technological shifts in how we "see" the body and, more specifically, whether there are specific gendered effects as we naturalize and normalize the VHP® body as "real" anatomy and physiology. In the 1990s, Evelyn Fox Keller wrote that "what we see as we gaze at the secret of life is life already, and necessarily transformed by the very technology of our gaze."[44] Her observation was made in an earlier era of biotechnological advancement yet remains an astute commentary on the social constructions of (scientific) reality. In a similar vein, Margaret Lock and Sarah Franklin, both renowned medical anthropologists, recently wrote that "the cultural analysis of visual, textual, popular, discursive and national forms of representation of the body requires paying attention not only to embodiment itself but to biology as a site of knowledge production, moral dispute, and economic worth."[45] Removed to the realm of the visual, the VHP® is one such representation: It is a "biopolitical object."[46] Trademarked, commodified, and constituted as a medical model with the ability to be manipulated at will, the VHP® is not simply a neutral representation of the human form. The VHP® substantiates the medical profession's dominance over the representations of bodies in the industrialized world, and the bioscientific practices from which the VHP has emerged further "reify, isolate, decontextualize and abstract [that scientific body] from real time, actual location, and social space."[47] Some have argued that virtual technologies are more democratic and have liberatory potential in that one can escape the physical limits of sex, race, class, and age via the electronic frontier.[48] How can these claims be sustained when we see the ways in which socially entrenched and value-laden concepts—like gender, age, and race—are reproduced in technologies like the VHP®? With the erasure of gender, age, and cultural heritage, one wonders if the VHP® should not more aptly be named the *In*visible Human Project.

Acknowledgments

A very special thank you to my "Anthropology of the Body" (2001) graduate seminar group: Deirdre Snelgrove, Laura Ford, Jean MacDonald, and Jacqueline Schumacher for their fertile discussions of this topic. I also would like to thank Ken Little, David Murray, Luigi Bianchi, and, especially, Rusty Shteir, Bernie Lightman, and the entire York Advanced Research Seminar Group 2001–2002 for their insightful and helpful comments on an earlier draft of this work. Thank you to my research assistants, Amanda Lipinski and Andre Goldenberg, for work completed during the summer of 2001.

Notes

1. M. J. Ackerman, "Accessing the Visible Human Project," *D-Lib Magazine* (1995): 1–5; hdl://cnri.dlib/october95-ackerman.

2. Ibid., 1.

3. See, for example, the National Geographic Society's 1975 film *Man: The Incredible Machine.*

4. cf. Gary Downey, Joseph Dumit, and Sarah Williams, "Cyborg Anthropology," *Cultural Anthropology* 10 (1995): 264–65.

5. Catherine Waldby and Lisa Cartwright have done much of the groundwork in the critical and cultural examination of the VHP®. See, for example, Lisa Cartwright, "A Cultural Anatomy of the Visible Human Project," in *The Visible Woman: Imaging Technologies, Gender and Science*, ed. Paula Treichler, Lisa Cartwright, and Constance Penley (New York: New York University Press, 1998), 21–43; Catherine Waldby, "The Body and the Digital Archive: The Visible Human Project and the Computerization of Medicine," *Health* 1 (1997): 227–44; Catherine Waldby, "Revenants: The Visible Human Project and the Digital Uncanny," *Body and Society* 3 (1997): 1–16; Catherine Waldby, "The Visible Human Project: Data into Flesh, Flesh into Data," in *Wild Science: Reading Feminism, Medicine and the Media*, ed. Janine Marchessault and Kim Sawchuk (New York: Routledge, 2000), 24–38; and Catherine Waldby, *The Visible Human Project: Information Bodies and Posthuman Medicine* (New York: Routledge, 2000).

6. Michel Foucault, *The Birth of the Clinic: An Archaeology of Medical Perception* (New York: Vintage, 1975). See also Alan R. Petersen and Robin Bunton, eds., *Foucault, Health and Medicine* (New York, Routledge, 1997).

7. Lisa Cartwright, *Screening the Body: Tracing Medicine's Visual Culture* (Minneapolis: University of Minnesota Press, 1995).

8. For a superb and more extensive analysis of the erasure of "race" in the VHP®, see Cartwright, "A Cultural Anatomy of the Visible Human Project."

9. Paul Rabinow, "Artificiality and Enlightenment: From Sociobiology to Biosociality," in *Zone 6: Incorporations*, ed. Jonathan Crary and Sanford Kwinter (New York: Zone, 1992), 234–52.

10. Ibid., 245.

11. Sarah Franklin, "Life Itself: Global Nature and the Genetic Imaginary," in *Global Nature, Global Culture,* ed. Sarah Franklin, Celia Lury and Jackie Stacey (London: Sage, 2000), 188–240.

12. Fifteen gigabytes is equivalent to approximately fifteen thousand floppy disks. Ackerman, "Accessing the Visible Human Project," 1–2. See also the Visible Human Project® Fact Sheet at http://www.nlm.nih.gov/pubs/factsheets/visible_human.html.

13. Anonymous, "The Visible Man," *Life* 20 (February 1997), 40–43.

14. A recent addition has been made to the male data set. The film images taken during the original milling process now have been digitized so that the images are available at a higher resolution: http://www.nlm.nih.gov/research/visible/getting_data.htm.

15. http://www.crd.ge.com/esl/cgsp/projects/vm/. In addition, there are currently nine other tools for use with the Visible Human™ data set, which offer, for example, volume rendering, animation, surface extraction, texture manipulation, and three-dimensional modeling: http://www.nlm.nih.gov/research/visible/tools.htm.

16. "Visible Human Project Fact Sheet," http://www.nlm.nih.gov/pubs/factsheets/visible_human.html.

17. One anatomy professor or laboratory assistant at fifteen of the sixteen medical schools in Canada was contacted by phone and asked: 1) Is your anatomy lab still using human cadavers? 2) Are there any plans for a virtual anatomy system? 3) How are the cadavers used? 4) How many students per cadaver?

18. Anatomy of nerves and muscles; interactive human anatomy; interactive clinical anatomy; anatomie de l'appareil locomoteur. From an interview with Jean Deziel, Université de Montréal, 2001.

19. Interview with Jean Deziel.

20. See http://www.nlm.nih.gov/research/visible/animations.htm for a full listing of the applications of the VHP®.

21. Michael Ackerman, VHP Project Director, NLM Office of High Performance Computing and Communications, 1992.

22. Foucault, *The Birth of the Clinic*.

23. Colin Samson, *Health Studies* (Oxford: Blackwell, 1999), 9; Foucault, *The Birth of the Clinic*; Waldby, "The Visible Human Project: Data into Flesh, Flesh into Data."

24. Alan Sekula, "The Body and the Archive," *October* 39 (1986): 3–64. For critical analysis of the stereoscope of an earlier century, see also Jonathan Crary, *Techniques of the Observer: On Vision and Modernity in the Nineteenth Century* (Cambridge, Mass.: MIT Press, 1994).

25. Allen Feldman, "Violence and Vision: The Prosthetics of Terror," *Public Culture* 10 (1997): 24–60.

26. Ibid., 45.

27. Joseph W. Lella and Dorothy Sawchuk, "Medical Students and the Cadaver in Social and Cultural Context," in *Biomedicine Examined,* ed. M. Lock and D. R. Gordon (Dordrecht: Kluwer Academic Press, 1988), 125–53.

28. Ibid., 138. See also Michael Soppol's *Dream Anatomy*, a web-based curatorial history of anatomical imaging based on the NLM's recent exhibit of the same name at http://www.nlm.nih.exhibitions/dreamanatomy.

29. Waldby, "The Visible Human Project: Data into Flesh, Flesh into Data," 27.

30. Feldman, "Violence and Vision," 45.

31. Linda Hogle, "Tales from the Cryptic," in *The Cyborg Handbook*, ed. Chris Hables Gray (New York: Routledge, 1995), 203–18.

32. Thomas McCracken, ed., *New Atlas of Human Anatomy* (China: MetroBooks, 1999). In addition to the plethora of websites, children's, and technical computer programs devoted to applications of the Visible Human Project®, there is a growing number of text-based VHP materials (e.g., *Visible Human Journal of Endosonography*).

33. Ludmilla Jordanova, "Medical Images of the Female Body," *Sexual Visions: Images of Gender in Science and Medicine between the 18th and 20th Centuries* (New York: Harvester Wheatsheaf, 1989), 134–59. Cf. Suzanne E. Hatty and James Hatty, *The Disordered Body: Epidemic Disease and Cultural Transformation* (Albany: State University of New York Press, 1999).

34. This perpetuates the historical link to the earlier days of autopsy when the corpses of criminals and others of little means and less power regularly were used for dissection and anatomical illustration modeling.

35. Dowling, "The Visible Man," 41–44.

36. Cartwright, "A Cultural Anatomy of the Visible Human Project," 33.

37. Cf. Donna Haraway, *Simians, Cyborgs, and Women: The Reinvention of Nature* (London: Free Association Books, 1991). Nina Lykke, "Between Monsters, Goddesses and Cyborgs: Feminist Confrontations with Science," *Between Monsters, Goddesses and Cyborgs: Feminist Confrontations with Science, Medicine and Cyberspace*, Eds. N. Lykke and R. Braidotti (London: Zed Books, 1996), 13–29. Simon J. Williams, "Modern Medicine and the Uncertain Body: From Corporeality to Hyperreality?", *Social Science and Medicine* 45 (1997): 1041–1049.

38. Sarah Franklin and Margaret Lock, eds., *Remaking Life and Death: Toward an Anthropology of the Biosciences* (Santa Fe: School of American Research, 2003).

39. See, for example, the cd-rom, *A.D.A.M. The Inside Story* (Atlanta: A.D.A.M. Software, 1997), or McCracken, *New Atlas of Human Anatomy*. Both use the digital anatomy of the Visible Human exclusively.

40. http://www.nlm.nih.gov/research/visible/getting_data.htm.

41. http://www.dhpc.adelaide.edu.au/projects/vishuman2.

42. http://www.nlm.nih.gov/research/visible/tools.htm.

43. Cf. Jeannette Batz, "Breast Intentions: Enlightening Medical Students about the Female Body," *On the Issues* (1995), http://www.echonyc.com/~onissues/breast.htm.

44. Evelyn Fox Keller, "The Biological Gaze," in *Future Natural*, ed. Sally Stafford (New York: Routledge, 1995), 120. See also Petra Kuppers, "Visions of Anatomy: Exhibitions and Dense Bodies," *Differences: A Journal of Feminist Cultural Studies* 15 no. 3 (2004): 123–56.

45. Margaret Lock and Sarah Franklin, "Animation and Cessation: The Remaking of Life and Death," in *Remaking Life and Death*, 21.

46. Waldby, "The Visible Human Project: Data Into Flesh, Flesh into Data," 36; Waldby, *The Body and the Digital Archive*.

47. Margaret Lock, *Encounters with Aging: Mythologies of Menopause in Japan and North America* (Berkeley: University of California Press, 1993), 371; Jonathan Simon, "The Theater of Anatomy: The Anatomical Preparations of Honor Fragonard," *Eighteenth-Century Studies* 36, no. 1 (2002): 63–79; Lesley Sharp, "The Commodification of the Body and its Parts," *Annual Review of Anthropology* 29 (2000): 287–328.

48. Cartwright, "A Cultural Anatomy of the Visible Human Project"; Hatty and Hatty, *The Disordered Body*; and Haraway, *Simians, Cyborgs, and Women*.

Index

Page numbers in *italics* represent illustrations.

Redfield, Mark, 76, 77

Rembrandt, *Flora*, 11, *11*

representations: and anatomy, 358–74; of the body, 337–57, 358–74; and early modern medical imaging, 339, 340, 353; in ESHRE publications, 339; of female doctors, 267–88, 289–314; of the goddess of nature, 57–62, *59*, *73–74*; of human reproduction, 337–57; of male doctors, 315–36; of naturalists, 28–53; politics of, 289–314; of women in medicos, 332; of women in photographs, 267–88, 289–314. *See also* iconography

reproductive technologies, 337–57

Ripa, Cesare, *Iconologia*, 17

Roberts, Mary, 219

Robertson, Minnie, 273

Romanticism: literary culture, 178; natural history collecting, 45–46; naturalists, 47–48; and women, 23

Roosevelt, Theodore, 128

Rosenblum, Naomi, 148–49

Rosse, Lady Mary, 151, *152*

Rosse, Lord William, 151, 229

Royal Society of London, 17, 243, 250, 306

Rudge, Anne, 243–45, 249; *Pittosporum fulvum*, 244–45, *244*

Rudge, Edward, 243–45, 249

Rudwick, Martin, 218

Samson, Colin, 367

Sant, James: *Admission of Lady Fellows*, 257–58, *258*; *Admission of Lady Fellows* overpainted by unknown artist, 258, *259*

"Satin Bower-Bird (*Ptilonorhynchus holosericeus*)" (John and Elizabeth Gould), 94, *95*

satire, 41–43, 183–84

Schaffer, Simon, 238n39

Schelling, Friedrich Wilhelm Joseph, 72–73

Schiebinger, Londa, xviii, 17, 74, 302–4, 306, 340, 342–43, 348, 349

Schiele, Bernard, 293, 301, 304

Schiller, Friedrich, 73, 74; *The Mission of Moses*, 62; "The Veiled Image at Sais," 6

Schlegel, Friedrich, *Lucinde*, 76

school children visiting museum at the turn of the twentieth century, 120, *121*

science as writing, 6, 17, 26n24, 216, 234, 367

Sclater, P. L., 101, 102

"scopic regime," 367

scrapbooks, 175–86; opening page, 176, *177*; page with *China* and the *Conchologist*, George Spratt, 182–83, *183*

Secord, Anne, 22, 112, 199, 217

Sedgwick, Eve Kosofsky, 77

Segner, Johann Andreas von, *Natural Science*, 68, 69

Sekula, Alan, "The Body and the Archive," 367

self-fashioning. *See* identity

self-presentation, 267–88, 289, 298, 301–2; in visuals, 38, *40*, 40–41, 112, *113*, *114*, *115*, 117, *118*, 214–15, *215*

sexual ambiguity, 57, 63, 74

sexual difference, xx, xxiii–xxiv, 21, 74–77, 85–109, 111, 117–18, 340; and Darwin and sexual dimorphism, 120; L. Summers's pronouncement on, xvii; and museum display, 125–29; representing human as male, 369; and sexual identity, 74

sexual selection, theory of, 85–109

Shapin, Steven, 307

Shelley, Mary, *Frankenstein*, 46, 170, 173, 186

Sheridan, Louisa Henrietta, 180; "The Adventures of an Album," 176

Shortland, Michael, 77, 78

Shuchman, Miriam, 293

Sibthorp, John, *Flora graeca*, 18–19

"Side view of male Argus pheasant, whilst displaying before the female" (Wood), in *The Descent of Man*, 2nd ed., 102–3, *103*

"The Skinned Man," anatomical wax figure, 349, *349*

Smith, Dr. Frazer, 275

Smyth, Charles Piazzi, 151

Smyth, Jessie, 151

Solander, Daniel, 42–43

Somerville, Mary, 217

Sonnerat, Pierre, *Voyage à la nouvelle Guinée*, 35, *36*

Sontag, Susan, 149

spirit photograph with medium Sarah Power, *155*

"Spotted Bower-Bird (*Chlamydera maculata*)" (John and Elizabeth Gould), 94, *94*, 101

male Argus pheasant, whilst displaying before the female," engraving in
The Descent of Man, 2nd ed., 102–3,
103
Worster, Donald, "romantic thinking,"
125
Wordsworth, William, 45–46

Young, Robert, as Marcus Welby, M.D.,
332, *332*

Zirpolo, Lilian, 10
"Zoë the Nuthatch": by Eliza Brightwen,
202–3, *203*; by Francis Carruthers
Gould, 202–3, *203*